STANDING ORDERS, ROGERS' RANGERS

1. Don't forget nothing.

2. Have your musket clean as a whistle, hatchet scoured, sixty rounds of powder and ball, and be ready to march at a minute's warning.

3. When you are on the march, act the way you would if sneaking up on a deer. See the enemy first.

4. Tell the truth about what you see and an army depending on us for correct infor all you please when you tell other folks about t don't never lie to a Ranger or officer.

5. Don't take any chance you don't have to.

6. When we're on the march, we march single file, far enough apart so one shot can't go through two men.

7. If we strike swamps, or soft ground, we spread out abreast, so it's hard to track us.

8. When we march, we keep moving 'tildark, so as to give the enemy the least possible chance at us.

9. When we camp, half of the party stays awake while the other half sleeps.

10. If we take prisoners, we keep 'em separate 'til we have had time to examine them, so they can't cook up a story between 'em.

11. Don't ever march home the same way. Take a different route so you won't be ambushed.

12. No matter whether we travel in big parties or little ones, each party has to keep a scout twenty yards ahead, twenty yards on each flank, and twenty yards in the rear, so the main body can't be surprised and wiped out.

13. Every night you'll be told where to meet if surrounded by a superior force.

14. Don't sit down to eat without posting sentries.

15. Don't sleep beyond dawn. Dawn's when the French and Indians attack.

16. Don't cross a river by a regular ford.

17. If somebody's trailing you, make a circle, come back onto your own tracks, and ambush the folks that aim to ambush you.

18. Don't stand up when the enemy's coming against you. Kneel down, lie down, hide behind a tree.

19. Let the enemy come 'til he's almost close enough to touch. Then let him have it and jump out and finish him up with your hatchet.

Major Robert Rogers, 1759

TAX FRAUD & EVASION: THE WAR STORIES

First Edition, March, 1989, MacPherson & Sons Publishers, Ltd.

Printed by Laurent's Printing & Services, Phoenix, Arizona.

ISBN: 0-9617124-6-5

Other Books by Donald W. MacPherson

April 15th: The Most Pernicious Attack Upon English Liberty
(2nd Edition, 1988)

Tax Fraud & Evasion: The War Stories, Part II
(Planned publication: March, 1990)

Acknowledgements & Credits

This book was "engineered" by my son Ryan ("Hogo") MacPherson, who, at age 14, has become a desktop publisher. Ryan was assisted by his brother Nathan, age 9, "President of Chuck & Joe Shmoe Companies, Incorporated." Credit & thanks are also due our word proccessors, Debbie Arthur & Nancy Hall, & proofreaders, Scott MacPherson, Ajay & Anita Lowery of the *Justice Times*, Charles & Linda Riely, & Rick Dalton. Finally, a special thanks to my wife Barbara for her ideas, proofreading, & encouragement. Sun Tzu and Mao Tse-tung quotes are from *Revolutionary Guerrilla Warfare*, edited by Sam C. Sarkesian (Precedent Publishing, Inc., 1975). Che Guevara quotes are found in *Che Guevara - On Guerrilla Warfare* (Frederick A. Praeger, Inc. , 1962). Other chapter heading quotes are from *The Morrow Book of Quotations in American History* , Joseph R. Conlin (William Morrow & Co., Inc., 1984).

Notice from the Author & Publisher

Under the *First Amendment* to the *United States Constitution,* this book advocates ideas. It is not intended to give to the public general nor specific legal advice. The author writes both facts & opinions. Opinions are those of the author only. Except for actual transcripts, facts are reported to the best of the author's recollection, & from file notes. Chapters 6 & 7 contain actual trial transcripts. Other quotations are based upon recollection & file notes, unless noted by "transcript." Chapters are written to be read in the order presented. *Italics* are used for emphasis, thoughts, & legal citations. Profanity of paratroopers in Vietnam is authentic & is quoted for sake of realism.

For Barbara

Who can find a virtuous woman? for her price *is* far above rubies.

The heart of her husband doth safely trust in her, so that he shall have no need of spoil.

She will do him good and not evil all the days of her life.

She seeketh wool, and flax, and worketh willingly with her hands.

She is like the merchants' ships; she bringeth her food from afar.

She riseth also while it is yet night, and giveth meat to her household, and a portion to her maidens.

She considereth a field, and buyeth it; with the fruit of her hands she planteth a vineyard....

Strength and honour *are* her clothing; and she shall rejoice in time to come.

She openeth her mouth with wisdom; and in her tongue *is* the law of kindness.

She looketh well to the ways of her household, and eateth not the bread of idleness.

Her children arise up, and call her blessed; her husband *also* and he praiseth her.

Many daughters have done virtuously, but thou excellest them all.

Favour *is* deceitful, and beauty *is* vain: *but* a woman *that* feareth the Lord, she shall be praised....

Proverbs 31

Table of Contents

I offer neither pay nor quarters nor provisions; I offer hunger, thirst, forced marches, battles and death. Let him who loves his country in his heart, and not on his lips only, follow me. Giuseppe Garibaldi

OPENING STATEMENT

If you are afraid of your own government, Major Mac, you might as well move to Russia. You were willing to volunteer twice for Vietnam, spend eighteen months there, mostly in combat, as an Airborne, Infantry platoon leader and then company commander with "the Herd," the 173rd Airborne Brigade (Separate), and now you should tremble at the thought that you are being tailed by Treasury Agents? Airborne Infantry lieutenant ("LT"), promoted to captain at age 24. On a daily basis, you walked through "the Valley of the Shadow of Death," yet "fearing no evil," despite the boobie traps, to which you lost so many good men, punji pits, and VC lurking in ambush at every bend in the trail. Lest we forget too soon, what would those with whom you served , and yeah even those who died for you, now think, their mocking words echoing from the grave, "Gone soft on us, LT? Where'd you pick up that case of jitters, Captain Mac? Forget your daily malaria pill? You taught us that 'There are no athiests in foxholes,' and that 'There is nothing to fear but fear itself.' Now you gonna cower from some pimply-assed bureaucrat who, back in '68, didn't want to leave his mama while we volunteered for Airborne School and then 'Nam? "

"It's those Treasury agents who, if they were any smarter, wouldn't have to work for the government. But then, they like smoking cigarettes and drinking that 'lifer juice' coffee. They wouldn't as much as make 'assistant to the assistant douche bag packer' at Cam Rahn Bay. Remember, Lt. Mac, you were the 'Black Hawk' platoon leader, and you, the 'Ranger Dude,' showed us how to sit quietly in ambush when it would rain on us all night long. But we were patient and long-suffering and out to get those kills, that 'body count.' And afterward, we searched and poked at the stiffs while you pointed out 'Look here, you Herd dudes. Flesh and blood, the real thing. Charlie is human too. He eats, sleeps and craps, and for us he'll pay the supreme price - die. He came to die, so let's do him a favor. See the blood, his brains and his guts? No superhuman, this Victor Charlie.'

"Give us a break, LT. Cut us some slack. What are you gonna do now? Say what we used to say when the choppers got caught by the monsoons and we sat stranded on Monkey Mountain for weeks without resupply, eating the monkeys we could shoot out of the trees: 'It don't mean nothin?' You went on bush with us all those times, and 'it don't mean nothin?' The Gooks would just love it, LT. You go right ahead and back off, Dude. Don't you do

1

nothin' now. It might be too scary for you. But before you cop out, do us one last favor.

"Write a letter to Sergeant Will. Remember? He limps now. Got shot up giving chase to those Gooks. And, oh yeah, Sergeant Stafford. He's alive, but doesn't sleep too easy with all that pain caused by the pistol shot from that NVA Lieutenant he was after in the banana grove. Remember? The one 'Crazy Horse' wanted to deal with in his own way. You haven't forgotten 'Crazy Horse' Audrain, have you, Captain Mac? West Point, Airborne, Ranger, Infantry, Marine, Indian. Wanted to slit that NVA's throat, but you said 'no.' What would Audrain say about Treasury Agents? And LT, don't forget Sergeant Williams. Of course, you can't write to him, but we'll give him the message. He's doin' just fine with us. But you ought to write to his folks again and tell them again and again and again what a good soldier he was, and what an inspiration to us all. But please, please, don't tell them you're gonna cower in the face of the enemy.

"Remember that young kid just in country two weeks , boobie trapped up at Bong Son, wasn't it? And remember what you said at the funeral service where we had the men line up, jump boots next to the M-16 with fixed bayonette, stuck in the ground, a symbol of the fallen soldier. What you said then was a far cry from that command you used to give us when things looked up tight. 'Fix bayonettes!' Warning us to prepare for close-quarter combat. So what was it you said for that young kid who died for his country, only two weeks in 'Nam, something about you being worthy? And, oh yeah, remember PFC ...." Stop. Stop, damn it! That's enough. You made your point.

Those were my thoughts in the summer of '79, almost ten years after I had left Vietnam, when I believed I was being followed by Treasury Agents. It was not just out of paranoia. I had just won my second criminal tax trial without realizing initially the import it would have on my professional *and* personal life. Attorney and close friend Mark McClellan and I had represented Charles Riely in our first case of charges of willful failure to file federal income tax returns. Charles was, I learned after the verdict, a well-respected leader within the nation-wide "tax rebellion." After the verdict and an article in the *Spotlight* , a national, right-wing newspaper, the phone was beginning to "ring off the hook." Calls of congratulation, plus requests, "Will you defend me if I'm criminally charged with tax offenses? I haven't filed in ten years. No lawyer will touch my case with a ten-foot pole." Jim Friend, my first federal trial client, had promised before Charles' trial, "You win Charles' case, and you'll have more clients than time to talk to 'em." I paid little attention when he said it. Now his prophesy was ringing true. At the same time, I was being followed. By whom? Clients leaving

2

my office complained that they were being followed. I hired a private investigator to find out who, if anyone, was tailing me. He reported he could not figure it out, but *he* was being followed. A brief period of paranoia followed.

What have I gotten myself into? Are these tax protesters such enemies of the State that they aren't as much as entitled to a defense? I thought. That did not square with my legal training at West Point twelve years before I went to law school. *Why won't other lawyers handle the cases? Are these tax protester defendants that unpopular? Or are the lawyers afraid of the IRS?*

After wrestling with these thoughts for several days, I concluded that, *yes, lawyers were afraid.* I speculated that they were no doubt afraid not just because of the reputation of IRS for abuse of power, but because lawyers had "tax skeletons in the closet." They did not want to risk audit and possible criminal investigation. Maintain that low profile. *The wheel that squeaks the loudest gets the grease.* This led me to several other conclusions.

First, I decided I did not deserve to live in the United States if I was to live in fear of my own government. And more important to me, I did not deserve the respect of those with whom I had served in combat. I did not even deserve *self-respect.* Second, what better candidate to handle unpopular cases than a combat vet who has not made over $12,000 a year prior to graduation from law school. No skeletons to fear there. What better candidate than a man who has always hated bullies and liked to root for the underdog. Besides, was I not taught in law school that lawyers had an *ethical obligation* to represent not only the indigent but the unpopular client? Tax protesters, it seemed, were high on the list of the unpopular with the IRS, the Justice Department, the federal judges, the public in general and, in the final analysis, the juries.

I was driven further to these conclusions during my fourth case in New Hampshire. There, I had been led to find local counsel because I was not admitted to practice in New Hampshire. Local counsel would serve only to introduce me to the court and file the paperwork necessary . I interviewed by phone a prospect to whom I had been referred by one of the tax resisters. The prospect was a young fellow, not long out of law school, with whom I could relate. A Marine lieutenant and Viet vet brother, in private practice, still in the Marine Corps Reserves. "What's the case about?" he asked. "Charges of willful failure to file federal income tax returns, misdemeanors. Mark and I mean to take the IRS to the cleaners; put those bullies in their place. Our client was a plumber who committed, in the eyes of IRS, the mortal sin of helping sponsor in Concord a meeting of tax protesters. His name was on the flier. He, the emcee, rather than the speakers, became the prime target. They want to put this guy in jail for three years." "Uh, let me see.

Uh, I don't think I want to be involved in your case," the Marine Corps attorney said. "Why not? What's the problem? You got some kind of conflict of interest?" "No." "What then?" "Well, uh, I filed late last year." "How late?" "A couple of months." "So? Did you pay all the taxes you owed plus interest and penalties?" "Yeah." "Then what's the problem?" "Well, I'm married, have two little children, and I'm just getting started in my law practice." "Fine. Me too. I've got three sons. The third, Nathan, was just born June 6, D-day, the same day I was promoted to major in the Army Reserves. I'm in Special Forces, assigned as an instructor with the Special Forces School out of Fort Bragg, North Carolina. I still don't understand. Technically, IRS could charge you with willful failure to file timely or failure to pay timely, but what they'd have to prove is that you intended to violate the law. Did you intend to break the law? Why did you not file and pay on time?" "Procrastination. Just put it off." "No sweat, GI. You can file that motion next week, have me admitted on the case, and you just have to run the paperwork down to the courthouse once in awhile." "No. I think I'd better not get involved...."

I could not believe my ears. This jar-head, gyrene was *scared to death.* A combat vet. Faced the VC and NVA, but cowered before the IRS. I was more-so disgusted because I had from West Point sought commission in the Marine Corps rather than the Army. I like the unity of the smaller force, the *esprit de corps*, "semper fi," the Marine Corps motto, "always faithful." I still maintained high regard for the Marines, and here a Marine Corps lieutenant, Vietnam vet was shirking his duty on the field of battle. I just could not believe it!

Almost ten years later, I have finally put pen to paper and revealed for all to witness the basis of that Marine Corps officer's fear: the mystique of criminal tax prosecutions. We fear that which we fail to understand, and we fail to understand for reason no one has brought us to knowledge. "Woe unto you, lawyers! for ye have taken away the key of knowledge.... " *Luke* 11:52.

In general, with rare exception, there are four types of publications regarding civil and criminal tax cases. The first category is the publication of the IRS. But you will not find an IRS consumer publication on criminal tax prosecutions, only "secret" publications such as *The Special Agent's Handbook* , which describes in technical terms how agents are to investigate the target, and what makes a good case for prosecution. The second type is the treatise, written by lawyers or accountants *for* lawyers or accountants. These books explain in *legalese* the legal doctrines and case holdings. No human element; just cut and dried cold facts and law.

Next is what I call the "silver bullet" of the tax protester, the book presenting themes which, in my opinion, no matter how legally correct or logical, will never be adopted by the federal courts on *any* level. Theories such as "wages are not income", "the *Sixteenth Amendment* was never properly ratified", "I'm not a person required," "the court is without jurisdiction," or "the income tax is voluntary." However correct the theory might be, what federal judge, pray tell, will put an end to *April 15th,* that *day of infamy,* with one swift stroke of the pen? Last is what I call the pablum: those "how to" books written often by the insiders, former IRS lawyers or agents. These books, while presenting some inside information as to how the system is supposed to work, make such bold, astute observations as "there is a difference between tax evasion and avoidance." "Pamby-Amby" is the phrase I have coined, derived from "Namby-Pamby." In the main, the reader no doubt comes away fearing what remains the mystique of the criminal tax case. Two of the rare exceptions to the "how to" category are two books by an IRS outsider, that lion-tamer and good friend, Dan Pilla of St. Paul, Minnesota, who deserves some V's for valor. (*Winning Publications,* 1-800-553-6458.) Like many of my clients, and unlike the Marine Corps lieutenant from New Hampshire, Dan has proven "fearless in the face of enemy fire."

Tax Fraud and Evasion: The War Stories . This book is not in the main about issues, but about people. Their beliefs, their courage, their stand. What happens to them mentally, physically and financially. They have, after all, the temerity to raise the issues, "to go where no man has gone before." What *has* happened to these people mentally, physically and financially? Read in this book the documented cases IRS will never share with you: ironworkers and doctors, airline pilots and housewives, plumbers and publishers, farmers and engineers, politicians and preachers. This is their story as much as it is mine.

Although to understand their "war stories," you must have the backdrop of what in the world of legal doctrine and procedure is occurring, do not forget that what occurs here is *human conflict.* Once you get past all of the tax statutes passed by Congress, the rules of evidence and of criminal procedure, interpretation by the courts of the laws and the rules, you are left with human drama. *Conflict.* IRS special agent versus citizen target. Justice Department prosecutor versus defense attorney. The final arbitrator of this combat is the jury of twelve. That which is public record is but one-tenth of the story. The *flesh and blood war stories* are intended to cut through the legalese to the end that you will be brought to understanding, and through understanding harbor fear no longer. Nor will the *Monster,* discovered as a paper tiger, any longer intimidate you, the sovereign citizen, the master. *Beast-master.*

This is not to say that tax matters, both civil and criminal, are to be taken lightly. Quite to the contrary, you will learn of IRS' arsenal and how to avoid it. And if non-filing tax protesters can obtain from a jury an acquittal, what fear should you have?

According to IRS statistics, in 1986, 101 million, 750 thousand individual tax returns were filed with IRS. Of those persons filing a return, only 2,954 were indicted with a tax-related crime, meaning if you filed a return, your chances are around 35,000 to 1 that you will *not* be prosecuted. After winning about 83% of their cases, IRS succeeded at time of sentencing in placing 1,475 of those one hundred million plus individuals in jail, meaning your chances, if you filed, against you spending any time in jail for a tax offense are around 69,000 to 1. Those statistics include *all* tax-related prosecutions. If we eliminate the four categories of "fraudulent tax shelters," "illegal tax protesters," "narcotics-related" and "Bank Secrecy Act (Title 31)" (currency transaction report and other money-laundering violations), the odds are around 70,000 to 1 that you will *not* be prosecuted and 146,000 to 1 that you will *not* spend any time in jail. The odds, in fact, become better if we add to the almost 102 million who filed returns around ten million individuals the IRS believes did not file a return but were, IRS claims, required to file a return. In an effort to sleep better at night, ask yourself this: even if you make $100,000 per year, would *you* spend $2,954 (3% of your earnings) for 2,954 $1 chances at winning a $101,750,000 simple lottery, knowing your chances are around 35,000 to 1? Probably not.

With these odds, what tools of enforcement does IRS have but intimidation and to play on your fears? Bullies at work have, throughout history, become legend. SS, KGB, and IRS. Ubiquitous initials. Oh, and do not forget *Gestapo. We, the People* are as much to blame as Congress and IRS for the mystique.

Failure to file an income tax return, failure to pay income taxes, and attempted income tax evasion are *not* crimes in this country. Not yet anyway. For those acts (or failures to act) to constitute a crime, one first must act with *specific intent* to violate the law; knowing what the law forbids or requires, one must set out with the specific purpose to violate the law. *Willfulness. Specific criminal intent.* Ignorance of the law *is* an excuse. Congress has declared that the tax laws are so complex that ignorance of the law is a defense so far as it goes to the citizen's state of mind; or, in other words, so far as it tends to negate willfulness.

Second, the government must assemble *evidence* and prove beyond a reasonable doubt to the satisfaction of twelve jurors that you *intended to violate the law.* If good faith belief or misunderstanding or reliance on the advice of counsel is raised, then the government must, in effect, prove beyond a reasonable doubt that you did *not* believe in good faith or did *not* in good faith rely on the advice of your attorney or accountant. At least some federal appellate courts hold that the belief or misunderstanding is *subjective*, not objective. This nuance means, in the final analysis, that it is not even relevant whether what you believed was right or wrong, or whether the jury determines it was reasonable or unreasonable for you to so believe what you claim you believed. All that matters is whether you in fact *believed* it. Put another way, the government must, then, prove beyond a reasonable doubt that you did *not* believe what you claim you believed.

Is it any wonder then the fine-tune processing by IRS and Justice Department of criminal tax cases? After two years of investigation by the IRS special agent of the Criminal Investigation Division (CID) and review by his supervisor, plus further review by Chief of CID and IRS District Director, the case then goes to the office of District Counsel, the IRS lawyers, for review. Then to Justice Department in Washington, D.C. for review, where it may remain for another year or two. Then back to the local U.S. Attorney for further fine-tuning and additional investigation, if necessary, and the ultimate prosecution by way of grand jury indictment or, in the case of misdemeanor rather than felony, by a charging paper signed by the U.S. Attorney, called an "Information." A long, arduous pipeline. For the *Beast* can ill afford to lose criminal tax cases. If IRS cannot succeed in putting behind bars those it believes to be tax cheats, what then the impact upon the remaining one hundred million and our system based upon "voluntary compliance?"

With mystery, mystique, lack of knowledge, lack of understanding, there lurks nearby the close cousin: intimidation. Fear is close on the heels of intimidation. What better way to cut through intimidation, fear and its step-sister, bluff, than to place you, the sovereign citizen, in the observer's tower, in the courtroom and behind the scenes, incognito, to witness the real flesh and blood of *the war stories*. See the enemy mount the attack by way of the skirmish line. Hear the whine of bullets closely overhead and the unforgettable whistle of incoming artillery. Smell the cordite and the stench of burning human flesh.

How do you take advantage of the tax laws and stay out of jail? Do you not find it bizarre that even with all the fear and intimidation, we still have a system which recognizes charitable contributions made to a church, including those placed in the offering plate on Sunday without the use of an offering envelope? Are you then, because of lack of receipt, to not claim the deduction? No way. Such was not the intent of Congress. Have you willfully intended to violate *26 U.S.C. Section 7203* , which provides a year in jail and a $10,000 fine for anyone who willfully fails to keep adequate records by your failure to keep records of the amount placed in the plate each Sunday? Not hardly. And what of your contribution of clothing, toys and other household goods to *St. Vincent de Paul* or *Goodwill*? Fair market value is what the law requires. Nothing more, nothing less. Use your best estimate and take a legitimate deduction. You earned it; take it.

Just how far can you push IRS and not be prosecuted? What are the "limits of the tax law?" What must IRS prove? The answers are found in the criminal tax cases that are *won*! *The proof is in the pudding*. If an Arkansas woman who did not file a tax return for eighteen years beat IRS at criminal tax charges, by what should *you* feel intimidated?

Consider this analogy: you go to a haunted house as a child and under cover of darkness are frightened by ghosts and goblins. Your imagination runs wild while at the house, and later you attempt, without success, to stave off recurring nightmares. In effort to put the matter to rest, your parents take you during daylight hours back to the haunted house and show you the tricks of the trade. The props used. That goblin was but one-sixteenth inch cardboard. Cardboard which, even as a child, you could rip apart with your bare hands. Don't you feel silly? The nightmares go away.

Likewise for me was the myth of the Viet Cong. Victor Charlie. V.C. Was he invulnerable? Did the night belong to Charlie? We took the initiative, took the night from Charlie, beat him on his own turf. Although Charlie was a master as a sapper, sneaking past trip flare wires and claymore mines, naked but for shorts, carrying on his back satchel charges and slipping like an eel through layers of concertina wire, coming to die, we often made him pay the supreme price before he failed in his mission. I looked without any horror or glee at pieces of arms and legs scattered in the sand, rotting in the noon-day sun at the fire base of the 101st Airborne Division near Phan Thiet, Vietnam. *The dirty bastards. It was them or us.* Patton had said to his men before they engaged in combat, "When you put your hand in a bunch of goo that a moment ago was the face of your best friend, you'll know what to do.... You don't win wars by dying for your country; you win wars by making the other poor bastard die for his."

Just like the ghouls and goblins in the haunted house, Victor Charlie, I had learned, was not invulnerable. Steeled and well-honed, perhaps, but not imaginative. Not even always tactical, as I discovered, my men sneaking up on him in the rain from which Charlie was attempting to shelter himself, under a poncho, eating a bowl of rice. More concerned about protection from the elements and his empty belly, it costs him his life, my men coming from behind, blowing him away before he as much as sensed their presence. Nor did he show a great deal of discipline creeping back to the hooch at night to sleep with mama and visit the kiddies, pat

8

the dog, only to be surprised at break of dawn by our ambush. His body withstood the tearing of bullets no better than the one-sixteenth inch cardboard withstood the tearing at the hands of the child.

The paper tiger. The bureaucrat, also known as *bureaurat.* If the IRS agent was truly competent and was not lazy, why had he not struck out for business on his own? Coffee and cigarettes and federal service retirement pay? The paper tiger exposed by the light of day. But who would dare to turn on the switch, or open the curtain, for this vampire *Monster* to be exposed to sunlight?

What does Vietnam combat have to do with criminal tax trials? Plenty - if your defense lawyer is "Major Mac," the "courtroom commando." How well I have learned, and applied to the courtroom battleground, the principles of guerrilla warfare, according to Mao Tse-tung:

> To defend in order to attack, to retreat in order to advance, to take a flanking position in order to take a frontal position, and to zig zag in order to go straight.

Mao (China, 1937) was himself a student of Sun Tzu (China, 500 B.C.) Sun wrote:

> Now war is based on deception. Move when it is advantageous and create changes in the situation by dispersion and concentration of forces. When campaigning, be swift as the wind; and leisurely march, majestic as the forest; in raiding and plundering, like fire; and standing, firm as the mountains. As unfathomable as the clouds, move like a thunderbolt. When you plunder the countryside, divide your forces. When you conquer territory, divide the profits...

> To be certain to take what you attack is to attack a place the enemy does not protect. To be certain to hold what you defend is to defend a place the enemy has not attacked. Therefore, against those skilled in attack an enemy does not know where to defend; against the experts in defense the enemy does not know where to attack. Subtle and insubstantial, the expert leaves no trace; divinely mysterious, he is inaudible. Thus he is the master of his enemy's fate.

"Now you're crackin', Captain Mac. You do remember. You remember it so well you'll never forget. It was 4 November 69 and we were in the coastal area, where a Navy barge containing 300 claymore mines had washed ashore, captured by the VC. That young kid had been in country only two weeks when he stepped on the detonation device buried on the sandy trail. You had a squad as

9

security walking point, and after six men walked over the device, that young kid, only nineteen, hit it just right. You were quick to call the medivac chopper, but it was too late for that kid. Not old enough to grow more than peach fuzz; not old enough to shave. You were later despondent, sitting in the shade on your steel helmet, writing to his parents. Now you're crackin', Captain Mac. You wouldn't forget that kid, knowing he's here with us. And you wouldn't forget what you were moved to read the day you held that memorial service just outside the hamlet we were sent to protect: 'Dear Lord, lest I continue in my complacent way, help me to remember somewhere out there a man died for me today. So long as there must be war, I must ask and answer, am I worth dying for?'" Who indeed would dare take on the IRS?

"I have a secret and dangerous mission; send me a West Point football player," were the words of General Marshall during World War II. I have a secret and dangerous mission for a criminal tax defense lawyer. Send me ... West Point, Airborne, Ranger, Infantry, Jump Master, S.C.U.B.A., combat veteran? Or Marine RECON? Navy SEAL? TOP GUN fighter pilot? Air Rescue? SAS (British Special Air Service)? French Foreign Legion? Mercenary? You get the picture. The two main ingredients should be obvious: the defense lawyer candidate makes use of logic and has physical courage. He is, for example, an Army Airborne Ranger hooking up his troops at a mere five hundred feet, preparing to make a night combat jump into Grenada. (Five hundred feet is too low to depend on a reserve chute in event the main chute fails to open, but it affords the enemy little time to shoot targets from the sky.) And he has been served with a grand jury indictment, a piece of paper in which the grand jury charges that his client, a schoolmarm, allegedly conspired to defraud the United States of America, subjecting her to five years in prison. This soldier, a hired gun, bodyguard, trained to "march to the sound of the guns," takes a deep breath of air, his body becomes rigid, steeled, and he bellows that first of nine commands of the paratrooper jump master. Above the loud drone of the engines from the old Air Force C-119 "flying boxcar" aircraft, he issues that first command to those young paratroopers dependent upon him, the leader, to direct them to jump from the aircraft at just the right moment,   G-G-G-E-E-E-T-T-T R-R-R-E-E-E-A-A-A-D-D-D-Y-Y-Y....

Know the enemy and know yourself; in a hundred battles you will never be in peril. When you are ignorant of the enemy but know yourself, your chances of winning or losing are equal. If ignorant both of your enemy and yourself, you are certain in every battle to be in peril. Sun Tzu

POINTMAN   Chapter 1

Company commanders are *not* supposed to act as pointmen. But in Vietnam there were no rules except the rules of the bush - the law of the jungle - and he who was in charge set the rules. This was true for patrol leaders of any rank: squad leaders (sergeants), platoon leaders (lieutenants) and, at the highest level, company commander (a captain). If you were of any higher rank, you were normally closely scrutinized. The battalion commander (a lieutenant colonel) was usually to be found in the rear fire support bases (FSB), and for him, the closest to combat was by way of his command and control helicopter (C&C).

"A platoon leader's war," they called it. In the bush, you were remote. No battle "line of demarcation" but the circular or triangular perimeter of the FSB. In the bush, or boonies, especially in areas of triple canopy, you were on your own. Even if you might be fifteen minutes from your battalion commander by chopper, it was a long distance by foot, and at such time as the chopper was overhead, what was the battalion commander to see through the triple canopy? The first layer was two hundred feet above ground, the second one hundred, the third layer fifty feet. On the ground you were in charge, only to answer later if you screwed up.

This day I had chosen for several reasons to be pointman, even though I was a captain and the company commander. None of the reasons justified the risk, but then it was a risk I was willing to take. I was not an ordinary risk taker, but for the most part a logical "end justifies the means" *calculated* risk taker. (The pointman led the way and was first in line, was the eyes and ears of the unit, alert first about the boobie trap, be it trip wire or punji pit. It was his responsibility to spot the ambush, or smell the sniper or cookfire ahead.) *I am a jungle cat. I am one with my element, not foreign to it. I am like Tarzan, raised, if not born, of the apes. I don't walk through the jungle nor am I king of the jungle. I am the jungle. We are one.*

Good pointmen are volunteers. They become high on being on point. When you are first in line, the adrenalin flows, not merely because of the danger, but because of the constant satisfaction to curiosity, the searching with eyes and ears, the question of what is over the next ridge or around the next bend in the trail. Curious not only for the enemy, but the terrain as well. The flora and fauna, the change in elevation. Navigating, tracking, sensing, protecting, with hairs on end as antenna. Insects and animals are not alarmed at the approach of the pointman. He is not part of the jungle; he *is* the jungle.

This is not to say that pointmen go through a Vietnam tour crouching and creeping as seen in John Wayne's *The Green Berets*. Creeping and crawling is exhausting and takes place only in close proximity to the enemy. Walking point becomes second nature without conscious concentration. The awesome responsibility of acting as the eyes and ears of the patrol or squad or platoon or company causes the adrenalin surge which, in turn, causes the senses to take over. *I am not in the jungle. I am the jungle.*

Company commanders are not supposed to walk point. Privates First Class (PFC) walk point. The company commander, a leader of one hundred fifty to two hundred men, remains behind the first platoon of forty. Even the platoon leader, a lieutenant, the field manuals say, does not walk point.; the lieutenant is to walk behind the first of his four squads of ten men each.

This day I walked point because I wanted to. The enemy was close by and I was bored, itching for action. My itch would soon be satisfied in a physical contact with the enemy I never expected. I would, within a matter of minutes, have one hand on the throat of the enemy with one hand covering his mouth, deciding whether to reach for my knife and slit his throat or spare him for intelligence purposes. Blowing him away with my rifle was out of the question. As pointman, I was creeping and crawling through a well-vegitated, small stream bed up to a group of hooches believed to contain the enemy. By reason of stealth, I had surprised one from behind.

It was not that I was interested in being a hero. Pointmen do not become heroes. They either survive or do not survive. As the saying goes, "there are but two types of soldiers on the battlefield: the quick and the dead." Pointmen do not even get Bronze Stars. Because they are not officers, they typically get an Army Commendation Medal, whereas officers who do not as much as see beyond a desk in the rear are awarded Bronze Stars. But that is the politics of war.

Ironically, the position of pointman is not necessarily the most dangerous. It was not uncommon in Vietnam for several men to walk past a boobie trap without harm. Once, as company commander, I brought in from the battalion a mine sweeping team. We were on a "pacification" mission near villages and I was losing many men on boobie traps, usually claymore mines, which spray lead pellets of death. Word was that a Navy barge had washed ashore and the VC had possession in my area of operation (AO) three hundred claymores. The terrain in our AO consisted of thick hedgerows with a network of trails. It was nearly impossible as one stepped over a clearing made through the hedgerow to see a trip wire. Also, as we were a few hundred meters from the coast, the trails were of sand. Typically the VC would set up a claymore in a hedgerow or even bury it in the sand and place the charging device on the trail under the sand for a GI's footstep.

Cynical as I was, I tested the ability of the mine sweeping team by burying in the trail a silver gum wrapper. Since the claymores are set off by a triggering device containing metal, I presumed that if the mine sweepers could pick up a gum wrapper of tin foil, they could surely pick up a claymore. I was impressed with their abilities and we proceeded down the trail. *If they were so good, how the hell did they miss that claymore?* The first six men following the sweepers missed it as well. Number seven stepped directly on the device and was killed instantly. Nineteen years of age, he had been in the country two weeks. And pointmen in an ambush situation may fair better than the main body. Under ambush doctrine, those ambushing wait until the *main body* is in the kill zone, which may leave the pointman well out of the zone.

Pointmen do not have to be good navigators, but it helps. Typically, I used a point team of three or four men - two or three pointmen and one navigator. In areas where terrain permitted, the pointmen walked abreast if two, or spear-shaped if three, with the navigator behind and in the middle, checking map and compass. The disadvantage of two or more pointmen was that the pointmen had to not only remain in contact with one another, but as well check periodically with the navigator who directed them with an arm signal. In rapid movement, it became an often frustrating proposition because pointmen might race in the wrong direction and the navigator would end up whispering or whistling to draw their attention. This did little for security of the pointmen, in particular, and the unit as a whole. Therefore, ideally pointmen were good navigators, as well, glancing periodically at compass, memorizing headings and terrain, thus precluding periodic map checks. It is hard to keep your eyes on the jungle and read a map at the same time. The pointman/navigator, first to walk the trail, would be covered by his "slack man," the second man, when map or compass checks were made.

But good navigators were scarce in Vietnam. I was a good navigator and pointman. Not naturally. On my left shoulder above the *173rd Airborne Brigade (Separate)* patch was sewn the covetted *Ranger* tab representing two months of arduous training in the Georgia mountains and Florida swamps with little sleep and food, and with emphasis on the ten-man patrol. We learned to trust a compass rather than our sense of direction both day and night. Having spent a year in Vietnam as platoon leader and staff officer, I was well experienced with the terrain and the topographical maps. As I flew over mountainous terrain by chopper and looked at ridges and valleys, fingers and saddles, my brain automatically transferred what I saw in three dimensions from the air to a two dimensional topographical map. The same applied in reverse. After the exhaustion of Ranger School, Vietnam for me was *duck soup.*

This day I decided to be pointman for additional reasons. I was experimenting in Vietnam with an age-old tactic. But for my company it was new as to the local terrain and enemy situation. If it was to go wrong, it was to be *my* responsibility. Also, spirits were low among the men for lack of recent contact and frustration in locating the enemy. Here, in the flatlands, we knew where the enemy was; it was just a matter of sneaking up on him properly. *Surreptitiously and under cover of darkness. Stealth.*

Having spent eight months in the central highlands as a platoon leader and another two as company commander, I had received a new mission. We were attached to a mechanized company at a fire base near the coast. The flatlands. In the mountains, the war had made me a Daniel Boone, Kentucky woodsman in search of Indians. The country was vast, the Indians scarce, though we were not without our share of skirmishes. Although finding the enemy was frustrating, the advantages of the highlands were this: we were on an even keel with the VC. We looked for them; they avoided us. Occasionally they looked for us. (One fire base was nearly *overrun* at Di Linh; one of our platoons was massacred by a VC company near my old platoon AO outside of Bao Loc.)

In triple canopy mountainous terrain, it is easy to get lost and hard to be found. We became trackers of blood trails, elephant dung, and footprints. We raided base camps, threw hundreds of tons of rice into flowing streams, burned villages and called in air strikes. The enemy was elusive, but at least we kept him on the run and, for the most part, at bay. We became so accustomed to leaches they became a mere nuisance, rapidly killed by a squirt of insect repellent.

"Lewis and Clark" is another proper analogy for my highlands experience. The problems of survival from the elements became as much a priority as avoidance of VC ambushes. Navigation, food, water, shelter from the wet monsoon, and the excitement of new terrain discovered became my daily existence. At such time as our battalion strategy departed from what I called "the Dak To Syndrome," company commanders were permitted to send platoons on their own. I had arrived in Vietnam and taken command of a platoon in April of 1968 after the Tet offensive of January, during which the 173rd faced head-on with a NVA (North Vietnamese Army) regiment at Dak To. Battalion and company commanders had thereafter visions of NVA regiments again sweeping down on

14

173rd units. As this fear subsided, the platoons began operating on their own and we later increased our saturation with "hawk teams," also called "hunter-killer teams," of six to ten men on their own but usually within supporting distance of one thousand to five thousand meters. In bolder moments, we operated more independently, much like LRRPS (long range reconnaissance patrols).

Thus I was, like Boone or Clark, on my own in a wilderness, in radio contact generally, but not always, with a rendevous for resupply every four to ten days. It was exhilarating. The independence. The responsibility. The control. The fire power. If need be, I had at hand Air Force bombers or Cobra helicopter gun ships, plus battalion artillery and sometimes mortars. In inclement weather, the air support was nill. We were usually out of range of the battalion 4.2 inch mortars and had ceased since the days of the Dak To Syndrome to hump the 8.1 inch mortar.

One memorable event was taking my platoon, as pointman, through mountain wilderness for days, heading for a large river, catching ridge lines for ease of travel, navigation and communication due to elevation. No less exhilarated, I suppose, than Lewis and Clark when they reached the Columbia River was I as I approached the edge of the ridge line and viewed the river and its valley below. No doubt the first man - not just first white man - to see the river from that vantage point. *Man, talk about John Muir and the Sierra Club, this is wilderness with a capital W*, I thought.

I had walked around spiderwebs across the trail commanded by a spider as big as my fist. Orangutans ran past our positions. Gorillas climbed trees, appearing at first to be VC with black pajama shorts. Camouflaged insects never seen by *National Geographic* shared my dinner. Deer barked in the draws at dawn, and one evening at dusk, as I sipped hot cocoa, my spine chilled hearing the unmistakeable sound of a tiger's roar, not within one hundred meters below our position. Other evenings on other knolls (we always sought the high ground), I was deafened by the roar - yes - roar - of tree locusts. They all started at once, as if an alarm had sprung. These locusts became for us nature's clock. It was time to set out the claymores and trip flares, for there were but fifteen minutes of twighlight remaining.

We had become one with nature by sight, sound and smell. We did not bathe for months at a time, unless you count monsoon showers or swollen stream crossings. Camouflage stick was impractical as unshaven, dirty faces served the purpose. Fatigue jackets (shirts) were repeatedly recycled from wet perspiration to dry. Over a thirty-day period our jackets provided a sour, vinegar-like odor which over time became comforting. It is your smell and you are used to it. No talking, only whispers. (Some GI's have to be *reminded* and even *taught* to whisper.)

Logistics for me after a short time in the bush was down to a science. I learned to travel light. As platoon leader, I needed to be on my feet constantly, and, if not on point, navigating behind point. I learned to exist with the bare essentials: four to six canteens of water, purification tablets, four days of chow, which could be stretched to ten, poncho liner (a light, space-age blanket), foot powder. A ditty bag with cocoa, cream, Nestee, Start orange drink powder, matches, and heat tablets, plus my small portable radio with earphone, toothpaste and brush, Dentyne gum, insect repellent. A waterproof bag with extra pair of socks, wool jungle sweater, black nylon t-shirt, plus a navy poncho, all packed in a ruck sack (backpack with metal frame). Machete, patrol cap, green towel, small spy camera, lensatic compass, note pad, writing paper, paperback book, M-16 rifle, cartridge belt with loaded magazines, map, fragmentation grenades, regular grenades, smoke grenades, Marine K-bar knife, can openers, demolition knife, and flashlight. I could slip my ruck sack over my back without assistance, leaving me totally independent, as necessary, from my comrades. Typically on the move, the platoon would rest off the trail, sitting on their rucks, watchful. Observation posts/listening posts (OPs/LPs) would move out to the flanks, front and rear. I would venture to the front or flanks for a map and terrain check, or perhaps a look for a patrol base location.

I wore a set of jungle fatigues with pants tucked into jungle boots (to keep out the leeches), no underwear (to prevent *crotch rot*), a *drive-on rag* bandanna, steel helmet with camouflage cover. I carried the frag grenades in shirt pockets and my map in the leg pocket. I attached my compass to my breast pocket with a nylon shoelace, using it constantly. Also in the breast pocket I maintained pad and pen, plus a small and large can opener, *P38* and *B52*, named after the WWII airplanes. (It was said in WWII that the *P38 Lightning* was the Army Air Corps' best flying machine, thus the name for the Army's best machine since the *Lightning*, a small can opener, an indispensable machine for the *line doggy*. The larger *church key* opener was named after the larger plane. This was all logical, at least to the *dog face*, or infantryman.)

Smoke grenades were kept for the most part in my ruck, or sometimes in my shirt pocket. I did not carry what the Army issues as combat harness or load-bearing equipment, which we referred to as *LBJ*, for *load bearing junk*. I found the World War II and Korea-type web gear of the Army imcompatible with the ruck. Also, unlike many GI's, I felt insecure with hand grenades dangling off my web gear. Vines could pull out pins. (One day I lost to vines my gold Rolex watch for which I had paid $250 at West Point.)

It was amazing how much fatigue shirt and pants pockets could hold. In fact, if we ventured out on patrol from a base camp, we often stuck one canteen and a little chow in one leg pocket, and squeezed a poncho liner in the other. That way, if we decided to remain overnight (RON), we had the bare essentials. The other choice was to try to get back to base before dark and worry about being ambushed because we were too tired to be alert. The ruck fit high on my shoulder, where it belonged, and it became a part of my body.

Much of my time in the mountains was during the wet monsoon season, during which rain and cold became a major enemy. (In Vietnam, there are two "monsoons," wet and dry.) We were constantly at risk of trenchfoot and had difficulty getting foot powder. "Those rear echelon motherfuckers [REMFS] enjoy coke, beer, USO shows with Bob Hope, whores and TVs, and we can't as much as get foot powder or extra socks," complained my platoon sergeant, Gary Evans, "Big G," from Memphis, Tennessee. "This stupid gook war gonna break my mind." Grunts of the 173rd, euphemistically called *the Herd*, had a reputation for being unruly. They fragged officers (threw fragmentation grenades), or shot them in the back, wore beads and earrings, and hung chains of VC ears around their necks. While their officers became alcoholics in the rear, grunts turned to marijuana in the field.

I wore just the fatigues with sleeves rolled up until dusk, when it got cooler. Then it was time for T-shirt, jungle sweater shirt tucked in (to maintain body warmth) and Navy canvas parka. When we were on our own as a platoon of twenty to thirty grunts, I would locate higher ground, set up a perimeter using a clock system, and set out OPs/LPs. We then took turns *chowing down* and setting up one or two-man hooches with ponchos. Two men snapped ponchos together, tied the corners off to trees, and drove in two stakes to the middle at each end. The hooch was kept but two or three feet off the ground so as to prevent a high profile to VC onlookers. I usually preferred hard ground over air mattresses because mattress rolling was noisy, and I invariably slid off the mattress or downhill on it. In rocky terrain, I blew just a little air into the mattress. While rolling on an air mattress makes a lot of noise, snoring was a bigger problem. We had to awaken our comrades to keep the noise down.

We discovered that termites eat through a mattress in a matter of minutes and have insatiable appetites. When dealng with red ants and termites, there was only one alternative: move. Also, we were at risk of what we called *airborne ants.*, ants which, I swear, waited on branches until you walked under, and then leaped from the branch onto the back of your neck. No parachutes. There were also a lot of flying ants. The worst were what we called *piss ants*: small red ones which were probably of the fire ant variety.

In wet monsoon weather, I was soaking wet and wore the Navy poncho constantly. It also served as a good windbreaker and insulator. Once I settled down under the hooch, I removed my soaking socks, dried my feet, applied powder, and put on the dry socks and boots. It was not smart to sleep with your boots off, and for reasons of security, I insisted my men sleep with their boots on and only lightly inflate their air mattresses. The wet socks, I would hope, would dry under my poncho liner by body heat. Even a wet poncho liner kept me warm, and, out of the rain, it would dry by body heat. (God bless the inventor of the Army poncho liner!) With dry T-shirt and jungle sweater, wet shirt and parka, and dry poncho liner over my head, I usually dried by body heat in a matter of hours, lying under the hooch, protected from the rain. Ambush was a different matter: no hooch, soaken wet throughout the night.

We took turns at watch, but if it rained hard, it did little good. The rain was deafening and the jungle pitch black. I adapted and generally slept well, except when on ambush. When we traveled as a company, the platoons took turns in sending out a one-squad ambush. Also, when we traveled in company mass, we had the additional hassle of digging at least foxholes, if not building bunkers, and clearing fields of fire with machetes. The *Dak To Syndrome*. In the case of bamboo, it made such a racket that the VC could hear us for miles. (A field of fire is a pathway cut for clearing a firing lane, so that rounds find their mark - the enemy's chest.)

It was always my belief that we were better off in platoon-size, even hawk-size teams, so as to better saturate the area, yet be within supporting distance of one another. Bunkers made excellent targets for the Russian-made B-40 rockets carried by VC and NVA. My biggest fear was setting up a base camp with such clamor that the VC would know our position. It was then their choice: attack or leave the area. In either case, we were the loser. Resupply every four days or more by chopper presented the same problem: it drew attention to our position.

Dinner was my big meal. We preferred the freeze-dried food provided for *LRRPS* which we referred to as *lurps*. But they were scarce. My favorites were beef with rice and spaghetti. A little fresh onion or Tabasco sauce gave it a lift. I made a heat tablet stove by cutting air holes into a small, empty C-ration can with the B-52, heated the water, and then poured it into the lurp pouch, allowing it to sit. Delicious. The C-rations were not as good, but of those I preferred the spaghetti and meatballs and beans with franks. I might have poundcake for dessert and top it off with some hot cocoa.

For breakfast, I typically had only cocoa, maybe some C-ration poundcake or an almond roll, and I would not eat much during the day. At lunchtime, I usually ate only peanut butter, jelly and crackers and some fruit. I snacked on fruit or candy bars during the day for energy. I repeatedly requested from *the home front* care packages to include exotic foods such as crabmeat and condiments like ketchup and tartar sauce. After eighteen months of Viet Nam C-rations, I came home craving condiments, a habit I have maintained to this day.

So the big advantage of being in the central highlands was that we were on equal footing with the VC so long as we traveled quietly in small groups as a platoon or hawk team. I felt most secure, in fact, under the hawk team concept, and liked the idea of numerous ambush sights. When we operated as hawk teams, it was not during the wet monsoon season and we did not erect a hooch, but rather slept under the stars. Also as an extra safety precaution, because we were so limited in number, we ate at one location, moved to another location at dusk, and *reconned* at the same time our final location, and then after dark moved into our final position. We were easily outnumbered and our best strategy was not to be seen. The disadvantage was that we could not set out trip flares or claymores in the dark, but I preferred, for security reasons, night movement over mines or early warning devices. A blanket of darkness was our best security. We usually set up along trails, hoping for some action. Because our friend became the dark, moonlit nights became a problem, especially in areas where vegetation was more sparse.

In the latter part of my second tour I felt most insecure. *Pacification*, then *Vietnamization*, which meant we were to secure the villages (showing that we had won the war) and then turn the war over to the South Vietnamese. Fat chance. Not only did the enemy have a fix on our positions, we were forbidden from patrolling beyond limits, and, due to proximity to villages, the friendlies were forbidden to fire without approval from higher headquarters even if fired upon first. The rule was this: get shot at, duck, call battalion and tell them the direction from which you are receiving fire, battalion calls the province chief, the province chief checks the sector on his map and determines if permission should be granted, the province chief tells battalion, battalion tells us. "You gotta be shittin' me," so sayeth the troops. "Sorry, no can do, motherfuck."

We did what came natural to survivalists, but that which was unnatural for West Point captains: disobey a direct order. Add to the scenario one important step: before calling battalion, I would receive a call from a platoon several clicks (a click is one thousand meters) away drawing sniper fire from the sand dunes to their east. Nothing but sand between the platoon and the deep blue sea. A platoon was supposed to request my permission and I then would pass the word on. This was President Nixon's way of winding down America's involvement in Vietnam, reducing the casualty rate, and obtaining "peace with honor," - all at *our* risk, not his.

Of course I was duty bound to give the order. No winks nor smiles. This is what the Army calls CYA ("cover your ass"). But it was understood without saying that the local commander, the squad leader in this case, not the Commander-in-Chief in Washington, the President of the United States, made the decision. "Shoot first, ask permission later." *Court martial me. What are they going to do - send us to Vietnam?* Battalion understood. The province chief understood. It was the *unwritten and unstated law.* Law of the jungle. Survive. Kill or be killed.

The highlands also held the advantage of plentiful, potable water and cover from the sun and temperature, all of which were related. Fresh water was more plentiful in the mountains as the result of more rainfall, resulting in mountain streams and springs. Also, our consumption of water was much lower in the mountains due to lower temperature as a result of both the altitude and the triple canopy. We did not see much of the sun in the highlands, whereas we roasted on the coast.

The flatlands or coastal plains were not without their advantages for us during late summer of 1969. There, the VC were not only plentiful, they were easily found. Not in large numbers; but in small squad-sized groups of eight to twelve. Because it had been the armored cavalry or mechanized infantry (MECH) which had worked the area extensively, rather than grunts or ground pounders, the VC had been lulled into a state of complacency. They returned each night and sometimes even during the day to their hooches and families in the rural areas without threat of American foot soldiers. They were confident of their simple early warning device: the sound of track vehicles which can be heard for at least a mile.

We were for a time attached to a MECH infantry company which, except for regular highway patrolling, remained within a perimeter defense near Highway 1, the main South Vietnam north-south artery. Upon arrival, it was unclear who would be the lead officer - the MECH commander or me. Remembering well the concept of unity of command, I inquired of my battalion commander and the decision was made: we were attached to the MECH and therefore their commanding officer (CO) was in command. I was bothered by this for several reasons.

First, the MECH had become too defensively oriented. Although they assisted with the regular daylight patrols on Highway 1, they seldom utilized foot patrols, LPs/OPs or ambushes outside their perimeter. As MECH *track heads*, as we called them, they were comfortable with the security of the tracks and the fire power available. They utilized the armored personnel carrier (APC), a tank-like tracked vehicle. A *moving coffin.* I was uncomfortable even around a track: it serves as a sitting duck or a slow moving target.

I was not without MECH experience, having served two months with the Fifth Infantry Division (Mechanized) at Ft. Carson, Colorado when still a West Point cadet in the summer of 1965. *Third Lieutenants*, they called us. I commanded a weapons platoon and had experienced the intensive training of an Army Training Test (ATT). And so, I was well aware of the limits as well as the capabilities of mechanized infantry.

Second, the MECH unit to which I was attached was experiencing some shell shock or battle fatigue as the result of a high casualty rate during their patrols of Highway 1. Tracks are susceptible as easy targets for a command or pressure detonated boobie trap, as well as ambush. One B-40 rocket fired by a twelve-year-old VC would not only stop an APC dead in its tracks, but kill a squad of infantry within or even on top of the track. *Coffin on wheels.* For this reason, and due to the heat, infantry in Vietnam typically rode on top or walked behind or alongside the tracks. For me it was still not desirable: the sitting duck target drew enemy fire. *Bigger they are, harder they fall.* Thus, I was not thrilled with the prospect of joint patrol operations and, as it turned out, they were few and far between because we were far more effective in the bushes on foot, alone.

The *tread heads*, on the other hand, were relieved to see us. Our mission was to find in the bushes complacent VC, thus taking from them the offensive and desire of initiative. An enemy on the run has little desire to regroup and attack. We were to patrol extensively utilizing the track camp as our base of operations. As Airborne Infantry, we were glad to get out of the perimeter and into our own element.

Attacks on the perimeter were rare. The VC need not bother since they could pick the battleground: tracks in the open on patrol. This, of course, was a major principle of guerrilla warfare: the guerrilla selects the battleground. *He who fights and runs away, lives to fight another day.* A tiger which leaps onto the elephant's back can take bites one at a time, leaping back into the jungle after each bite.

Therefore, the situation boiled down to this: we knew where to find the enemy by approaching the hooches shown on the map. The challenge was simply to catch them by surprise. Considering that we were watched constantly by VC or VC sympathizers within the village just outside the base camp, our ingenuity and imagination were greatly challenged. *Outsmart the fox.*

We were consistently inconsistent. Borrowing from Ranger techniques and tactics, we sent out patrols, ambushes and LP's/OP's by varying time, place, route, number of men, and equipment carried. We assumed always that we were watched. We utilized the ruse, diversion, demonstration and feint. For example, we might patrol at dawn within the village, drawing a lot of attention to our presence, and while occupying the eyes and ears of VC or VC sympathizers at that location, another patrol would slip into the bush in another direction. Or a patrol might leave obviously headed north, but once they were in the bushes they would circle around and head south. Another trick was the stay behind patrol. A patrol with, say, twelve men would leave late afternoon and return at dusk. They would enter the perimeter wire when it would be just dark enough to make it impossible for villagers to count the number of men. Three remained in the bush.

Because we knew the general location of the VC who returned to their hooches at night, and because the hooches were, at two to three clicks, within walking distance of our camp, the biggest problem became barking dogs. After all of my sophisticated military training, my nemesis was a dog! It was extremely difficult to sneak up on a group of hooches with several dogs, any of which might be awake. Dogs have a great sense of smell, and Americans smell a lot different than Vietnamese. Typically, we planned our arrival so that we attacked at dawn. Not only did this give us the element of surprise, but as well, we hoped the dogs would be asleep. Not so. Often, they awoke during our approach. Because of women and children within the hooches, we were not able to merely shoot up the area at random.

I therefore developed other tactics. If we had a good idea of the route of escape, we placed a small ambush force on the route. Two small forces, then, of three to five men each would approach from the bush at dawn from two sides. On the third side, perhaps a trail or other likely avenue of escape, I placed a third team. The first two teams approached cautiously, the dogs barked and the VC fled through the likely avenue and were gunned down. If we lost the fleeing VC due to other escape routes, we shot the dogs and tried the same tactics days later. It was just a matter of time before *papa son* would again visit home. The problem was it seemed the VC had an endless supply of dogs. No wonder, considering they added dog meat to their diet of rice.

As the result of both boredom and frustration, I developed another tactic which provided more excitement than success. I carried a light anti-tank weapon (LAW) which is a small, discardable bazooka-type weapon which fires once. (We never discarded LAWs for reason the VC could make some use of them.) As I observed a VC (if they were young and ran, they no doubt were VC) run from a hooch at dusk where the VC was out of range of our M-16, I fired the LAW. *Whoosh, kaboom.* I think some world records in the 100 meter dash were set.

My former West Point roommate, Dean Kunihiro, was of particular assistance to me during this phase of my eighteen months

22

in Vietnam. When Dean and I were promoted to captain in June of 1969, I became company commander of Charlie Company and Dean became battalion intelligence officer (S-2). Dean had ready access to a chopper, so together we flew aerial recon by chopper, searching for likely VC hideouts. We then planned for the operation of my six-man "Hawk teams," or "Killer-hunter teams," coordinating with the battalion recon platoon which was under Dean's control.

Dean was frustrated: he wanted to be in the thick of the action, having spent only a short time as platoon leader in the boonies before his promotion to captain. Dean and I together graduated from Airborne, Ranger and the Infantry Officer Basic schools, and we were then assigned to 82nd Airborne Division at Fort Bragg, North Carolina, arriving December, 1967. Desiring to go to medical school, Dean chose Chemical Corps rather than Infantry branch. (He figured his chances of Army assignment to medical school were better from Chemical Corps.) Thus, Dean was "detailed" Infantry branch for only two years, and the "plumb" of company command was not to be his; it was reserved for "career Infantry officers." *Infantry. Queen of Battle. "Follow Me!"* Afterall, are not the missions of *all* other branches in essence to support the Infantry? Basic mission of the Infantry is: "close with and kill the enemy." *Shoot. Move. Communicate.*

One day Charlie Company had particular luck with what I called "Ft. Benning tactics," meaning *by the book* of The Infantry School in Georgia. On a daylight patrol, we targeted a small group of hooches. As we approached we heard young male voices and believed VC to be in the area. The hooches were in the open surrounded by a sparsely wooded area. Using the clock system, with our location at six o'clock, I sent one squad around the left skirting the woods, dropping off men so that six o'clock to nine o'clock to twelve o'clock was covered. Likewise, on the right for six o'clock to three o'clock to twelve o'clock. The headquarters, which included me, Sergeant Cox and two RTOs (radio telephone operators), remained at the six o'clock position. We waited. After an hour or so the chattering stopped, the meeting having broken up, and I heard one crack of a shot followed by a dull thud, as if someone fired a single shot into a tree or log.

One of my men, brand new in country and on his first patrol, alone at the ten o'clock position, was observing a trail when a male with a Soviet-made AK-47 rifle, accompanied by a female, walked rapidly down the trail. This man kept his cool, took a bead on the male VC, fired one shot, and hit him squarely in the head. The woman fled. My grunt was not sure what to do about the young lady since she did not have a weapon. I explained later that if she was an obvious VC she was fair game, with or without a weapon. *If she was with VC then she was VC. Guilt by association.* We then closed the noose on the remaining five VC with children. It was getting dark, and fearing a counter-attack or ambush, I pulled back to a small knoll about two hundred meters away where we set up a tight perimeter. I left one squad in a dry river bed watching the main trail. After hearing a lot of movement, they became spooked, fearing they were being surrounded. Knowing firsthand the tricks darkness can play, I yielded to the request of their squad leader to join us on the knoll, which they did. We watched carefully to see that they were not closely followed, as now it was becoming very dark in the woods.

I now had two squads, five VC, and a few children on a small hill in the middle of nowhere with no cover but a few trees. I chose not to dig in for reason of noise security. I felt that while the VC might suspect we were on the hill, they would not know *for sure* unless we made a lot of noise. We were vulnerable, but our only other alternative was to withdraw to the base camp, some five clicks away, or to another location, at the risk of ambush. I elected to remain, spotting our position with artillery rounds.

Although the spots, actual rounds placed at my direction thus bracketing our position, ascertained our general position, I felt the VC might be discouraged from attack if they knew of the fire power readily available. But we were in for a long night.

The VC persisted in probing our position. It was now pitch black and we could see nothing but did hear movement. Without definitive targets and not knowing the size of the enemy, I had the men hold their fire, lest we give away our firing positions. *Hold your fire 'til you see the whites of their eyes.* Our noise security was compounded by the men, women and children we held captive. The men and women had their hands tied behind their back while I trusted that the small children would remain with their parents. I felt that restless children would grow more restless if their hands were tied. We had no interpreter and learned that much of the prisoner commotion was due to the calls of nature. We were humiliated no less than our prisoners by the urinating and defecating within a few feet of us, the captors. I could recall no Infantry School textbook which dealt with that problem. Dawn came none too early, but we remained cautious. After sweeping the area with one squad, I moved the patrol to a clear area, called for a chopper, and evacuated our catch. Our mission now: more of the same, the hooches by what we called on the map the blue line. The river.

So here I was pointman, inching my way up the river bottom trail, watchful of boobie traps and expecting VC dashing my way any second. *Hauling ass. Capping up.* As company commander, I was carrying a CAR-15, a "sub-machine gun" which is a short barrelled version of the M-16 with folding stock. I had chambered a round long ago when we left the base camp and now quietly and carefully moved the safety switch from the semi-automatic to the fully-automatic position. *Quick a-go-go.* Nothing like a spray of 7.62 milimeter to ruin a guy's day when his objective is fleeing down a trail. I was all eyes and ears, now in a crouched position. Slowly. *Take it easy. No hurry. You've got all day, Captain Mac.*

Behind and covering me as slack man stalked Sergeant Cox, behind him my two RTOs, back a way so that any radio transmissions would not be heard at my location on point. I had two radios so that I could simultaneously effect communication with my company elements and battalion headquarters. Within minutes I could have available artillery or gun ship support. The second RTO walked cautiously backwards as rear security. The first RTO was responsible for the flanks.

The hairs on my arms were on end. Antennae. I could sense the enemy. I was now committed on the trail and at the highest level of concentration. *I am a cat.* I was made up of nothing but eyeballs and ears. The hairs on my arms and neck were more than antennae now; they were feelers, feeling even the difference in density of the air. It was all an illusion, of course, but it was the power of my mind. I allowed the illusion to become reality.

He first appeared on my left flank above me on the hillside. I froze. Just as expected, just as we had planned, as my elements moved in from the north, and east, their presence was detected and this gook, at least, was *fixin' to dee dee* (run) out the sierra whisky (southwest). The blue line, running from northeast to southwest was the most logical choice as an avenue of escape for it provided the best available cover and concealment from an enemy approaching from the north and east. We purposely did not approach from the west. He moved with purpose, but slowly, quietly and cautiously down the slope. *How many more?* My eyes darted left, front, right, left, front, right. A small gurgling from the stream to my right flank was the only sound. I seemed to stop breathing. My heart was not pounding. *Has it stopped?* With the adrenalin soar, I had no fear, only anticipation.

As he continued at an angle down the slope, I remained frozen and had not yet drawn a bead on him for fear my movement would give me away. At the point on the trail at which I crouched, there was little concealment from the underbrush or from trees, and less cover in event I was fired upon. He had not yet faced me, and appeared to be looking for something. I watched in anticipation for a weapon. None. He stopped, turned his back to me, now a mere twenty-five meters away. I could hear him breathing forcefully, from fear, not from his movement which had been purposeful but slow. *What is he doing?* Cache on the side of the hill? A small cave? *Probably his AK or a Chi Com carbine.*

I could read Cox's mind. Though his breathing, like mine,

seemed to have stopped, I could sense his presence behind me. *Let's blow him away and ask questions later.* I sensed the RTOs had frozen about fifteen meters back, and from lack of any sound of the radio rushing noise, knew they had turned off the radios. At least I *hoped* they had turned off the radios. Take no chances with noise discipline now. It took but a few seconds to turn a radio on; it took less to take a bullet through the heart.

I considered opening fire with a spray of bullets, with the result one VC killed in action (KIA). Or a single shot through the head. *Crack, thump.* Just like dead wood. It is no wonder they call it *dead wood between the ears*, I thought. Whoever started that one knew that a bullet directly into the head sounds like one into a tree stump. But if I fired, there were risks. I would give away our position and be caught in a draw with little cover and concealment. Return fire by other VC could ruin my day. If this gook moved north or northeast back up the hill, he would fall within our net. If he proceeded south or southeast down the hill, I would move forward and converge with him on the trail still with, I hoped, the element of surprise. If he came toward me, well, we'll see ....

The VC pulled a ruck from the small cave and began moving down the hill toward me, backwards. The ruck appeared full, and from the way he was carrying it - heavy. *No doubt now. VC.* Twenty meters, fifteen, then ten. *He still doesn't see me!* He was watching for the enemy from the direction of the hooch he had left. *Or is he watching for his comrades to link up?*

No time to decide. He has moved backwards down the hill to the trail and stands with his back to me a mere five meters now. He breathes heavily. Too late now for any further thinking, for I know he will have to turn in my direction to move down the trail.

I slowly rise, bring my CAR-15 to my shoulder and take a bead on his head, my finger relaxed but pressured against the trigger. He turns, sees the barrel in his face, drops the ruck and shakes like an autumn leaf. He is too shocked to shout initially, to run, to do anything but to shake. *My God. It's a kid about twelve years old, unarmed but obviously VC.* While I consider the trigger, Cox reacts quickly, for which I thank him later. He jumps past me and with one sweep covers the boy's mouth and knocks him to the ground. I start to draw my knife quickly from its sheath, my other hand on the gook's throat, CAR-15 now by my side, and the kid begins to panic, trying to scream. Rather than draw the knife, with my free hand I help Cox cover his mouth. The lad's attempts worry us and cause us to be only stronger with our grip and more purposeful. The first RTO, *the Professor*, watches the trail ahead, though he has moved no closer. Cox, the boy and I remain on the ground. Observing the universal sign for silence, our forefinger over the lips, he quiets when I withdraw my hand from his throat. *If we can keep him quiet now, no need to kill him. God, a twelve-year old boy and I almost blew him away at point-blank range. No one would have blamed me. He is no doubt the enemy.*

While Cox holds the boy down, covering his mouth with one hand, I advance forward. The boy, no longer fearing immediate death, has relaxed a little. By hand signals, I tell the others to remain. We have said nothing. I make little commotion. I sense more VC ahead.

I inch my way up the trail, close to where it crosses the stream. On the other side is the trail and then banana groves and elephant grass in a very thick marshland. The southern route, though slower, provides the greatest concealment for the enemy. It is impossible to run through elephant grass without leaving a trail, but the trail can become a maze of trails, any of which may bear a boobie trap, punji stake pit, or spider trap, which is a VC in a hole with a thatched, hinged roof ready to spring up and fire. I do not like the thought.

As I continue to inch my way in a silent low crawl, I hear whispers. I then observe through the bush across the creek no more than ten meters away two VC with weapons. Grown men. *Damn, I can reach out and touch them.* They are preoccupied and do not see me. *Probably discussing which way to go if the enemy soldiers in fact come upon the hooch, as would be indicated by the chickens and dogs. Perhaps they are waiting for the boy. A rendezvous? I am back to square one. Some predicament. Shoot or wait? Are there more? Wouldn't it be nice if my other elements arrive at the hooch and five or ten VC decide to run down the trail and right into me? I've got twenty rounds locked and loaded, and my CAR-15 can fire at a rate of ...? That's how many seconds to fire twenty rounds?* I estimate I'll hit three to five with the first burst and lock and load a second magazine while remaining in the prone position. Chances are any shots taken at me by the remaining VC will be high. *Grenades? Damn, I'm in the lowland. Any VC at the hooch has an easy grenade target.*

I contemplate my fate and that of the VC as I remain frozen. Minutes slowly go by. My eyes dart left, front, right, left, front, right. *The VC are to my right flank. No wait - they're gone! Where in the hell did they go? They were so close. Are they moving in on me?*

Noises now in the hooch area. Whistles and other bird sounds. I recognize them as my men and, with some hesitation, signal back with whistles. Slowly we link up. The trails lead through the swamps to the south and southeast. For reasons stated, I decide not to pursue. Chances of catching them in the maze of swampland are slim to nil. I climb the hill to the hooches. Women and children only. The requested chopper comes for the boy. Through interrogation, we learn later that he is indeed VC, trained by NVA in the area. His father and uncle have escaped. How they disappeared before my eyes I still have not determined. This much is certain: *He who fights and runs away lives to fight another day....*

In April of 1969, after receiving the *Vietnamese Cross of Gallantry with Silver Star,* I wrote from Vietnam the following:

The war continues the same for us, bombing halt or no bombing halt, peace talks or no peace talks. Despite the frustrations encountered, the eight months I spent on line as a rifle platoon leader were the most satisfying of my life. The satisfaction came not just from the knowledge that I was serving my country in a commendable manner. As much, it came from living and fighting with the *young kids* in the platoon I led. Enough tribute cannot be given to the line infantry man fighting in Vietnam.

Averaged out, he is nineteen years old, a high school graduate and married, with one child -- or, one on the way. He is not *Soul Brother* or *Non-Soul Brother,* he is *Garbage Man, Quick-draw, Gringo, Bluegrass, Goose, Kid, Pedro, Big G, Top, Featherr,* or *Doc.* Race, religion, or color are not his enemy. He is simply *an American, a line doggie,* one who gets the job done because *someone has to,* if for no other reason. He is not without his doubts, fears, regrets, and other wars with his private feelings. At the least, he has affections to fight for. Too often he goes home a creditor -- the debt never to be repaid. God is his pointman for, as Helen Steiner Rice says, "No one walks so close to God as those who walk so close to death." He is called *boonie rat,* but he has a spirit capable of love, compassion, faith, integrity, humor, charity, sacrifice, and endurance. But most especially he has *courage,* and the courage he desires and prizes *is not the courage to die decently, but to live manfully.* If he lives to be twenty, he is a MAN.

There are only two kinds of soldiers on the battlefield: the quick and the dead. Author unknown

CRAZY HORSE   Chapter 2

I first met Frank Audrain when, as company commander, I was on patrol in the central highlands. *Lt. Frank Erwin Audrain, West Point Class of '68, Airborne, Ranger, Infantry, Marine, and part Indian.* He was walking in my footsteps when we first met. *"Cherry, FNG,* Fucking New Guy," my seasoned RTO proclaimed. A new lieutenant joining *the Herd.* Fresh fatigues and boots. His compadre, Sergeant Stafford. The two had been to Ranger school together. Stafford, from Tennessee, had a tatoo that covered half his back. Blond and handsome, about nineteen, he had attended the Non-Commissioned Officers School of six weeks - *shake 'n bake* - and was therefore staff sergeant E-6 at an early age. His tour of Vietnam would be short-lived, due to his encounter in a banana grove with an NVA lieutenant armed with a semi-automatic pistol.

Audrain, descendant of a French Canadian trapper grandfather and Indian grandmother, looked like a character out of *Northwest Passage.* He was made of steel, but soft spoken. At more than six feet, he was lean, dark complected, high cheekbones. What was most remarkable was his obvious sense of purpose. He had a way of being relaxed in an intense mode, and being intense to the extent that looks could kill. His jawbones gave away the intensity building inside; they constantly quivered. Nicknamed by his men *Crazy Horse* for his Indian heritage, his fearless fighting, and his less than adept manner by which he could hold his liquor, Frank would have a lasting encounter with Stafford's NVA lieutenant. You do not shoot *Crazy Horse's* friend in the stomach at close range and walk away without repercussions. Without liquor, *Crazy Horse* could be crazy.

Although Frank was but a year behind me at West Point, I had not known him. The West Point Corps was made up of some four thousand cadets. But I learned later the high respect his classmates held for him. The Corps was divided into four regiments and Frank had graduated regimental commander. From his hometown in Reno, Nevada, he had enlisted in the Marine Corps and attended one year at the University of Nevada prior to his admission to the Military Academy. Thus, he was a year older than me.

It was one day, while on patrol in the coastal flatlands, that some of Frank's men had surprised some VC and their NVA lieutenant advisors at a hooch. They shot up a couple of VC, one of which was gunned down by an M-16 as he ran, the other laid dying when I arrived with our medic, the doc. Here I was, kneeling at a hooch a couple of yards from this elderly, dying VC who had a sucking chest wound. The doc was working on him, there was gunfire all around, and I was talking to battalion on the radio, advising of the situation. *Crazy Horse* was on his way. Anxious. His first squad, which he usually used as point and were the biggest hell raisers, was led by Stafford and they were involved in the shootout. *Crazy Horse* was not about to miss any of the action. But before he arrived, this is what happened.

I am on one knee, on the radio talking to battalion, my RTO, *the Professor* (because he looked like one), is kneeling beside me, his M-16 at the ready. A couple of feet away lies this dying VC with Doc working on him. The two NVA advisors had fled from the hooch a few yards away, into a banana grove, which was about ten feet lower elevation. Sergeant Stafford and one of his buddies, Jones, had chased after the NVA and were scurrying in the dense vegetation. We anxiously awaited. Intermittent firing was taking place by other squad members who were chasing more VC into the woodline. The VC were returning fire and there were some bullets overhead, but nothing dangerously close. In any event, there was no cover. The best we could do was take the prone position.

So I continued to talk on the radio, with the sounds of all these shots being heard by the battalion commander and other staff officers, and I am sure they are thinking I have contact with a VC battalion, and I am trying to reassure them with my slow drawl, "This is Charlie Six, we've got contact, one VC KIA, one VC WIA, call up the dust off (medivac helicopter) if you want to talk to the WIA. Won't last long. Some VC fled to the woodline and we've got two NVA in a banana grove, just to my November (north)." As I am talking on the radio, I am interrupted by one shot in the banana grove and a cry "He shot Stafford. Stafford's hit." It's Jones. With this, as I continue to talk on the radio, Stafford's best buddy in all the world, and the best pointman in the unit, Smith, who is acting as my security along with the RTO, kneeling a few feet away, rises, leaving his M-16. Without as much as pulling a knife, he leaps into the banana grove, scurrying after the NVA that just shot Stafford. I continue to drawl into the mike. It all happens in a flash. Next, I see a lot of banana trees taking a beating, hear a lot of cursing by Smith, yelling for Stafford, "Where are you? Stafford, are you okay? Where the hell's Stafford?" Unarmed, Smith is after a guy who obviously has a gun and shot his best friend.

I am still talking on the radio, now with this, "Break. We've got a friendly WIA, make that urgent now on the dust off. I repeat, one friendly WIA; request dust off ASAP." As I continue to talk, I see this young NVA emerge from the banana grove, charging directly toward me with pistol in hand. He is not firing at us. His eyes are wild with fear. Smith is a foot or so behind him, bare handed,

30

ready I suppose to break this guy's neck. We do not have Stafford yet. He is still in the banana grove. The NVA is thirty feet away and coming straight for me. Professor raises his M-16 and with single shots, starts putting some rounds into him. I am still talking on the radio, and now the sounds of Professor's M-16 shots are going right into the mike, and I imagine some anxiety on behalf of the battalion commander and the staff officers, who must be curiously listening to our company's contact.

This NVA keeps coming. He is ten feet away now, his weapon raised, but not fired. Smith about to tackle. Professor is methodically pumping rounds into his chest. No panic. No *quick-a-go-go*. Just single shots. I continue to talk in my slow drawl. It is as if I am watching a movie, and it is not really happening, and I am just continuing with my business at hand.

Finally, the NVA drops right at my feet, having taken about ten rounds in the chest. As he hits the ground, all firing ceases, the movie including sound track, frozen. A still frame. There is not a sound. The world has stopped. Then there is one gross gasp from the old VC being worked on by the Doc. Doc looks over to me with his hands raised in a gesture of hopelessness. It still seems the world has gone silent, but for Doc's voice. "Well," he says matter-of-fact-like, "the old man's gone." I get the impression he died more of shock than his wounds, having just witnessed the NVA's unsuccessful charge on our position. Charge or flight from Smith? Smith is now back to his M-16 where he left it, picks it up and is ready to put some more holes into this dead NVA, and I tell him, "No, don't waste your ammunition. Let's take care of Stafford."

Now the other men in the squad are out to the woodline, securing our position. By this time Frank has shown up and is pulling Stafford out of the banana grove. Doc is looking after him. Stafford has been shot in the stomach and is in bad shape. The dust off we hope is on the way. We have also captured a second NVA with a pistol. The one who shot Stafford. Smith chased down the wrong guy! They tie the POW's hands behind his back and sit him by a tree.

With Frank is another squad. We are still taking some sniper fire from the trees. I continue to talk on the radio. I have some cobra gun ships on the way; in a few minutes they arrive. "Where do you want 'em, Charlie Six?" the cobra pilot requests, very nonchalant, as if delivering the Monday morning milk bottles to the back door step. I have two cobra ships at my disposal, armed with 5.2 inch rockets, and they can fire with pinpoint accuracy. We continue to take sniper fire from the tree line, only about seventy-five meters away. "Sniper in the tree line seventy-five mikes direct whiskey. Been a pain in the ass." "Roger," says the cobra ship. They are flying in echelon, meaning not quite abreast, one slightly trailing the other, flying directly from the east. Rockets let loose just over our heads and with, as I said pinpoint accuracy, the rockets land just where I want them. No more sniper fire. After directing the cobras for another fifteen minutes, things settle down and we have the area entirely secured and negative enemy fire. We pop smoke for the dust off and they take Stafford. Boy, is Frank mad. I trust he will cool off.

I am back on the horn (radio) with battalion, coordinating my next move, setting up a CP (command post). Frank walks over. He has been visiting with the NVA prisoner. The NVA has remained with his hands, and now his feet, tied, seated against a large tree. Some of Frank's key NCO's have been visiting with him also. From his uniform we know he is a lieutenant, an advisor to the VC local cadre.

Frank says to me very coolly, calmly and casual-like, as he pulls out his knife, "Sandy, " using my childhood nickname, "I'd like to have a serious talk with this NVA lieutenant. I don't like his attitude. I don't trust this rope we've used to tie him up. Too bad if he tries to escape. He might fall on my knife."

One day on a hilltop bunker, Frank told me of his marriage to Dana McDougal, whom he called Dani. She was an airline stewardess when they met on a blind date at West Point. Dani was petite and Frank told her she looked like a squirrel and asked her back to the Academy for another weekend date. On the second date, as she got off the bus, Frank had for her a little squirrel doll. Madly in love, they married soon after Frank graduated. As Frank reported to me in Vietnam, Dani was pregnant with their first child and remaining with her folks in North Dakota. So here is this straight-laced, former West Point regimental commander who stood tall in his dress gray uniform with five stripes on each shoulder and handed a little stewardess a squirrel doll as she got off the bus. This was the same Frank Audrain whom they called *Crazy Horse*, who wanted to cut up into little pieces an NVA lieutenant. Frank was the only guy I knew who, going into combat in Vietnam, fastened the chin strap to his helmet. Even John Wayne did not do that in the film *Iwo Jima*. If you were a company commander in Vietnam, you no doubt would want Audrain: Marine, West Point graduate, Airborne, Ranger, Infantry, ... Indian.

I had not been company commander long when Frank arrived. After eight months in the bush as platoon leader of 2nd Platoon, *Mike*, in Charlie Company, which was made up of four platoons: *Lima, Mike, November* and *Oscar*, following the phonetic alphabet, I was sent against my will to a staff position. During my seventh month as platoon leader, I had been offered battalion recon platoon, which I took as an honor because, typically, the best lieutenant in the battalion received the position. At the time, I was the most experienced lieutenant in the unit. Recon platoon was independent, on its own in search of the enemy. Its mission was to locate, not fight, the enemy. It operated much the same as LRRPS: far into enemy territory. Recon platoon is the "eyes and ears of the battalion." For days they might sit in the bush doing nothing but watching a trail or road. The recon platoon leader works directly for the battalion intelligence officer (S-2), a captain. At the time, it was tempting for me to take the position, for my new battalion and company commanders were less than confident and we were again under the *Dak To Syndrome.*

Captain Crowe, commander of Charlie, had received a direct commission from NCO. He had spent two other tours in Vietnam with Special Forces, but was a *cherry* when it came to handling a hundred men in combat. Special Forces captains handle an A-team of only twelve men, whereas majors command a Special Forces company of four A-teams. Although Crowe seemed to have great confidence in me, he was hesitant to let the platoon run independently. He had fears, I am sure, that we would be overrun by an NVA battalion, if not a regiment. In addition, he became irritable due to personal problems. Back in the *real world* (the United States), his father was dying. Captain Crowe and I had our share of field arguments, morale was low in the company, and I was generally disgusted with the whole situation. It did not take me long in the bush to conclude that the war effort was futile. But, as the saying goes, "it's not a very good war, but it's the best we've got." I was a professional soldier, having chosen, as they say at West Point, *the profession at arms.* I had *marched to the sound of the guns.* Thus, the move to recon and independence was tempting. But I was too loyal to the *Black Hawks,* a platoon nickname I had inherited. Guys like *Garbage Man, The Greek, Gringo,* and *Big G.*

I loved my platoon and could not bear to leave it. I discussed it with them, as we had a few days stand down in the battalion dump. That is right, after weeks in the boonies, we finally got a few days of supposed rest in the rear area, but as if we were a deserted stepchild whom everyone in the battalion rear wanted to forget, we were placed out at the airstrip to guard the aviation fuel drums. We were adjacent to the dump. No trees. Just a dump. The REMFs enjoy the hot chow, movies and TV, though our battalion camp at Bao Loc was no country club. Bob Hope never showed up there. But we were used to being the bastard child. *The Herd.* On a good day, we were happy to get a coke or two a piece. Warm. And the staff officers wondered why these guys smoked pot. "Piss on the battalion. Piss on recon platoon," my RTO told me. My only calling was with the *Black Hawks.* Their words echoed in my mind: "Wow, man. This bullshit gonna break my mind. These

33

battalion dudes don't know jack shit. This is bull fucking shit. These fuck-nose mother fucks don't know which way is up."

I turned down the recon offer, but my days with the *Black Hawks* were numbered. I neared the point of incorrigible and was sent out of the battalion to Task Force South at Da Lat, location of the summer presidential palace, the "garden city" of Vietnam, high elevation and ideal climate. I can just hear the battalion Doc whispering to the battalion commander, "combat fatigue." Typical rotation plan for lieutenants was this: six months in the field as platoon leader, six months on staff. Also I assumed *the Herd* wanted to be fair with the junior officers by spreading around both opportunity and risk. Let the lifers get their tickets punched.

But I did not volunteer for Vietnam to receive, in the words of *the Herd*, "assistant to the assistant douche bag supply officer who supervised pimply-assed second lieutenants burning shit." *Ash and trash*, they called it. Sergeants and lieutenants in disfavor ended up in charge of the *shit-burning detail*. Each day human feces from the latrines were burned in fifty-five gallon drums cut down. The stench was overwhelming. Responsibilities included supplying what we called *crab powder,* or *crap powder,* to the latrines, another important REMF job. For every combat soldier in the field it took, they said, ten REMFs to support him.

We did not as much as go near the latrines if we could avoid it. Crabs. One of my men sent in a joke to *Reader's Digest* for print: "*The Herd's* method of getting rid of crabs when you return to the States: go to movie theater and take with you hidden in your pocket a large ice pick. Buy a large buttered popcorn on the way in. During the movie, begin to eat the popcorn and open your fly. When the crabs come out to eat the popcorn, kill them with the ice pick." *Reader's Digest* was not interested. I asked *Reader's Digest* to print a different kind of story. *Helmet Grafitti.* I was intrigued by the manner by which GIs decorated their helmet covers and the slogans used. "Slack off." "Give me slack." "Ho Chi Minh is a Fag." "FTA (Fuck the Army)." "This Army is FUBAR (Fucked Up Beyond All Repair or Recognition)." "Getting Over." "It Don't Mean Nothing." And for the pointman, "Don't Follow Me, I'm Lost" or "God is my Pointman." One of my pointmen, Kidd, wore a helmet with a big dent in the side. In a bunker one night, he was hit with a B-40 rocket. Did nothing but give him a bad headache. Rather than have the helmet replaced on the next resupply, he wore it. His brown badge of courage. Kidd would later become a casualty and be sent to a hospital in Japan. Walking point in some heavy brush, a stick entered his ear and punctured his ear drum. Kidd later reunited with us. We were surprised and elated.

The Herd was cynical about everything, but never failed to generate through the rumor mill word that *the Herd* was headed home. I think *the Herd* was headed home every month of the eighteen that I was there, from May of '68 to December of '69, with one month home. *The Herd* did not return to the States, where it was deactivated, until '72. And it was rumored that the Army Corps of Engineers estimated that with the billions spent on the war, the United States could have, in the alternative, leveled the entire country and black topped it for one large north-south air strip for bombing runs to North Vietnam and China.

"War is our business and business is good" was a motto of young officers training in 1967 at Ft. Benning, Georgia before making the trip over the pond. There, they filmed *The Green Berets,* and I was in the drug store one Sunday morning in town when in walked John Wayne and his son. Wayne was looking for the most powerful cough medicine. He had a bad cold.

I could not imagine a future without Vietnam combat since at least as early as 1966, my junior year at West Point. In 1964 I had read Robin Moore's *The Green Berets,* and, by 1966, was playing Sergeant Barry Sadler's album *The Green Berets:*

> Put silver wings on my son's chest,
> Make him one of America's best.
> He'll be a man, they'll test one day,
> Make him one of the *Green Berets.*

Our professors and tactical officers at West Point returned to their alma mater from the combat zones with hair-raising tales of daring do, their multi-colored chests corroborating it all. Some had been advisors in the early '60's. "You don't know the friendly from the enemy; they all wear black pajamas. If they shoot, they're enemy...." The Military Assistance Command, Vietnam, (MACV) forces had acted in a limited advisory capacity and lived with their Vietnamese counterparts, suffering the Vietnam diet. "Happiness in Vietnam is a dry fart," a Marine Corps Major told me.

The war began to change in March, 1965, when President Lyndon B. Johnson deployed the Marines to Danang. The "elite" 173rd Airborne Brigade (Separate), the first Army unit deployed, arrived in May. The 173rd was separate because it was not part of a division commanded by a general. Brigades are usually commanded by a bird (full) colonel, a rank which follows lieutenant colonel, major, captain, first lieutenant, and second lieutenant. (In two short years, I had moved from second lieutenant to captain, age 24, company commander. The forces of supply and demand. *War was our business and business was good.*)

In 1967, we had received at West Point not just returned MACV advisors, but returned combat commanders. They proudly wore on their right shoulder the patch of the 1st Cavalry, the 101st Airborne Division, or *the Herd*. As a future infantry officer, it was not a question of would I be going to Vietnam from West Point, but *when*: six months, nine months, one year from graduation? First, the pipeline: Airborne and Ranger Schools, plus the Infantry Officer Basic Course at Ft. Benning. (There was a debate over whether West Pointers were in need of the basic course. We were not, but suffered through it anyway.) Another issue: how much non-combat experience it took to hone a second lieutenant to be of battle mettle. About ninety days.

Why Infantry? West Point graduates were given, within the limits of their class rank, branch choices: Engineer, Finance, Chemical, Armor (tanks), Infantry, Artillery, or Medical. Engineers were the choice of the *hives* or *engineers*, the top ranking cadets, as compared to the *goats*, which were in the bottom one-third. The Corps of Engineers was always the first branch to go as to slots available for graduating cadets. Although I was just within the bottom one-third and had played defensive end for the *goats* in the *goat-engineer* football game played the week that Army played Navy (*as the goats go, so goes Army*), I still had choices of Armor or Artillery. But Infantry had been in my blood as early as 1963, my first summer at West Point, just as the military had been in my blood as early as 1952.

My father, Malcolm Douglas (Mac) died of a heart attack at age 29, when I was but two years old. I was born on April 22, 1945, the third of three children. My brother, Douglas Malcolm (Doug) was four years my senior, and my sister Margo Ann was two years older. My mother, Patricia Ann Vockell was of pure German parentage - William Henry Vockell and Corrine Yeager - whereas my father's side was Scottish. MacPherson means "son of the parson." My father's grandmother had been a preacher in the 1920's for a Methodist women's group, exorting against child labor.

As a boy, my father had attended Admiral Farragut Academy and dreamed of an appointment to the U.S. Naval Academy at Annapolis, Maryland. But he had rheumatic fever as a boy, which likely caused a weakened heart condition and untimely death. A broken eardrum kept him from military service in WWII, and as Director of Public Relations for Ralph H. Jones Company, an advertising agency in Cincinnati and New York, he was responsible for their U.S. War Bond drive. In 1944 he was radio campaign manager for Governor Bricker of Ohio when he ran for the vice presidency of the United States with presidential candidate Dewey.

My parents had met and dated at Withrow High School in Cincinnati, Ohio, where my mother's father had his own machine tool shop. He was patriarch of a family of two boys and two girls and ultimately eight grandchildren. A Republican and great fan of both MacArthur and Eisenhower, he looked like Truman. I am old enough to remember the Korean War and my grandfather's disgust at Truman for his discharge of MacArthur. *Old soldiers never die, they just fade away.*

Thus, with the untimely death of my father, I was raised in my grandparents' home. In first grade, for reasons to this day beyond my understanding, I was sent to a Catholic military boarding school run by nuns. I was not even Catholic, but soon learned the true meaning of discipline at St. Aloysius Military Academy in Fayetteville, Ohio about fifty miles north of Cincinnati. I thought my grandfather stern, but as a six-year old, I had new discoveries at military school: Ivory soap melts in your mouth faster than any other (for those who talk when they should not), and a green stick on the back of your bare legs in a cold shower room hurts far more than a paddle. And, if the cadet next to you holds his arms around his head, it is a good clue that someone behind him will start slapping him soon, and maybe you as well. Although a good student, I ran away in first grade, only to be caught the same day and sentenced to three months of raking leaves during afternoon play period.

We slept in a large dormitory with rows of beds, like something out of a James Cagney reformatory school movie. The nuns slept in private rooms, one at each end of the dormitory. Because I was Episcopalian rather than Catholic, I was the only cadet not to receive "First Holy Communion" with my class, despite my required catechism training. Being somewhat ostracized, this caused me at an early age to become an over achiever. I became the best student in the class. I had learned my lesson well from the punishment tour of leaf raking. And it was homesickness more than rebellion that caused me to sneak out a lavatory window and make the run.

The days went too slowly and I looked forward to holiday furlough and reunion with my mother, brother and sister, grandparents, aunts, uncles, and cousins, all of whom were very loving. My brother Doug was at military school with me, but due to our four year age difference I did not see much of him. Margo attended a Catholic boarding school a few miles away, Brown County Academy. My mother traveled door to door, "Avon calling."

During the entire summer months, my brother, sister and I attended a Catholic camp, Fort Scott, in New Baltimore, Ohio, about fifty miles west of Cincinnati. There I developed camping skills and a love for horses and the outdoors. Also, Doug and I became excellent swimmers. Somehow my mother had obtained partial scholarships for our attendance at boarding schools and Fort Scott. After we had attended the camp several years, they had to

37

create new merit badges. Doug, Margo and I had already earned everything they had to offer, having attended all summer rather than two weeks like most campers. My counselor and riding teacher, Dave Vollman, became my first *adopted father*, and a lifetime friend.

St. Aloysius visitor's day was on Sunday. Watching through the bay window in a playroom, I waited anxiously for sight of my mother's Chevrolet Belaire on the oval drive which led up to the academy buildings. One by one, classmates left me to visit with their parents. My eyes left the oval drive only to check the large wall clock behind me. By 2:00 p.m. I was alone and light rain began to fall. In the window reflection I could see the tears rolling down my cheek. *She wasn't coming. Why wasn't I told?* The metaphorical umbilical cord was that day cut. *I am not six years old. I am a soldier. I am strong. I am independent. I stand alone.* In later years, the adult cry became, *I am Infantry, Queen of Battle. Follow me!*

After my second grade St. Aloysius closed, and Doug and I were transferred to Millersburg Military Institute in Millersburg, Kentucky, non-denominational. There, as a boy-soldier, I received a trophy for highest grades in my fourth grade class, having remained a serious student. By then I had adjusted well to military life, plus the school did not have nearly the strict atmosphere. Instead of Catholic mass, I heard old-fashioned southern preaching.

It was on our first hike, during my West Point first summer in 1963 that I learned the *cry of the Infantry*. We reported July 1 to *Beast Barracks* and I had adjusted well to the military and discipline, though I had attended public schools since Millersburg, in Greenwich, Connecticut (5th and 6th grades) and Woodward Junior and Senior High Schools in Cincinnati (7th through 12th grades). In high school I found myself much a loner and quiet leader, excelling in academics and swimming, though I liked and participated also in football, baseball and track. Swimming was my forte and I had set school, pool and Southern Ohio District records in the butterfly in ninth grade. I grew up on the television series *Men of Annapolis* and *Men of West Point*, plus the John Wayne, Gary Cooper, Jimmy Stewart, and Robert Mitchum movies; and I always dreamed of an academy appointment. As a result of my mother's second marriage to an architect, a marriage which lasted a mere two years, we moved from Cincinnati to Connecticut in 1955. On the way we stopped in Washington, D.C. and then Annapolis. That for me did it. I was academy bound. I even wrote to Annapolis as early as ninth grade. Then as a high school sophomore, it became Air Force Academy, but my lack of 20/20 vision (20/30 and 20/40) and "combination red-green color blindness" (failure to pass the dot test) drew me to West Point and

Grant, Lee, Patton, Pershing, MacArthur and Eisenhower. I knew little about the regular service, but I knew what I wanted. After all, I religiously watched the Army-Navy game each fall: Pete Dawkins of Army, Joe Belino, and finally Roger Staubauch, of Navy. I had watched Roger play in high school in Cincinnati. (In reading one of Roger's biographies recently, I discovered that one of his coaches had been Bernie Cincheck, my Fort Scott camp swimming instructor and a tremendous motivator. *Small world.*)

Finances became a strong consideration. After two years in a small town in Connecticut and my best childhood days at ages 12 and 13, we were back with my grandparents in Cincinnati. My mother was back to work full-time. I was not as strong in swimming in high school as in junior high, and I had doubts about an athletic scholarship. Aside from academics, I took myself too seriously and considered Ivy League: Brown & Dartmouth. They declined my admission saying I did not have enough money to attend. Spring of my junior year I traveled to Wright Patterson Air Force Base in Dayton, Ohio to take a full physical exam. I still had hopes of squeaking through for an Air Force Academy qualification. (Ironically, that same day at my high school my good friend Pete Johnston, a year ahead of me, received at a "class awards day" assembly his appointment to the Air Force Academy. Pete, a national skydiving champion and one of the top cadets in his Air Force Academy class, was killed in March of 1966, a few months before his graduation. He had received a scholarship to attend post graduate school at George Washington University in international relations and I have no doubt that today he would be a U.S. senator, if not an Air Force general. His skydiving club performed for a spring break audience at the Academy and his main chute failed. After hundreds of jumps, he miscalculated and was too late popping the reserve.)

Knowing by June of 1962 that of the three major academies, Air Force, Annapolis and West Point, I was medically qualified only for West Point, my goal was set. That summer, at age seventeen, I traveled alone by plane to New York City, then to West Point by bus to participate in an indoctrination tour sponsored by the Defense Orientation Conference Association (DOCA), a military junket group by which civilians are able to see first-hand what soldiers do. (Jack Nolan, who had his own advertising agency in Cincinnati and was a good friend of my mother, was a member of DOCA and invited me to attend.) The DOCA group ate with cadets in the mess hall, toured the facilities and watched the cadets in action at both West Point and Camp Buckner, the summer training ground. At historic Thayer Hotel, I had dinner with the group, the leader of which had two sons, both of whom were seeking Annapolis appointments.

Next to me sat General Westmoreland, in his last year as

superintendent of the Academy, and who had been informed that I wanted to attend West Point the following year. Little did I suspect then that my life in later years - in Vietnam - would be so influenced by this man. Westmoreland proceeded to ask me a litany of questions taken from the West Point annual profile: Boys State? "No." *But I was a delegate for Hi Y, a Christian organization that sent delegates to the state capital in a program much like Boys State. Why doesn't he just ask me what I did do?* "Captain of the football team?" "No." *But I did letter in varsity football and swimming. Aren't those questions on his list?* "Class valedictorian?" "No." *But I was in the top 5% of my class. Doesn't he want to know that? And I was in National Junior Honor Society. No, I'd better not go into that because I wasn't invited into Senior Honor Society, even though I had the grades. I had gotten into a fight Sophomore year and punched out some kid in a bowling alley parking lot across from the school grounds. One of my buddies had used a home-made brass knuckle on another kid. The police investigated and my reputation with some of the teachers had been tarnished.*

Frustrated by what I years later learned to be the *West Point blockhead mentality*, which meant a fixation on litany rather than search for the truth, I became more determined. I even wrote Westmoreland and asked that since he had met me he could surely tell what an outstanding candidate I was and would he please write for me a letter of recommendation. He declined under the bureaucratic theory that his membership on the academic board precluded him from making recommendations.

Having no doubt in my mind what I wanted, I returned to high school that fall, more determined than ever, and began the long application process. Had I not been appointed, I likely would have joined the Marines out of restlessness, despite my college qualifications. I could not as much as picture myself at a civilian college. But God was on my side. My mother, bless her heart, with whom I was very close, yet, at the same time, from whom I remained very independent, was then working at L. M. Prince Company, opticians in downtown Cincinnati. She daily rode the bus and was for her three children forever the martyr. One of her customers was a Mr. Rollman, owner of Rollman Department Stores in Cincinnati. He personally knew Congressman Rich from our district, and I suspected later that during my high school years Mr. Rollman must have contributed heavily to both Rich and the Republican Party. (The final irony to this was my support of conservative Republicans in the eighties.)

Congressman Rich could either appoint from the qualified pool of candidates a principal and several alternates, or have the academy make the choice. I never met Rollman nor Rich, but always wrote and updated them with my latest accomplishments. In December of

1962 I received the principal nomination. I was elated; a lifetime dream come true. In February I gave up the state swimming meet to take my final physical and mental exams, riding the train from Cincinnati to Ft. Benjamin Harrison, Indiana. By letter dated April 22, 1963, my eighteenth birthday, the Academy told me I was accepted and to report July 1. In June of 1963, after graduating twenty-sixth of six hundred in my high school class, I trained for my West Point entrance by running on golf courses in the evening. Then I again flew alone to New York City to catch the bus from Times Square to West Point.

I had kept my promise to my father and to George Washington. At the Academy there stands a huge statue of Washington on horseback with outstretched arm pointing, as if to say, "forward, men!" As the DOCA activities had ended the summer before, I had walked alone from the hotel along the walk overlooking the Hudson to the plain, the flat parade ground, and to the Washington Memorial. It was late afternoon and quiet. I was moved by the Academy atmosphere, and, with great perseverance, I looked up at Washington and promised my father, George Washington, and myself I would be back the following summer. I prayed, asking God for the West Point appointment.

Now it was July 1, 1963 and I stood at attention at the edge of the plain, a stone's throw from the Washington statue. But I was not alone. I stood with a thousand other new cadets, heads uncovered and shaven, dress gray pants, white shirt with gray epaulets, right hand raised, as we swore an oath to support and defend the Constitution of the United States, against all enemies, foreign and domestic.

So fellow West Pointer Frank Audrain wanted to cut this NVA lieutenant into little pieces and he was serious. God, was he mad. Several times I had to walk from my command post over to the tree where the prisoner was sitting, looking scared to death, and remind Frank it was not a good idea. Frank, mostly alone, sometimes with a few of his key men beside him, would sit or stand and just look this guy in the eyes. Slowly and methodically, Frank would proceed to sharpen his knife, saying nothing, his jaw bones quivering more than usual. We continued to await a second chopper to pick up the prisoner. *Dust offs* headed directly to the hospital, but this prisoner was due for interrogation by the South Vietnamese. I later had occasion to observe some of their methods.

During our Vietnamization duty in May of '69, we were co-located just outside of key hamlets with the South Vietnamese and the *Rough Puffs,* Regional and Popular Forces, the Vietnamese version of the reserve and national guard. But for these *weekend warriors* it had become a full-time position, for their country was at civil war. For me it was a very insecure feeling, sharing a perimeter

41

with soldiers who pranced around proudly in Army-issue field jackets in the hot sun, and constantly had us jumping by shooting birds. I reckoned that these soldiers had no reason to be in any hurry. Their country had been, at least intermittently, a combat zone since World War II; and, as they well knew, there was no early end in sight. At the Paris peace talks, they could not as much as agree yet on the shape of the table. I longed for the Central Highlands and the security of mountains and triple canopy.

If we took prisoners, we sent them back to the S-2 for interrogation. When the South Vietnamese made the capture, we had no input. Activities of our ally were none of our business. South Vietnamese torture techniques were both simple and effective. The first I observed required only a bench, towel, soap and water, and the second a 12-volt battery and two wires.

We were just outside the hamlet within our joint U.S.-South Vietnamese perimeter. I felt ill, having just mixed for the first and last time a Darvon pill with a warm beer. The Vietnamese had within the perimeter a *coke hooch*, which offered to GI's black market cokes and beer. I typically did not touch beer, but one of the NCO's walked by and offered it. I was feeling so lousy with a tropical headache and a Darvon was not working, so I mixed the two. After dry heaving a couple of times, my head was spinning. I walked from our end of the perimeter fifty meters or so to the south end to clear my head. The Dai Yui (captain in Vietnamese) was, as I observed, in charge of an interrogation, South Vietnamese-style.

The POW, a young VC of about 20 years, was on his back on a bench, his legs tied, and his hands tied behind his back and under the bench, his head over the end of the bench. He was securely blindfolded. A towel was placed over his head, and the captain ordered soapy water poured over the towel. This, I was told by the interpreter, caused a prisoner to drink in effort to breathe, and eventually run out of breath. The sensation was one of drowning. But the flow of water would stop in time to allow a few gasps of air, thus causing repeated drownings without death. The soap added to the victim's stomach discomfort. After an hour of this, the VC's slow memory gradually improved.

In the case of the battery torture, I did not stay around to watch. I was later told by one of my NCO's the details of the methodology. A female VC was tied on a bench on her back, legs spread, and naked. After securing a ground for the battery with one of the wires, her tormentors repeatedly touched her with the positive end. The location was her most sensitive area, known as the inner labia, which for those of you who slept through biology, means the inner layer of the vagina. For males, testicles serve the purpose.

So what had this NVA lieutenant, *Crazy Horse's* potential victim, heard about South Vietnamese and U.S. interrogations? If given a choice, which tormentor would he select? Had he heard of the U.S. rumored practice of taking several POW's for a ride in a helicopter and accidentally dropping one out at one thousand feet altitude? It was claimed that such a practice quickly lubricated the tongues of the VC onlookers.

I never observed any such practice. *The Herd* was less subtle: they often avoided taking prisoners, which I believed to be an error for reason of the need for intelligence. Yet, I could at times appreciate their attitude. When I was platoon leader, a grunt in another platoon had been blinded by a VC grenade. The VC had been captured and held his hands in the air proclaiming "Chu Hoi," which meant, "I surrender." Trained in the ways of the Geneva Convention, the GI approached an apparently unarmed VC, whereupon the VC let go of a small grenade held in his hand. He obviously had not heard of Geneva, much less a convention held there. A few weeks later, some men of the same platoon surprised from the rear three VC in the bush at close range. They shouted "Chu Hoi," to which the VC immediately responded by dropping their AK-47 rifles, turning, and repeating with earnest faces, "Chu Hoi, Chu Hoi, Chu Hoi." To this, one of the GI's, a friend of the blinded grunt answered, "No can do, mother fuck." Placing the M-16 on *quick-a-go-go* , he, it was told to me, "blew away those sorry ass mother fuck dinks." Looking at their sprawled bodies, he proclaimed, "You better get your defecation in sequence" which meant "your shit in order." "You fuck-nose mother fuck gook. Fuck you, all of you fucking gooks."

A *Herd* practice no less subtle was that which dealt with this rule: *if they run, they're VC*, which had replaced the MACV rule, *if they shoot, they're VC*. (After deployment of a number of U.S. combat units in Vietnam, it became too risky to wait to be fired upon.) When I first arrived as platoon leader, my men told me of a sergeant who in his final months in country, on the brink of insanity, if not well over the line, made it a practice to shout to elderly field workers, "Dee Dee mao, motherfucker gook, dee dee mao," which meant, "get the hell out of here." As the farmer ran down the rice paddy dike, away from the GI's on the trail, he was promptly gunned down by the sergeant. "Mike Six [platoon leader], this is Mike Three [squad leader, sergeant]. We got one VC KIA here. Was capping up as we approached. Searching now for weapons." (A GI's grenade could always supply the weapon justification.) No public announcement via the AN PRC 10 ("the prick ten") radio was made concerning the taking of the VC's ear. The soft badge of courage. This was "shit-house rumor," all of which I believed, and for good cause.

Perhaps reaching only the brink of insanity, the worst I condoned was the stamping of two-pronged jump wings, the parachutist badge, in the forehead of a dead VC and placing in the mouth a *Herd* patch of blue and white, our calling card. *We came, we saw, we conquered.* "Don't fuck with *the Herd.*" "You fuck with *the Herd* and you're a dead man." "Don't fuck with us you pussy-ass motherfucking VC," was the warriors' cry from a 19-year old PFC. "Fuck with *the Herd* and *the Herd* will bring the dam dam all over your sorry-ass mother fucking heads." (I concluded after having spent only my first day as a platoon leader with *the Herd* that few in *the Herd* could speak as much as a phrase without adding for spice, "mother fucker." It replaced a favored stalling tactic of others, the "ah' or "and," for it gives the speaker more time to think about what he is going to say next, but without actually pausing in his speech.)

I had not observed assassination, only monitored it by radio when I was on graveyard shift in the TOC (tactical operations center) of Task Force South, during my staff assignment in Da Lat. "Sea wolf in position." (Submarine was offshore.) "Roger." "Dolphins wet." (Navy SEALS in the water.) "Dolphins dry." (SEALS on the beach.) "Mission accomplished." (VC suspect assassinated.) In a village in the Phan Thiet area, an individual was suspected to be a VC or VC-sympathizer. But he was a village chief and it became a political hot potato for both U.S. and South Vietnamese armed forces. An easy, logical solution: "By stealth and under cover of darkness, assassinate the bastard and blame it on the VC. *Eliminate with extreme prejudice.*" Here was the application of the guerilla warfare principle against the guerilla himself: *He who fights and runs away, lives to fight another day.* Or, as Sherman said after burning Atlanta during the civil war, "War is hell."

What hell, then, was conjured up in the mind of the NVA lieutenant as he tried not to observe *Crazy Horse* sharpen his knife? Was he relieved to hear the womp, womp, womp of the incoming chopper? With what unit and for how long had he served? What was his purpose in the area and what was the location of his command? To these and hundreds of other questions, I never learned the answer. Within a few hours he was dead. Not by the knife of *Crazy Horse*, but by a weapon more invincible. A chopper flew the NVA back to the rear for interrogation. But no sooner had he arrived when he was dead. Shock. Pure shock. *Crazy Horse* had literally scared him to death.

Crazy Horse had established a rapport with his men comparable only to my relationship with the *Black Hawks*. In fact, I felt Frank had done a better job than I had, or perhaps because of me as company commander. The morale was high. We were killing gooks. (General Omar Bradley, West Point Class of 1915 said, "Leadership is intangible and therefore no weapon ever designed can replace it.") Our major casualties were from booby traps. For a few

44

months at least we acted like we owned the countryside. Frank's men had to be restrained, they were so anxious to catch VC by surprise and gun them down in their own backyard. It was probably this overzealous attitude which cost Frank, Sergeant Will.

Will, an American who was from Panama, was another *shake 'n' bake* NCO. Short, lean and muscular, he was our fastest VC chaser. He was Frank's platoon sergeant. On one patrol, between the coast and mountain ridges, he led a squad, giving chase to some VC. He was shot badly in the thigh, after killing several gooks, shooting on the run. The gook that shot him was killed by Will and awarded by Will's men the jump wings stamped in his forehead. I did not see Will again, and had remembered with affection the day he asked me to a *high noon* show down with a couple of new men who thought they were tough guys. Frank was patrolling the bush while Will and I were at the MECH base camp.

These two NFGs had been given that typical stateside choice: jail or enlist. Disobeying Will, they had left the base camp, found some beer in the nearby village, and were *whore shopping*. We had to find them before they either got killed or killed somebody in the village. I decided I would let Will handle it; I would be back up. We found the FNGs in the village, and as we approached, they *locked and loaded*, weapons at a forty-five degree angle, pointed to the ground, finger on the triggers. We did the same, weapons pointed in the air. We motioned for the villagers to clear out, a process which had begun by the metallic click of the chambered rounds. I moved to the left side, and remained ten meters behind Will. I wanted a clear shot, if necessary. We said nothing. Intense eye contact. *This is a test. This is only a test.*

Without hesitation, Will moved up to the man on his right, knowing through sound, that I had moved left. He brought the barrel of his M-16 to the man's neck, while at the same time putting his face within an inch of the FNG's, as he switched from semi to full automatic. He said, in taunting fashion, very slowly, "Quick a-go-go, wanna dance?" Reaching out his hand for the FNG's M-16, he slowly asked, "Who's in charge of *the Herd?*" No answer. Who was bluffing whom? Will pressed the barrel harder into the man's neck, no longer reaching for the man's weapon, and asked again, louder this time. "Who's in charge of *the Herd?*" The other FNG remained frozen. I began to whistle, casually, as I flicked the safety switch to automatic, keeping the stock on my right hip bone, barrel pointed to the overcast sky. After some hesitation and a conclusion that this was no bluff, the FNG answered, "*The Herd* leader." Pressing the advantage, raising his voice further, but slowly, Will asked, "And who is that?" "You" "You, what?" "You are, Sergeant." "You are sergeant, what?" "You are, Sergeant Will." Gritting his teeth, a whisper now, Will said, "You shit ass FNG. I am your momma. I eat pussies like you for breakfast, if the VC don't blow your shit away first. Put that safety on, haul your ass back to the perimeter. I catch you down here again, your *piss ant* ass is grass, and I'm a lawn mower. Move out smartly, airborne." They did, and later accepted the ways of the *Herd,* and *the Herd* accepted them. I would miss Will.

I last saw *Crazy Horse* in 1975, when my wife, Barbara, and I and our first son, Scott, visited with Frank and Dani and their two daughters at Ft. Bragg, North Carolina, where *Crazy Horse* was a company commander with the 82nd Airborne Division.. He went on to Command and General Staff College, then to Korea as aide to the commanding general. Ultimately he returned to command an infantry battalion, *creme de la creme,* for the Infantry officer. I have no doubt he will someday be a general. But his left breast will forever be without one Bronze Star medal earned in Vietnam combat.

Frank told me the story in 1970 at Indiantown Gap, Pennsylvania, where I was training ROTC students during my tour as Assistant Professor of Military Science at the University of Cincinnati. Frank, who had been wounded twice when I was still in country, had made it safely back to the world, his wife, and their newborn daughter. While in Vietnam I had radioed to him the news from one hamlet to his position in another: he was a father. He had just narrowly escaped death when he stepped on a claymore firing device in the sand. The claymore fired but was facing backwards. Apparently, the VC who placed it couldn't read the English print, which stated, "Face this side forward." So now I am meeting him in a hotel lobby for a long-awaited reunion, but *Crazy Horse* is uptight. Dani has not come yet to the lobby to join us for dinner and Frank is in a hurry to tell me something. He is really serious, and I am thinking, *Oh no, Stafford died or Sergeant Will died, or something awfully terrible has happened.* But Frank says, "nothing like that," but the words do not flow so easily and I can tell that he is really uneasy, under pressure of Dani's imminent arrival. He does not want her to know what he is about to tell me. He half whispers this story.

His tour in Vietnam was up, he left *the Herd* and was in Cam Rahn Bay to catch the big freedom bird home. His last night, so he thought, and he goes to the officer's club for some drinks, has too many, and watches a USO girlie show. The girl out on the floor is dancing a seductive dance and is being edged on by the claps and yells of well-lubricated officers. Clad in only so much as to leave little to the imagination, the dancer is doing the alligator and the snake on the floor, writhing around, and then on her back, thrusting her hips in the air. Except for Frank, the crowd goes wild. Frank's problem is this: he is just out of the boonies in the midst of other officers he perceives to be, and most of whom probably are, REMFS. He misses *the Herd* and feels guilty. His troops are on ambush, or getting shot at, or trying to avoid booby traps, and the war to this girl and the REMFs is one big party. He becomes disgusted by the whole scene.

Frank breaks through the line and shouts to the dancer, "Get up." It has come to him in a flash. *The absurdity of it all. The drunken officers, who as REMFs do not know the barrel end of an M-16, and this dumb broad acting like an animal. Stafford shot. Will shot. Other men dead. And for what? A pussy show in the O club?* The band plays on, hoping Frank will give up his demand. But Frank is both stubborn and stoic: *Marine, West Point, Airborne, Ranger, Infantry, Indian ... and now Cong killer.* "I said, get up! Put your clothes on!" She refuses, and Frank goes forward. No one attempts to restrain him, as he pushes through the crowd to the center of the circle, and continues to yell at the dancer. Still, no one attempts to restrain him. This guy is better than John Wayne: he kills people with his looks. Because she refuses to obey his commands, *Crazy Horse* gets down on the floor and like an animal, bites her right in the crotch. The MPs arrive and things do not go well for Lt. Audrain the following day. Brought before the Adjutant General, , he is informed that he will go home soon, but late and without his well-earned Bronze Star.

I looked at Frank, hugged him, and said, "The story's worth a lot more than the Bronze Star." He smiled. Dani and their little girl arrived, and the subject was closed. We had a nice dinner. For at least a few hours, *the Herd* was reunited.

War is the realm of chance. No other human activity gives it greater scope; no other has such incessant and varied dealings with this intruder. Chance makes everything more uncertain and interferes with the whole course of events. Karl Von Clausewitz

During the early part of the third century B.C., the rivalry between Rome and Carthage for control of the western Mediterranean led to over a century and a half of warfare, what became known as the Punic Wars. Though it was the Roman republic which would prevail in the end, those expensive lessons taught the Romans by the great Carthaginian general Hannibal formed the basis of present military doctrine in the United States. From Hannibal and other *Great Captains Before Napoleon*, as taught by the Department of Military Art and Engineering at the United States Military Academy, West Point, New York, there was developed "the principles of war": *offensive, initiative, maneuver, surprise, security, simplicity, mass, economy of force, and unity of command.* Hannibal was included in that list of *Great Captains Before Napoleon:* Alexander the Great, Hannibal, Ceasar, Gustavus Adolphus, and Frederick the Great. Alexander the Great "with courage, endurance, intelligence and skill ... completed the conquest of the entire then-known world, marching over 19,000 miles in his eleven years of campaigning; and all this before he was thirty-two." Hannibal no less rose to the occasion. For, as the saying goes, "Great captains go hand-in-hand with great events." As Hannibal took his army over the Alps invading Italy, defeating the Romans time and time again, the Romans complained of Hannibal's unfair tactics, his use of stratagem instead of relying upon what was then "the time-honored stand up method of fighting." Hannibal was smart enough to not only utilize the principle of *surprise* but to exploit its advantages.

After the major defeat of the Roman Army at the Battle of Trebeia, in which Hannibal utilized a ruse to draw the Roman Army across the river, it was time for Hannibal to make his next move from northern Italy to central Italy toward Rome. There were two major routes: the eastern route was the easier and well-traveled way, while the western route led through difficult marshes but afforded Hannibal an opportunity of a turning movement. Thus, the latter was the choice of Hannibal. By forced march through treacherous terrain, Hannibal succeeded in placing his army between the Roman army and Rome, thus forcing the Romans "to seek battle in order the rectify [their] strategic position." This, then, the turning movement, led to the Battle of Lake Trasimene.

A mountain range runs along the east side of the lake with a small defile between the lake and the mountains. Reaching the lake first, Hannibal took his army through the defile and camped at the southeastern part of the lake, discovering through his scouts that the Romans had bivouacked at the northern end. Through his intelligence sources, he expected the Romans to attack the following day and knew of the Romans' habit of neglecting "to secure their march by properly disposed security detachments." In other words, Hannibal could expect the Romans to walk straight through the defile without flank security on the east. Thus, he placed hidden in the foothills the bulk of his calvary on the north, his light infantry in the center, and his heavy infantry in the south.

Just as planned, the Roman general advanced early in the morning with not only lack of flank security but with a fog which restricted observation. As the head of the Roman column engaged Hannibal's heavy infantry in the south, making little progress, the remainder of the Roman column bunched up, finding "itself crowded in the four mile defile between the mountains and the lake. The trap was set. Hannibal gave the order to his calvary to close the northern end of the defile and struck the east flank of the contained column with his light infantry. The result was surprise, panic and slaughter. Over three-fourths of the entire Roman Army, some 40,000 men, were captured or killed."

Historians have recognized that the individual Roman legionary was a far better fighting man than his opponent, the Carthaginian. Nor did Hannibal ever outnumber the Romans. The armies were equal in the way of equipment. What, then, was the answer to Hannibal's success? "Generalship. Hannibal used his forces in accordance with a well-conceived plan and took full advantage of the psychological forces so important in war.... Thus, by the simple effectiveness of his plan of battle, Hannibal destroyed the morale of his enemy and nullified his powers of resistance. Again, as on the Trebeia, the intellect of the great Carthaginian was the deciding factor between two forces which in other respects were evenly matched." In writing of the *Great Captains Before Napoleon*, our West Point instructors taught us that the great captains "penetrated beneath the surface of the military dogma of their times and revealed that success in war, as in any other undertaking, follows him who has the intelligence, energy, courage and imagination to exploit fully the means at his disposal." No less true in the art of criminal trials.

Doing battle with the IRS, the firm of MacPherson & McCarville, P.A. takes on the three major divisions: Examination (civil audit), Collection (collection of taxes and delinquent returns), and Criminal Investigation Division. In the civil battleground we have faired well. For example, IRS alleged that one of our clients, a Boston businessman, owed in excess of two million dollars in taxes, interest and penalties. The client had utilized the foreign triple trust program of tax avoidance promoted by Karl Dahlstrom, which you will read about later in this book. The client had relied on advice from accountants and attorneys and, with the case under Kirk McCarville's command, we succeeded in saving our client over a million dollars! IRS agreed to not only drop the fifty percent civil fraud penalty, but as well the five percent negligence penalty. Kirk could tell of hundreds of other "civil tax war stories" in which we succeeded, as did Hannibal, in overcoming great odds. But this book is mainly about the third major division, the Criminal Investigation Division, and prosecutions brought for tax fraud and evasion.

IRS' arsenal is formidable: felony charges of conspiracy, attempted tax evasion, false tax returns, to name but a few. Plus misdemeanor charges of failure to file a tax return, failure to supply information, failure to keep records and failure to pay the tax. But all criminal tax charges require of the government proof to the jury beyond a reasonable doubt that the defendant acted willfully and intentionally, that is, with specific intent to violate the law which he knew and understood. The all-too-familiar adage, "ignorance of the law is no excuse," does *not* apply to tax crimes and other crimes which the courts have regarded as so complex that they defy common understanding. Ignorance of the law *is* an excuse, at least so far as it goes to the issue of intent. In other words, a defendant can demonstrate his *good faith misunderstanding* of the law. As well, he can develop a defense of reliance upon advice of others, especially professionals trained to so advise him: accountants, CPAs and attorneys. Thus, one way to insulate oneself from criminal prosecution in the area of uncertain law is to seek out and rely upon specific advice of an independent, competent counsellor. Of course, for the defense to be viable, you must disclose the full facts, and once advice is given, you must "follow it to a T."

A "not guilty" in a criminal tax case does not necessarily end for the accused problems on the civil battleground. There the IRS may employ its weapons of civil fraud penalty (50% of the tax), negligence penalty (5%), interest, plus liens and levies upon wages and property. (No, the state homestead exemption *cannot* withstand attack by a subsequent IRS tax lien!) But the accused is not without his own civil battle plan. One weapon, heretofore "secret," which you will learn more about later in this book, is bankruptcy. Contrary to popular belief, tax debts *can* be discharged in bankruptcy! IRS is led, through our efforts, down the defile between Lake Trasimene and the mountains to the east. In the early morning fog, the trap is sprung.

One client, a doctor, was charged with willful failure to file income tax returns for several years. After hearing from us his options, both civil and criminal, learning that a win in the criminal case would not end his civil woes, and that civil woes could be remedied by the bankruptcy ambush, he decided to plea. *He who fights and runs away, lives to fight another day.* The doctor pled guilty to one count, the remaining counts were dismissed. At sentencing, he filed all back tax returns, "self-assessing" over a hundred thousand dollars in tax debts, and received from the judge probation and a fine. The fine is now paid, the waiting period under the bankruptcy rules passed, as we have been crouched, patiently awaiting the IRS army of agents in the mountains east of Lake Trasimene. It is early morning, the fog remains, and IRS had entered the defile....

Once a criminal case is accepted by CID for criminal investigation, a special agent is assigned as the agent in charge and typically will be joined by an assistant from the civil division, a revenue agent, who will make tax calculations for both civil and criminal purposes. The criminal calculation is always less than the civil, the government not wanting to prove any more than absolutely necessary in a criminal trial. After the investigation, which averages two years, and bureaucratic pipeline approval of the recommendation for prosecution, the charges are brought by way of a grand jury indictment in the case of a felony, or by an information in the case of a misdemeanor. (The details of an actual criminal investigation, "from A to Z," will be covered in *War Stories, Part II.*)

Prior to trial, the government is obligated to disclose to the defense any and all evidence it intends to use in its case in chief, meaning its case brought prior to any defense case. The same is required of the defense. This, then, leaves open, contrary to criminal procedure in many state courts and contrary to civil procedure in both state and federal courts, the element of *surprise*. Documents utilized for the purpose of cross-examination of witnesses during the opponent's case in chief need *not* be disclosed prior to trial. Nor must the defendant disclose his list of witnesses unless he agrees, for reason of strategy, to do so in exchange for information from the government. The government is required only at the commencement of trial to disclose its witnesses and must give to the defense after each witness testifies any sworn statements or grand jury testimony of the witness. Because all documents and witnesses are not discoverable prior to trial, this leaves room for stratagems by both sides, especially the defense.

After hearing pretrial motions, the case is set for trial and the jury is selected. First, *voir dire* questions to the jurors to ferret out bias or prejudice in the case. Most federal judges do not permit counsel to question jurors except through written questions asked by the court. Each side is given "pre-emptory strikes" in addition to opportunity for removal of jurors "for cause"; i.e., those jurors who

51

admittedly cannot sit "as a fair and impartial juror."

After opening statements (the defense can reserve, giving opening prior to the defense case in chief), the government presents its case in chief, calling witnesses and offering evidence. The defense cross-examines and after the government's last witness, the defense presents its case in chief, if any. In rare instances, the government will bring a rebuttal case after the defense's case, against which the defendant is entitled to bring sur-rebuttal. The law as determined by the court is settled upon with written jury instructions or charges. (Prior to the late 1800's, our courts permitted the jurors to decide the law and the facts, which means they could defeat a law by voting "not guilty," called "jury nullification." More on this in *War Stories, Part II*.) The prosecutor gives closing in two parts, having the last say for reason the burden of proof is always upon him. After closing, the court reads to the jury the instructions and oftentimes gives to the jury not only the documentary evidence but the instructions in written form. The case is then considered submitted to the jury; the jury deliberates and reaches its verdict.

In the event of a conviction, the defendant can appeal to the U.S. Court of Appeals for the circuit controlling the district in which the case is tried and, if not successful there, can petition the U.S. Supreme Court. On appeal the case is either affirmed, reversed and remanded for new trial, or reversed with acquittal ordered. Watch now for application of "the art of war" to "the art of courtroom combat" and that adage "twice armed is he who hath a cause that's just and thrice armed is he who gets his blow in first." As taught by West Point Military Art and Engineering instructors, we cannot create opportunity for greatness; we can only seize it.

Sun Tzu, who wrote *The Art of War* in China about 500 B.C., became a master at guerrilla warfare. Sun taught flexibility of operations, reliable intelligence, attack at vulnerable points of one's own choosing, stealth, ruse, and surprise. He wrote:

Now an army may be likened to water, for just as flowing water avoids the heights and hastens to the lowlands, so an army avoids strengths and weaknesses. And, as water shapes its flow in accordance with the ground, so an army manages its victory in accordance with the situation of the enemy. And as water has no constant form, there are in war no constant conditions. Thus, one able to gain the victory by modifying his tactics in accordance with the enemy's situation may be said to be divine. Of the five elements, none is always predominant; of the four seasons, none lasts forever; of the days, some are long and some are short, and the moon waxes and wanes.

He knoweth the way that I take. When He hath tried me, I shall come forth as gold. Job 23:10

TEXAS PREACHERS   Chapter 4

As is the case with many of my clients, I read about Jean C. Hylton, housewife and Justice of the Peace candidate, well before I heard from her. By the time I received the call from this patriot extraordinaire, her Texas accent obvious, I had read in the *Spotlight* of her ordeal. *Spotlight*, far to the right and a favorite of many of my Constitutionalist clients, had written how a Chambers County, Texas housewife had succeeded in having the County arrest and prosecute two IRS agents of the Criminal Investigation Division (CID).

The agents were Thomas E. Artru and Michael E. Rentsch. I delighted in the way Jean spoke their names - in total contempt - with her Texas accent, as if gritting her teeth. Artru and Rentsch had come onto the Hylton property, crossing numerous "Posted No Trespassing" signs. Living on the property was V. R. Hylton, preacher and former crop duster Constitutionalist; his wife, Jean; their daughter, thirteen year old Debbie; and son, David, age twenty-three. There was another daughter, Janet, married to an Assembly of God pastor and living in Ohio. She and her husband had one son, Lance, age four, and the family had observed the agents leaving the property.

Jean was home alone the afternoon of November 4, 1981, when the agents appeared flashing badges, handing over their cards. Armed agents like these often appear in pairs without warning or appointment, hoping to catch the unwary housewife off guard. Little did they know, but how well they should have, Jean was too much their match. God and the Constitution were on her side. I was called to become her bodyguard.

There were few in Chambers County, Texas just east of Houston, who were not familiar with the name V. R. Hylton. As would be testified to by a County judge and prosecutor, nary a sole drove down Highway FM 563 in front of the Hylton fifty-acre property without taking notice of the many "Posted No Trespassing" signs. The Hyltons have a beautiful home with lake and a sand and gravel pit. They acquired the property in 1974. But not only were the Hyltons aware of their Constitutional right to privacy as guaranteed by the *Fourth Amendment* , the Hyltons took affirmative steps to put the world in general, and the IRS in particular, on notice that their privacy was to be respected. The *Fourth Amendment* provides that "The right of the people to be secure in their persons, houses, papers and effects against unreasonable searches and seizures shall not be violated and no Warrants shall issue but upon probable cause supported by Oath or affirmation and particularly describing the place to be searched and the persons or things to be seized."

The Hyltons had recorded at the County courthouse in August, 1976 a declaration that all government officials, local, state and federal, and IRS agents were not to trespass. In addition, they mailed the declaration to IRS and IRS maintained it in a Hylton file. The Hyltons posted as many as seven signs, one of which was four by six feet. The agents would, of course, later lie under oath and claim they never saw such signs, despite the fact that during their afternoon surveillance they drove slowly in front of the property at least seven times looking for entrance to V. R.'s gravel pit. (In retrospect, subsequent to the lies under oath given by Artru and Rentsch, the Hyltons and/or I should have filed a complaint with the U.S. Attorney's office for prosecution for perjury, not that I am optimistic that any action would have been taken.)

As the two agents drove up Jean's driveway, she went outside to the front side patio to meet them. She had observed that afternoon that they had repeatedly driven slowly in front of the house as if they were looking for something. Thus, she had expected the confrontation, and, home alone with her daughter, was prepared to deal with the agents.

Indeed, the agents were in search, not only for V. R.'s gravel pit, but for David Hylton, who was under IRS criminal investigation for failure to file federal income tax returns. Interestingly, neither V. R. nor Jean were under criminal investigation for their alleged failure to file. Both the agents and Jean were armed with a tape recorder, thus there was no conflict in the testimony as to what next transpired. Rentsch began, struggling with his tape recorder, "Just a second. We both seem to be having our recorders going on here. Ah, my name is Michael Rentsch." Jean shot back, "Would you spell that? Would you write that down for me right there please?" "I'll spell it for you." "Why I can hardly see," Jean said. "Yeah." "It's what - 6:15 p.m. - and it's dark. I can hardly see." Rentsch added, "Ten after 6:00." "Well?" "My name is Michael E. Rentsch, " flashing his badge. "How do you spell that?" "Rentsch." "R-e-n-t-s-c-h?" "Uh huh." "Okay. And what is you ..." "I am a special agent." "A special - agent with who?" "The, uh, Criminal Investigation Division of Internal Revenue Service." "Criminal Investigation Division?" "Yes ma'am." "Okay. What is your address?" "300 Willow - Room 302." "Okay." "That's in Beaumont." "Okay. And what is your telephone number?" "It is 839-2442." "Okay. And what is your supervisor's name?" "Jeff Ruffin." "How do you spell that?" "R-u-f-f-i-n." Jean, turning to the other agent said, "Okay. And what is your name, sir?" "Thomas," the other agent answered, flashing his badge. "Mr.

54

Thomas? "No. Thomas - first name." "Okay." "Middle initial E. Last name Artru - A-r-t-r-u." "Okay. And your address, Mr. Artru?" "Same. All information is same." "Okay. Information same. Okay, uh ... " Then cutting in, Rentsch said, "Ma'am. Ma'am." Undaunted, Jean continued, "Gentlemen, I'm going to have to read the Privacy Act of 1974." Impatient, Rentsch responded, "I will allow you to read the Privacy Act." J. Hylton: "Uh. It provides that each federal agency inform individuals whom it asks to supply information of the authority of the solicitation of information and whether disclosure of such information is mandatory or voluntary. Okay. Is this mandatory or voluntary? " Artru answered, "All we want to know is David Hylton at home?" Maintaining charge, Jean shot back, "I'm asking *you* a question. Is this information mandatory or voluntary?" Returning a volley, Artru fired back, "I'm asking *you* a question and I'm not going to answer any questions. All I want to know is David Hylton at home?" Still undaunted Jean firmly stated, "Mr. Artru. Uh, I'd like to know the law - title and section - that gives you jurisdiction to ask these questions. Would you please cite that law for me?" "It says right there on my credentials, ma'am, Artru again flashing his badge." Struggling to see the badge in the dark, Jean said, "Okay. Could we - would you. If you'll let me see it, I'll write it down or else if you'll ..." "Well, I. All I want to do is ask - is David Hylton at home?" "I'm asking you the law, title and section - that gives you jurisdiction." "We're not going to answer any questions ...," Artru responded firmly. "To, uh, ..." "If David Hylton is at home, we would like to speak to him, to ask these questions. If not, we're going to leave." "Mr. Artru," Jean commanded. "I'm not going to answer any questions for you, ma'am." "Did you and uh - Mr. Rentsch - do you gentlemen realize that you are *trespassing on private property*?" "Well, we are going to leave. Would you have Mr. David Hylton contact either one of us at the telephone number on here and we will leave," Artru sheepishly answered, handing Jean a business card. Relentless now, Jean firmly stated, "I want to know the law, gentlemen, that gives you the jurisdiction to come and ask questions on this property of David ...." (Transcript.)

Refusing to answer, Artru and Rentsch left the Hylton property. The agents had proceeded onto the Hylton property without a search warrant in total disregard of the "No Trespassing" signs, the declaration filed with IRS, and Hylton's *Fourth Amendment* rights. Jean acted without hesitation, filing that night a criminal complaint against Artru and Rentsch. Having read the Texas Criminal Trespass statute, she lodged her complaint with the County Justice of the Peace, Josh B. Mayes, who in turn the next day forwarded it to the County Attorney Eugene T. Jenson for possible prosecution.

The initial complaint resulted in the arrest of Artru and Rentsch, under which they were required to execute appearance bonds. In the second complaint that Jean filed with the County Attorney, she alleged that the agents entered "a habitation" without consent, under a theory that because the agents came upon the patio, this constituted "a habitation." Entering of a habitation versus just entering property would cause an increase in the offense from a Class B to a Class A misdemeanor, thus resulting in an increase in potential penalty from jail confinement of 180 days and $1,000 fine or both, to jail confinement of one year and $2,000 fine or both. (The government would later make much of the two complaints and, in addition, point to a third complaint, which was not intended by Mrs. Hylton, but typed by Jensen's secretary, alleging the agents had refused to leave once they were told to leave. Jenson had insisted on an *original* complaint and Jean was asked by Jenson's secretary to sign a blank complaint, which she did, trusting the complaint would be prepared accurately, which it was not.)

Jean's first complaint, tracking the Texas Criminal Trespass statute, Section 30.05 of the penal code, stated that on or about November 4, 1981, Artru and Rentsch did "intentionally and knowingly enter property and the said habitation of Jean Hylton without the effective consent of the said Jean Hylton, and the said Michael E. Rentsch and Thomas E. Artru, acting together, did then and there have notice not to enter said premises in that Jean Hylton, the owner of said premises, had signs posted to be reasonably likely to come to the attention of intruders and the posted signs warned Michael E. Rentsch and Thomas E. Artru not to enter said premises." Jenson found Jean's complaint and tape recording sufficient to warrant prosecution and arrest of the two IRS agents. Jenson, short and fat, would qualify as County Prosecutor for Hazard County and fit right in with Mayor Boss Hogg. In addition to Jenson's determination as to the adequacy of the complaint, Jenson would later testify before the federal Grand Jury which indicted Jean that Jenson was afraid of vexatious or harassing litigation by Jean or V. R. His fear, thus, was as well a factor in his decision. V. R., it seems, had a habit of filing, as his own attorney, million dollar lawsuits against government officials, and with the suits filing *lis pendens* actions, meaning liens against the defendants' property pending outcome of the suit. It was no wonder, as everyone in Chambers County knew, you did not go uninvited on the Hylton property in Wallisville, Texas.

Jenson did not want to prosecute the complaint and did so only because the judge ordered him to do so. Jenson told Jean, "I am Lord over my parish [county]" and that the Hyltons had sued him for one million and fifty five thousand dollars. Jean said, "I didn't sue you, V.R. did." Jenson replied, smirking, "Well, maybe not, but you sure do some pretty typing," suspecting Jean, not V.R. had typed the complaint.

For years, the Hyltons had maintained an ongoing feud with IRS and other governmental agencies. It was no wonder that their property had become their refuge, their last bastion of God-given Constitutional rights. The line of demarcation had been drawn in a silent truce - a truce violated when Artru and Rentsch dared cross the line and venture into Hylton territory. It was much like the Hatfields and the McCoys, those long-feuding families of the West Virginia hills, or as if one challenger had stated to another after drawing with his foot or a stick a straight line in the dirt, *"Cross that line and be prepared to deal with me."* As a country fundamental preacher, V. R. probably would have said, *"Be prepared for the wrath of almighty God."* For V. R., the *Fourth* had become most recently his highest battle banner.

The Artru and Rentsch incident was but a skirmish in the ongoing Hylton versus oppressive government war. In 1979, V. R. had been charged with obstruction of justice and resisting a federal officer in the performance of his duty. (Details in *War Stories, Part II.*) IRS was highly displeased with not only V. R.'s personal conduct but his influence on others. He was instructing citizens from all walks of life concerning not only the *Fourth Amendment* rights, but as well *First* and *Fifth*. The indictment, filed January 20, 1982, alleged that Jean and V. R. "were leaders of a semi-organized tax rebellion movement and, as such, the Defendant and her husband have not paid federal income taxes since 1975.... As part of her tax protest activities, the Defendant, Jean C. Hylton, attempted to cause officials of Chambers County, Texas to arrest and initiate criminal charges against a United States District Judge and deputy United States Marshalls ... The Defendant's son, David Hylton, was also a member of the tax rebellion movement and has filed no federal tax returns or paid federal income taxes for the years 1978 through 1981." During Jean's criminal case, I would represent not only Jean but as well assist David and V. R. by preparing for their filing *pro se* (as your own attorney) a motion to strike the language concerning V. R. and David for reason that it was damaging to their reputations.

The indictment went on to allege that Jean approached Mayes and Jenson "in an attempt to cause those County officials to issue warrants for the arrest of the Special Agents and to initiate criminal trespass charges for the purpose of obstructing and impeding the investigation of David Hylton." It was the government's theory, as outlined in the indictment, that Jean "did corruptly endeavor to intimidate and impede two officers and employees of the United States of America who were then acting in their official capacities as criminal investigators under Title 26, United States Code, and that said Defendant attempted to prevent two Special Agents of the Internal Revenue Service from asking questions of David Hylton by causing Chambers County officials to initiate criminal trespass charges against said agents." Under this, Count I of the indictment, intimidating or impeding federal officers, Jean faced a maximum penalty of five years and a $50,000 fine. Then in Count II, the Grand Jury alleged that by the same actions on November 4 and 5, 1981, that Jean "willfully endeavored by means of misrepresentation and intimidation to obstruct, delay and prevent the communication of information relating to a violation of a criminal statute of the United States by her son, David Hylton, to criminal investigators, and that said Defendant caused Chambers County officials to initiate criminal trespass charges against two Special Agents of the Internal Revenue Service." This, the obstruction of justice charge, could result in a maximum penalty of five years and $50,000. The indictment was signed by Warren A. Butchman, Jr., foreman of the Grand Jury, and by James L. Powers, Assistant United States Attorney.

Ironically, although I did not know the Hyltons prior to the *Spotlight* article, I had represented one of their acquaintances, an airline pilot and former Marine Corps fighter pilot, Les Kaegler of Kerrville, Texas. Of all my clients, Les is the only one I never met personally and one of several who died during my representation, and one of two who was murdered during that representation. Kaegler's case received national attention, including an article by syndicated columnist Sylvia Porter, for reason that he was the first in the nation criminally prosecuted for use of what the IRS would call the "Church Scheme" or "Mail Order Ministry." Like many airline pilots, including the "Braniff Ten," a criminal case later brought in Fort Worth, Texas in which I would be involved, Les had followed the lead of Kirby Hensley of the Universal Life Church (ULC) in Modesto, California. I can remember in the early '70s, before I went to law school, Hensley appearing on CBS' *60 Minutes* and pronouncing that he was against tax exemption for any church, but if it was good enough for Billy Graham and good enough for the Catholic Church, it was good enough for him. Hensley, who claims he can neither read nor write and appears a character out of an Elmer Gantry novel, could "sell snow cones to Eskimos." But to IRS, he has been "a snake oil salesman," selling just one of the many tax protester schemes.

ULC would amass a claimed membership of ten million due in large part to the landmark ruling in which IRS challenged ULC's tactics and status. In upholding the exemption, U.S. District Judge Battin, presiding in that case, wrote a passage often quoted by ULC and other "family churches:"

Neither this court, nor any branch of this government, will

consider the merits or fallacies of a religion. Nor will the court compare the beliefs, dogmas, and practices of a newly organized religion with those of an older, more established religion. Nor will the court praise or condemn a religion, however excellent or fanatical or preposterous it may seem. Were the court to do so, it would impinge upon the guarantees of the *First Amendment*. *Universal Life Church, Inc. v. United States*, 372 F.Supp 770,776 (C.D. Calif. 1974).

Thus, mail order ministries proliferated, including Life Science Church, of which one branch, Life Science Church of New York, was headed by Bishop Larry Ranucci, a former carpet layer I would later defend in the United States District Court for the Southern District of New York in Manhattan.

In 1981, Les was prosecuted for income tax evasion by James Powers, an ambitious but stupid Assistant United States Attorney, who was out of control. (Years later Powers would leave the Houston office and join the U. S. Attorney's office in Tampa, Florida, where he would prosecute another client of mine.) Simply put, Powers was a pompous ass, blinded by not only his own ambitions to be appointed by the President of the United States as U.S. Attorney, which was never to be, but by his vindictiveness toward tax protesters in general and the Hylton family in particular. *Hatfields and McCoys. Powers and Hyltons.*

I was called to represent Les in his appeal after the jury had convicted him in what turned out to be a close case. His trial attorneys had raised good faith belief in the legality of his actions as a defense and the jury deliberated several days. Les called me, dissatisfied with his trial counsel, and we discussed the appeal. We agreed on the terms of the fee and I was on the case.

First order of business was to read the trial transcript and discuss the case with trial counsel, which I did. There was no need for Les to appear in Phoenix, so we continued our discussions by phone. From his voice, I pictured a man who was strong-willed, no nonsense, but willing to listen to my advice. He sounded the part: *Marine Corps fighter pilot* . In fact, for Les, airline jockeying was not enough. He had purchased a T-28, an old Air Force prop trainer with glass canopy. It guzzled gas and, like all old prop trainers and the fighter planes of World War II, it had a personality of its own - large, overbearing and very loud. (A personality not unlike many of my Constitutionalist clients.)

Les was out on bail pending his appeal and was restricted to the Southern District of Texas but for travel required by his job with Texas Airlines. Having developed the facts of his case, I was working out an appeal strategy for a brief I never had to write. Les skipped. Soon after, the government filed a motion for a hearing in

Houston. Now Les and I had a real problem. If Les showed, he would be immediately arrested and charged, assuming the government had enough evidence of his flight. Bail jumping is a felony with a maximum penalty of five years and $50,000. But if Les failed to show, that in itself would be evidence of bail jumping. Moreover, how could I defend against the serious allegations without Les' presence to assist me? Would the court proceed without his presence?

I did what I typically do in compounded situations: take ten steps backward, be objective, apply logic and examine all the alternatives, play out all the scenarios - worst case, best case and several in between . My duty to Les was to advise him. The government was claiming that he was last seen fleeing into the woods from a small airport in Tennessee. The airplane he had landed contained, according to Drug Enforcement Administration (DEA), Customs and IRS agents, the largest single cache of cocaine seized to date in the United States. Arms and ammunition, including automatic M-16s had been allegedly found at a house he had purchased. Les, the government alleged, was not only in violation of his bond condition, but he had become a leading drug runner. Based on the drug allegations, IRS had proceeded with a jeopardy assessment for non-payment of taxes, seizing the Kaegler home in Texas, where Les' wife, Holly, and their several small children resided. Under jeopardy assessment statutes, IRS could not only lien, but immediately seize property where they alleged that due to anticipated flight of the defendant, or for other causes, the ultimate payment of the taxes was in jeopardy.

In applying my logic technique, I uncovered the only available defense to an untenable situation. The hearing was set, but since this was a new action, and because I was counsel of record on the appeal only, the government could not complete service on Les without serving him personally. Nor could they prove constructive notice. Without notice and opportunity to be heard as guaranteed by the *Fifth Amendment Due Process Clause, United States Constitution,* how could they then proceed against Les?

I filed papers for Les, entering a special appearance and pleading to jurisdiction, thus not waiving the notice and service argument and making the point that the court did not even have jurisdiction (power) over Les personally, nor over the subject matter. In my affidavit filed with the court, I declared that, although I had talked to someone who identified himself as Les subsequent to the government's action and advised him of the hearing, I had no way of knowing Les' identity by voice because I had never met the man. The case was assigned to Judge Carl O. Beu. I flew to Houston and met Holly and her brother in the courthouse to prepare for the hearing. Judge Beu first heard me out on the notice issue, reserved ruling, and had the government proceed with its evidence. According to the testimony, Les had piloted a plane to Gatlinburg, Tennessee. He must have been tailed by a DES or Customs surveillance aircraft because at the small terminal he was confronted by Customs Agents. They wanted to search the cargo. Les consented and, as the agents proceeded, he and another man slipped out of the terminal and were last seen running into the nearby woods. That is the last the government would see of Les alive. IRS, working with Customs and FBI then seized the Tennessee home, the private airplane and the T-28. In the home, they found clothing and weapons.

Les continued to call, but only from phone booths. Again, I could only assume it was Les, for it sounded like him, but then he was also the man I assumed was Les when we first talked. Les would not disclose his location but did tell me he was with a group which was protecting him. I pictured an armed encampment somewhere in the Oklahoma or Arkansas hills.

We were retained by Holly to handle the jeopardy assessment and attempted to at least save for Holly and the children the Texas house. Les and Holly had placed the house in trust, thus offering us perhaps a technical defense because the conveyance had occurred well before any drug running dates alleged. Kirk McCarville, my "partner" (used loosely and not in the tax sense, since technically we had formed a corporation), would handle the civil matters.

The government moved to dismiss the appeal due to "abandonment by flight." With the evidence presented and with no Les to come forth, to the government's motion I had no defense. Judge Beu never did rule, probably aware that the issue would be moot by way of indictment and warrant for the arrest of Les for bail jumping. The State of Tennessee had located and charged Les' son. Represented by Tennessee lawyers, the son was later convicted and sentenced to several years. The feds kept their hand in the matter and we were contacted by the U.S. Attorney's office in Nashville. Having made the biggest coke bust to date in the U.S., the feds believed they were really onto something big. They suspected that Les had been making regular drug runs from somewhere in South America, probably Columbia, through Florida or Texas. They hoped to cut a deal with Les, coordinate with the Texas U.S. Attorney, and bring him in from out in the cold. With Les, they could go after Mr. Big, identity unknown.

Through the "patriot network," I was hearing rumors that Les was in an armed encampment, somewhere in the mountains of eastern Oklahoma, protected by Mr. Big. Or was it the CIA that was involved? Rumor had it that Les was running guns to the Contras in Nicaragua in exchange for payment of cocaine. With insufficient federal funds authorized to fund the Contras against the

Communist-supported Sandinistas, the CIA had reportedly found an easy method of funding. (As history has shown through the Iran-Contra scandal, such a rumor does not appear farfetched.) As a fearless pilot desperate for money, disenchanted with the federal system of "justice" since his conviction, and a risk-taker at heart, was this Les' way of getting even and at the same time making some good bucks? But for Les, was it a "calculated risk?" A federal Grand Jury was investigating and the U.S. Attorney was looking for Les and his partner with whom he had fled.

Thus, Kirk began negotiations with the U.S. Attorney's office for a deal Les could live with, such as dropping the drug and bail-jumping charges, felonies, in exchange for his return to Tennessee and cooperation. At first, Les appeared to have no interest, but apparently his fugitive status and the confinement to the armed encampment began to wear on this free-spirited pilot. With each phone call to me, I sensed he progressively leaned toward "coming in from out of the cold."

What happened next can be plausibly explained only by the following: our office phone was bugged by Mr. Big or the CIA, the U.S. Attorney's phone was bugged by Mr. Big or the CIA, Mr. Big or the CIA had an insider with the U.S. Attorney's office, or any combination of the above. Les was leaning strongly to cutting a deal. Kirk was to fly to Nashville, meet with the Assistant U.S. Attorney (AUS) and cut a final deal for Les' approval. There were numerous telephone calls between Kirk and the Assistant U.S. Attorney. Les would surrender at Nashville. Kirk met with the AUS in Nashville and discussed the terms of Les' surrender. Flying back to Phoenix that night, Kirk arrived home around midnight and received a call. Les was dead. Murdered. His body washed ashore near Miami, Florida, his death made to appear as an accident. His head had collided with a moving propeller of an outboard motor. We could only conclude Les knew too much about CIA operations, or Mr. Big, or both, and had been "terminated with extreme prejudice." Mr. Big was never prosecuted. There was more to the CIA story, as we discovered in the civil tax proceeding. And IRS had little evidence of the millions in drug income alleged. (Details in *War Stories, Part II*.)

Just as Vietnam had become a small world in that I repeatedly came into contact with high school and West Point classmates, including roommates and other friends or acquaintances, so was it with the Constitutional movement, or as IRS claimed, the "illegal tax protest movement," only more so. Here, I repeatedly came full circle, retained by a new client only to learn of his connection with prior clients. So long as there was no conflict of interest, it only served to make life more interesting. As we said in Vietnam, "it's a small war."

So it was that Mrs. Hylton, whom I had read about in the *Spotlight* , with whom Les and Holly Kaegler were fellow patriots, called me to inform me she had been indicted by a Grand Jury for interference with IRS agents and for obstruction of justice. Powers would prosecute. The *Spotlight* article was pre-indictment, lauding Jean for her courage in petitioning her government for redress of grievances by filing the complaint against Artru and Rentsch. My first reaction to the indictment was disbelief. Were Powers and the U.S. Attorney's office more stupid than I had originally thought? My second reaction was outrage. What was there left of the *First Amendment* right to petition the government for redress of grievances if a Texas housewife was to be charged and convicted of obstruction of justice for filing a criminal complaint which made true allegations of conduct by federal public servants? The *First Amendment* guarantees that "Congress shall make no law respecting an establishment of religion or prohibiting the free exercise thereof; or abridging the freedom of speech or of the press; or the right of the people peaceably to assemble and to petition the government for redress of grievances." Powers was not only blinded enough by his own vindictiveness and ambition, but he would trap himself by the government's justification for the charges by claiming the absurd: Jean C. Hylton lied about the presence of "No Trespassing" signs on the Hylton property. Locked into the lie, the government's own agents were locked into their testimony. Or was it the other way around: had Artru and Rentsch become so desperate as named criminal defendants that they lied to Powers about the signs in effort to preclude a conviction? A simpleton could merely drive slowly in front of the Hylton property and ascertain that the signs had not only existed but had been there for sometime. Would not the Hylton neighbors confirm it? Were Artru and Rentsch afraid of conviction, having read the Texas statute which made crystal clear that their act constituted a criminal offense, a statute that did not require proof of criminal intent?

Another scenario I considered was this: *Big Brother* had a habit of using a big stick against the little guy in an effort to not only justify the governments illegal acts committed, but to silence forever that sovereign citizen and others who would dare speak out. *The wheel that squeaks the loudest gets the grease.* What kind of defense could V. R. and Jean Hylton, non-filers for years, often *pro se* litigants and "leaders of this semi-organized tax rebellion," possibly muster against James Powers, a federal Grand Jury, and the backing of the U.S. Department of Justice in Washington? "Dare to file a criminal misdemeanor complaint against one of our agents and your reward: two felony counts with a maximum jail time of ten years!"

This was the same bureaucratic mentality I was determined to accept at West Point and had learned to detest in the Army and while working for the federal and state government as an Area Extension Agent, Community Resource Development, Virginia Polytechnic Institute and State University. *The end justifies the means.* *Might makes right,* as Machiavelli so succinctly put it in *The Prince.* But the likes of Tom Paine, Sam Adams, Pat Henry, Jim Madison and Tom Jefferson had a different view: the government is always suspect as a potential tyrant; the only safeguard is the common law and a contract known as the *Constitution,* by which there was formed a republic. For Jefferson in the *Declaration of Independence* recognized that God is the Divine Protector. Who then is the enforcer of this contract and by what means? The people are the enforcers by the mechanism of the rule contained within Article VI, Clause 3, wherein the contract requires that "Senators and representatives before mentioned, and the members of the several state legislatures and all executive and judicial officers both of the United States and of several states, shall be bound by oath or affirmation to support this Constitution; that no religious test shall be ever required as a qualification to any office or public trust while under the United States." And where any oath taker did violate the sacred oath, in the future the Divine Protector would deal with the perjurer, while as to the present, the contract authors surely had enough foresight to trust that another oath taker, as true to his oath, would march to the cry of the oppressed. If I was serious enough to take an oath, at age 18, whereby I swore to defend the *Constitution of the United States* against all enemies, foreign and domestic, to the end that I volunteered twice for Vietnam, where I would daily deal with *Doctor Death,* thus "marching to the sound of the guns," was *Big Brother* so foolish as to believe I would shirk my duty to God and to Country, and not become Point Man for Jean Hylton?

I had learned a lot about the petition for redress prior to the call from Jean Hylton. Not from high school government class, West Point, or even law school. Why was it contained within the *First Amendment* , except that it was at least as important as free exercise of religion, free press, free speech and right to assemble and associate? My clients repeatedly made reference to it in their correspondence with IRS and other bureaucrats, a habit I in turn picked up. Simply put, it is the right to gripe, blow off steam, verbalize, to put the potential tyrant on notice that you are serious about violation of your rights or other misconduct by the *Beast.* We are the sovereign; they are our servants, else why the term *public servant* ? They work for us. We delegate only so much authority as is specified and must constantly maintain the reigns. *Eternal vigilance is the price of liberty,* as Jefferson put it. Otherwise, government becomes as was noted by Pamphleters in the

1600 and 1700's, that *Monster of Monsters*. The *Monster* is bound by the chains of the Constitution. Only apathy and non-exercise of the people's rights can loosen those chains. Jefferson had complained within the Declaration of Independence, "In every stage of these oppressions we have *petitioned for redress* in the most humble terms. Our repeated petitions have been answered only by repeated injury. A prince whose character is thus marked by every act which may define a tyrant, is unfit to be the ruler of a free people."

It is not mere coincidence, I have concluded, that while the right to petition is the last enumerated right within the *First Amendment*, it is immediately followed by the *Second* : "A well-regulated militia being necessary to the security of the free state, the right of the people *to keep and bear arms* shall not be infringed." Thus, the founders foresaw the need for a self-executing clause within the contract. *Amendment One* permits the blowing off of steam for the contract enforcers, the people. But if the *Monster* does not remain within the bounds of the chains, enforcers have available other remedies. The *Monster* would call it "anarchy," a term overlooked by Jefferson when he said:

> Prudence indeed will dictate that governments long established should not be changed for light and transient causes; and accordingly all experience has shown that mankind are more disposed to suffer while evils are sufferable, than to right themselves by abolishing the forms to which they're accustomed. But when a long train of abuses and usurpations pursuing invariably the same object evinces a design to reduce them under absolute despotism, it is their right, it is their duty, to throw off such government and to provide new guards for their future security.

From the first call from Jean, in which she informed me of the indictment, I learned that she could not afford to pay me very much money. Although our firm was not one of any means, having only two attorneys at the time, and though I was personally doing no better than financially struggling with the rest of middle class America, I really had no choice but to accept the responsibility. If nothing is to be left to the right to petition, then what remained worth fighting for? Petition was the key: it is not just the right, it is the execution of *all* rights. It is not coincidence that court filings at the first level, as well as on appeals, are called "petitions"; e.g. petition for temporary restraining order, petition for rehearing, petition (to the U.S. Supreme Court) for *certiorari*.

First, I had Jean send to me the tape, news articles, the complaint against Artru and Rentsch and the indictment, and most important, for my curiosity and for points to be made at trial: the photographs of the "No Trespassing" signs. After reviewing the evidence, there was no doubt in my mind. The agents had seen the photos and their defense to an unlawful intrusion was to deny their existence. To lie. Would they not look foolish stating before a jury that they intentionally passed seven signs which clearly posted "No Trespassing?" If asked whether they were familiar with the Texas statute which made it a misdemeanor to so trespass, they would be faced with a no-win answer. If they answered they were *not* familiar, they would be hit with the "ignorance is no excuse" argument, and as well look foolish for reason that as law enforcement officers they were*not* familiar with state penal statutes. If they answered that they *were* familiar, then they would be admitting to the crime. At issue for the IRS, then, was not only the case against Artru and Rentsch, but as well a civil suit by the Hyltons against IRS, and Artru and Rentsch for violation of their *Fourth Amendment* rights, a *Bivens* suit. In *Bivens v. Six Unknown Narcotics Agents,* the first case of its kind before the U.S. Supreme Court, the court held that a citizen can sue individual agents for violation of Constitutional rights. Bivens, acting *pro se* from prison, had filed a complaint against the agents for unlawful entrance into his home, illegal arrest, illegal search and seizure. The agents had cuffed Bivens behind his back and beat him in front of his wife and children.

The first order of business was the prosecution of Artru and Rentsch. Since Jean was the complainant, dare she take the stand as complainant and testify, thus not only waiving her *Fifth Amendment* right against having to be a witness in a criminal case, but giving up the element of surprise saved for her own criminal trial? But what surprise? The conversation between Jean and the two agents had been tape recorded. Technically, the prosecutors could introduce the tape against both the agents and Jean. But at serious doubt was Jenson's ability and desire to take these agents *to the cleaners, put them in a sweet pea,* as my junior high school football coach used to put it. Sylvestor Stallone had a phrase for the Pepsi Generation, *Eye of the Tiger.* Jenson did not have the toenail of the tiger, much less the eye. The strategy and tactics developed in Jean's case illustrate not only the applicability of global warfare when dealing with IRS in particular, and the government in general, but as well demonstrate the chess game lawyers play. Not only must you plan your next move, you must anticipate that of your enemy and plan several moves in advance.

Jean felt I should assist in the prosecution, thus ultimately protecting her in the criminal case. In addition, she had hopes that the agents would receive their just reward - conviction - by way of prosecutor Jenson, even though he was intimidated by the *Beast.*

Poetic Justice. Not only was Jenson intimidated by IRS, he was more so intimidated by the Hyltons and their reputation for million dollar suits against bureaucrats.

We decided, then, that the best defense was a strong offense and that we should posture ourselves in Jean's criminal case with a criminal conviction of Artru and Rentsch, despite the risk of having Jean take the stand in their criminal case. If the agents were convicted, how could it be said that Jean committed an offense by filing a complaint, thus setting up the government for a motion to dismiss on impossibility as well as *First Amendment* exercise by Jean. But the government had its own strategy, and the case became a game of *Twixt*, or *Feudal* . (In *Twixt* , a game by which players must make a connecting bridge across the board by making individual moves, players must think three or four plays ahead. In *Feudal* , each player has an army made up of men who have different moves, the same moves as in   Chess. The major difference, though, is that every time it is your move, you can move *every* man! Thus, the possibilities become mind boggling.)

First, the government, defending Artru and Rentsch, moved the county court judge for removal of the case to federal court, based upon federal subject matter jurisdiction. Jenson did not as much as object, and prior to Jean's call to me, the case had been ordered to the United States District Court for the Southern District of Texas in the Galveston Division before Judge Gibson, the same judge who had presided over V. R.'s case. I traveled to Galveston and did my best to prod Jenson, who was shaky at best. Rumor was Jenson had serious personal problems. His wife had died and he was residing in an unkept house. It did little for his reputation that as a white, southern Texas prosecutor, he was living with a black woman. His knowledge as the county prosecutor of several years was seriously lacking, as was shown during his testimony at Jean's trial.

Despite the frustrations, for me it was worth the trip just to watch IRS CID agents plead not guilty to criminal charges. Judge Gibson permitted Jean as complainant to sit at the prosecutor's table and he honored my request to assist her in assisting the prosecutor, since she was my client in the criminal case brought against her by, in essence, IRS, which in essence was Artru and Rentsch. So, I sat between Jenson and Jean. Here was a real twist. I was placed in a position of assisting in a prosecution of those responsible for prosecuting my client. Rare indeed is the opportunity for a criminal tax defense lawyer to assist in the prosecution of IRS special agents. As they say, *Don't get mad, get even.*

But my hands were tied. Jenson did little more than go through the motions in presenting the evidence: Jean's testimony, the photos, the tape recording. The story was told but we were ambushed not on the facts, but on the law. In the case of *Foster v. U.S.*, 296 F.2d 65, 67 (5th Cir. 1982), the U.S. Court of Appeals for the Fifth Circuit had held that when the performance of his duty requires an officer of the law to enter upon private property, his conduct, otherwise a trespass, is justified. The government was not entirely stupid. Rather than file a motion to dismiss prior to the evidence, they had waived jury trial and moved to dismiss on the strength of *Foster* at the end of Jenson's case in chief. In a matter of minutes the judge ruled, acquitting Artru and Rentsch. We urged Jenson to take an appeal, as the law was unsettled among the circuits. Even if Jenson was dead in the water within the Fifth Circuit, perhaps the U.S. Supreme Court would hear the conflict among the circuits. He refused. Any leverage we had, was now lost. We had taken not our best shot, but the only shot we had, and it was now the government's turn.

I had some tricks of my own, due more to Powers' stupidity than my own abilities. On Count II of the obstruction charge, Powers had shot himself in the foot. In that count, the grand jury charged that Jean obstructed justice by interfering with the witness about to give evidence to federal investigators investigating the suspect. A serious shortcoming, however, was lack of a witness. It was Powers who assisted the grand jury in returning the indictment, the same prosecutor, who I argued, should have known that clearly the law in the Fifth Circuit is that in order for an obstruction charge to stand, there must be A, a suspect, B, a federal investigator, and C, a witness. The suspect and the witness cannot be one and the same, as declared by the Fifth Circuit in *U.S. v. Cameron,* 460 F.2d 1394 (5th Cir. 1972). Notwithstanding the clear import of this case holding, Powers had succeeded in having the Grand Jury return an indictment on Count II. *Rubber stamp.*

Typically, targets of a criminal investigation might threaten, intimidate or even kill a witness. Or, as in the case of Iran-Contra and Lt. Col. Oliver North and his secretary, Fawn Hall, evidence is destroyed by shredding or otherwise. Here, there was no such conduct. Under criminal investigation, David Hylton had the right of silence as guaranteed by the *Fifth Amendment, U.S. Constitution.* At worst, Jean's action and subsequent complaints would prevent Jean from being confronted by agents about the whereabouts of David. In other words, at the very worst, Jean *obstructed herself,* an impossibility under the statute. Because Jean was not A, the suspect, nor B, the investigator, she was C, the witness. Jean as witness then had obstructed herself from giving information to the investigators about her son, David, the suspect.

Of course the government's theory was broader: Jean's complaint which resulted in prosecution of Artru and Rentsch obviously resulted in bringing to a halt the investigation of David

Hylton by Artru and Rentsch, a precedent which might serve to chill the aggressive tactics of IRS special agents. IRS could ill afford such a precedent. Principle, then, was at stake for both sides: Jean's right to petition; the *Monster's* claimed right to intimidation of targets, witnesses and family members of both.

Prior to trial, I filed a brief putting the court and prosecutor on notice as to the defect of Count II. I did not move to dismiss, waiting until jeopardy had attached by the swearing of the jury to spring the ambush. Of course, I could have waited until after the jury was sworn to raise the issues, but would have done so at the risk of a District Court and, later, an Appellate Court, holding that I waived the issue by not putting the court on notice prior to jeopardy attachment. In response to my brief, Powers moved to dismiss Count II, which was granted by the court. (As part of the chess game, this was also a judgment call as to whether we should perhaps go to jury trial on both counts with the hope that District Court would dismiss Count II at the end of the government's case in chief, thus causing a loss of credibility for the government in the minds of the jury. It became a balancing test, which leads to a decision by the commander. *You can delegate authority but not responsibility.*)

In my typical style, I went further than setting the government up on a motion to dismiss Count II. Since the duty of the prosecutor was to see that justice be done and advise the grand jury of the law, as well as protect the accused, how could it be that a grand jury advised by a diligent prosecutor could indict on obstruction of justice when, under the facts, the crime was impossible? Simple. When the prosecutor is Powers, or any other prosecutor maddened by his own ambition and vindictiveness. Powers, obviously, had misled the jury and obtained that rubber stamp indictment. *A prosecutor can obtain an indictment against anything not nailed down.* A cliche close to my own military heart. *If it moves, salute it. If it doesn't move, paint it.* (When President Kennedy visited Ft. Bragg, North Carolina, home of Special Forces and the 82nd Airborne, the paratroopers were instructed to not only paint the rocks white, but to paint the grass green!)

Based on this notion that the prosecutor is duty bound to protect the accused and that he is to seek justice, not necessarily convictions, I filed a motion to dismiss due to prosecutorial misconduct and grand jury abuse on the theory that Powers had intentionally misled the grand jury on the law concerning obstruction. In 1935 the Supreme Court discussed the duty of the United States Attorney:

> The United States Attorney is the representative not of an
> ordinary party to a controversy, but of a sovereignty whose

obligation to govern impartially is as compelling as its obligation to govern at all; and whose interest, therefore, in a criminal prosecution is not that it shall win a case, but that justice shall be done. As such, he is in a peculiar and very definite sense the servant of the law, the twofold aim of which is that guilt shall not escape or innocence suffer. He may prosecute with earnestness and vigor - indeed he should do so. But, while he may strike hard blows, he is not at liberty to strike foul ones. It is as much his duty to refrain from improper methods calculated to produce a wrongful conviction as it is to use every legitimate means to bring about a just one. *Berger v. United States*, 55 S.Ct. 629.

The *Berger* type motions have become a regular part of my arsenal: prosecute the prosecutor or persecute the persecutor. But Jean's case became more bizarre than usual. Because we trusted Judge Gibson more than we could trust a jury, and because we feared Powers would be permitted to put Jean and her entire family on trial as tax protesters, despite no tax charge, we waived the jury, a Constitutional right guaranteed by the *Sixth Amendment*. I discovered, to my chagrin, that the *Monster* had a right to trial by jury not mandated by the Constitution nor by common law, as is the case for the accused, but by right vested upon them by Congress by the Federal Rules of Criminal Procedure.

On the hearing on pretrial motions, Judge Gibson permitted me a limited evidentiary hearing and Powers magnanimously offered himself as a witness. Smiling as ever, Powers had innumerable lame excuses for his oversight on the obstruction charge. The judge denied our demand for non-jury trial and for dismissal due to grand jury abuse and prosecutorial misconduct, and for violation of the *First Amendment* right to petition the government for redress of grievances. Worst of all, considering that we were now set for jury trial, he denied our motion *in limine*, which was our objection to introduction by Powers of evidence concerning Jean's protest activities, including her alleged physical attack upon a U.S. deputy marshal at the time of V. R.'s arrest. It was a lie; they had the wrong woman. Here, then, was a tax case which had become an obstruction of justice/intimidation and interference with IRS agents case which was developing again into a tax case with assault mixed in and, as a defense to the assault, mistaken identity. How could Powers, a man of such little restraint, wield so much power? *Only in America*. (A motion *in limine* seeks an advance ruling on the admissibility of evidence.)

Whether Powers got out of the kitchen because he could no longer take the heat or, in fact, had a more pressing matter, I can only suspect the former. I viewed the government's situation as a quagmire akin to Vietnam; *the tar baby syndrome.* Another analogy are those many instances where the government, wearing blinders, insists for example that it can build a bridge for one million dollars. Halfway across the river it concludes that it will take ten million. Rather than allow half of a bridge sit as a monument to bureaucratic stupidity, the government proceeds, blinders in place, to build the ten million dollar bridge which was supposed to cost one million. Then the bridge falls down. Robert McNamara, Secretary of Defense, and his army of Harvard computer whiz kids always had the underlying solution to Vietnam: technology. Yet a twelve-year-old farmer, barefoot and dressed in black pajamas, carrying an outdated carbine brought the most powerful nation in the world to its knees. Stupidity. *Don't miss the forest for the trees.* Having every confidence that Jean ultimately would be vindicated by some court for her exercise of the right to petition, I stood in awe, watching our all-powerful United States government take more swings at tar baby. Whatever the reason, prior to trial, Powers was replaced by George A. Kelt, Jr., later to be appointed U.S. Magistrate in Houston.

I was disappointed that I was to be denied the opportunity to do battle with Powers, not just because of my own ego. I believed as did Jean that he was so vindictive that he might destroy his own credibility before the jury as indeed he had already done before his peers, judges, and court personnel. I had read of his courtroom antics in the *Kaegler* transcript (an intelligence source) and had observed Powers firsthand in another case I had handled in which the defendant and his wife pled guilty and were granted probation and no fine. In that case, one of obvious overkill by Powers, a government tactic which serves only to strengthen my own attack, the couple had filed, in lieu of regular tax returns, returns exercising their *Fifth Amendment* and other constitutional objections. On the strength of their objection that the money of account was no longer real money, *funny money* or *fiat money* for reason it was no longer backed by gold or silver, they had requested a return of tax dollars paid in through withholding. Rather than levy misdemeanor charges of willful failure to file federal income tax returns, Powers played Elliott Ness: in addition to the misdemeanor failure to file charges, he had the grand jury charge felony counts of conspiracy, willful attempted income tax evasion, mail fraud, wire fraud, and false claims.

The clients were torn as to their decision. They wanted to go to trial on principle, believing they stood a chance of acquittal on the basis of good faith belief. The husband was stricken with terminal cancer and had been given estimates of but six months to one year to live. They owed, in fact, very few tax dollars. Thanks to Powers' reasonableness on plea negotiation, I was able to obtain for our clients an offer of plea to one count misdemeanor, failure to file, with dismissal of the remaining counts, which is highly unusual. Typically, the Justice Department will not approve downgrading of tax offenses from felony to misdemeanor. Here, they were probably willing to do so because of the husband's health.

The couple had moved from Texas to California in search of work where the wife was waiting tables. They did not have a penny to their name. At sentencing I had asked for probation and no fine. Powers became the object of courtroom ridicule by all with his serious plea for a substantial fine. The judge, a reasonable King Solomon-type, wanted to know from Powers from what source the fine would be paid, and Powers, with his boyish grin could give no answer. Expressions of the courtroom personnel: clerk, bailiff, court reported and law clerk, said it all: Powers, a man who would, if his wish were met, be appointed by the President of the United States as United States Attorney for the Southern District of Texas, could not as much as be taken seriously by those who worked with him on a daily basis. *The court jester, the fool, would be King.*

In 1979, I had dealt with another prosecutor out of control, one who supplied me with some of the personality traits for one of my Justice Department fictional characters in my first book, *April 15: The Most Pernicious Attack Upon English Liberty.* Jake Schneider and his associate, Curtis Nash, prosecuted in New Hampshire a failure to file case against a "brain-fried John Bircher" named Bob Judge, who had filed *Fifth Amendment* returns for a few years. Bob, a plumber of very modest means, lived in rural New Hampshire with his wife and two small children. At age forty, having not been blessed with children, they adopted a child. By the grace and wisdom that only God provides, his wife was soon pregnant for the first time. Now fifty, they reared the two small children and their dog, Skipper. But Bob's real sin in the eyes of the *Monster* was not his failure to meet up to his claimed duty to file tax returns, upon which he owed very little money. Rather, his high crime was to dare sponsor a New Hampshire meeting at which those infamous tax protesters would speak.

Not a public speaker himself, Bob merely introduced the several speakers, but it was Bob's name that appeared on the flyers. *The wheel that squeaks the loudest gets the grease.* To watch and listen to Jake, one would think that Bob was Al Capone, public enemy number one. Curtis Nash, on the other hand, I liked. Curtis, a black man, was reserved, and I could tell had no personal animosity or vindictiveness against tax protesters. Only doing his job. In fact, as I was to learn, the most inexperienced prosecutors were typically given the job of prosecuting tax protesters. It was a job no one wanted and no one enjoyed, except Jake. In addition was the fact that many of the protesters represented themselves, thus not creating

72

much in the way of challenge for a prosecutor flying all the way in from Washington, D.C.

Perhaps deep down, Curtis, as a black man, could relate to underdogs such as Bob Judge. After all, was it not Martin Luther King who preached civil disobedience in effort to bring about change? (The Ninth Circuit in a criminal tax case opinion would later state that civil disobedience of the tax laws was not a proper means by which to effect political change.) What, prey tell, is the difference between objecting to tax monies utilized for the murder of the unborn by way of government-subsidized abortions and seeking a meal in a restaurant which serves only white people?

It was not that I really disliked Jake, I just had no respect for him. Like Powers, I saw him as a baby. In fact, they each maintained a "baby-faced" appearance. In Bob's trial, Jake repeatedly went into temper tantrums. He was determined to win at all costs. At all costs to the defendant, his counsel, the judge, the jury, and the entire justice system. Schneider was on a collision course with destiny. It was only a matter of time.

At trial, I brought out before the jury the fact that at the Holiday Inn on the evening of the meeting that Bob had helped sponsor, two IRS CID agents who later investigated and recommended prosecution of Bob, drove through the parking lot slowly. While one drove, the other read into a small tape recorder the license plate numbers of every vehicle in the lot. Those attending the meeting would dare attend and listen to public speakers who would dare to seek a change in public policy made by the best Congress money could buy. *We will maintain the status quo. Dossiers. KGB will learn from our tactics.* (Of course, far worse it was for those whose tax matters were investigated, those who had not attended the protest meeting but had stayed the night at the Holiday, their car parked in the lot. *The sin of coincidence.*)

Although Bob had the courage to withstand Jake's barrage on the witness stand in the criminal trial, the jury saw the case otherwise and found him guilty. The judge, who had amused us by his comment on a trial exhibit, gave Bob probation. Bob went home to his wife, two young children, and his black and white spotted mongrel Skipper, his name pronounced as only they can in Massachusetts or New Hampshire: "Skippaaahh." One of the books Bob had read and upon which he had relied concerning his fear of retaliation, thus justifying his claim of *Fifth Amendment* right to silence on his tax return, was *None Dare Call It Conspiracy* by Gary Allen. The book provides a "Conspiracy 101" textbook for John Birchers. To this, the judge had commented, "Oh, I read that. Good book."

On another case, I had learned that for at least some of the young prosecutors within the Justice Department, Jake had become an idol for his aggressive use of the grand jury. *It's only a matter of time,* I thought. He is no guerilla warrior. He will expose himself, as he has become his own worst enemy. I was not at all surprised to hear over the radio in 1984 that the Justice Department for the first time in the history of this nation sought to restrain the publisher from printing a judge's opinion. Prior restraint on *First Amendment* rights, called abhorrent by any freedom-loving nation. The Department obtained initially a temporary restraining order which added fuel to the media fire. What was being said about a federal prosecutor by a federal judge that was so defaming that it should remain secret? A lot when the object is Jake Schneider, his conduct in court and before the grand jury. *U.S. v. Kilpatrick,* 575 F.Supp. 325 (D. Colo. 1983).

Thus, in 1982 in preparing to ambush Powers, I could not help but think back on my 1979 experience with Schneider. Now my chance was lost; battle with Powers would await another day. I would have to endure many more days of lying in wait patiently, soaking wet, my hand on the firing mechanism of the claymore mine, hoping that when Powers came to the fork in the path he would come to me in the dark. *Walk this way, Jimmy. The trail is easier over this way. A shorter route. Make it easy on yourself. The night is long and you are weary. Be kind to yourself. Charge some helpless housewife and let Major Mac and the First Amendment bring the damn damn on you.*

I was not at all pleased with the Hylton jury. They did not as much as wiggle in their seats or change positions. They seemed transfixed. Did they blink? Breathe? Were they drugged? Expressionless, even during the lighter moments of the trial. Despite prosecutor Kelt's attitude of reasonableness, he proved to be no pushover. Though not personally vindictive, like Powers, he would drive every nail to the bone. The morning of trial, he offered Jean a misdemeanor plea. I could tell he did not like the case, the nightmare he had inherited from that idiot Powers. We stood in the hallway of the antiquated Galveston courthouse negotiating. If Jean would agree to plea to a misdemeanor, the felony charge would be dropped. Probation, no fine. Just a pound of flesh in the name of principle. We could find some obscure law to which she could plead. Maybe spitting on the sidewalk? Or had she used the Woodsy the Owl symbol in violation of federal law? Maybe even a no-contest plea - one reserved for the likes of political defendants such as former Vice President Spiro Agnew. Anything to make this *tar baby* go away. "Let go of me, tar baby," said Brer Rabbit, "or I'll toss you into the briar patch." Tar baby said nothing and Brer Rabbit, his left fist stuck in tar baby, reeled back with his right fist aiming right for tar baby's nose....

It was Jean's call. My duty was to advise her of alternatives and play out the consequences by way of worst and best case scenarios. My own conscience would not permit me to advise her by terms other than those couched in contingencies. "If you want to minimize your risk, and *if* you want to minimize your costs, knowing full well your abdication of principle, then ...." My duty was to my client, but my client had become more than flesh and blood in the person of Jean C. Hylton of Wallisville, Texas. It was Miss Liberty herself. No, I could not be blinded by my own principle which had caused me to take the case at a financial loss. It was tempting, but my first duty was to my client, even above my duty to the *Constitution,* for the duty to the client is a duty underwritten within the *Sixth Amendment* in which it is guaranteed that a defendant in a criminal case shall have a right to counsel. It's your call, Jean.

Jean, after seeking a moment of divine guidance, required even less time to decide. She had been promised by His Word. As in *Psalm 94:16,* she had laid out the fleece. She was but an instrumentality. She was not the issue. Powers was not the issue. IRS was not the issue. This was a war between principalities. A war that was long ago fought when Lucifer was bound in Hell. A war that would again be fought as proclaimed by John in *Revelation,* Chapter 19, verses 11 through 16:

> And I saw Heaven open and behold a white horse; and He that sat upon him *was* called faithful and true, and in righteousness he doth judge and make war. His eyes *were* as a flame of fire and on his head were many crowns; and he had a name written that no man knew but he himself and he *was* clothed with a vesture dipped in blood: and his name is called the Word of God. And the armies *which were* and having followed him upon white horses clothed in fine linen, white and clean. And out of his mouth goeth a sharp sword that with it he should smite the nations: and he shall rule them with a rod of iron: and he treadeth the wine press of the fierceness and wrath of Almighty God. And he had on *his* vesture and on his thigh a name written: King of Kings and Lord of Lords.

Either the *First Amendment* held for all a promise or it was not worth the paper on which it was written. Besides, there were a number of federal appellate judges, additional oath-takers, who stood between Jean and the jail cell.

We were smart enough to hedge our bets. Practically speaking, we assumed Judge Gibson would be at least as lenient with Jean as he had been with V. R. Thus, in event of conviction, probation was expected. But a different risk loomed for Jean. She had run unsuccessfully twice for Justice of the Peace in Chambers County and planned to try again. With a felony conviction, she would be barred from voting, much less running for public office, until her probation time had run and her civil rights were restored. Was not the Constitution more important than her political aspirations?

The trial became more bizarre than the pretrial proceedings. *Fact is stranger than fiction.* That, and much more, I had learned in Vietnam. While on the pacification mission, a sniper fired at me and I heard the round go well overhead. A few minutes later I received a call on the radio from November, 2nd Platoon. Their platoon leader, Lt. Schweitzer, with but a few weeks remaining in country, had been hit in the arm. Nothing serious; the round had little momentum when it hit, but it was enough to earn him the Purple Heart and an early freedom bird home. The bullet, intended for me, had traveled hundreds of yards to November's position where Lt. Schweitzer sat eating a can of peaches. Similarly, on my first day of combat, I stood above ground waiting my turn to jump into a fox hole my platoon sergeant and I were digging. It was almost chest-deep when he yelled "Damn you, Lieutenant!" thinking I had struck him in the shoulder with a shovel. I looked down to see hot metal buried in the flesh of his right shoulder. Shrapnel. Our 81 mm mortars were registering rounds a thousand meters out from our position. Incredibly, a piece of shrapnel had not only managed to fly the distance, but had come directly down into the fox hole into Sergeant Rodrigues' shoulder while I stood outside the hole inches away.

Again, during our pacification mission, one of my new men was careless with his shotgun, fired it accidently, and a pellet passed through the body of a cute eight-year-old girl. We called for medivac. A few weeks later, she was returned to her mother and I visited the village to watch her play as a normal child. Her body bore two small band aids - one on her chest and one on her back. The steel ball had miraculously passed through the center of her body and out her back without as much as touching a bone or vital organ.

And was that any more or less bizarre than the circumstances surrounding another eight-year-old girl, a *Mountagnard?* When I was platoon leader, we had launched a combat assault by helicopter into a densely forested area. After some enemy contact, we located what we believed to be a VC village. Our company commander had us draw back and called in the Air Force which dropped 500 pound bombs. I was then sent with my platoon up the mountain to see what was left, if anything, of the village. The company commander was wrong. These were not VC. They were *Mountagnards,* mountain people. Fortunately for them, they had escaped the wrath of the bombers for I found no evidence of dead bodies. On the other hand, I found little evidence of *anything*. I walked through one bomb crater after another, smelling a distinctive smell that gets caught in your nostrils and causes difficulty in breathing. The U.S. Air Force had succeeded in blowing the entire village off the map. The only thing remaining were a few tree stubbles. That evening as dusk approached, my men were out setting up claymore mines and trip flares in front of our position. An eight-year-old *Mountagnard* girl walked right into our perimeter. Five minutes later, she would have hit a trip flare and been blown to pieces by the claymore. Was she the sole survivor of her village? Perhaps off the mountain picking flowers or chasing her puppy dog? No doubt about it! I had been prepared for the bizarre.

On the mistaken identity issue in Jean's case, we played it out no different than Perry Mason. The officer who had claimed that Jean had grabbed him around the neck and was choking him was either a terrible liar or he could not identify his own mother. V. R., who had, because of Jean's request, not come to court for reason he would subject himself to the jurisdiction of the *Beast,* told me the officer had also falsely identified another man alleged to be part of the courthouse scuffle. The man he had identified as Campbell, an airline pilot, was not Campbell at all. Therefore, V. R. and I planned it so that Campbell sat in the front row during trial while Charles Warix waited in the hall. During my cross-examination of the officer, I asked him about Campbell and pinned him down to absolute certainty. I wanted him bolted in a box before I lowered the boom. Too often, attorneys feel they clamp down the witness with certainty, but leave him room to squirm. *Anchor the witness.* In addition, the line of questioning that gives rise to an anchored witness adds an air of interest for the jury by the way of suspense. Raising my voice, I asked the officer, "Are you absolutely certain, officer, that you can identify Campbell?" Of course he responded "yes," since he wanted the world to know he was a highly competent law enforcement officer. I walked Jones in from the hallway through the large double door, had him stand in front of the judge, jury and witness, and he was identified as "Campbell." I then returned him to the hallway. *Dramatics.* I asked, in *Columbo* fashion, as would Peter Falk, "Oh, by the way, Officer, just one last question. Do you recognize the man on the front row, third from left?" This was Campbell. "Never saw him in my life." "Are you absolutely certain?" "Yes." "Would you stake your professional reputation as a law enforcement officer on it?" "Yes, sir." Whereupon Campbell rises and identifies himself as Campbell.

Other jurors would have fallen off their seats. The only thing they love better than seeing a witness nailed is seeing an attorney nailed. "Know how to tell when a lawyer is lying? When his lips start moving." "Know what's brown and black and looks good on a well-dressed lawyer? Two dobermans." "Know what you call three lawyers up to their neck in sand? Not enough sand." But this jury did not as much as change their expressionless expressions. We were in trouble and I knew it. *Thank God for the First Amendment and our federal appellate system.*

Warix testified about the choking incident, identifying the woman whom Warix obseved choking the deputy. Warix identified her by name and description. It was *not* Jean Hylton.

We, who had no burden of proof, had demonstrated beyond *any* doubt that one of Jean's principle accusers was either totally incompetent or a liar or both. Yet, the jury did not as much as raise an eyebrow. *Maybe in south Texas folks are more laid back than I thought? IRS got the jury rigged? Stacked?* I could not figure it out. And while VR roared with laughter when we recounted for him back at the motel the cross-examination, he then turned serious. "Don't trust that jury. Don't trust none of them Texas jurors."

The officer's testimony had indeed become crucial because of the government's attempt to destroy Jean's good faith motive. By showing a woman who would grab a marshal by the throat in an effort to protect her husband, the prosecutor had shown, he would argue, a woman who would lie about "no trespassing" signs to protect herself. They were, after all, tax protesters, cheating not just the system, but law-abiding citizens like you and me, requiring of us more of our fair share to make up for the lost revenues on account of their intent to evade. This vicious Texas woman had absolutely no respect for authority.

The testimony of Artru and Rentsch likewise was, I thought, crucial. Although credible witnesses in addition to Jean would testify that signs had been posted, I wanted to attack the government by showing to the jury that its agents would intentionally lie as part of a vendetta against the Hyltons. I drew a simple diagram, a technique I have often used and with which, as an engineer, I feel comfortable. Apply simple logic. Make the jury feel as if they are at the scene. Assist them in visualizing what actually occurred.

Displayed on the chart was the highway and the Hylton property. I had the two agents testify about how many times they drove slowly in front of the house. They were looking for signs of David and V.R.'s gravel pit, where they might find David working. They admitted that they passed slowly in front of the house at least seven times, yet they insisted that they saw not a single "no trespassing" sign. I counted on the chart each time they passed in front of the Hylton property. They were lying through their teeth. Justice of the Peace Mays, with whom Jean had filed the complaint, testified likewise about the signs, as did Jenson. Mays commented that you could not drive down Highway FM 563 without seeing the signs.

Since the government had urged that Jean had lied about the

signs, I felt we should show not only her complaint as true but the government vendetta. Their burden was to prove that Jean had corruptly interfered with IRS agents. Unlike most criminal tax statutes which require willfulness or knowingly, here, only the word corruptly was used. I was able to find only scant authority for the meaning of the word by researching the legislative history. Since it in effect meant with malice or without good faith, then I concluded that good faith was a defense much like good faith belief in legality is a defense to willfulness in a criminal tax trial. But I was up against the same government who had brought us Vietnam, Watergate, and the prosecution against Mrs. Garber, also of Texas, who had received money for her rare blood and was prosecuted for income tax evasion for her failure to report her blood proceeds. Any interference with the law, Kelt argued, was for ill purpose.

For all of the haggling over Mrs. Hylton's complaint, and her good faith exercise of her *First Amendment* rights, in the end it apparently meant nothing to the jury. The government argued bad motive on the part of Jean, bringing out the million dollar suits against government officials. Jenson, believing in his naivete that grand jury testimony would forever remain sealed and secret, was surprised to learn that defense attorneys obtain grand jury testimony of witnesses who actually testify at time of trial. He first denied that one of the motives in bringing the prosecution was his fear of retaliation if he had not brought the criminal case against Artru and Rentsch. The prosecutor impeached him through his grand jury testimony, to which Jenson said, "I thought that was secret, Judge."

The court instructed the jury that the government must prove beyond a reasonable doubt three essential elements: first "that the defendant endeavored to intimidate or impede an officer of the United States;" second, "that the officer was acting in an official capacity under the Internal Revenue Code;" and third, "that the defendant's acts were done knowingly and corruptly." "Endeavor" he said, "means any effort to try to accomplish evil purpose that the statute was designed to prevent." "Corruptly" he stated, "means the specific intent to intimidate or impede an officer or employee of the United States" while "specific intent" he continued "means more than the general intent to commit the crime. The government must prove that the defendant knowingly did an action which the law forbids (or knowingly failed to do an act which the law requires) purposefully intending to violate the law. The word knowingly ... means that the act was voluntarily and intentionally and not because of mistake, accident, or other innocent reason."

The difficulty for us, however, was that in effect the government had succeeded in putting Jean on trial not simply for the complaints she had filed against the IRS agents, but for her alleged attack against the marshall, an act for which she was not technically charged. Under the "similar acts" doctrine, the government was able to have the jury consider her alleged act of assault and battery in determining "the state of mind or intent with which the Defendant committed the acts charged in the indictment." The Judge continued stating that, "where proof of an alleged act of like nature is established by evidence which is clear and conclusive, the jury may but is not obligated to draw the inference and find that in doing the acts charged in the indictment the defendant acted knowingly and corruptly and not because of mistake or accident or other innocent reason." In other words, as to the similar bad act, the government only had a burden of proving that the act was committed by the standard of "clear and conclusive" and if they first met that burden, then the jury could in effect find Jean guilty of the assault and consider the assault in considering her state of mind. Then, there was the defense portion of the instruction, which merely stated, "However, if you find the defendant did the acts charged in the indictment with a good faith belief that such were a legitimate exercise of her legal rights and not with the purpose or intent of committing the offense, then you will acquit the defendant." Whether the jury found Jean guilty of a similar act, we will never know, but they deliberated a mere three hours before reaching a verdict of guilty on the charge of intimidation or impeding Artru and Rentsch.

I was angry more than disappointed. *Those blockheads. Can't I make them understand the issue here?* But of course I had been limited in my presentation by the jury instructions on the law. With great emotion I urged the judge in open court to, notwithstanding the jury verdict, dismiss on legal grounds on the basis that the *First Amendment* protected the actions of Mrs. Hylton and that her purpose, whatever that might be, was not at all relevant. Without conceding her motive, I urged that her actions, whatever her motive, were protected nonetheless than speech, which for example, suggested that the president be shot. Speech is protected so long as it does not invite imminent lawless activity. For example, while a speech which suggests that the president be shot is protected, that which urges people to grab their guns and go shoot the president is not. In fact, members of the Black Panther Party, I discovered through my research, had been acquitted on *First Amendment* grounds for their suggestion at a meeting that the President be shot. In the courtroom, packed with Jean's supporters, you could have heard a pin drop at the conclusion of my argument. Law plus emotion. We had nothing to lose now.

The judge commented that my argument was persuasive but he denied the motion. Was this "damnation with faint praise?" Who cared how persuasive it was. The only thing that mattered to me was whether or not he would free my client. Sentencing was set and we now had the chore of informing V. R., who was waiting back at the motel, of the verdict.

V. R. is one of those strong-willed, charismatic individuals who, when you first meet him, you feel like you have known him all of your life. I first met him on my initial trip to Wallisville, at the same place Jean had met Artru and Rentsch - on the home patio. I had stayed in the Hylton home and knew them to be not only devout constitutionalists, but devout Christians. V. R. was preaching as guest preacher at numerous churches and was in the process of forming a new independent church. Each day of the four-day trial, he awaited on the balcony of the Holiday Inn in Galveston, watching over his four year old grandson, with whom he was closely attached. Like a kid awaiting the return of his parents, V. R. paced the balcony, anxious to receive the daily trial reports. This day, I could tell he expected that for which he had prayed that morning: acquittal. He did not have to await our words; our expressions told all. Except, I felt different this time after a loss. I was in a strange kind of mood, different from the depression I usually feel after the court clerk or the jury foreman read "we the jury do find the defendant ... on count one, ... guilty as charged ...."

After the verdict, Jean and I dutifully reported to the probation officer, who wanted to know from Jean if she chose to sign waivers of her right to privacy. Probation officers file with the court prior to sentencing a presentence report based upon a background investigation, which includes family, school, employment, and finances. I advised Jean she had *Fourth* and *Fifth Amendment* rights not to disclose anything, but must realize that her lack of cooperation would be noted to the judge and considered. *Between a rock and a hard place.* Again, it was Jean's call. She declined the officer's request. Had she endured the ordeal of trial by prejudiced jury only to now waive her privacy rights? Not hardly. As we left the courthouse, I felt that my anger had immediately worn off. While Jean remained totally disgusted, I felt elated. It was not until I saw V. R. that I realized why.

I had felt before in a time of travesty that same elation. *Faith springs hope eternal.* It was 1970 and I had returned home from Vietnam and was teaching the Reserve Officer Training Corps (ROTC) at the University of Cincinnati and occasionally dodging rocks from demonstrators. As part of the assignment, I became on a rotating basis with all other officers, a SAO, Survival Assistance Officer. There were two types of assignments. The first was to go with an NCO to the home of the parents or wife of the deceased, be the first to advise them that their son or husband had just been killed in Vietnam. This was, by far, the worst job. The second was to handle all funeral, insurance, and award matters for the family, becoming in effect executor of the estate, legal advisor, financial advisor and trustee. The same officer and NCO team could not act in both capacities on a single case for the simple reason that the next of kin abhorred the sight and memory of the officer and NCO tasked with the responsibility of bringing the worst kind of news.

On my first SAO case I had the second task, and in dress green uniform, upon which were fixed my airborne wings, Combat Infantryman's Badge, and numerous ribbons for eighteen months of Vietnam service, including several Bronze Stars, Air Medals, and the Vietnamese Cross of Gallantry with Silver Star, I went on a Saturday to a poor section of Cincinnati to visit with the family of a nineteen year old boy killed in Vietnam. I was twenty-five, wore captain bars, and my gold and black Ranger tab over the blue and white 173rd Airborne patch. *Herd* company commander. *Point man.* Rather than the "flying saucer" hat which I thought made officers look like bus drivers, the garrison cap, I preferred the "overseas cap" with a parachutist patch, the "railroad tracks" or captain bars over the patch.

The house was white, two-story frame, with a large front porch. On the porch sat a middle-aged, heavy set man, a city bus driver. I had been briefed by the first team. The soldier's father. I felt embarrassed by the vehicle I drove, a 1959 Corvette convertible with hard top on, customized, painted GTO gold with red interior, 325 cubic inch engine, 375 horsepower, four on the floor, the vehicle for which I had paid a former high school classmate $1200. The walk from the curb to the porch steps, some fifteen yards, was the longest of my life. I dare not look down nor to the side, nor to the grey Cincinnati sky, but only directly into the father's eyes. The father who had lost his only son in a war which I knew had been a total waste. I dare not tell him that his boy died in vain.

"Guess you're the officer they talked about. Going to help us out here, huh?" His eyes glistening. I felt mine glisten with his. "Yes, sir. Captain MacPherson." As he rose from the rocking chair, I, having climbed the set of stairs to the wooden porch, reached out my hand. A firm handshake. He was a huge man, some 300 pounds, with a great hand, a firm grip. "I'm really sorry about your son, Mr. ____. I'm here to help all I can, but I feel helpless." "Come on in, Captain," as he headed for the front door, turning to wipe the tears from his cheek. "You sure you're a captain? You look too young to be a captain." "Yes sir, captain at age 24, second lieutenant to captain in two years. A young man's war, as they say. But then you know that better than anyone ...," somewhat regretting that I had again opened into a tender area. Through the front door we entered into the modest living room. "Yeah, my son Johnny, he was only 19. Here, say hello to Mrs. ____, and my brother and his son, and over here my daughter-in-law, Sally. Did you know

Johnny had a wife? Married only three months before he went over." I am shaking hands with all these people, looking around the living room, not much different than my grandmother's house in which I was raised. Floral carpet, modest furniture, wall hangings, a mirror, freestanding lamps, coffee table, sofa and chairs. "This here's Captain MacPherson, sent by the Army to assist us with everything." *What's that there, that photograph on the mantel over the fireplace? Johnny?* I moved to a large photograph of Johnny, a strikingly handsome lad. *Never to again breathe breath into his strong body.* I pause to take in the photo, a uniform picture probably taken at the end of basic training, as so many soldiers do for their parents. They always make for good birthday and Christmas gifts or for no occasion at all. The proud parents never hesitate to display it in the most prominent place in the house. As I looked at the picture, no one had yet sat back down and you could hear a pin drop. *God, what do I say next?*

"Here, sit down over here, Captain," the father breaking the silence that seemed to last an eternity. "What are all those ribbons for, Captain? You must have seen a lot of action, huh?" asked Johnny's uncle. My mind is racing. *Keep cool, Captain Mac,* I tell myself. I am perceptive enough to see what is happening. First, I have got a serious problem. Technically, I look after the next of kin, who happens *not* to be the parents who knew their son 19 years, but this 18-year old girl, too scared to speak, who probably got to know Johnny in the back seat of a '57 Chevy a year ago and has been married to him but a few months. But she gets the insurance proceeds. And Johnny's articles of clothing and the other personal property which will later arrive in an Army footlocker. And she, not the parents, decides the funeral arrangements. Already, I sense the parents were against the marriage and have not gotten along well with Sally since Johnny took the big bird to Nam. And they, no doubt, plan to be in the driver's seat as to all of the survival assistance matters. *But that problem, Captain Mac, can wait. God, what's happening here?"* "You married, Captain?" the uncle asked, his twelve year old son looking on with both admiration and fascination. "No sir, not much time to settle down, you know. West Point, then Airborne, Ranger, and Infantry School, a few months with the 82nd Airborne at Ft. Bragg, North Carolina, then the last eighteen months in Vietnam. I volunteered to go over and then to extend an additional six months to take over as company commander when they promoted me to captain." I can see his eyes; he's counting the damn ribbons! "Know what you mean," chimes in Johnny's father. "Told those two love birds to hold off. Wouldn't listen to a word I said. Or that of their mother." The wife, standing awkward, looks at the floor, remaining silent. She is still in a state of shock. *This is not happening. This is not real.*

83

This is all a bad dream.

In a mind's eye flash, I am reminded of the Norman Rockwell painting of the young soldier returning to his neighborhood from World War II. He lives in one of those brownstone row houses in a large city, is about to climb the stairs, dufflebag in hand, the whole neighborhood is looking out the window with smiles on their faces. The day of reunion, of great joy. He has made it back. Not so for Johnny. Now my mind's eye moves quickly (the other Rockwell painting) to the living room scene in which the prodigal son had returned, the center of attention in the living room and the family members are not sure what to ask, they are just all aglow at his presence, that their son and grandson and brother has returned home, a small dog on the floor by his feet, young siblings scurrying around in the excitement ... *No, wait, that's what's wrong here. God, no. I'm a surrogate for the son and God no, for the husband too. I'm young, not much older than Johnny, returned from the war and single. I'm the substitute. I'm Johnny.*

Finally, the wife speaks, a frog in her throat. "Can I ask you a question Captain?" "Yes, ma'am." "When will they bring Johnny home? When will I see him?"

This, then was the beginning, and it got a lot worse. I was tactful in explaining on the phone to Johnny's father about my duty to the young widow. I also suggested to the widow the awkward situation. With me as liaison between the two factions, she became agreeable. We all went together to the funeral home. Joint decisions were made, though it was always an uncomfortable situation. A relief in a sense, because the tension between the widow and Johnny's family cut through some of the sorrow. The funeral itself was awkward, when the parents insisted on riding with me in the first limousine. There was not room for all of us, so I tactfully went with the wife in the second car. She and her roommate in following months would suggest I meet them at the Ironhorse, a country bar and dance house. She was lonely and was no doubt falling for me out of heartbreak, on the rebound. I was not Captain Mac, I was Johnny. I had no interest in her and was engaged to Barbara, having sent to her from Vietnam a pearl ring that I ordered through a PACEX (Pacific Exchange) catalog. Thank God, too, I had joined a fundamental Baptist church. No smoking, drinking or dancing. That provided for me the excuse to Sally. That, and my busy schedule.

I felt saddened by her loss and her loneliness. I invited her and her roommate to our Sunday evening revival service at Landmark Baptist church to which they respectfully declined. It was a standoff. I did not feel so bad declining their invitation now. Landmark had 6,000 in Sunday School with 100 buses. For me, what a Godsend.

What became the most poignant moment for me in my life, aside from the porch scene, was at the grave site. After a twenty-one gun salute and the playing of taps and the folding of the flag, I presented the Stars and Stripes to the widow, "Ma'am, from a grateful nation." We remained only a few moments, but not Johnny's father. As the funeral party drifted down the hill to the line of cars with me escorting the widow who had one arm in my arm, the other grasping the flag, Johnny's father refused to leave. Down on his knees, with one huge arm around the casket, he was crying out, sobbing, "No, Johnny, no. My only son. I won't let you go. They can't take you." He was not about to allow the casket to be lowered in the ground.

There was not much we could do. The funeral director remained patiently. Attempts by family members to lift the father and bring him to the car failed. For how long he stayed there, I do not know. We walked patiently to the car, waited a few minutes and drove away. My thoughts in the car were only regrets, blaming myself. *God, I wish I'd known Johnny. What was he really like? Was he a good soldier? What if I had extended another six months, would our paths have crossed out there somewhere? Would that have made a difference? There, but for the grace of God go I. Why Johnny, Lord? Why not me, Lord?*

With the folded flag, the blue cloth with white stars on the outside, Sally wiped the tears as we drove away from the cemetery. I used a handkerchief.

My next assignment was worse. I was the first to tell a black woman her only son had been killed. Records showed a younger sister living with her mother. There was no father. The mother and daughter lived in a tenement building on the outskirts of downtown Cincinnati. It was a Sunday when I got the call, and I was unable to locate an NCO to go with me. I asked for a police patrol car, not because I feared for my safety, but because I suspected the worst: hysteria. In fact, I was at the time living in my old neighborhood, not far from the University of Cincinnati, a neighborhood which had come, due to "white flight," predominantly black. I lived on the second floor of an apartment, one block from the house in which I had grown up. The house was sold by my grandmother in 1961, when I was a high school sophomore. Within the apartment complex I was the only white tenant, a fact about which my mother and others were not happy. But I had returned from Vietnam more so a rebel. I had slept and eaten and fought alongside black men. Why not live in a black neighborhood, especially since it was close to the University of Cincinnati and cost a mere $95 a month? I could then afford my Vette, my bird dog Tag, and a horse. Other housing was available, but expensive and as the skin flint I was, I stubbornly chose the black apartment building.

As I reflect back on the decision, it was more than rebellion. I was warned about repeated robberies in the area. I do not think I was ready to leave the combat zone altogether. I was under decompression, requiring calculated risks. I kept my Winchester 30-30 loaded and should have had cause one night to use it, but did not pay attention to what Tag was trying to tell me. I heard the doorbell to the room next door where there lived a man who loved the symphony and had invited me on several occasions to go. I peered through the peephole and observed two black men wearing black berets. Friends, I assumed. They left. I should have been more suspicious, but it was Friday evening and I was tired. My door had screwdriver marks which I had reported to the landlord. Tag, no doubt, had discouraged the attempted illegal entry. So as I watched television, hearing a commotion next door and assuming my neighbor had returned with his friends from the symphony, and telling Tag to stop his whining and barking at the wall that separated the apartments, my neighbor lost his television and stereo.

So entering the black ghetto as a white Army officer in uniform was to me of no moment. I feared for the well-being of the next of kin. With a police officer alongside, I rang the doorbell. The mother answered, took one look at me, wailed, trembled and ran for the kitchen, screaming, "Go away, I can't see you. You're not here." To her daughter, "Tell this man to go away, he's not here, I don't see him." *Another young man killed in Vietnam. Damn you, Johnson. And you, McNamara, you idiot sticks. You both deserve to be hung and quartered.* The mother wanted the nightmare to go away. It could not be true. Her only son. The sister was not yet in a state of hysteria. She was in shock. She was about fourteen and invited us in. The visit was brief. I simply stated that I was heartfully sorry that her only son had been killed in Vietnam, and the next day the SAO team would arrive to assist her. The mother was not listening, still disbelieving. *This is not happening, this is a nightmare. This white captain is not here.* As I left the building, I knew that the next day the SAO, a black lieutenant colonel and Vietnam vet, would take over. Another surrogate son. Surrogate brother. *Is there any legal limitation on the number of families by which you can be adopted,* I thought.

Case number three was bittersweet. I was given the mission of driving several hours into rural Ohio to award to the parents a bronze star medal earned by their only son who had been killed in Vietnam a year prior. Time will heal all wounds? I remembered to stand extra tall as I parked in front of the white, three-story Victorian home, typical of the rural Midwest. Turn of the century architecture.

I was being watched, I could feel, from the living room. I maintained my military gait up the walk, rang the bell once and was met by the father and mother. Norman Rockwell, here's another setting. These folks in front of their home, should have graced the cover of the *Saturday Evening Post*. After exchanging pleasantries, the parents expressed that they were annoyed with the Army for the delay. In my hand was the Bronze Star medal and citation for bravery in action, which I read standing in the living room. They walked me to a show case separating the front parlor from the kitchen. Enclosed were photos of their handsome son, the ribbons, medals, and written citations for meritorious service and valor. He was nineteen when he was killed. I stayed only long enough to be respectful and polite, not wanting to open old wounds. It was too late, thank God, for a surrogate son. They were dealing with their grief in their own way: a sitting room monument. Also encased was the folded flag, the blue background with white stars showing. Again, the proper fold. Some people had bowling trophies on their mantel. These folks? Well they just had their son displayed in the showcase. *God, do I scream or cry. For how long will they maintain this vigil? No doubt forever. What do you do, wait two years and move the showcase to the garage? Maybe the attic. How about the basement? Five years? Ten?*

More awards were due, and as I shook hands at the front door, I promised to do my best to cut through Army red tape and hasten the paperwork. It was a long walk for me from the house to the Vette. Again, embarrassed by this hot rod which their son should be driving around town, dating high school cheerleaders. I could feel them watch my every step. *Why should I feel so guilty to be alive and in one piece? Why me, Lord? And Isaiah said, "Who shall I send? Send me, Lord." And I had gone. But I had returned.*

As I drove off slowly, not looking back, I again realized, this was not a young man from a wealthy neighborhood. The college deferral of course. Law school deferral. These were just middle class, regular folks. Of course, the wealthy could always buy off a doctor who would grant a medical exemption. *Damn you Johnson. Damn you McNamara. You should both see this now and you both deserve to rot in hell for eternity. How could you be so stupid? How could you lie to us so much?*

It was General Patton who said, "You don't win wars by dying for your country; you win wars by making the other son of a bitch die for his country." Added to that is my corollary: If you are rich you do not serve your country by giving your life in the war; you serve your country by making money off the war. *Nineteen years old.* I had been in control during my visit within the house. As I started the engine and drove away, it was then that my eyes began to glisten. *Must be that dual exhaust system. Have to check for leaks.*

On the fourth assignment, a young lieutenant from Cincinnati had been killed in a helicopter crash. He had been aide to a general.

Captain David Britain, West Point Class of '66, a year ahead of me, volunteered to take the assignment out of order. David had received his Purple Heart for going down in a helicopter. He had been aide to a general. Ironic enough? The dead lieutenant had taken Dave's Vietnam slot when Dave rotated back to the states. *But for the grace of God, there go I,* Dave had thought.

As my mind is racing through my SAO assignments, akin to my duty to inform V.R. of the verdict, I am riding with Jean and Janet and Debbie and my mind races to the fifth and last SAO assignment from which I have discovered my high spirits of the moment. A black sergeant shot by his own men while outside the perimeter. By accident or not, I am not told, but of course, the official line is accident. I am further instructed that I should do all I can to persuade the young widow not to request a viewing of the body. Too messy, I am told. *A cover up?* I wonder. After meeting with the young widow several times, I received the impression that either she really did not have a lot of remorse due to trouble in the marriage, or it still has not sunk in. At first, like most, she did not want to believe it, claiming there must be a mistake. Then she grew increasingly callous awaiting shipment of the body. She insisted the casket would be opened. I volunteered to view her husband first, then advise her further.

Thus, here we were one afternoon, the day of the evening wake. A decision was to be made whether or not this woman should see the torn up head of her husband. He had been gunned down by an M-60 machine gun, I was told. Okay, pal, here goes. I have probably seen worse. Go ahead, open it up, as I braced for the worst. I was both relieved and curious. A few scars on the face and head, but nothing shocking. I so informed the widow, who was satisfied, who then viewed the body and was satisfied it was, indeed, her husband, and we proceeded with an open casket wake. *What's up with those guys back at graves registration in Vietnam?* I had of course heard the horror stories of mistakes where the wrong body would be sent to the family. Many families insisted on viewing the body, whatever the condition, just to be sure that there was no mistake that their son might still be alive in Vietnam or perhaps a POW. If graves registration had screwed up the instructions on this case, how many times had they sent the body to the wrong address? Or, had they failed to send the instruction not to open the casket with one that should not have been opened? An assignment to graves registration: a fate worse than death.

At the funeral the next day, the deceased sergeant's grandmother again appeared. The sergeant, his name Jack, had lost his mother as a young boy and was raised by his grandmother. Grandma was a charismatic Christian lady and the funeral service rocked the Cincinnati hills with black spirituals. I could not help but sway with the rhythm. It was hypnotic.

> Oh happy day.
> When Jesus washed.
> When my Jesus washed.
> He washed my sins away.
> Oh happy day.
> Yea, it's a happy, happy day.

As the service closed, the grandmother went to Jack's casket before it was lowered into the ground. *Oh, no,* I thought. *A repeat of Johnny's father, the busdriver.* But the mood here was different. Grandma was not wailing, she was rejoicing, talking to Jack. As if no one was present, she was declaring, "Jack, I'll see you in the morning, yes sir, sweet Jesus. Jack, I'll see in the morning." What was the meaning? Was there a favorite saying between Jack and Grandma when she tucked him in to bed? No, I understood perfectly. Grandma was old. She was rejoicing for Jack and for herself. With not long to live, she would soon see Jack and Jesus in everlasting life. That was the morning. Grandma was not in any hurry, but she would just as well see Jack in the morning. *Faith springs hope eternal.*

As V.R. came down to help unload the car, he and Jean embraced and then had words about a jury that was not smart enough to come in out of the rain. Jean was in the dumps; I was rejoicing. V.R. looked at me like I was crazy. "Faith springs hope eternal, V.R.," I said. "Believe me, it's going to be all right in the morning. We are just clay in the Master's hand. Today the jury has served our purpose. Mark my word. You won't be disappointed." V.R. looked me dead in the eye and believed every word I said.

As for Jean's political career, that was ruined by the media which took as truth the false allegations of the IRS. In one article reporting on the upcoming election in which Jean faced Josh Mayes, a sixty-seven year old Wallisville rancher who had been the Justice of the Peace since the resignation of another man in 1977, the paper referred to the federal indictment against Jean, and that she and her husband V.R., owners of an "excavation company on their thirty-three acre homestead have not paid federal income taxes since 1975 and their son, David, who Mrs. Hylton says is studying to be a minister, has not filed a federal return or paid income taxes since 1978." Jean lost the election to Mayes.

On June 10, 1982, Jean was contacted by a reporter and in turn called me. She had been acquitted. She had been awaiting her sentencing and Judge Gibson had reconsidered on his own my motion for dismissal on *First Amendment* grounds and had ordered that under the law, the conviction could not stand. (I later learned that Jean had written to the judge, giving her side of the case and requesting that the judge again consider my *First Amendment* argument.) "The gravamen of the government's case is that the defendant in lodging her complaint did not act in a good faith assertion of her own rights, but rather with the specific purpose and intent of obstructing an IRS investigation into the criminal liability of her son," the court wrote:

Hence, the government contends that she can be convicted because she acted with an *obstructionist heart*. The court disagrees. Even assuming the evidence to establish beyond any doubt that the defendant acted with the sole purpose of obstructing the investigation of the two IRS agents, the court finds the application of the criminal law to the facts and circumstances of this case constitutes an impermissible infringement upon the *First Amendment* right of the defendant to petition the government for redress of grievances. Accordingly, even construing the evidence and reasonable inferences therefrom, in a manner supportive of the jury's verdict, the court holds that the defendant has committed no offense prescribed by 26 U.S.C. Sec. 7212(a).

The court went on then to cite from Supreme Court cases from which I had cited, quoting that the petition for redress of grievances is "among the most precious of the liberties safeguarded by the *Bill of Rights.*" In a footnote the judge noted that whereas the government had contended that there were no trespassing signs posted on the property at the time the agents entered, "the evidence, however, overwhelmingly points to a contrary conclusion." In other words, the judge did not believe Artru and Rentsch any more than we did. But why so then the jury? The judge also noted that "It is clear that responsible officials in Chambers County were aware from personal knowledge that conspicuously posted signs adorned the Hylton property prior to the occasion in question." Also in the footnote the court noted there was no evidence that Jean "brought any undue influence or pressure to bear on the officials of Chambers County to bring criminal charges against the two special agents," noting however, that although Jenson testified at trial that complaints appeared proper, he had also testified before the grand jury that his fear "of vexatious or harassing litigation by the defendant or her husband, was a factor in his decision to file the criminal charges." Next, the government appealed. Because Jean had not been acquitted by jury verdict, they claimed a right to appeal to the U.S. Court of Appeals for the Fifth Circuit. *It's not over until it's over.*

Again calling Jean "a leader of an organized tax rebellion" in its brief to the Court of Appeals, the government complained that if Judge Gibson's decision is upheld, it would open "the floodgates for tax protesters to engage in a number of criminal acts directed at agents under the guise of asserting their own constitutional rights." I would have answers for this as well as for the government's claim that they had found no case "in which criminal prosecution resulted from a situation similar to the instant case."

In my third point in my brief before the Fifth Circuit, I urged that the cases relied upon by the government which were brought under the "corrupt intimidation" statute were cases in which the defendant clearly threatened force or use of force against an IRS agent. In one there was a scuffle between the defendant and an IRS agent. In another a threat by way of display of a gun cartridge box and statements regarding violence and killing and "what a man might do when backed into a corner," and the third, a threatening letter in which the defendant said to the agent, "I have an itchy trigger finger, more deadly than when I was overseas." I continued: "The government has warned this court that if Judge Gibson is upheld, this court will thereby open 'the flood gates for tax protesters to engage in a number of criminal acts directed against agents under the guise of asserting their own constitutional rights.' But agents of our government are not without judicial remedy, by way of civil suit for malicious prosecution, or otherwise. To extend the government's logic one step further, the government would have a sovereign citizen convicted of interfering with his Congressman by having a million letters of income tax protest mailed to the Congressman. Obviously, the Congressman's staff would be burdened, and perhaps even 'threatened and intimidated.' But what all this points to is the real design behind the right to petition.

In my brief I continued, "Our Government fears anarchy, but it is the right to petition, and only that right, that offers a republican form of government the 'safety valve' needed whenever freeborn men delegate to a few such vast authority to act. For it is the sacred right to petition which guards against frustrations of natural men, which frustrations lead to anarchy and bloodshed.

"This realization is not without historic precedent, for it was within the *Declaration of Independence* unanimously adopted in Congress, July 4, 1776, at Philadelphia, that Thomas Jefferson declared:

In every stage of these oppressions We [the people] have petitioned for redress in the most humble of terms: our repeated petitions have been answered only by repeated injury. A prince, whose character is thus marked by every act which may define a tyrant, is unfit to be the ruler of a free people.

"But the right to petition was not formulated by Jefferson, nor anyone within the Colonies, for it was founded upon the oppressions of the freeborn by a tyrant King in England during the 1600's, in the form of that infamous charge: seditious libel."

For my fourth point, I urged that *Mrs. Hylton has been charged, in effect, with "seditious libel," a charge abhorred by freeborn Englishmen and abolished by the First Amendment right to petition for redress of grievance.*

"Government concedes that 'We have found no case in which criminal prosecution resulted from a situation similar to the instant case.' If one limits his search to American jurisprudence, the reason is simple. Since the *Bill of Rights,* the right to petition has been accepted as such a simple, primitive, and natural right that even a prosecutor of the most perverted genius has not imagined such a vile prosecution as the one against Mrs. Hylton. And if one researches the full history of the right to petition, one is invariably led to its root: the infamous charge of 'seditious libel.'

"No more valuable an instrument of repression was known in England during the 1600's save that born of the Star Chamber: the crime of seditious libel. In an era of universal and savage intolerance, the charge proved most useful to kings, bishops, prosecutors and judges hostile to religious and political freedom.

"Yet it had no foundation at common law. Rather, it was the brainchild of the keeper of the Star Chamber procedure, Sir Edward Coke, appointed by the King in 1606 as Chief Justice of Common Pleas. As a sideline, Coke was also a judge of the Star Chamber, that infamous court of inquisition in which no rights were afforded the accused, only the opportunity to swear and confess to the alleged crime.

"And in 1606, Coke prosecuted in Star Chamber the first case of seditious libel: he 'obtained the defendant's confession to composing and publishing a scandalous set of verses on two of England's highest clergymen.' The case drew little attention and drew Coke to widen his Star Chamber jurisdiction. *See also* the case of *John Lamb* (Star Chamber 1606) (seditious libel; repeating a seditious libel was also punishable as seditious libel).

"Coke then proceeded to develop the theory, without foundation, that truth is no defense to seditious libel. Truth of the allegations became even an aggravation of the crime!

"Freeborn Englishmen were prosecuted and convicted of seditious libel for any oral or written statement, however true, which shamed the king, his court, one of his appointees, his honorable clergy, or was otherwise in 'derogation of the king's crown and dignity.' Any criticism, by petition, preaching, or publication, which concerned the royal dignity and was in prejudice of the king, was considered seditious libel. The practice was soon broadened to

92

quiet religious dissidents. And, in 1678, the twelve high judges of England declared seditious libel punishable at common law, whereupon, cases were brought in Court of Kings Bench, the Star Chamber having been abolished in 1641.

"Thomas M. Cooley, in his A Treatise on the *Constitutional Limitations*, Volume 1 at 728, quoting from Story, *On the Constitution,* stated, that the right to assemble and to petition is one which "would seem unnecessary to be expressly provided for in a republican government, since it results from the very nature and structure of its institutions. It is impossible that it could be practically denied until the spirit of liberty had wholly disappeared, and the people had become so servile and debased as to be unfit to exercise any of the privileges of free men. . . ."

I continued in my brief, "The charge against Mrs. Hylton cannot stand, as it is illegal under the *First Amendment* right to petition, the common law, the 'law of the land' (Magna Carta 1215) and as Jefferson declared within the Preamble to the *Declaration of Independence,* the 'Laws of Nature and of Nature's God.' It is against this very risk of anarchy, anarchy which Jefferson so eloquently justified, that the Petition for Redress guards.

"The *First Amendment* is, according to Supreme Court 'interpretations,' by no means absolute, although the amendment does state in no uncertain terms: 'Congress shall make no law ... abridging ... the right of the people ... to petition the government for a redress of grievances.' What room is there, in these words, for regulation by law? Not enough, Mrs. Hylton submits, to criminalize the acts of a freeborn citizen who files with proper state authorities a genuine complaint against officers of the federal government.

"If Mrs. Hylton's conviction is to stand, what man will dare to open his mouth, much less to use his pen, against even the worst governmental administrators, yea, even against a President who may be most corrupt and even confesseth to it? And if Mrs. Hylton's conviction stands, it then should be denominated high treason, for as surely as it is a seditious libel, it is just upon the heels of treason.

"The charge against Jean C. Hylton, a freeborn sovereign citizen, is a most pernicious attack upon English liberty."

My research on Jean's case had led me to history of England and the Colonies in the 1600 and 1700's and inspired the writing and title of my first book, *April 15th: The Most Pernicious Attack Upon English Liberty.*

Without oral argument, the Fifth Circuit on August 1, 1983, upheld Judge Gibson's opinion and concluded "that Jean Hylton's actions represented an exercise of the right to petition for redress of grievances in its pristine form ...." The court stated "Having thoroughly reviewed the record and the district court's holding, we have concluded that Hylton's actions represented a legitimate and protected exercise of her right to petition for the redress of grievances. The record clearly reveals that Hylton placed a high value on her right to personal privacy and genuinely attempted to protect her rights through the orderly pursuit of justice - filing of citizen complaints with a reasonable basis. Although we do not condone the Hylton's continued opposition to this nation's tax laws, we likewise cannot condone the imposition of criminal sanctions for Hylton's exercise of her constitutional right." *Two wrongs don't make a right.* In the end of its opinion, the Fifth Circuit, quoting from a decision of the Seventh Circuit, added, "The possibility that a citizen who feels himself to have been abused by a particular federal official may take satisfaction when the official gets his perceived due is too human for *First Amendment* protection to depend on its absence."

The *First* and *Fourth Amendments* still live in Wallisville, Texas, at least as to the fifty acre homestead of V.R. and Jean C. Hylton. After the Fifth Circuit's decision and a petition for re-hearing by the government, which failed, the government did not attempt to take it up with the U.S. Supreme Court. The Hyltons have not been bothered by the IRS since. As to County Attorney Jenson, there is an unbelievable footnote to this story of Jean C. Hylton. (Details in *War Stories, Part II.*)

In 1988, V.R. and Jean wrote to me, "These are the main scriptures that we feel the Lord chose to commission us unto 'His own purpose and grace.'" Included were *Psalms* 94, verse 16, and *Ecclesiates,* Chapter 10, verse 4:

Who will rise up for me against the evil doers? *or* who will stand up for me against the workers of iniquity.

If the spirit of the ruler rise up against thee, leave not thy place; for yielding pacifieth great offences.

To this day, the Hyltons have refused to yield.

I must study politics and war so that my sons have liberty to study mathematics and philosophy, geography, natural history, naval architecture, navigation, commerce and agriculture in order to give their children the right to study painting, poetry, music, architecture, statuary, tapestry and porcelain. John Adams

BAPTISM BY FIRE   Chapter 5

For my close friend, Mark McClellan and me, schooling in constitutional law and legal defense of the underdog against the *Monster* all began with a printer named Charles Riely and an unincorporated association in Mesa, Arizona known as the Arizona Caucus Club. Mark, now a Baptist minister and missionary, was one of my ROTC students when I returned from Vietnam. Due to my influence, including my classroom and field instruction on insurgency/counter-insurgency/guerilla warfare, Mark chose the same path as I, minus West Point: Airborne, Ranger, Infantry and Special Forces. I had attempted, without success at the time, to influence him toward Christian activism for at the time I was teaching a class of three hundred twelve-year-olds in Sunday School at Landmark Baptist Temple in Cincinnati, an independent fundamental church. I joined soon after my return from Vietnam. In fact, it had been another friend, Dick Rose, a Marine Vietnam vet, with whom I had attended Woodward High School in Cincinnati, who had just joined Landmark and invited me to attend.

John Rawlings of Tyler, Texas, a tent revivalist, had built a church with one hundred buses and six thousand in Sunday School. (The buses picked children up for Sunday School throughout greater Cincinnati.) It was one of the fastest growing churches in the nation. He was not one to mince words: "America needs God. We don't need more dope, more whiskey, or more pornographic literature. America needs God!" After strong preaching, John would at time of the traditional Baptist invitation turn tender with a soft voice, "Now won't you come to my dear Jesus, and let Him save you?"

Nor did John Rawlings shy from political subjects as most preachers who, in my opinion, have been bought out by the *Monster* through the carrot of tax exemption. "I don't appreciate Congress at all. If the Postal Workers deserved a raise, they should have got one in the first place." (The postal strike was ended when Congress in 1970 gave the Postal Workers a raise.) And the ego of the businessmen and liberals on the Supreme Court, as well, were regular targets of Preacher Rawlings. "Listen to me, businessmen, self-made. There is going to be a price you'll dearly pay if you don't get right with God and follow your Christian conscience.... We get all riled up over whether a little black boy and a little white girl are going to go to school together. We would not have these problems if we had pure hearts. We won't have pure hearts until we accept the loving kindness and tender mercy of the Lord Jesus Christ."

Rawlings' preaching was a lesson for me. At West Point those principles, in which I already believed, became ingrained: God, Country, Family; Duty, Honor, Country. West Point brought me from belief to conviction. In Vietnam I had opportunity to apply my convictions. And from Rawlings I learned not to be shy about stating them publicly. Thus, I developed a natural courtroom style of saying it like it is, not mincing words, going for the jugular and raising and lowering my voice for emphasis. It was not something I consciously developed, but rather it came naturally with emotion. Jurors expect emotion and drama. Without it, they are disappointed. I would not disappoint them.

Mark received a four year ROTC scholarship and had attended two years at Arizona State University in Tempe. At the University of Cincinnati, he became a BMOC, "big man on campus", a cadet major, and graduated a Distinguished Military Graduate, receiving a Regular Army commission. He was off to sow his wild oats, which included a tour with the 101st Airborne Division at Ft. Campbell, Kentucky, and one in Panama, where he attended the U.S. Army Jungle School.

Meanwhile, at the time of Mark's graduation in 1971, I was leaving the Army and turned down Rawlings' offer to become a church staff member. I had researched on my own time deferred giving methods of large Christian ministries and I had met with the director of stewardship at Rex Humbard's Cathedral of Tomorrow in Akron, Ohio. Rex had developed at the time the largest nation-wide television ministry and was viewed on more than five hundred stations. I discovered the key to financial development of large ministries: estate planning and deferred giving. Eight out of ten Americans do not have as much as a will, much less trusts which can save income and estate taxes. Under an aggressive stewardship program, the church prepares for the church member or television listener through a network a will at no cost or obligation. By means of tax savings devices such as the Clifford Trust, charitable trust and charitable remainder trust, the Cathedral of Tomorrow was obtaining millions in property, businesses and cash. (Later they came under SEC attack for their annuity program because they had insufficient monies on reserve.)

Having discovered the Cathedral's plan, I was asked to implement it for Landmark. But I reckoned that "blood runs thicker than water," for I had observed John's use of his sons in the ministry. Harold, the oldest who had married Barbara and me, was the associate pastor and had graduated from that conservative, fundamentalist institution in North Carolina, Bob Jones University. Herb, the second oldest whom I really liked, was music director, but also a business manager with no business background. (Part of my recommendation to the church was to apply business principles to church work.) Herb had flown me in a small plane to Akron. Another son was a gospel singer, while the youngest, George, was in law school at the University of Louisville. I therefore asked Pastor Rawlings to defer his offer for reason that I had been offered a research assistantship at Utah State University in agricultural economics. I trusted that I would be able to apply what I learned there for the good of Landmark if he was still interested in a couple of years. I had hoped to get into farm and ranch management, which also tied in with church work because large ministries such as the Cathedral of Tomorrow were receiving farm and ranch properties, as well as other businesses. If George, as a new attorney, was to become involved, he would no doubt head up the program. I could manage the properties. In addition, I had dreamed of the opportunity to go west. So, resigning my Regular Army commission in July of 1971, and accepting a reserve commission as captain, Barbara and I, with our newborn son, Scott, moved to Utah.

That summer I had hoped to do some church free-lance consulting work and apply to other ministries what I had learned in my study for Landmark. While I had taught at the University of Cincinnati, I had attended an MBA program in the evening. It struck me that churches should be run by business managers who are qualified, especially where they were developing rapidly into business areas associated with the church. For example, Cathedral of Tomorrow had its own TV studio and a tremendous TV ministry which required marketing. Landmark had its own record production company and nation-wide radio ministry. Fascinated by these issues, I often visited the UC law library and studied the Tax Reform Act of 1969, under which Congress gave churches five years to depart from businesses not related to church activities or face the consequences by paying income tax on the income from those businesses. Rex Humbard had been under considerable attack for ownership by the church of a girdle factory for which he paid no tax on the profits. I was intrigued by all this and seriously considered law school at the time, but I did not want to spend three years booking it, and really dreamed of being the ranch/property manager of the many properties I had hoped churches could acquire through aggressively marketing their stewardship program. I also felt the stewardship information should be shared with smaller churches by way of a "Christian Consulting" firm.

In the spring of 1971, in anticipation of my June departure from UC, I had written to many of the large ministries with my ideas.

One recipient was Jerry Falwell and the Old Time Gospel Hour in Lynchburg, Virginia. He never as much as responded to my letter, and I found it ironic years later when I was living in Virginia but 20 miles from Falwell's Thomas Road Baptist Church that Falwell came under attack by the federal government for alleged mismanagement of monies. As part of the settlement, Falwell agreed to subject his ministry to some review by a board of visitors made up of esteemed businessmen in the community. Preachers, especially independent fundamentalist preachers, I had found, were not only independent, but stubborn. This was years before formation of Moral Majority and Falwell's entrance into the national political scene.

Thus without any job offers from any of the many churches to which I had written, Barbara, Scott and I spent the summer in Philadelphia, staying at Barbara's parents' home, for they were away for the summer. She and Scott flew to Philadelphia and I drove for reason that I still had the Vette. Despite our growing family, I was too stubborn to give it up. I drove it alone to Utah. (My bird dog Tag-a-Long had died before my departure from the University of Cincinnati.) Barbara and Scott followed me to Utah by plane.

My first contact with Barbara had been by phone in January of 1964. I was a plebe (first year) at West Point, swimming against Villanova, which is in Lower Merion, Pennsylvania, close to Merion, where Barbara, her two older sisters and parents lived. Upon leaving the swim meet, I met her sister Marilyn who was pinned to a West Point yearling (sophomore), Bill Otto. Marilyn told me she had a sister all of 15 and I phoned her from our motel. I was 18. Barbara had a date that evening, but the following summer at Camp Buckner, about thirty miles outside of West Point where yearlings undergo intensive military training for the summer, a bunk mate by the name of Pete Hagan said he had a date with Barbara Hubsch. Pure coincidence. Bill had set Pete up with Barbara during our plebe year. I met her that weekend, sparks flew, and we dated off and on for six years before deciding to tie the knot in Cincinnati in September of 1970. There was an additional irony. When I assumed responsibility for the new AO in the coastal area of Vietnam, I went to meet with the company commander of the 1st of the 50th Mechanized Infantry, who was currently responsible for the area. Because the VC and NVA by that time had broken down into small squad-sized units, the 173rd had decided that it would be best to locate their paratroopers on foot rather than to continue with patrols by armored personnel carriers (APCs or Tracks). The Track Company Commander was none other than Pete Hagan.

Bill and Marilyn married soon after Bill's graduation from West Point in 1966 and, during their tour in Germany, they learned of the death in Vietnam of Bill's best friend. Bill volunteered for Vietnam, leaving his wife and young son, only to return to the states soon after with a knee injury. After leaving the Army in 1970, Bill became a physician, Marilyn an attorney. They now live in Boca Raton, Florida. Their oldest son, Kemp, attends Wheaton College and their other son, Rob, is a yearling at West Point.

During my years at West Point, I "adopted" the family of Al Webeler and his wife Mardette from Cincinnati. They have three daughters, Jeannette, Kathy and Laurie, and I became a friend of the family through a common interest in horses. I nicknamed Al "Shane," after the Allan Ladd movie of the same name. Shane and Mardette have likewise become adopted grandparents of my three sons, Scott, Ryan and Nathan. During 1969 through 1971, when I taught ROTC at the University of Cincinnati upon my return from Vietnam, my major interest was horses, with the dream that someday I would move out west and have my own ranch. Only one-half of the dream has been fulfilled to date: ten years residency in Glendale, Arizona.

While at the University of Cincinnati, several of my students were law students under a ROTC two-year program which provided a deferment for graduate school and law school students, a popular program considering the draft was still well underway and U.S. forces invaded Cambodia in 1970. Law certainly related to my interest in the church work, but I was, despite eighteen months in Vietnam, still somewhat restless and not ready to make the commitment.

During the summer of 1970, I trained ROTC cadets at Indiantown Gap, Pennsylvania. I was still the gung ho motivator, challenging my students at pull ups and the one mile run. On night patrols in the mountains, I had fun demonstrating night navigation by compass. The patrol became totally disoriented in the blackness of the mountain woods by not keeping an eye on the compass. To their amazement, I led them directly back to the patrol base several thousand meters away. (I had watched the compass and simply used the back azimuth.) The cadets were, therefore, well impressed with the benefits of Ranger training.

On graduation day two strange things happened. First, in double timing the company of one hundred and twenty cadets to the parade ground, I called cadence as I had learned through West Point, Airborne and Ranger schools, the type of cadence we had utilized throughout the summer.

> I wanna be an Airborne Ranger,
> I wanna live a life of danger,
> I wanna go to Vietnam,
> I wanna kill some Viet Cong.

Continuing with the hypnotic cadence, I would call out, with the troops repeating, "All the way ... Airborne ... Ranger ... Infantry ... Special Forces ... can do ... up the hill ... over the hill ... through the hill ... so good ... can't stop ... feels good ... so good ... bayonet ... feels good ... so good ... kill!"

The Kent State incident had occurred in May after President Nixon had ordered the Cambodian invasion. (Some of my cadets were from Kent State and understandably confused by the political-military crisis of the time.) We were withdrawing from Vietnam. We had lost 58,000 lives, and mothers and girlfriends dressed in pretty summer dresses were walking on sidewalks to the parade ground. It was a festive time. The brass, the full colonels and generals, did not like the Ranger chants. Not now. It was no longer fashionable to be a gung ho militant, despite the fact I was charged with the responsibility of training cadets who might visit Southeast Asia within a year. Vietnam - the Fun Capital of the World. I was charged with the responsibility of teaching young men how to kill. Kill or be killed. I also reminded my troops, perhaps unfairly, since there was no fair comparison between World War II and Vietnam, that Patton had told his men, "Some day when you have your grandson on your knee, and he asks, 'What did you do in the war, Grandpa?' you won't have to answer, 'Well, I shoveled shit in Louisiana.'" I reluctantly changed the chant to traditional songs.

> Ain't no use in looking down,
> Ain't no discharge on the ground.
> Ain't no use in looking back,
> Jody's got your Cadillac.
> Ain't no use in looking 'round,
> Jody's got your girl and gone.

As we reached the parade ground I saw the visiting general and his aide, a Captain Cecil. *Small war, small world.* In 1968, when I first arrived in Vietnam and was assigned to *the Herd*, I went to the airport at An Khe to board a C-23 Caribou Army aircraft for my flight to Bong Song. Off boarding the same aircraft was First Lieutenant Cecil, West Point Class of 1966. Though we had not really known one another at the Point, he recognized me and came over for a chat. He looked haggard. It was no wonder. The 173rd had just taken a beating at Dak To. *"Watch your step. Keep your powder dry. You'll do all right."* He did not want to talk about much else. What else could he say? Now on the parade ground at Indiantown Gap, he smiled and looked relieved. *Herd* brothers. I, like he, had made it back in one piece. It now made sense to him.

100

The crazy captain causing one hundred and twenty graduating cadets to call out militant chants like "Kill" was not only West Point, Airborne, Ranger, Infantry. He was a *Herd* brother. Spirit of *the Herd*, a unit disbanded in 1971. "Stack arms. Furl the colors."

The Cecil irony came full circle when, in 1985, sixteen years after departing Vietnam and after fifteen years of refusing to deal with it, I bought my first book on Vietnam, *The Vietnam Experience* - a multi-volume set. The volume I had purchased was *A Contagion of War*. It took another two years for me to read any of it. When I did, I found "Dispatch from Hill 875" in which Pulitzer Prize winning correspondent Peter Arnett described his 30 hours spent with the "173rd Airborne paratroopers during their bloody struggle for Hill 875 - climax of the month-long battle of Dak To." It was his Thanksgiving eve 1967 report in which he opened with:

War painted the living and the dead the same gray pallor on Hill 875. For fifty hours [starting Sunday] the most brutal fighting of the Vietnam War ebbed and flowed across this jungle hilltop and by Wednesday was still not over. Death picked its victims at random and broke and twisted their bodies. At times the only way to tell who was alive and who was dead amongst the exhausted men was to watch when the enemy mortars crash in. The living rushed unashamedly to the tiny bunkers dug into the red clay on the hilltop. The wounded squirmed toward the shelter of the trees that had been blasted to the ground.... Of the sixteen officers who led their men across the ridge line of Hill 875 on Sunday, eight were killed and the other eight wounded. Of the thirteen battalion medics, eleven died.... The days pounding steadily reduced the platoon commanded by First Lieutenant Bryan MacDonough, 25, from Ft. Lee, Virginia. He started out Sunday with twenty-seven men. He had nine left mid-day Tuesday. If the Viets keep this up, there'll be none left by evening, he said ....

Followed by Arnett's dispatch was a more detailed description of the battle. It was First Lieutenant Gerald T. Cecil who, because he was C-Company's only Ranger qualified platoon leader, drew point that day. Moving cautiously and utilizing the clover leaf tactic by which the patrol periodically sends out flanks security on clover leaf movements to discover enemy locations, if any, Cecil found that despite his precautions he led his company into an NVA battalion-size horseshoe ambush. One hundred against two thousand. The only way to survive was reliance on the Air Force's five hundred pound bombs, many of which had missed their mark, falling on friendlies. Forty-two men in the company were killed by a mistake.

It was no wonder Cecil looked haggard the day I boarded the C-123. His valor earned for him the Distinguished Service Cross, second only to the Medal of Honor, an award given PFC Barnes of Cecil's company. Barnes, watched with horror as the NVA killed both men of one machine gun team. With the NVA ready to gain the perimeter line, Barnes "dashed across a bullet-swept slope, slid in behind the machine gun, and poured fire on a squad assaulting the perimeter ...." Barnes killed nine soldiers and that repulsed the attack. Later, when Barnes had run out of ammunition, he "backed away from the machine gun and got up to search for more M-60 belts when he saw a Chinese hand grenade drop among a half dozen severely wounded soldiers. To shield them, Barnes threw himself on the grenade just as it exploded. His action cost him his life, but it saved others...."

In Utah in 1972, as I worked on my thesis in land use planning for my Masters Degree in Agricultural Economics at Utah State University, Logan, job opportunities were scarce. Again, I considered law school, but had had enough of the books. At 27, I was just young enough to join the Marine or Air Force aviation program, and I almost did. I had been serving with a Special Forces unit of the Utah National Guard as detachment commander. Our team was the SCUBA specialty. I leaned toward remaining in Utah if possible, but our families were in Philadelphia and Cincinnati, so I took a position with Virginia Polytechnic and State University at Appomattox, Virginia. Because I did not have 20/20 vision, I was offered by the Marines and Air Force a reserve commission as navigator. As much as I wanted to fly, I could not see myself navigating rather than taking the controls.

Moving to Virginia after obtaining my Masters Degree, I learned about the politics of land grant colleges and universities and rebelled against the status quo. My job was Community Resource Development Agent, responsible for four counties. I was to assist local communities in seeking their own destiny. I would cut through bureaucratic red tape, both federal and state, and help develop parks, bring in industries, etc. I developed a slide/tape presentation on land use planning about which a group in Albemarle County had heard. They were forming a citizen's action group to protest the activities of a gravel pit which had expanded near a residential area, thus causing breathing problems for residents. The County Board of Supervisors was against any protest; the gravel pit owner, I concluded, was a political crony. I was supposed to clear my visits through the county agent who was paid by the county, the state and the feds. Thus, to me he was a political pawn of the local board. In addition, he or the board or both had complained to our headquarters at Blacksburg, Virginia. "Don't have MacPherson come down here and show that program, thus making trouble here in Albemarle County. This group is a bunch of loud-mouth troublemakers." I was told not to show the program.

Now I had a real struggle. The citizens, as taxpayers, had paid for the program and had every right to see it. My salary was paid by state and federal funds. The irony was that Albemarle County was Jefferson country, location of the University of Virginia, which he had designed with its serpentine walls and majestic columns.

Typically, I develop analogies. So for the Albemarle situation I developed the following story, which no one would print. It goes like this: A group of citizens in Albemarle County wanted to protest certain political action by the then governing body. The group was led by an energetic, imaginative man who wanted to make to the group a dynamic presentation of the issues by reading from a document he would prepare. But he needed help. Not far was a resource person who had researched much that would be of aid to this political activist. The activist and all citizens were entitled, because of their tax dollar, to the resource product as it had been paid through the public treasury. The resource person was forbidden to present the fruits of his public service labor which would be of great assistance to the activist. For this very reason, the activist was without his resource and, therefore, could not complete his document nor present his idea. Rather, he for years sat idly by as the document lay on his desk gathering dust, with nary a sentence, which began, "*We the People ...*" (The activist, of course, was Thomas Jefferson, who authored the *Declaration of Independence.*) Since I was forbidden to give the presentation but was not forbidden to deliver it, I did the latter. *More than one way to skin a cat.*

My wife and I always had joked about how we neither go looking for trouble nor ask for it; it just seems to gravitate our way. While in Virginia I attempted to join the Virginia National Guard, having had a successful career in Utah. I presented my credentials and was told there would be no captain slot made available to me. "Why not? You said you've got some openings." "You're right about that, but we hold them for our native sons. We've got some first lieutenants soon to make captain. We want to hold the slots available for them." "What do you mean by native sons?" "Virginians. Natural born and raised Virginians." I could not believe it. The slots were manipulated to the end that the first lieutenant native Virginians would have captain slots available at the time of promotion at the expense of a highly qualified combat veteran captain. On a salary of only $12,000, I turned to Big Brother, Department of Labor (DOL), who turned a deaf ear.

"Discrimination must be based on race, religion, color or national origin." "What about state origin?" I asked. An attorney for DOL responded, "Congress hasn't yet addressed that issue." My letter of complaint was published in the Reserve Officer Magazine and caused some stir but no results. Even the liberal American Lawyers Guild had no interest.

Next, VPI wanted to charge against me leave time for my two weeks spent as a reserve officer at the Infantry Officer Advanced Course at Ft. Benning. I was not trusting anything to Big Brother this time. I drove to the University of Virginia law school and did my own research. VPI was dead in the water wrong under federal law which states that reservists cannot in anyway be penalized for reserve duty. When I quoted for VPI's personnel office the appropriate federal law, they conceded.

Then Barbara's great aunt died. She had left the three girls $3,000 each. The Philadelphia lawyer who wrote the will and named himself as executor, thus responsible for probating the estate at about 12% of the gross, said the girls get only $2,000. I responded saying that that sounded rather steep and shouldn't all the costs of administration be pro-rated somehow across the board so that the three sisters would not be docked unfairly? An elderly gentleman, his response was: "The judge has approved it this way for years." That did not make it right, and again I was off to the library acting as my own lawyer. With results of my research, I sent him a blistering letter pointing out how, if he and the judge had done it that way for years, they had done it improperly. We wanted our money, not to mention justice. He conceded.

At the same time I had read Norman Dacey's book, which had sold millions of copies, *How to Avoid Probate*. Addressed is the abuse by lawyers of the probate system and the fact that most lawyers will not suggest to their clients an inter-vivos (living) trust for the purpose of avoiding probate because it cuts the lawyers out of their own fee. I was intrigued. The New York Bar had prosecuted Dacey for practicing law without a license, but he ultimately won on *First Amendment* grounds. He had promoted ideas.

The stage was being set.

Finally, I had a run-in with the Virginia Bicentennial Commission (VBC), a bureaucratic group formed for promotion in Virginia of the bicentennial era, the 200th anniversary of the formation of the country. I had encouraged them to agree to finance a joint project with VPI, the writing and publication of a directory of resources for citizens and small communities interested in development of bicentennial projects. They agreed but balked when my first draft included the People's Bicentennial Commission, a radical group which attacked big business and big government and undertook such projects as asking people on the street to read and sign the Declaration of Independence. (Most people refused, calling the document Communist.) I cried *First Amendment* to the VBC and they gave in; People's Bicentennial Commission was listed as a resource in the publication.

Barbara, Scott and I had visited the University of Virginia, Wake Forest, Washington & Lee, and William & Mary law schools. I applied to University of Virginia, Wake Forest, and some sure bets including Oklahoma City University (OCU) and the University of Akron. I was accepted at the latter two and chose Oklahoma because it offered day and evening programs. I would have to work my way through law school, having used up much of my GI Bill benefits in Utah. I was upset with the other schools. I had not been admitted due to their refusal to recognize that my GPA of 2.3 at West Point was not bad considering that West Point was on a 3.0 system, not a 4.0 system like most colleges. They paid no attention whatsoever to my 4.0 grade point average in my masters program at Utah State. The bureaucratic idiots ignored me and I felt it was high time anyway to get out of the southeast, especially central Virginia. In my two and a half years there I developed my own theory: those who get further than the Appalachian Mountains were a different breed than those who remained for the very simple reason that the former had the gumption to cross the mountains. Central Virginians consider themselves aristocrats of some sort. Many I had met in Appomattox County, a county of only ten thousand, had never as much as left the county to venture into the city of Lynchburg, only twenty miles away. In trying over fifty cases in twenty-four states, I later learned the differences were even more attenuated than I thought, for this reason: the eastern United States has been under government control a good one hundred years longer than the western states. Arizona did not even become a state until 1912!

I considered law school in Utah, Colorado or Arizona, but figured Oklahoma was about as far as we could afford to move the family. Also, OCU gave me a loan. Law would, I trusted, provide me with the knowledge to defend my own rights (be my own bodyguard), and become financially independent through my own business, probably store-front lawyer. (I was also inspired by my uncle, Richard Morris, a lawyer and sole practitioner in Cincinnati who had, I observed in my youth, not only obtained financial independence but practiced "freedom of thought.") In 1975, when I left Virginia for law school in Oklahoma, there was a move afoot to reduce the restrictions on lawyer advertising and I reckoned I could make it on my own. It was not that bar associations were opening the door, but the Supreme Court rulings tended to protect free exercise of *First Amendment* rights on even a commercial basis. VPI wanted me to remain and eventually get a PhD. But with a PhD I figured I could not hang out a shingle and state "Dr. MacPherson, PhD in Economics" and expect I could become financially independent.

In August of 1975, at age 30, at the wheel of a U-Haul truck with Barbara driving the Chevrolet Blazer we had purchased in Utah, carrying our two boys, ages 4 years and 9 months, we left Virginia without looking back. I had been accepted to law school in 1974, but due to Barbara's difficult pregnancy with Ryan, waited another year to attend. Meanwhile, Mark, now in Panama, had grown weary of the military bureaucracy and was ready for a change. "Let's join forces for law school in Oklahoma," I had said with enthusiasm. "Why not?" Mark was accepted also, but being late with his application he had to start in the evening program. Still single, he lived in the dorm and drew GI benefits.

Oklahoma City University is a private United Methodist school with an excellent reputation in Oklahoma. Many of the adjunct professors are practicing lawyers and judges. U.S. Senator Boren graduated there, became governor and then senator. I never met the man, but this was another personality with whom I would come full circle in that in 1987 he would be a leading figure in the Iran-Contra investigation, an investigation that targeted one of my clients. (Details in *April 15th*.)

I was pleased with our class make-up which included about one-half old-timers, like myself, in search of a second career. There were several Air Force pilots in the class who were now flying as reservists. I was amused to hear from the dorm students talk of "the iron man" they had observed. "He runs for miles without tiring and does hundreds of push ups. In his room he has many Peruvian artifacts and is always reading the Scripture. Like Billy Jack, he drives a black jeep and is armed with only a bow and arrow. You should see the photos he has of a bear in the Colorado mountains ripping his jeep top." Mark R. McClellan. *Rambo* before his time.

Influenced by Campus Crusade for Christ, Mark had become a Christian after returnung fromPanama and, while at law school, he waivered between law and the ministry. Before we graduated from OCU he married Cindy, a Southern Baptist whose sister was a missionary. With their three sons, they would leave for the Guatemala mountains in 1984, but not before Mark and I formed a formidable team against the *Monster*. Many an IRS agent would remember my relentless cross-examination; many a prosecutor would be stung by the jury appeal of Mark's preacher-like rhetoric. *Smooth as silk*. I would take on the government's case and deal with all the technical issues, giving opening statement. Mark would prepare and present the defendant and give closing argument. On occasion we split closing between my attack on the government agents, and Mark's remarks about the good faith belief and conduct of the accused. Mark's closing was like an altar invitation. "Now won't you come to my dear Jesus and let Him save you?" Mark and I had a natural chemistry; we could, it seemed, read one another's minds, in and out of the courtroom.

As I began law school, Barbara and I had decided that she would stay home with the boys. One parent absent was enough. Our boys were not, we were determined, to become "latch-key kids." It made a difference as we watched their academic progress. Initially, I worked part-time for a branch of the U.S. Department of Agriculture (USDA) as an "enumerator." I called myself a "cow counter." USDA was always doing surveys, collecting data on the number of acres of winter wheat in Oklahoma, the number of calves in a spring crop. With my Agricultural Economics background, I required no training. So, up to the limit of days I could skip class, I was in the outback of Oklahoma day and evening interviewing farmers. While I was impressed by the Okie spirit, I was dismayed to discover how readily farmers and ranchers waived their privacy rights and disgorged every intimate detail about their financial and business affairs. Of course, *Big Brother* was supposed to be their friend. Once you become subsidized in the mouth of the *Monster*, you relinquish the chains. On rare occasion, I was told to get lost in terms far less than kind. Having lived in ten states, I remember Oklahoma most for its wind, friendly people, and OU football. (They broadcast the games on radio speakers within the major department stores.) In Virginia, the first question was always who your family was; in Oklahoma they care about what you can do, not from whence you came.

My wife and sons saw little of me and I lost twenty pounds in the first two weeks of law school. But I made Dean's List and then Law Review. The second year, I took a law clerk position with a downtown law firm at $3.00 an hour, working mornings and attending class afternoons and evenings. I left the house before 8:00 a.m. and returned at 10:00 p.m. On weekends I studied and wrote Law Review articles.

Third year, in need of more money to live, I took a job with the Oklahoma City Community Council as manager of its million dollar Comprehensive Employment Training Act (CETA) program. *Big Brother* at it again, this time doling out our well-earned dollars to charitable organizations such as Salvation Army and Boy Scouts to hire the unemployed. What was all this money doing in Washington in the first place? I did not stop to ask. A survivor, I was being paid $1,000 a month. One of the board members repeatedly spoke out against the financial involvement by the feds with a private organization. Little did I know I would in years to come develop the same attitude, the same rhetoric. *If you're not part of the solution, you're part of the problem.*

Mark was having problems with his love life. He was crazy about Cindy, but Cindy said she would soon be leaving on a mission. I taught Mark, four years my junior, a little about female psychology. "Mark, tell her since she's going off on a mission, you've decided you might as well date other women." "Yeah, okay, Mac, might as well. Not getting anywhere this way." He did, to include a "Miss Oklahoma." Cindy did not like the idea, and Mark and Cindy were engaged and married soon after. I was best man.

My first trial was against Mark. He and I took a law school course in trial practice together and we were to try a case in front of a jury made up of senior citizen volunteers. I represented a dentist sued for malpractice. The professor's text provided through the professor, and unknown to the students, information given to other students who acted as witnesses. We had to interview them. The plaintiff, a young man, had complained that he had no use of his right arm due to improper administration of anesthesia. Through my witness investigation, I learned of the plaintiff's injury in a baseball game. Mark and I each even had an expert witness and, with our competitive spirits, we really went all out to do in the other guy. I spent many hours reading medical treatises in the law library. At trial, I anchored the plaintiff on his testimony, that he had no prior injury to his arm. "You are absolutely certain that at no time during your twenty-four year life span have you done injury to your right arm." "Right. No injuries." "You're positive?" "Yes." "Any *minor* injuries to your right arm?" "No." "You're positive?" "Yes." "Ever play baseball?" "Yes. Before the injury." "Tell the jury now what injuries, if any, were sustained as a result of baseball." "Object, Your Honor. Asked and answered." "Overruled. You may answer, but it is beginning to be a little repetitious, counsel." "None. None whatsoever." Having sufficiently anchored him on his lies, leaving no room to recant without looking worse a liar, I called several unbiased witnesses who testified to the baseball injury. The jury found for my client in a matter of minutes. While I often kidded Mark about our first trial, he and I both took seriously the admonition: anchor the witness before lowering the boom. Otherwise, he will look for room to squirm loose from discredit to his veracity. IRS special agents would attempt to avoid at all costs being anchored. With me asking the questions, they usually did not succeed.

After two and a half years of year-around law school, Mark and I finished in December of 1978. We sat for the Oklahoma Bar, purchasing the review materials, but refusing to go to the classes. "We can read faster than anyone can talk," I said. He agreed. After the last day of exams, he began his drive to Arizona in search for work. Having loved the state as a student for two years at Arizona State University, he had made up his mind.

He wanted me to come, but I said he could play pointman and scope out the job opportunities. Immediately he obtained a clerk position with the trial practice and personal injury firm of Warner &

McCauley. Mark was led to the firm through an associate, Harry Cawood, a member of the Christian Legal Society which Mark and I had joined. Mark but loved Harry and Al McCauley. Al, originally from New York, had been a claims adjuster for an insurance company for some fifteen years before going to law school. Rochelle ("Rocky") Streble was the firm's paralegal.

In March, I drove the family to Arizona with the notion we would scope it out, and if we liked it I, along with Mark, would sit for the July bar exam. I had never been to Arizona. We liked it, and I applied for the bar exam. At the time, the passing rate was only fifty percent, an efficient method of cutting out the competition. In April, I was sworn into the Oklahoma Bar, but had no desire to remain in Oklahoma. My plan was this: if I passed the Arizona Bar, we would move to Arizona; if not, it would be Colorado Springs where I would dig ditches, if necessary, take the February bar exam and settle. We decided it would be our last move, if at all possible. Again, I purchased bar review materials and studied in Oklahoma while my competitors attended cram classes. I continued with Community Council, which was located at the YMCA, where I worked out daily. Through the help of Barbara's father, we had purchased a house during law school and had it on the market for sale.

In October of 1978, I received a call from the Arizona Bar that I had passed. Soon after the house sold and we loaded a Ryder truck with help of friends. We ran out of room and I had to tie chairs on the roof of the cab, bicycles on the back. I towed an old VW Karman Ghia I had purchased for commuting, and on top I tied mattresses and the TV antenna. Barbara followed again in the Blazer we had purchased in 1973. The two boys took turns riding with me in the truck. If ever there was a picture of Okies fleeing the dust bowl, this was it.

After interviewing with some Phoenix firms, I decided I did not go through law school to work for someone else. Financially, as a result of equity in our Oklahoma house (we had hit the market just right) plus some insurance proceeds as a result of my mother's death from cancer of the bone marrow in summer of 1978, just after I had taken the Arizona bar, Barbara and I figured we could take at least a six month risk. We purchased a Glendale, Arizona four bedroom home with pool for $80,000 with a $30,000 down payment - $10,000 from the equity in the house and $20,000 from insurance proceeds. Our mortgage was only $500. I elected to share an office with two attorneys on the east side of town, but I did not buy there because housing was more expensive. Both the elementary and high schools were but a half block away from our house, and Barbara was pregnant with our third child, due in June. *The American dream.* We had earned it.

In Oklahoma I had been a Reservist and needed the money from attending monthly drills. Our mission was to test other units and as infantry assignments were not available, I was cross-trained in intelligence work. This proved invaluable in dealing with IRS a few years hence. Initially, I joined a Special Forces Unit, the unit with which Mark stayed. Once in Arizona, I applied for and obtained an instructor position with the Special Forces School in Fort Bragg, North Carolina. I spent several summer months training Special Forces officers in the mountains of Utah and later reluctantly relinquished this position due to my criminal trial schedule. On June 6, 1979, anniversary date of D-Day, 1945, I was promoted a major and our third son, Nathaniel Kyle was born. Barbara and I had chosen the name Nathaniel for its Biblical significance.

Mark was doing well at Warner & McCauley and had developed a special friendship with Rocky. He came to me in January 1979 with a criminal tax case. He wanted my help, since I had at least taken the tax courses in law school. (I received a C, which at OCU was not a bad grade.) *U.S. v. Jim Friend.* Jim, a construction worker, along with several co-workers, had been charged with willfully and knowingly filing a false form W-4, the withholding statement filed with employers. He faced two years in jail. The defendants, along with thousands of others working for Bechtel and at other construction sites, had filed exempt or W-4E, claiming exemption from withholding. Payroll clerks honored the forms signed under penalties of perjury. Uncle Sam and the Arizona Department of Revenue had caught on, and a major tax protest was under way. IRS, with help of the Justice Department, intended to nip the movement in the bud. Across the country, and especially in Arizona and California, thousands were filing *Fifth Amendment* returns. A *Fifth* in conjunction with the W-4E was a real threat to the IRS system of "voluntary compliance." (Agents would later testify that voluntary compliance means that "you're required to volunteer." It reminded me of the Army's system of obtaining volunteers. "All right men, I need three volunteers." [silence] "I'll take you, you and you.")

In search of a law practice, I was handling everything from DWI to divorce to landlord/tenant disputes. I was appearing in traffic court, before the Justice of the Peace on criminal matters (preliminary hearings) and in Superior Court. I had yet to try a case. *Friend* was a case which offered opportunity for a criminal trial in federal court. *The big boys.* On the phone, I told Mark, "Sure, I'm interested. Let's get together." That is when I met Charles Riely and Rocky, which caused a 90 degree turn in my path. Ninety degrees to the right, and I was already at least as far right as General of the Army Douglas MacArthur, one of my West Point heroes.

Charles, Rocky, Mark and Jim came to my office on East

Camelback Road in Phoenix. Charles, always polite and mild mannered, had an engineering background from Purdue and had his own printing business. "A modern-day Ben Franklin," Mark and I called him. The Caucus Club held meetings on a regular basis and published Constitutional literature. Not a membership organization, many of its associates were filing *Fifth* and claiming exempt. Rocky had worked for IRS. I liked that. She became our intelligence officer. Good with accounting, she was equally fearless. I later learned of her Jewish heritage and hardship. She had spent time in a prison camp. Jim was the antithesis of Charles: a large, boisterous roughneck with a beard and big cowboy hat with a feather. Ironically enough, an Okie. I should have known. Jim had a criminal record "as long as your arm," including armed robbery and possession of a sawed-off shotgun. Although he appeared rough as a cob, I perceived immediately his sense of principle, despite the criminal record. After interviewing him and reviewing the facts, I came to the simple conclusion. Jim was innocent. *Pure and simple: innocent.*

The major irony was that prior to the charge, Jim had no connection with the Caucus Club nor tax protesters. Like most construction workers, his pay had fluctuated and he had considerable travel and away from home expenses. Since IRS already had for the year what Jim expected he owed, he wanted to stop withholding for the remainder of the year. At the job site, he heard of W-4E, which would do it. When that did not work, he was told to file ninety-nine allowances, which caused the same result through the computer. For the government, it did not look right. Their position was that to qualify for exempt status, an individual had to incur no tax liability for the prior year and anticipate none for the current year. But what was the meaning of tax liability? What if you got a refund as Jim had for the prior year and anticipated a refund for the current year? Therefore, no big deal. Jim, like all the rest, signed as W-4E and ninety-nine under penalties of perjury.

But to IRS tax liability did not mean what you owed when you filed, it meant any payment of tax due at *any* time during the year. To them, it was due when it was earned. Taxation at the source. That is not what the form said. Tax liability does not appear on a 1040 and it is not defined in the Code. As Rocky explained all this, I became more intrigued. My adrenaline was flowing. *Those bastards. Why all the fuss?* A childhood expression from Cincinnati had come to mind. *So wadda ya wanna do, make a federal case out of it?*

Why, then, had IRS prosecuted Jim? This was my first class in IRS Human Relations, 101. IRS wrote Jim letters which he ignored. On a Sunday evening, after dark, when Jim was asleep, two IRS special agents from the Criminal Investigation Division

(CID) from Phoenix, came up to his house. Jim lived in a remote area of the Arizona mountains. The agents, armed with badges and guns, and flashlights, wanted to question Jim about his W-4. In his own style, half asleep, he told them to "Go to hell."

A second irony developed. Taking the offensive, I wrote a pretrial motion for dismissal for the agents' conduct in trying to question Jim at his home after dark, in a remote area. Jim had a phone and a mailbox. I decried the *Gestapo* tactics and hit a government funny bone. I learned prosecutors did not appreciate attacks on the government, despite the fact that they have every intention of putting my client behind bars. The irony was that the prosecutor was a brother Ranger, Ken Fields, now on the defense side of the fence, after years as an assistant U.S. Attorney. After my motion to dismiss had been denied, Mark and I met Ken and we traded Ranger stories. I said, "Look, Ken, this guy's not a protester. He made a mistake, he owes no taxes. He'll gladly file a new W-4 exempt." Lesson No. 2: *It's too late to say you're sorry*. Ken said, "No way, that's like the bank robber who said 'I'm sorry, here take the money back and let me go.' Wait till you see this guy's rap sheet. It's as long as your arm." Trial was set before Judge Walter E. Craig, on senior status. For Mark and me, it was *baptism by fire*. No lawyer mentor, no book on the shelf about defending tax protesters. In fact, no books on defense of W-4s, though we did study the numerous treatises on tax fraud and evasion. Enter Peggy Christensen.

Peggy was "the fat housewife from Missoula, Montana with a blue jean jacket," as she liked to tell the story about how she assisted a public defender in Utah obtain an acquittal for a tax protester. Trained as a nurse, Peggy had ridden off with a "biker", Bob Christensen, and learned first-hand about the *Constitution*. Bob was the teacher. Peggy soon became a legend in Montana and nation-wide among tax resisters. The Montana housewife who judges would permit give assistance at the defense table. Peggy visited with Mark, Rocky and me in a strategy session. She told us to forget the law and what we had learned in law school. Rather, we should appeal to the twelve-year old mentality. "Don't be afraid to ask the obvious. Assume nothing. If IRS says they assume, go to the board, write the word assume, and show to the jury it makes an 'ass (out of) u (and) me' Appeal to the common sense. If the agent can't make tax law understood by the jury, how was your client to understand it? Does the agent really understand it? Test him every inch. Smile at jurors." (I rarely could smile, due to my seriousness of purpose and natural frown.) "Take command of the courtroom. It belongs to *We, the People*. If IRS uses a hypothetical, stick it back in their face with 'Now hypothetically speaking, if the defendant's house burned down and he had no insurance, wouldn't he be entitled to a large deduction, the value of the house?' If IRS claims a man is entitled to only five allowances based on 'anticipated itemized deductions,' then ask if the accused wouldn't be entitled to a deduction if he had a theft or fire loss and no insurance proceeds. When the agent answers 'yes,' ask if the IRS checked with the police department or the fire department. *Put them to the test."*

Peggy had already been involved in several winning cases. She had our attention. She left us with a trial transcript of a winning case. I studied it. We were ready to do battle in the pit. Mark and I, the two "Cincinnati Kids," were now well-trained for our *baptism by fire.*

And what of this federal income tax, and the *Sixteenth Amendment* to the *U.S. Constitution?* Senator Richard E. Byrd, Speaker of the Virginia House of Delegates in 1910, speaking out against passage of the *Sixteenth Amendment* , warned:

> It (the *Sixteenth Amendment*) means that the state must give up a legitimate and long-established source of revenue and yield it to the Federal government. It means that the state actually invited the Federal government to invade its territory, to oust its jurisdiction and to establish Federal dominion within the innermost citadel of reserved rights of the Commonwealth. This amendment will do what even the *Fourteenth* and *Fifteenth Amendments* did not do - it will extend the Federal power so as to reach the citizens in the ordinary business of life. A hand from Washington will be stretched out and placed upon every man's business; the eye of a Federal inspector will be in every man's counting house.
>
> The law will of necessity have inquisitorial features, it will provide penalties. It will create a complicated machinery. Under it businessmen will be hauled into courts distant from their homes. Heavy fines imposed by distant and unfamiliar tribunals will constantly menace the taxpayer.
>
> An army of Federal inspectors, spies and detectives will descend upon the state. They will compel men of business to show their books and disclose the secrets of their affairs. They will dictate forms of bookkeeping. They will require statements and affidavits. On the one hand the inspector can blackmail the taxpayer and on the other, he can profit by selling his secret to his competitor.
>
> When the Federal government gets a strangle hold on the individual businessman, state lines will exist no where but on the maps. Its agents will everywhere supervise the commercial life of the states....

*My center gives way, my right is pushed back, the situation
excellent, I am attacking.* Ferdinand Foch

OKLAHOMA PIPEFITTER   Chapter 6

The case of *U.S. v. Friend* was first assigned to Judge Carl A.
Muecke and later transferred to Judge Walter Early Craig, I believe
for reasons of convenience. Judge Craig then was on senior status
and it was typical, I learned later, that judges on senior status would
take cases, especially misdemeanors, which bogged down the other
judges' calendars. This, I felt, often worked to our advantage
because the senior judge, with less of a calendar burden, was more
patient with us, the issues and the defendant. In addition, it was
interesting that Judge Craig was a descendant of Jubal A. Early, a
famous Confederate general and West Point graduate, class of 1865.
We began trial May 22, 1979.

In his opening, Field stated, "This is a tax case. It's simply the
first charge that on April 19 of last year this individual sitting over
here, Mr. Friend, was employed by Bechtel Corporation, St. Johns,
Arizona, and as such, he went to work there; he was required to fill
out a Form W-4, setting out the number of withholding exemptions.
He supplied false information to his employer because he claimed he
was exempt from taxation. [Not so; he claimed he was exempt from
withholding.] Form W-4 states: If you claim exemption, you have
no liability for the prior year and you anticipate none this year. That
wasn't the case. He did, in fact, have a liability in the year 1977,
the evidence will show. And he could reasonably have anticipated,
based on his salary, that he would have a tax liability for 1978. The
second charge is September 29, the same year he filed another W-4
claiming 98 withholding exemptions [it was allowances that he
claimed], and he knew he was probably only entitled to seven total.
He was still at Bechtel, still drawing a wage as salary. This also
was a false statement. . . . He was contacted by the IRS saying 'you
can't do this, you can't be allowed to do this.' He filed another W-4
on August 15. September he filed another claiming 98. In
November he was contacted by criminal investigative agents. A
short time after the agents' visit, he comes back and files another
one claiming seven. Now that is the high point of the government's
evidence. It's not all the evidence you are going to hear, but that's
what the government's evidence generally is."

In my opening statement, the first I ever made other than trial
practice in law school, I wanted to make clear to the jury that Jim
was not some type of "tax protester." This was especially so
considering that the government strongly suspected that Friend was
a rabid tax resister. He was not. Not yet. I looked the jurors
straight in the eye and stated, "I'd like to point out from the start

what kind of case the evidence will show this to be. This is *not* a tax protester or resister-type case. We are talking about a tax*payer*. The evidence will show the defendant received an income for 1977. It will also show that he has recently filed, although he hasn't received to date his *refund* for 1978. The evidence will show that he expected to receive a *refund* for 1978. The defendant, if you look at the wages of the defendant, the evidence will show we are not talking about somebody in the 50% bracket, somebody making millions of dollars. We are talking about a working man, and a construction worker for Bechtel up at St. Johns, married with some children. In fact, the evidence will show that on the 1977 return, he took a *standard deduction*. Filed a *1040A* in 1977. Didn't even itemize deductions. So that is the kind of *taxpayer* we are talking about. The evidence will also show that, as a construction worker, as you probably know, he is subject to layoffs and subject to fluctuations in the market system."

I wanted to make clear for the jury we were not talking here about a sophisticated man, and as well wanted to put the jurors on notice early of our attack against the government, an attack based on bureaucratic confusion. "The evidence will show that there is a great deal of confusion here. We are talking about many different terms, many different forms. For example, the evidence will show that the information [charge sheet of the prosecutor] deals with the *withholding exemption certificate*. The evidence will show that the defendant *didn't even sign* a withholding exemption certificate. He signed a withholding *allowance* certificate! You are going to learn some strange things, the evidence will show, as to different terms. You will learn that exemption basically means a head count. Counting people. That you *are* entitled to an allowance for an exemption, but you are *not* entitled to an exemption for an allowance .... The evidence will show there is a great deal of confusion about what is a *tax liability*. A great deal of confusion as to what payments and credits are allowed for withholding allowances of any credit for income tax withheld .... The evidence will show that the IRS Code - their Regulations, their publications and their forms - do *not* define tax liability. Nor do they give you an example. Nor do they refer to some line on the tax form and say tax liability is indicated on line such-and-such of your 1040. The evidence will show that tax liability is a *very confusing* term and misunderstood by many. The evidence will show that it has been misunderstood by many, many employees of Bechtel. So that gets to again looking at the exhibits. Look at those letters, put yourself in the shoes of the defendant with regard to finding intent here."

As I soon would learn from experience, my detailed opening was probably a mistake, tipping our hand by giving out details of what we intended to show. Rather than sticking with the plain statement that the evidence would show there was a lot of confusion concerning different terms, I laid it all out, taking a chance, giving up the element of surprise, allowing the prosecutor, if he wished, to be more prepared. But he was not. And for me, this was "baptism by fire."

As its first witness, the government called Greg Post, chief timekeeper of Bechtel Power Corporation. Bechtel had a power plant in St. Johns where Jim had worked and filed his W-4s. Mark and I had developed a four-pronged attack, all related to the element of intent. First, we would show that the IRS, itself, was confused on the Form W-4, especially the requirements for filing exempt or a high number of allowances. Second, we would show that Bechtel, itself, was responsible for not only misinformation given to employees, but encouraging employees, through their timekeepers, to claim exempt if the employee wished. Tied to this was our third point, our bandwagon defense, showing that many employees like Jim were confused and, relying on the timekeepers and lack of guidance from IRS, had filed exempt or a high number of allowances. Fourth was Jim, himself. He was just a construction worker from Oklahoma, an *Okie*, who did not pay a lot of attention to fine print or forms, and only did what he thought was right. How then could the jury find that he had acted with specific criminal intent or with willfulness?

On cross-examination of Post by Mark, the following: "Have you ever advised any employee to file exempt until they got their financial situation straightened out?" "Yes. Employees have asked me if they could file exempt and I said as long as we don't have anything on file you can, as long as we know ... " "Would their financial situation have been - whether they have or were having financial difficulties - have been a factor?" "I don't know. You know, I have had people ask me if they could claim exempt and I said 'yes.' Just tell them what we would do. That you could, you know, to read the statement. That is all. I have never advised. Somebody has asked me." "Would your timekeepers ever have advised anyone?" "It's possible." The stage was set for development of the reliance defense. The government, we planned, would call some of our best witnesses.

Next was Janice Skopinski, a revenue representative for two years working in the IRS collection division in Phoenix. Her job was to "assist taxpayers in preparing and completing delinquent returns and paying delinquent taxes." Skopinski was charged with the responsibility of giving taxpayers assistance by phone and, of course, she kept a memo of conversations. But was the memo detailed enough? On direct examination by Fields, she described her conversation with Jim. "Well, he called and wanted to know - he had received a letter from us questioning the fact that he claimed exempt on the W-4 from Bechtel and he called me to discuss it and find out what was wrong with it and why he couldn't claim it. What we were questioning, that sort of thing." "Do you recall what you told him?" "Not specifically. Based on the history, I get many calls exactly like that. We just advise them of tax liability if they have a liability the prior year and are anticipating one this current year, we are not exempt. I asked him the standard question. 'Did he have a liability in '77?' 'Did he expect one in '78?'" "Do you explain if they want to know what a tax liability is?" "Oh certainly." "How do you explain it?" "I use the standard explanation. Say if you have a thousand dollars withheld in '78 for taxes, you file your '78 return April 15 and you receive a refund of nine hundred dollars, you've got a liability of a hundred dollars. That is your liability. It doesn't necessarily mean that you owe on April 15 and you can't pay." "That is a routine answer?" "Absolutely." "And a definition that you give a taxpayer of exempt?" "Yes."

Now I realized my mistake, tipping my hand too much for Fields. Knowing from whence I came, Fields, a graduate of the Army Ranger School, was setting up ambushes. It was my turn for cross-examination. I had to stick it back in their face.

After learning that Skopinski had been with the IRS for seven years, I asked her about one of the exhibits. "It's a 1977 1040A, short form." "Filed by whom?" "James W. Friend and Linda L. Friend." "And would you tell me which line shows that they had a tax liability for that year?" "Line 13." "And would you read Line 13, please?" "Two thousand seven hundred and nine dollars." "Would you please read the explanation next to Line 13." "Tax on the amount on Line 10 (see instructions for Line 13 on page 12 and find your tax in the tax table on pages 14 through 25)." "Do you see the term anywhere 'tax liability'?" "No, sir." "Do any of those instructions that Line 13 refers to define tax liability?" "Not as such, I don't believe." "Do you know of any Internal Revenue Service publication, form, regs or code which defines especially tax liability?" "I don't know that." "You do not know the answer?" "No, sir, I don't know the answer." "Now, you mentioned a minute ago you defined tax liability by an example. I'm sorry. I kind of missed that example. [Inspector Columbo] Would you repeat that?" "A thousand dollars withheld and you get a refund of nine hundred dollars, your liability for that year was a hundred dollars. You file your tax on April 15."

Here the court intervened with questions of the witness, the judge, truly inquisitive, seeking the truth. "Do you use the phrase 'tax due' and 'tax liability' interchangeably?" "No." "What is the difference?" "Well, tax due is usually construed as after prepaid credits and there is a balance due on the return. If there were a withholding or estimated tax payments." "Tax due after prepaid credits, right?" "Yes." "In other words, a person has paid some of his taxes already." "Right." "And so he gets credit for that and then, if there is a balance due, then that is tax due?" "Yes, that would be my interpretation, yes." "If he has overpaid it, what do they call that?" "That is a refund." "Okay, what is the difference - you tell me what the difference is between tax due and tax liability. You explained what tax due is. Now what is tax liability?" "It's the amount of tax on the income earned during the year." "Not taxable income, but tax on that income. In other words, that would be the total in the first instance where you - a taxpayer - pays some as he goes along and then makes his final return and gets credit for that and the balance he owes is tax due, but the total including what he already paid, if he hadn't paid it, would be tax liability." "Liability - well, not necessarily. If he hadn't paid it, it's regardless of that. It's the tax on the total amount." "It's the total tax, is the tax liability?" "Right." "Okay." *Thanks, judge,* I thought. *If it is not confusing now to the jury, it never will be.*

Now I thought I would test Skopinski, IRS veteran of seven years, with her knowledge of the W-4. "Would you please state what that exhibit is." "It's a Form W-4 filed by Mr. Friend claiming six exemptions, married status." "And what is the title of that exhibit?" "Employee Withholding Allowance Certificate." "*Allowance* Certificate?" "Yes." "What is the difference between an allowance and an exemption?" "I can't answer that question. I don't know." "*How long* have you worked for IRS?" "Seven years."

Given the fact that Skopinski had testified, in effect, that she would have given the advice to Jim Friend over the phone concerning the rules on W-4 exempt and tax liability, I had to take a chance and test her. Jim told us that she never gave such information, never gave such a definition. I believed Jim. Let's see what Skopinski is made of, I thought. I had her read from her log sheet, her "TDA history record," of the telephone conversations with Jim. "Mr. TP called upset. Stated he always claimed seven exemptions first half of the year and exempt status second half of year to break even at the end of the year." "'Mr. TP' - that is Mr. Taxpayer?" "Yes, sir." "That is Mr. Friend in this case?" "Yes, sir." "Do you have a personal recollection of this telephone conversation?" "No, sir." "Okay. You mentioned before we took the break as to a standard example, that is claimed tax liability. How long have you been using that example?" "I've been working the program about three months of this year and three months of '78. I would say for that period of time, we have used this same example." Test her first in the time frame. "So the three months of '78 would be what - October, November and December?" "August, September, October, I believe." "Okay. And the date of this form is what?" "August 17." "So you are saying that you used that example at the time that Mr. Friend called." "Yes." "Do you know *for a fact* that you used that example?" "Not particularly with him, no. I can't say that." "Would you - if you had, would you not have made some kind of a notation on your TDA history record that you have?" "Yes. I would usually say I advised of liability and that is the standard explanation for that." "And on this TDA we have before this court today, did you make that statement?" "No, sir." For emphasis now. "I'm sorry?" "*No, sir.*" "So chances are that you did *not* advise him as to that example, is that correct?" "It's possible."

So here was an IRS agent who led the jury on direct examination to believe that she definitely would have given the example of tax liability to Jim over the phone, and then on cross-examination again stated yes, that she used the example, but then when I pinned her down, pinned her ears back and asked "Do you know *for a fact* that you used that example?" she could not state under oath for a fact. Of course, I was taking some chances here, but I realized that even if she would have claimed that she knew for a fact, *I* knew that her log sheet had no mention of it. I could then make her look like a liar. Calculated risks. As to the log sheet, she may have answered that she did not write everything down, but then I would have gotten into the purpose of the log sheet and demonstrated how incompetent she was by not being complete and keeping a log of important matters concerning her contact with the taxpayer. It was what I call, for us, "a win-win situation." Bureaucrats tend to box themselves in by their own bureaucracy.

When I first got on Jim's case, I could relate well to his situation for reason that, as an Army Reservist reporting for two weeks of duty at Fort Benning back in 1974, we were asked to file with Finance a W-4. Since I had received a substantial refund in the prior year and knew that, through my regular employment, I was having enough withheld to cover me for the current year even considering the military pay, which was not much, I filed a W-4 exempt. No intent to violate the law. Like Jim, technically, I had been wrong. I thought "tax liability" meant owing on April 15th. The only real difference between Jim and me was that when he went to file exempt a second time, Bechtel would not permit it, saying IRS told them to take him off exempt. The Bechtel computer did not have an "exempt" entry; 99 was used. Therefore, Jim now unable to file 99, filed, with the advice of the timekeeper, 98 allowances.

It bothered me that one of the charges against Jim was that he had filed 98 "exemptions." Exemptions to most people meant dependents, including children and spouse. I brought out with Skopinski that, despite the fact the charge read 98 exemptions, he at no time had ever filed 98 exemptions, but rather 98 allowances.

Fields next called Tom Montalto, a Special Agent with IRS. Montalto, who had gone to Jim's home at 8:15 on a Sunday evening in November in Eagar, Arizona, which is near Show Low, which is near St. Johns, accompanied by Revenue Officer Jerry Orthway, described his purpose in meeting with Jim. "My purpose in meeting with him was to advise him that he was the subject of a criminal investigation and to advise him of his constitutional rights." "It was to talk to him about the investigation?" "Yes, sir." Fields, in his attempt to show criminal intent on the part of Jim, was about to demonstrate Jim's lack of cooperation with the agent. There was a double irony here. First, IRS agents are, by regulation, required to read to the taxpayer their *Fifth Amendment* right to remain silent since they are under criminal investigation. When that is done and the taxpayer refuses to say anything or refuses to answer certain questions, the courts have held that the individual has been "induced" by the reading of the rights and that the prosecutor cannot bring out in the trial refusal to answer questions. Such would constitute a comment on exercise of the *Fifth Amendment* , and thus render the right a "hollow mockery." Here, Montalto was never even given a chance by Jim to read from the rights card. But, as the second irony, Mark would succeed in keeping Jim's statements out even though the rights had *not* been read. A mere stroke of luck with the judge. In retrospect, it is my opinion that considering the circumstances, - Jim surprised after dark on a Sunday at his home, by two agents flashing badges - it would not have worked all that badly against Jim for the jury to know that Jim was less than cooperative. Montalto went on to explain his version of the meeting.

"Mr. Friend's residence is located on a large piece of property. I'd say approximately half an acre to an acre large. The home is set quite a ways back from the front yard. It is surrounded by about three foot wire fence, and there were a couple of German Shepherd dogs inside the fence. We were unable to approach the residence at all. Mr. Friend apparently heard the dogs barking at us, came outside, and began to approach myself and Mr. Orthway. I asked him if he was Mr. Friend and he stated he was. I identified myself as a special agent with the Internal Revenue Service. I displayed my badge for him to see, and attempted to carry on a conversation. There was probably fifteen or twenty feet between us. He did not come clear up to the fence. At that time, I advised him that he was the subject of a criminal investigation, that I would like to discuss it with him, but before I could discuss it with him, I would like to advise him of his rights. At that time, he stated that he did not want to hear." (McClellan) "Objection to any statement he made." (The court) "Don't worry. Overruled at that point." (Fields) "Please continue." (The court) "What did he do then?" "He stated he did

120

not wish to hear his rights. He did not wish to discuss it. I said fine and attempted to hand him a piece of paper with my name and telephone number where we were staying in Show Low at the motel, saying that in the event he wished to discuss it later, at least he would know who to contact and where we were staying if he wished to change his mind later. He refused to accept the piece of paper at that time. He said he didn't want to discuss it. However, he would listen to anything I had to say." "Did you say anything?" "Again, I advised him that he was the subject of an investigation and that, again, I would like to discuss it with him. He asked if I knew he was an employee of Bechtel ..." (The court) "I don't want to hear his conversation. I just want to hear what you did and what you did as a result of that." "... From that point on, I said very little or nothing. Most of the conversation was from Mr. Friend. After which time we did leave. He finally accepted the piece of paper and we did leave." (Jim had told the agents to "go to hell.")

At that point, Fields, wanting to get in what he thought to be incriminating statements of Jim, approached the bench and said to the court, "I think the defendant's statements to this agent are admissible. The agent attempted to advise him of his rights. He was not coerced in any way. The two dogs there were keeping them away from the house." To this, the court replied, "He could have written him a letter and made an appointment. I'm not going to let it in. He has to give it [the reading of the rights]." "He attempted to give it to the defendant." "He attempted to give it, but he didn't get it done. Talk about what happened later."

Taking a common sense approach, Mark's cross of Montalto was sweet and simple. "Mr. Montalto, what is your GS level with the government service?" "Twelve." "Do you have a GS-12?" "Yes, sir." "Pretty high up, I assume." "It's average." "You have a college degree?" "Yes, sir." "Did you call Mr. Friend and ask him for an appointment to come see him that night?" "No, sir." "Have you ever contacted him in reference to getting an appointment to see him?" "No, sir." "Do you know he had six children in his family?" "No, sir." "Did you know that his wife was sick?" "No, sir." "Did you attempt to explain anything to Mr. Friend?" "It was pretty much a one-sided conversation. There was a little back and forth talking, but there was no explanation given." "You did show him your badge?" "Yes, sir." "No further questions, Your Honor." Why is it IRS, charged with the responsibility of protecting citizens and protecting citizens' rights, insists on sneaking up on people in the dark, on Sunday evening, at their home? The answer is simple: they hope by catching the citizen off guard that the citizen will say something stupid, perhaps incriminatory. Thus, this bureaucrat who would rather be drinking coffee and smoking cigarettes back in Phoenix will cause the citizen to make the case against himself.

121

Less work for the bureaucrat; move to the next file. "Inventory" as they call it. Taxpayers are considered "inventory," like a box of Kleenex on the shelf!

The government's expert, an IRS revenue agent by the name of Robert Desiderati, who had been with IRS for eight years, had a Bachelor of Science degree in accounting and was also a CPA, testified that, in order for Jim to legally claim 98 allowances, he would have to have approximately $68,000 in "anticipated itemized deductions." Since Jim was entitled to seven personal exemptions, that would leave 91 allowances claimed, each one worth about $750 of itemized deductions. $750 times 91 was approximately $68,000. Of course, Jim had not claimed 98 because he thought he had $68,000 worth of allowances; he claimed 98, as we would show, because he wanted to claim exempt but they would not allow him to claim exempt. So he claimed the next best thing to the computer equivalent of exempt.

So Desiderati was not only an IRS agent for eight years, but a CPA. A know-it-all, I guessed. I decided that I would throw him enough rope and let him hang himself. But first the preliminaries. "Sir, I understand that you are quite familiar with the Internal Revenue Service forms. Is that correct?" "Most of them, yes." "Most of them including the W-4, the 1040 and the 1040A?" "Right." "... Now on the W-4, is there anywhere that it defines tax liability?" "On the W-4, itself?" "Yes." "I don't think it does, no. I have read it before. I don't believe it does discuss it." "You have been with the IRS for eight years." "That's right." "During your eight years experience, have you ever seen on a form of the IRS or any publication or regs or code that term 'tax liability' defined?" "I believe it is defined in the regulations in the section concerning W-4s." He then proceeded to read a complicated definition from the regulation that would take a CPA, plus a Philadelphia lawyer, to figure out, a definition that made reference to tax credits. It was just certain tax credits, not all tax credits.

There was a purpose for me in getting into these technical nuances. Mr. Bray, chief of the collection division of IRS in Arizona had, because of the W-4 problem with Bechtel, written a letter to Bechtel giving his definition of 'no liability.' I asked Desiderati to read from the very letter. "Now down to the last paragraph, the second sentence. Would you read that, please?" "'No liability means zero tax before tax credits.'" "Is that a correct statement?" "Well, I don't know what he means by a tax credit." "Well, if he means *all* tax credits, is it a correct statement?" "I would say not, no." "*You would say what?*" "It is not." "It is *not* a correct statement?" "Right." Hmmm. *IRS, itself, giving out incorrect information to Bechtel, which would in turn misinform the employees?* Plus I had succeeded in pitting one IRS employee

122

against another. *Divide and conquer. Dissention among the ranks.*

But had I gone far enough? I did not want to take the chance that I had not, and felt I could take calculated risks because I had the IRS publications and the issues were plain confusing. It was time to nail the coffin shut.

"Now do you know, sir, of any - within *any* of the publications, forms, codes or regulations that the IRS gives the taxpayer, of an *example* of how to fill out a W-4 where they explain any tax liability?" "I think there are some examples in the regulations on how to fill it out, but I don't know if they define the term other than what I have read." Remember, IRS is supposed to *help* taxpayers understand the tax laws. "Okay. Are you familiar with the publications of the IRS, such as Publication 17?" "Yes." "539?" "I don't recall that number." "Okay. How about Circular E?" "Well, vaguely familiar with it, yes." "Your Honor, may we have the witness shown exhibits K through S? Would you describe to the court, please, what these exhibits are?" "Defendant's K is Publication 17." "Excuse me. What is Publication 17?" "It's a booklet that the IRS publishes called *Your Federal Income Tax* , and it's to be used by individuals in filing their returns." "And what is the big difference between Publication 17 and the small booklet that they send you with your tax form?" "It's quite a bit thicker. Covers a lot more complicated areas, let's say." "More complicated areas?" "Yes." "With a lot of examples?" "There are examples. But this, you know, this covers things like capital gains and losses and that type of thing." "Okay." Logic: if IRS provided examples in one area, why not in another, especially where they knew taxpayers were confused? "Of course, the other one does, too. I'm not sure. Defendant's exhibit L is the 1979 edition of Publication 17. Publication 539."

"Defendant's exhibit M is the 1978 edition of withholding taxes and reported quota requirements." "Are you familiar with that publication? [He hesitates.] Take your time." "I don't know that I have looked at one for a long time." "Would you just describe its general purpose?" "I believe its general purpose is it defines what employees are, what an employer has to do, what his withholding requirements are." "Please go on." "Defendant's exhibit N is the 1979 edition of Publication 539. Defendant's exhibit O is Circular E of employer's tax guide. This is the circular which has the withholding tables in it. Defendant's exhibit P is Circular E. It's another one, I guess, for '79. Defendant's exhibit Q is Circular E Supplement. Defendant's exhibit R is Circular E Supplement, employer's tax guide for 1977. And Defendant's exhibit S is a pamphlet called *Understanding Taxes '79* , which I've never seen before." (This one was for *high school students.* Indoctrinate the sheep early; less chance then of graduating potential tax dissidents.)

"... Those publications are distributed to whom?" "Some to employers, I guess. Most of them to the employers. The Publication 17 isn't distributed. I think you have to purchase that. [Wrong; they are free.] I'm not sure on Publication 17." "But are they readily and fairly readily available to the taxpayer who would come to the IRS to ask for, say, Publication 17?" "I think they could go to the office and pick up a Publication 17, yes." "So if a man had a question about filling a W-4 out, he could come in and get these types of publications?" "Yes." "Now, *where* in those publications do they give an example of how to fill out a W-4?" "I don't know." "Do they define tax liability?" "I don't know that either." "Do they define allowance?" "I'm not sure without reading all of it. I can't tell you what is in there word-for-word." "Do they define exemption?" "I'm sure they do, somewhere."

"Would you turn to exhibit K. Would you turn, please, to page 22." "Okay." "And what does that section deal with?" "Tax withholding and estimated tax." "And did you see anything in there with regard to filing exempt?" "Yes. It says exemptions from withholding." "Do you see any *examples* in there?" "No." "Does it say *who* can file exempt?" "It only says if you incurred no tax liability for the past year and expect none for the current year, you can file." "Does it define tax liability in that section?" "No." "Okay. Please refer to page 23 of exhibit L." "Okay." "Is that basically the same thing we just looked at on page 22 of exhibit K?" "I believe it talks about exemption from withholding." "And does it say *who* can file?" "Only a person that meets the requirements. No tax liability for the past year incurred." "Does it *define* tax liability?" "No." "Give an *example*?" "Not in that paragraph, no." Stick it in their face. They want my innocent client behind bars for two years.

"... Would you consider yourself an expert as to Internal Revenue Code matters?" "Yes." Good; now throw him some more rope. "And that would include expertise with regard to the W-4?" "Yes." "... Sir, being quite familiar with the W-4 and having worked for the IRS for eight years, do you know for any reason why the IRS does *not* define tax liability or give a simple example?" "No, I don't." "Is there any IRS policy with regard to that that you know of?" "Not that I know of." "Have you ever suggested to anyone in the IRS they should define tax liability or give an example?" "No, I didn't." I did not dare ask him *why* not. Leave it be; he looks stupid enough.

I next attempted to demonstrate the flexibility intended for the W-4, that an individual could at any time of the year, based on his circumstances, change his W-4 and he would have to but "guesstimate." By this time, however, Desiderati was not about to give me what I wanted, probably realizing that I had already had him

124

eating out of my hand, step by step. After he was less than responsive to my questions, pretending lack of understanding, the court, probably impatient and truly seeking the truth in the case, asked, "It fits the circumstances to take his [my] line of questioning, a fellow who worked for two months and got laid off a month, then he went back to work, he could file another W-4 and he may work three months and get laid off for four months, and then go back to work and he would fill out another W-4, depending on his past experience compared with his year before, and he is guessing, but he is coming up pretty close." Boxed in now by the judge, Desiderati had no choice but to answer, "My guess is he could do that." Good, because that is just what Jim did. The government rested and it was our turn.

Mark first called Linda Flick, one of the timekeepers at Bechtel who testified in her own words what tax liability meant, "When they have incurred no tax liability means they do not owe any taxes at all." Great, that is what I thought it meant, at least in reference to April 15th. That is what Jim thought it meant. Another timekeeper, Becky, who, Jim recalled, gave Jim advice in filling out the W-4 exempt, was in the hospital sick, so we had to call some other witnesses.

Mark called Leander Jones and was able to slip some hearsay by. "To your personal knowledge, then, there were timekeepers during that time period that would inform their employees they could file 98 allowances?" "Yes, they were informed they could do that." "Did this happen very often during the time you were employed there? Weekly, monthly?" "Say again." "Did it happen weekly or monthly?" "To my knowledge it would happen maybe on people who came in. I personally assisted a number of people in changing their W-4s, but to my knowledge that went to exempt for allowances or whatnot and there were at least three or four of those a week." (Hearsay is a statement made by an out of court declarant offered for the truth of the matter; e.g. other timekeepers did say to employees, "You can file exempt."

Time for cross-examination. Ken Fields made the mistake, I believe, of asking too many questions, the answers to which he did not know, digging himself deeper and deeper. Perhaps he thought Jones was lying and needed to be tested. But the testing opened the hearsay door wider and wider. "Who by name in the timekeeping office advised employees that you are aware that they could file a 98 on their W-4s?" "Gregory Post, Rebecca Neele, Patricia . . . . There was a lady there by the name of Neele. I don't know her first name. Nola Prichard and Carla - I don't know her last name. She was a secretary." "They would be telling employees they could file a 98, but they couldn't file exempt, is that correct?" "That was." "Did they ever tell them they should file 98 exemptions?" "Say it

125

again." "Did they ever tell them they should file 98 exemptions?" "You said the word, what do you mean?" "In other words, you said your people were saying that the people could file 98. Did you ever see any of these timekeepers you just named fill out the form or explain to them how they could fill out a form to get 98 exemptions?" Risk hearsay, to our advantage. "Yes, they did explain it. However, to my own understanding, they did not particularly understand it themselves." (The Court) "Not the clearest thing in the world to read, is it?" "No sir, it isn't." Again, the judge, totally unbiased, was but merely seeking the truth. *Seek ye the truth and the truth shall set you free.* The truth was: it was very, very, very confusing.

A last ditch effort to discredit the witness, Fields thought he would bring out the fact that Jones had been fired. I liked Jones' explanation. Jones could fight along side me any day, on any battlefield. "Who discharged you?" "Again, that is a good question. I was told by Gregory Post my services were no longer required and I was terminated. However, when I approached Mr. Post on the tenth of September concerning my desire - personal belief being involved that I did not think it right to deny a person *due process of law* by changing their W-4, that it was a personal thing and that I would assist him in any other way possible by contacting people and having them come in, he said, 'Well, we will work something out.' And when I came in the next day we had a little chit-chat with Larry Ivy, his office assistant supervisor. He asked me how strongly did I feel about this and I said it was a very personal thing to me. *I spent nine and a half years in the Army and my country is very important to me.* And to deny a person anything I can't do that because I can't restore it. And so after I told him that he went and had a conversation with Larry Obey and Kurt Stafford and I departed Mr. Stafford's office and went back to the time shack and ten minutes later I was notified my services were no longer requested."

I felt we had the momentum, but my nature was to be *tenacious. The pit bull.* I next called the boss himself, William Bray, who was Chief of the Collection Division and had been with IRS *nineteen years.* In response to my question as to whether he regarded himself as an expert on W-4 matters, he answered smugly, rather than simply saying "yes," "I am thoroughly well-versed in forms W-4." Bray, remember, had written a letter to Bechtel, stating that "The issue of no liability in 1978 or anticipated no liability in 1979 as discussed in Internal Revenue Code Sec. 3402(n) *is misunderstood* by a number of your employees." I wanted to stick his nose in it. "Now, you have a statement that this is *misunderstood* by a number of your employees. How many employees are we talking about? A hundred, a thousand, three thousand?" "For Bechtel for 1978 that number was approximately forty-five hundred." "*Forty-five hundred*?" "Yes sir." "So forty-five hundred employees at Bechtel *misunderstood* the issue of no liability?" "I have to assume they misunderstood it because the exempt status was not correct in that - checking prior year returns we found that there was, in fact a liability for 1977, and therefore, the exempt status was not proper nor correct." "Do you know if Mr. Friend was one of those forty-five hundred who *misunderstood* the tax form?" "I don't know specifically in his case. I would assume in filing an exempt W-4 he had some knowledge of his prior tax situation." "But you don't know from your own personal knowledge as to what *kind* of knowledge Mr. Friend had? In other words, he never called you on the phone, wrote you a letter?" "I had never spoken to the gentleman at any time."

I next moved to a common sense question. If Bray was so intent on informing the employer of the problem, then surely he would be just as conscientious to inform by letter those employees who had "problem W-4s." Since he explained to employers tax liability, did not it make sense to explain it to employees? Bray read from his form letter written to the employee and I interrupted him. "Excuse me, sir, does it define tax liability, explain tax liability?" "No it does not. It states the Code sections *exactly* as they are written in the Internal Revenue Code." "The *Code section* defines tax liability?" "No, the Code section uses 'no liability.'" "So you don't have tax liability defined here, but you have the Code section so you go to the Code section and they say 'tax liability' but they don't have tax liability defined there, so then where do you go to find what tax liability means?" It was all so ridiculous. The circuitous route. The never ending circle of *bureaucrateze*.

Speaking of circles, I brought out with Bray an article that had appeared in the *Arizona Republic* newspaper, describing the W-4 problem and "tax fraud." In the article Bray suggested to taxpayers that if they had problems, they contact IRS Taxpayer Assistance. Of course, Taxpayer Assistance included people that did not know what they were talking about when it came to tax liability. I had Bray read part of the article. "But IRS officials say that employees deliberately or through misinformation who are illegally claiming to be exempt from withholding will have to pay back taxes when they file returns early next year." "Is that necessarily true, they will have to pay back taxes? Couldn't they still get a *refund*?" "They could still get a refund." "Does it say 'deliberately *or through misinformation*?'" "That's right." "Do you have any personal knowledge as to where that *misinformation* came from?" "No, I have none personally." Here, IRS had shot itself in the foot. On the one hand they advised the public of all this misinformation, and on the other hand charged my client, a construction worker who had relied on the *misinformation*. Mark and I would not allow them to have it both ways. Of course, through the article IRS did nothing to attempt to clarify the tax liability issue. Misinformation was worth mentioning but not worth unraveling. Was it too complicated for a news article?

Next, Mark called Scott Warren, another construction worker who testified that he had filed his W-4 based on advice from the timekeeper. "The timekeeper, her name is Linda Flick. She told me that it was legal to claim 99 allowances and that was different than exemptions because I knew I wasn't entitled to 99 exemptions. I told her that she better be sure about this because I didn't want anybody coming down on me about it. So she turned around and talked to two of her superiors in the office and they told her I guess that it was legal."

We were on a roll and Fields needed to stop the train. He figured that perhaps Friend or even Mark or I had put words into Warren's mouth. "Do you know Mr. Friend?" "I knew him on the job. I never met him before this trial." "Did you ever talk to him about W-4s?" "No, not Mr. Friend." "You talked to his attorneys about W-4s, is that correct?" "No, I just seen - I just saw his attorney this morning when I came in."

Mark was mad. The truth was Mark had interviewed Warren in the hallway and we had called him at the last minute, not knowing whether he would show up. We were unable to locate him and serve a subpoena and hoped that he would lend us support, for which we were grateful. Mark, a gentleman of high moral character, was not about to have a prosecutor impugn his character. Thus, on redirect examination. "Mr. Warren, have you *ever* seen me before this morning?" "Not before this morning, no." "Did you *ever* talk to me on the phone?" "No." "Did you *ever* know my name before this morning?" "No. I don't even know it *now*." I loved it. "You just talked to me for a couple minutes just prior to coming in here, is that right?" "Yes." "No further questions." Sweet and simple. Like me, a pit bull, Mark was not about to rest. *It's not over till it's over*. He next called Ray Garrett who testified that Flick had advised him that he could go 98 allowances and "I would have no problems."

Because Jim was "rough as a cob," Mark and I wrestled with whether we should call him to the stand. He was prone to flair up, perhaps lose his cool on cross by Ranger Fields. But Jim testified, and Mark and I, having lived for a number of years in Oklahoma, got a kick out of Jim's Oklahoma way of thinking, describing how it was he filed some of the W-4s. "Now what did you claim for allowances?" "Ninety-eight." "Why did you do that?" "The timekeeper told me I could. See, I entered fifteen like IRS told me and she told me they were going to take out a small amount of money, so it would all work out at the end of the year. And it didn't. They took out a lot more than what she said." "Were you upset?" "Yes, a little bit, so I went back to the time office. That is when we could still go to the time office by yourself. And I told the timekeeper you know, they were taking out too much money according to the IRS and she had some forms in there or tables, and she said no, that is what it is supposed to be. And I said, well they're taking too much money out. It's not going to come out at the end of the year. They're going to owe me a whole bunch of money. I said how about me filling out another exempt? She said, 'no you can't do that.' I said, 'okay.' She said 'fill out ninety-eight.' I said, 'ninety-eight what?' She said, 'ninety-eight dependents.' I said, 'I ain't got ninety-eight kids.' She said, 'well just fill out allowances then.' And she told me how to fill it out, down at the bottom, and I got seven exemptions. Seven kids or seven people in the household and she showed me ninety-one down here, and add them up to ninety-eight, and she said put ninety-eight there, and I did, and I signed it. Then she told me I would have to make fourteen hundred and some dollars a week before they could take any taxes out. And I said, 'well, if I make fourteen hundred and some dollars a week, I'm going to owe some more money so we'll all even out the same.' And I said, 'I don't anticipate working any more than forty hours a week so it should come out about right.' So I gave it to her and she filed it."

After going through the scenario of the agent's visit, the phone calls with IRS, and letters back and forth, Mark asked Jim what the next thing was he heard about his W-4. "Well, I worked on Saturday and the guy I worked with, he come up to me and he said, 'Jim, what is your middle initial?' I told him and he said, 'You know, you made the papers.' I said, 'do what?' He said, 'Yes, you was in the paper.' I said, 'why.' He said, 'You have been charged in federal court for a crime.' So I read the article and I had, so I didn't know what to do so I figured I better get a hold of somebody that was smarter than I was and I figured that would be an attorney, because I am charged with a crime and you're supposed to get an attorney. So I got a hold of you and Mac."

We introduced a tax return for 78 recently filed by Jim and his wife Linda, who had prepared the return. "Does the return entitle you to a refund, Jim?" "Yes, I think it does. Let me find, yes, they owe me $1,204.50. They ain't sent it yet." "Jim, do you understand all the figures and tax computations on that form?" "I understand two figures. The wages that I made and the money they owe me. I don't even, you know, pay attention to it. Linda takes care of it, that is her part of it." "Jim, when you filed your W-4 forms in 1978 that are in question here, what did you understand tax liability to mean?" "Tax liability is money you owe or they owe you. If I owe IRS money at the end of the year then I got a liability for them. If they owe me money at the end of the year, then they have a tax liability towards me." "Did anybody ever explain what tax liability meant to you during that time?" "I still don't. I'm not really sure what a tax liability is. As far as I know, it's money owed at the end of the year and they have always owed me money. I think almost always. Yes, I get a refund about every year anyhow. I didn't anticipate this big a return this year."

On cross-examination, Fields did little damage to Jim and asked him about the tax return. "Did you read it before you signed it?" "No, because I figured Linda knows more about what she is doing than I do. And I do trust my wife. If you can't trust your wife, you can't trust anybody."

In closing, Mark told the jury, "It's a case of a construction worker. It's a case of a man who works with his hands like a *carpenter*. [The Jesus analogy was intended.] A case where a man works with his hands and not his mind. We asked you or the judge asked you when you took your oath if you could evaluate the case without any kind of prejudice as to a man who did not appear the same as you did. Not dress the way you did, who may wear a beard or look differently, and I remember that you all acknowledged with a sigh that you did."

After a hung jury, the court acquitted Jim, an act of discretion, and in addition offered the jury his explanation. "And while I'm not obligated to explain why it may be of some interest to you to know the workings of the court's mind. This is really not too complex a case. The issue primarily being the state of mind of the defendant in filling out forms that were to be given his employer which were both correct and incorrect. It's obvious to the court that the defendant is not so sophisticated a businessman; that he makes his living with his hands. He is a welder and an electrician. He is not a CPA. He doesn't have a college degree .... So under the circumstances and in view of your extensive deliberations, it seems to me that the least we can say is there is a reasonable doubt as to the condition of the defendant's mind at the time he signed the W-4 forms that were turned into the employer. And, therefore, as I stated, judgment of acquittal - the motion for judgment of acquittal, will be granted." "Baptized by fire," Mark and I had proven ourselves "in the pit."

Physical courage which despises all danger will make a man brave in one way, and moral courage which despises all opinion will make a man brave in another. The former would seem necessary for the camp, the latter for the counsel; to constitute a great man both are necessary. Author unknown

ARIZONA PRINTER   Chapter 7

"Now, this case, as you probably gathered by now, is a tax case. It's a failure to file case, failure to file tax returns. It is not a technical tax case, but just simply whether this defendant willfully failed to file tax returns for the years 1972, 1973 and 1974. The evidence is mentioned in the stipulation - there has been a stipulation, he earned sufficient income in amounts that would require him to file a tax return. That stipulation will be read to you at the beginning of the government's case. Evidence of the failure to file. You will hear testimony. There will be exhibits and official transcripts of this defendant's particular account with the Internal Revenue Service, showing the fact there are no tax returns, acceptable tax returns filed for the years 1972, 1973 and 1974. Lastly, there will be evidence of willfulness that he willfully, that is knowingly, failed to file tax returns when he knew he had to. The evidence will indicate that he did file a particular type of form 1040 which is a form that people use to make a tax return. On this form 1040, two of the years in question he wrote or made certain notations, the notations being, 'Object, self incrimination.' For the year 1974 the 1040 had other notations on it relating to Federal Reserve System and other constitutional amendments.

"There will be testimony of a discussion he had with an Internal Revenue Service attorney, regional counsel, Mr. Richard Jones, as to why he submitted these peculiar - or these particular type of form 1040s instead of acceptable tax returns. He will state his reasons. There will be some evidence of his prior filing record prior to and including the year 1971, when he did file acceptable tax returns, not forms 1040 that were not acceptable. There will be some testimony about statements he made to special agents of the IRS investigating this case, indicating that he was playing a word game: 'What is money? What is a return?' - that type of thing. That, generally, is the high points of the evidence in this case ...."

Thus, the beginning of *U.S. v. Charles Riely* , on June 19, 1979 in the U.S. District Court for the District of Arizona, Judge William P. Copple presiding; for the government, Kenneth Fields, and for the defendant, Mark McClellan and Donald MacPherson.

Mark, forever the Baptist preacher, gave opening, "The Judge has particularly pointed out to you that you are not to make a decision on all the evidence until it is in. You are to consider the evidence throughout the trial in light of the presumption of innocence. I have a way of putting it that was written in the Scriptures that, "The first man who comes to plea his cause seems just until another man comes and examines it.' And that is our duty today. We will be examining the government's case.

"We will be cross-examining and presenting our own evidence and examining their case.... We anticipate that if it becomes necessary, Mr. Riely will read from and will offer exhibits in evidence from the documents and things he relied on this case. Senate Committee Hearings, books, articles, *United States Constitution*, Supreme Court and Circuit Court of Appeals case law, things he relied upon because you will have to see what his state of mind was and whether he acted at all times in good faith. We intend to show through that evidence that he, without question, relied on reputable documents, reputable sources to come to his decision as to how to act on his returns....

"The evidence will not deal in the slight with whether or not Mr. Riely was right or wrong. This is not to be the issue. The evidence will deal with whether he acted in *good faith* and whether he *reasonably relied* on what he relied on in the case: the *Constitution,* Senate Committee Hearings, other publications and documents ...."

Who was this Charles Riely? After graduating from college with a degree in electrical engineering, he was a man who dealt with logic. Because Charles had become a printer, Mark referred to him as a "modern day Ben Franklin." (Remember, "the pen is mightier than the sword." A printer's simple press is a far greater threat to the *Beast* than two airborne divisions. *Silence* the dissidents!) But what better description of Charles than from his own mouth as contained in the introduction to his 1981 book, *U.S. v. Riely* ? *Or Was It The Constitution v. the IRS?*

"Suddenly my study opened new doors - there were real problems facing the United States and I had been completely unaware of them. Mentally refreshed by my long self-imposed book ban, I now plunged into a deep study of the history of freedom and current political problems. The study isolated for me the source of our liberty and simultaneously exposed freedom's enemy. The proponents of freedom: the Colonists who staged the Boston Tea Party. The loyal men and women who supported George Washington in the struggle to overcome the Redcoats. The statesmen who forged the Constitutions of the young states. The delegation who met, and under Washington's guidance in Philadelphia, agreed to each and every Article of the *Constitution*. The great men who developed the resources of this once primitive land into a productive nation, and the women who raised and taught those men. America was great because she had strong, responsible law-abiding *families!*

"These families were not robots nor pawns for the old-style European Aristocrats to play with. They had their own values to judge their actions by and they did not fall for sophistry. They knew a person couldn't spend more than he made without going broke. They knew the source of wealth was industry and not the bank. They knew that paper money caused inflation and produced great evils in the nation. They knew that politicians couldn't always be trusted so they wisely didn't leave very much for the government to do.

"It worked. It worked so well that America became the land of the promise - the envy of the world. Emigrants came to work. Work they did, and they prospered. All were not pleased. There are always those who would rather use O.P.s During the 30's depression a bum would reply as to the brand of cigarettes he smoked: 'I smoke O.P.s.' The Aristocrats under King George became unemployed when Washington drove out the Redcoats. They, too, lived on *Other People's efforts*. America became great because America no longer loaded aristocrats on the backs of productive citizens!

"War, whether contrived or spontaneous, is doubly dangerous. The visible enemy is fighting from a distance. The invisible enemy can be the most dangerous. Wartime programs enrich speculators. Emergencies and excitement cover up a lot of graft. Secrecy and 'national security' cover the rest. Congress passes emergency measures and they become permanent after the war. The 'friends of paper money' glut themselves on the debts of war and enslave entire nations to work for them in peacetime through government-enforced taxation to repay the wartime 'debt.'

"Gradually, the succeeding generations of Americans, many born to a soft life because of the hard work of indulgent parents, forgot what was required to maintain liberty. Gradually the aristocratic types returned to power. In 1861 paper money returned. (A wartime emergency.) In 1913, paper money became the base of private bank control of the nation's money and credit. The Federal Reserve Act re-established the European banking empire on American soil! Jefferson turned over in his grave. Also in 1913, the people passed the Income Tax Amendment to tax Wealth for the benefit of the working class. (The Democrats proposed the Amendment in Congress in 1909.) In 1913, the Wealth slipped into tax-free foundations. Have you heard of the Rockefeller Foundation? The Mellon Foundation? The Carnegie Foundation, and so on? In 1933, Roosevelt prevented the bank from giving out any gold and in January of 1934 Congress made it illegal to use gold as money. In 1943, during the excitement of World War II, the Withholding tax went into effect and the burden was finally shifted on the back of the productive class. In 1963, on the day of President Kennedy's

133

funeral, Federal Reserve Notes, without any redemption clause, were distributed to the nation's banks. In 1965, copper/nickel tokens stamped to look exactly like U.S. coinage, were authorized by Congress. In 1968, the government stopped paying silver for Silver Certificates. In 1971, Nixon stopped paying gold to foreign governments. The quiet revolution was complete. The aristocrats were again safely in control. Billions for the friends of Congress: taxation for those who believed in democracy.

"Those who dared speak out were silenced. Some spoke anyway. The people weren't ready to listen. In the beginning inflation acted as a tonic - easy money - frequent pay raises - great government projects for the benefit of the people. Free lunch was in. Thrift and reason were out. Way out! Kennedy attempted to pass radical expensive social programs - never considered part of a free nation. He failed. Kennedy was martyred. Johnson passed his programs as though his martyrdom had sanctified them - remember? Goldwater ran for president in 1964. He spoke out and was made to look the fool. History has since proved that all he said was true.

"America went deeper into unreality. For the second time we fought a war that was never declared by Congress and was not supposed to be won! For the second time we got uncontrolled inflation. First in 1787 - the *Constitution* cured that one. The current inflation had reduced the purchasing power of the traditional U.S. Dollar unit of value to five cents. Still we hear that in a few years the 'Fed' will have inflation 'under control.' In a few years it won't matter - there won't be any value to 'control.'

"If you think by now that I am a rambling old fool, perhaps you are correct. But let me tell you just a little more. The full name of that book I mentioned earlier, the one that triggered my interest in all this, was *FOR IF IT "PROSPERS", None Dare Call It Treason*. My friend, it prospered. The federal government today has over 16 million direct and indirect employees, *not counting military*. The *Declaration of Independence* put it this way to the king: '[You are sending] swarms of officers to harass our people and eat our substance.' Today we have Kings, Earls, Dukes, Barons, Princes, Knights, and serfs, indentured servants and slaves. Only the names have been changed to protect the guilty.

"Okay, enough rambling. What does this all have to do with tax returns anyway? Follow this closely because I'm giving you the outline here - not the entire detailed story. The good part is the trial - and you are going to get it pretty soon. But first you need this background to really appreciate the story.

"We Constitutionalists say that the IRS is the biggest culprit. It feeds all the other monsters and acts as a national police force as well. It 'gets' the big ones - remember Al Capone? What you don't remember are all the millions who would do something about the problem if they had any money left after taxes or if they weren't afraid of the IRS! Who does have money after taxes? Why, the friends of paper money, of course! The tax-free organizations and foundations. Why don't they tell it like it is? Because they would lose their tax-free status! The same goes for churches. Schools and colleges would lose their grants. Public officials get audited. Simple, isn't it?

"Some attorneys say we're doing it wrong. We should pay the tax, sue for refund and raise the issue in court. Fine. Except it won't work. Never has and never will. A taxpayer does not have standing to raise a constitutional issue in Court because he 'only suffers with people generally' and is not 'particularly damaged' by the requirement to pay tax! These things are not understandable - you can only read them and see that the U.S. Supreme Court said them.

"In this brief sketch I am trying to show that the traditional, peaceful way to get the aristocrats off our backs is through test cases in the court system. NRA, Roosevelt's worst socialist program, was struck down by the court. No revolution, no street battles; just a good court case. The evils of Prohibition were struck down by so many court cases jamming the dockets that Congress proposed repeal and repeal the people did. How then can *We, the People* restore Limited, or Constitutional government when Congress is not interested? Ah, that is the *real* issue.

"Here it is. Trial by Jury is really Trial by the People. Our licensed and trained professionals: Judges, Attorneys and Professors, cannot understand because they are part of the problem! But a jury is not trained - they *can* understand! Further, a jury verdict is not reversible nor appealable by the government when it decides in favor of the citizen! So ... prepare a Constitutional Test Case (or thousands of them) and let the Jury decide the issue.

"Are you afraid of the IRS? Of course you are. Do you suppose it is possible for you to be both fearful and free at the same time? Are we free? Not as long as the IRS hangs the sword of Damacles over our heads! What is their power? Prosecution and jail. What information would they use against you? Your own Tax Return, of course.

"What protects us from having our own information used against us? The *Fifth Amendment* (put in the *Constitution* by the Founding Fathers to protect Communists from Joe McCarthy, remember?) states in part: 'No person ... shall be compelled to be a witness against himself in any criminal case ...' Did you know that you forever 'waive' or give up that right when you file a tax return? You do and the U.S. Supreme Court told you so.

"How can you file a tax return and not waive your Constitutional rights? Take the *Fifth* in answer to the statements you feel might cause you to be a witness against yourself...."

Which is exactly what Charles did, thus leading to the case of his prosecution, with Mark and I as defense counsel. Unlike Jim's case, there was not much here of a technical defense unless you wanted to call the *Constitution* a "technicality." Our plan was this: stick the *Fifth Amendment* in their face; dare the government to go around it, and show how Charles reasonably relied on government lawyers and publications in reaching the conclusion that he had no choice but to claim the *Fifth* on his tax return. To do otherwise, he would waive the issue. *"So whadda ya wanna do, make a federal case oughta it?"* "Yes," was the *Monster's* reply.

Before we eavesdrop on the persecution of "the modern day Ben Franklin," a couple of editorial comments. First, a brief overview of the politics of dissent.

While some readers may consider Charles, in particular, and "tax protesters," in general, less than patriotic, remember this simple principle: our country, the United States of America, to whom millions have sworn or affirmed allegiance is *not* the bureaucrats that sit in Washington; it is the people, *We the People*, through a representative ("republican") form of government. But what happens when that republican form becomes so distorted, so corrupt? As Charles has noted, "We have the best Congress money can buy." A remedy just shy of anarchy is simply this: *dissent*. Martin Luther King knew well the principle: *strength in numbers*. History hath, indeed, shown that when you surround the Washington Monument with a hundred thousand or more, you get someone's attention fast. This is much like the old joke about the mule: to get his attention you hit him over the head with a two by four. And King did get attention, not only the attention of Congress, but of those who not only believed in but practiced the principle of "the wheel that squeeks the loudest gets the grease." (As attorney and agent for James Earl Ray, sentenced to ninety-nine years imprisonment for the murder of King, and having read Ray's book chronicling his version of the events, I give it as my fixed opinion that it was *not* Ray who was responsible. Indeed, many black leaders agree. Details in *War Stories, Part II*.)

But which of you would dare step forward and form the ranks of the hundred thousand to march upon Washington in protest to our income tax system? Oh, I get it, you really *like* the system, really believe it is *fair*, right? After all, with the Tax Reform of 1986 Congress cut out many of the loopholes for "the rich" and "simplified" things. Sure. Now we have but three rates - fifteen percent, twenty-five percent, and thirty-three percent, and "watch my lips" President George Bush has unequivocally promised *no increases* during his term of office, a promise which, if kept, merely begs the issue. Do we need the disincentive devices of fifteen, twenty-five and thirty-three percent? For a man who has his own corporation, on his salary alone he is paying thirty-three percent on federal income tax, plus fifteen percent in social security "insurance," for a total of forty-eight percent. Add to that state income tax plus possible sales tax and city income tax. When will Americans get "mad as hell" to the end that Congress will be forced to act? My answer: not so long as the government steals from the American working class a nickel at a time through withholding and gradual tax rate increases. Did you know our country prospered until 1913 *without* the income tax, but for a short period of time during the Civil War? There must be a better way, such as a national sales tax, flat rate tax, even a federal lottery. Several states have not been shy about instituting lotteries to effect a financial bail out. Not one to gamble, I ask you: what is more immoral, more criminal, more socialistic than our present system of income taxation, a system premised upon "robbing Peter to pay Paul?" We have accepted the system as a way of life, and rather than deal with it honestly, millions have shirked their duty and responsibility and turned to cheating. The coward's way out. Run and hide. Rather than effect change through a two-pronged attack of political influence and popular dissent, as did King, we have abdicated to the enemy. And for those of you who hate King and what he stood for, consider this: he at least had the courage of his convictions, was willing to pay the "supreme sacrifice," and did so. Since *We the People* have surrendered our crown to the *Beast*, we get, as Charles would say, "the best government we deserve."

Getting the mule's attention. Until *We the People* act in mass - dissent, political action, civil disobedience - we will not have the Congress-mule's attention and will continue "to get what we deserve:" "paying through the nose." In a recent tax protester criminal case, a panel of three judges sitting on the U.S. Court of Appeals for the Ninth Circuit commented to the effect that "disobedience of the tax laws is not a proper means of civil disobedience." Then what, pray tell, is? Black civil disobedience effected political change through public school attendance and violation of state law, bus rides, marches and restaurant sit-ins. Vietnam protesters? Same methods: civil disobedience. In the '80s, it is the anti-nuclear armament and pro-life groups, willing "to pay the price" of jail. President Jimmy Carter's daughter, an activist against U.S. military assistance to Nicaragua, was, with others, acquitted of illegally disrupting college campuses recruiting efforts by the CIA. Her defense? *Necessity.* By one simple illegal act, she attempted to prevent a more serious illegal act: murder.

So what say ye, pro-lifers? Have you not read the principles of guerilla warfare as set out by Sun Tzu (500 B.C.), Mao Tse-tung (1927) and Che Guevara (1959)? *Cut the enemy off at the source, disrupt his supply lines.* At least one Vietnam War dissenter had the temerity to raise it. He filed a W-4 claiming six billion allowances, claiming those individuals over which he felt the protectorate, the lives to be saved by stopping the flow of tax dollars which added to the war coffer and the body count. Charged as was Jim Friend, with willfully filing a false and fraudulent W-4, he was *acquitted* on appeal, the court holding that his W-4 could defraud no one! "Hell, no, we won't go!" became the cry of the 70's. I have not heard yet a whisper from the masses of "Hell, nay, we won't pay." Only the silence of surreptitious attempted tax evasion. The underground economy. The shadow economy. But perhaps I am missing the point; perhaps the underground economy and intentional *successful* tax evasion is the true mark of the well-honed guerilla warrior. Who said guerilla warriors were honest?

Second, a brief comment concerning the money system, especially for those of you who have not studied the problem and do not take it seriously. If you were born, as I was, in 1945, or in an earlier year, you are old enough to remember, for example, the ten dollar "silver certificate." Perhaps you have a few as "collector's items." Ten dollars was, back then, backed by ten dollars in silver, *real money.* Perhaps you remember, as I do, that as kids we used to joke about how, at any time during banking hours, we could go to the bank and trade in a dollar bill for one dollar in gold or silver. We never did, of course, due to the inconvenience of carrying heavy metal in our jeans. And at Christmas from my great aunt and uncle my gift was a U.S. silver dollar. *Real money.* I can remember holding it in my hand, amazed by the shear weight. The government cannot print money at will *if* it is backed by a limited resource such as gold or silver. Unlimited printing of federal reserve notes (ferns) leads, of course, to unlimited inflation. Ask the peanut man from Georgia, Jimmy Carter. Remember twenty-one percent APR?

But all of this was known to the colonists, who coined the phrase, "It's not worth a Continental," paper money ("notes") not backed by gold or silver. How serious were the founding fathers concerning the sound money system? Volumes have been written by the fathers first, then historians. Remember at least this much: the National Coinage Act of 1792 provided a single penalty for debasing the coin. Death.

The government's first witness against Charles Riely was Charles Kahn, a revenue officer with IRS assigned to the Special Procedures staff for the Phoenix district. He had been with the IRS for twenty-nine years and had been a revenue officer for twenty-four years and was currently acting chief of the Special Procedures Branch. As acting chief, he was designated custodian of certain IRS records. Prior to trial we had received through the discovery rules copies of the documents Fields intended to offer through Kahn. I could not believe it. Here it was, my second case, and there was a glaring, obvious error committed by this gluttonous bureaucracy. Here they had charged Charles with failure to file for three years, yet for one of the years their own document stated unequivocally that a return had been filed. "Return filed." I thought I had been lucky with some of the breaks in Jim's case, but in Charles' case and in many cases to follow, I learned that it was the rule rather than the exception: the IRS was at best inept. Time now to zero in on Kahn as we listen to the direct examination by Fields.

"For the years 1972, 1973 and 1974, what does that transcript indicate?" "For the year 1972 column 'B' indicates 'no liability, no return filed.'" "1973?" (Mr. MacPherson) "Objection, your Honor. I don't believe - according to my exhibit, he has not read correctly from the document." (By Mr. Fields) "For the year 1972 again check the transcript and what does it say?" (Mr. MacPherson) "Could he please read it *verbatim*?" (The Witness) "I stand corrected. 'No liability, return filed.'" (Mr. MacPherson) "Thank you, your Honor." (By Mr. Fields) "What does that term 'no liability, return filed' mean?" "It indicates a form was filed and no tax liability was indicated on it." "For the years 1973 and 1974 what does the transcript indicate about returns being filed?" "It says 'no record of return filed.'"

So here I had it. Charles is charged with three years willful failure to file and for one of the three years their own records indicate that he *filed* a return. Had the government made a mistake as to that year in showing Charles had filed a return when he had not? Or just as logically, had the government made a mistake as to the other two years and shown that Charles had not filed a return when he really had? After all, the government had to prove beyond a reasonable doubt that Charles had not filed a return, yet their own evidence indicated otherwise for at least one of the years. Could I not I bootstrap the other two years with the logic that since he filed basically the same thing for the three years, if the 1040 constitutes a return in one year, it should constitute a return in all three years?

On cross-examination I wanted the one year in cement. "So a return was filed for the year 1972?" "That's what the transcript indicates." "Your Honor, may we have the witness shown the indictment in this case?" (The Court) "No, you may not have him shown the indictment in this case. He has nothing to do with the indictment. He is a witness, not the prosecutor." But I wanted to show the inconsistency of the government, charging on the one hand failure to file a return for 1972 and their own form on the other hand showing a return had been filed. "Sir, are you familiar with the charges brought in this case?" Two ways to skin a cat. If I could not show him the indictment, I would just ask him about the charges. But I could not believe my ears. "No, I am not." How could that be? Was this man being truthful? Certainly he is smart enough to know that he was not brought to the courtroom to introduce records showing the filing status of an individual without knowing it was a case of willful failure to file.

Next, I worked on another matter of logic: the document locater number. Rocky had taught me that IRS puts document locater numbers only on returns, not 1040s that are not acceptable as returns. For the 1040s filed by Charles for the three years in question, each had the document locater number. The government had introduced the "certificate of assessments and payments" which showed various columns of information. "Now, over in column F as in fox, what do those numbers indicate over in that column?" "Column F is the document locater number and that would be the number put on the return or the form that's filed." "Now, how are document locater numbers utilized? For what kinds of documents are they placed?" "They are placed on all documents." "On *all* documents filed with the Internal Revenue Service?" "All forms, yes." "If the taxpayer sends a letter to the IRS, does that letter get a document locater number?" "Not to my knowledge." "Do returns get document locater numbers?" "Yes, to the best of my knowledge." "So if a document filed with the IRS has a document locater number, that document would be a return, is that correct?" "Yes." *Good, because the exhibit and the 1040s themselves each show a document locater number.*

Now I wanted to show that perhaps someone made a mistake in preparing the forms which showed 'no record of return filed' for two of the years. "Who transferred the information from the return that is filed to the computer?" "The terminal operators." "And are mistakes ever made by terminal operators?" "Not to my knowledge. A human being could make a mistake. I would imagine mistakes happen if a human being is doing a job." "Mistakes are possible, then?" "In my opinion." "Then looking down at the bottom of the transcript where it says page 4, no record return filed, it is possible that a return was filed and it was never entered on the computer for some reason." " A form 1040 could have been filed. If it was not accepted as a complete return, it would be considered as not being filed as a complete and proper return." "And who would make that determination, the terminal operator?" "No, the Ogden Service Center or whoever has that function." "Do you know personally who would have that function?" "I do not." "So in other words, even though the transcript indicates 'no record of return filed,' it is possible that a return was filed, but somebody made a decision in Ogden not to have that information placed on the computer; thereby, that information not showing on this transcript, is that correct?" "It's possible that a form was filed. There's a difference between a

My father, Malcolm Douglas MacPherson, was raised in Atlanta and attended Admiral Farragut Academy as a boy, hoping for an appointment to the U.S. Naval Academy at Annapolis. A broken eardrum caused his disqualification, and during WWII he worked with the War Savings Staff. Named as director of public relations for Ralph H. Jones Co., advertising agency in Cincinnati and New York, he specialized in radio promotion and publicity. In 1944, he was radio campaign manager for Governor John Bricker (R., Ohio), who ran for Vice President on the Dewey ticket. My father died of a heart attack in 1947 when I was two years old.

My father and mother, wedding engagement, Cincinnati, Ohio, 1937.

My father, Philadelphia, around 1947.

My grandparents and their four children.
(My mother is in bathing cap.)

"Happy Days" of the late fifties. With grandparents, brother and
sister and cousins, I am second from right.

With brother Doug, Margo and one of the Sisters at S.A.M.A.

With my mother and sister Margo, St. Aloysius Military Academy (S.A.M.A.), Fayetteville, Ohio, where I completed first and second grade, 1951-53.

With Margo and Doug at Millersburg Military Institute (M.M.I.), Millersburg, Kentucky, where I completed third and fourth grade, 1953-55.

My first date with Barbara Joanne Hubsch of Lower Merion, Pennsylvania, at Camp Buckner, West Point, New York, August, 1964. I was 19, Barbara had just turned 16. We were married in 1970.

Barbara and I back at West Point, April 5, 1985, during the Life Science Church of New York trial in Manhattan (New York Carpet Layer).

With classmates of Company D-3, West Point, 1967. I am third from left, second row. Dean Kunihiro is second from left, first row. Dean served with me in Vietnam.

First year at West Point, age 18, 1963.

With friend "Fee Fee," age 9, during Vietnam "pacification mission," 1969. Here I am a captain, age 24, Company Commander with the 173rd Airborne Brigade (Separate), "the Herd."

Good friend and high school classmate, Pete Johnston, U.S. Air Force Academy. Pete, a national sky diving champion, was killed in March, 1966, a few months before his graduation. His main chute failed; he was too late with his reserve.

A tired Airborne, Ranger, Infantry Platoon Leader, Vietnam, 1968. "Black Hawk."

A few of the "Black Hawks," 1968. "Big G" is on far right; "Garbage Man" holds the M-60 machine gun; "The Greek" stands in center, shirtless.

With the Herd, central highlands of Vietnam, 1968. "Gringo" stands in center.

With Vietnamese "counter-part" during staff assignment, Task Force South, Dalat, Vietnam, 1969.

On R&R at the Australian sheep station of Max Cameron and family, 1968.

Stan Newton and I drove from Ft. Bragg, N.C. to Washington, D.C. to hand carry our request for Vietnam combat, 1967. We were platoon leaders with the 82nd Airborne Division.

Near Bao Loc, Thanksgiving, 1968.

In the village of An Hoa on the coast during pacification. With me is my combat friend "Steamboat," an intelligence officer later charged with murder. I wear his hat.

Company commander, pacification, 1969. My RTO, "Professor" is behind me. The two officers in background are MACV advisors.

"No athiests in fox holes." Vietnam chapel service conducted in the central highlands by Captain Curry Vaughn, West Point football player, Airborne, Ranger, Infantry, Chaplain. The troops called Curry "BAC" — "Bad Ass Chaplain."

Sergeant Will, coastal plains, shortly before he was shot, giving chase to the VC. Will was fast and aggressive, killing several VC.

In the "Tactical Operation Center," Task Force South, early 1969.

Walking away with pain from Herd funeral service, 1969. One of my paratroopers was killed on a boobie trap. Age 19, he was in country only a few weeks.

Major Frank E. Audrian (Crazy Horse) and family, 1976, less one Bronze Star medal. Frank was Marine, West Point, Airborne, Ranger, Infantry, part Indian.

Sunday School teacher, Landmark Baptist Temple, Cincinnati, December, 1970, with "Tag-A-Long."

Reunion with West Point roommate and Vietnam combat teammate Dean Kunikiro, 1978.

With "Crazy Horse" and NCOs, Vietnam, 1969. At left is "Marty," a former Marine.

With horse "Tommy," 1970.

My youngest son, Nathan during a poignant moment at "the Wall," the Vietnam War Memorial, Washington, D.C., August, 1987. We traveled to D.C. during my representation of "the Colonel," an Iran-Contra target. Nathan points to the name of a fallen West Pointer, Frank A. Rybicki, Jr., a close friend of Barbara and her family.

Receiving the Vietnamese Cross of Gallantry with Silver Star, First Lieutenant platoon leader, late 1968.

A Slip is as Good as a Mile

Big Cottonwood Canyon — Capt. Don MacPherson double checks ski bindings as he and other members of Utah National Guard's 19th Special Forces Group embarked on the weekend survival course starting at Solitude. No vacation, it was part of the winter survival course during which the group must learn to deal with for combat.

With Barbara and Mark and Cindy McClellan, graduation from law school, Oklahoma City University, May, 1978.

Jean and V.R. Hylton with son-in-law Billy Gibson, an Assembly of God minister.

For Mark and me, these two started it all: Charles Riely and Rocky Streble, 1969.

Bob Judge, Concord, New Hampshire, 1969. Bob dared sponsor an anti-IRS meeting.

With Barbara, Scott, Ryan and Randy Knowles (Vietnam Medic) and family, Kenai, Alaska, during the Pazsint trial, 1982.

Barbara and the boys with Jim Pazsint (Vietnam Helicopter Pilot), Anchorage, Alaska, 1982.

At press conference with Bill Davis (Arizona Senator), *Phoenix, 1986. (Glen Rabinowitz/Glendale Star photo)*

With the indomitable Rock Smith, Talkeetna, Alaska, 1981.

Ajay and Anita Lowery (Arkansas Publishers) *after victory, 1988.*

William Cohan with his son Gabriel (left) and my son Ryan during the Bryan trial, 1984 (Cayman Island Bankers).

With Barbara, Nathan and the "Fargo Five" (North Dakota Brakemen), *who beat the state at criminal tax charges, Bismarck, 1986.*

Barbara and (left to right) Ryan, Nathan and Scott, Honolulu, Hawaii, 1987.

Barbara, the navigator, research assistant, and photographer, Arizona desert, 1985.

On research and photo reconnaissance mission in the Arizona desert with the firm's Cessna 205, 1985.

With my "adopted parents" Al ("Shane") and Mardette Webeler of Cincinnati at our home in Glendale, Arizona, 1987.

form and a return." "What is the difference, sir?" "A return is a completed document properly filled out." "And what is the difference between a return and return information?" "The information that applies to that particular return should be associated with that return." "Is that an Internal Revenue Service regulation requirement or Code requirement?" "The Code requires that a return be filed. Section 6011 and 6012 of the Internal Revenue Code." "It requires that a return be filed?" "Be properly filed and completed in accordance with those sections." "From the transcript, sir, where it says on page 4, Column 'B' as in boy, for the year '72 it says 'Return filed.' So far as you can tell from this current transcript, that return that was filed for the year '72 *was a proper and correct return*?" "I can't answer that it was proper and correct. The Ogden Service Center determined that it was a return." "So it was a return as to the requirements you just indicated a minute ago as having at least the information on it that was required to constitute a return." "I don't understand your question." "Well, a minute ago you were explaining it was a return under sections, I believe you said 6011 and 6012, that somebody would make that determination at Ogden, the fact that a 'return filed' appears on this transcript would indicate to you that somebody made a determination in Ogden that what was filed for '72 was a return under the regulations." "That's correct." "If they indicated a return was filed, they assumed that that was a completed return." Obviously, he was attempting to squirm out of it, but was boxed in by the mistake made in Ogden, Utah.

As in Jim's case, the government next wanted to evidence, by way of an IRS Special Agent, IRS efforts to *assist* the taxpayer in clearing up any misunderstandings or mistakes. James E. Mason, Special Agent, was called to the stand and testified that he and Special Agent Allen Friedenberg had visited the Riely residence twice. According to Mason's testimony, Charles had told the agents, "If you will show me what is wrong with these returns, I will be glad to amend them." But, "it was pretty hard for us to do that because he hadn't identified those as being his, so we couldn't really get into a discussion of them." In other words, the agents were out to gather information from Charles, but until Charles admitted that he was the one who had filed the returns that the agents brought to the house and thought Charles had filed, the agents were not about to even discuss the returns. I ran into this IRS bureaucratic blockhead mentality time and time again. Do not do what is reasonable. Do not do what makes the most sense. Do not do what will get to the root of the problem. Just take it one stupid, cautious step at a time.

Mason also testified that Friedenberg "gave Mr. Riely his rights. Mr. Riely stated he was not clear as to what those rights were, and I just gave him a quick overview as to what they were, simply that he

141

had the right to remain silent, that any records that he might have submitted to us could be used against him and he could have the assistance of an attorney if he wished." Mark, on cross-examination, proceeded to demonstrate the irony; i.e. that here IRS was out complaining about Charles taking the *Fifth* on a return, but the first thing they wanted to do was advise him that he had the *Fifth Amendment* right to remain silent, a right which he had exercised on the very return about which they complained.

"Mr. Mason, did you personally explain to Mr. Riely his constitutional rights?" "No sir." "Who would have done that?" "The case agent, Al Friedenberg." "Did he tell him he didn't have to answer any questions if he didn't want to?" "Yes, sir." "So it certainly wouldn't be ill will on his part if he said 'I don't want to answer any questions,' then would it?" "No sir." "Was he explained his constitutional rights - he obtained them at that time or did he have them when you walked in the door?" (Prosecutor) "Objection." (The Court) "I don't' understand your question. You better state it again. It doesn't make sense." "Did Mr. Riely have those rights you explained to him *before* you walked in the door or at the time you explained to him that he had those rights?" (Prosecutor) "I still object, Your Honor. I don't understand the question." (The Court) "Constitutional rights belong to anybody from the day they are born, don't they?" (Agent Mason) "Yes, sir." (The Court) "And what you were doing was *reminding* him of his constitutional rights in the criminal context, right?" "Yes sir."

Mark decided to drive the point home as to the agent's lack of good faith; they were not there to really search for the truth. Their sole purpose in life is to gather evidence to be used in a criminal case. "Did you inform Mr. Riely as to what he could do to submit an *acceptable* return for the years in question?" "We would have *loved* to have done that sir, if he would have identified those returns. We didn't know if they were his returns or not. We were there to establish that fact. The reason we went the second time is because we had one more additional return, 1974. The first time we went there because we had the three. On both occasions he refused to identify those returns as being his." "After you told him he didn't have to answer any questions." "Al Friedenberg, which I thought he was bending over backwards, says 'It doesn't have any income on these returns for 1972 and 1973,' while we were in that area discussing that." "Did Mr. Riely tell you that he wanted to cooperate, that he wanted to know how he could do so without waiving any constitutional rights?" "Yes sir." "And if he had identified those particular copies of those returns, would he have not waived one of those rights that you had advised him of?" (Watch him attempt to skirt the issue.) "I think at the time, sir, they are not the copies, I think they were - it is our practice to bring the original, that they would be the vehicle of the crime if there was a crime. They were not copies." "You are stating you had the originals at that time." "Yes." (Back to the issue.) "Let me rephrase the question. Wouldn't he have been waiving his constitutional rights by answering questions about those returns that you had with you?" (Prosecutor) "Objection." (The Court) "Objection sustained. *It's obvious* ." Yes, indeed, by this time it was *obvious*. Obvious first that the agent wanted to skirt the issues as best he could by attempting to change the subject, attempting to get the jury to take their eye off the ball. And obvious the *Fifth Amendment* irony and the *Fifth Amendment* dilemma for Charles.

The prosecutor next called Richard Jones, a former IRS special agent who was district counsel at the time the IRS District Director recommended prosecution of the case. After some jousting between Jones and Mark concerning whether an individual could claim the *Fifth* on a return and whether or not Jones had read the U.S. Supreme Court case of *Garner v. U.S.*, in which the court held that an individual must claim the privilege on the return or forever waive it, the government rested.

Having not been totally satisfied with making all the points that I wanted to make with Kahn, I called him back to the stand as our first witness. I wanted to drive home the analogy: there was no significant difference between the returns filed for '72, '73 and '74, yet the IRS had determined that the 1040 for '72 *was* a return. I had him compare the three returns by line item, showing that they were basically the same, yet '72 had been accepted by IRS as a return filed.

Wanting to continue with the offensive, I called next to the stand Robert Erickson, the revenue agent who had been sitting in the courtroom and assisting the prosecutor with the case. He had not been called by the prosecution because we had stipulated that Charles had made sufficient income requiring him to file a tax return. I felt it was with this witness that I could demonstrate that information on a tax return *could* be used against someone, laying a foundation for Charles' beliefs, about which he would soon testify. I was stymied somewhat by Judge Copple, but did the best I could. "Other than no figures appearing on the form, what are some other things that might lead you to further investigation?" "In the course of my audit, if I find from deductions that there is a pattern of not having substantiation for the erroneous deductions, the underreporting of income and a pattern." "And those are shown by what figures on the return?" "No they are not. They are a lot of times determined through audit procedures that are used in my field examination." "Are they sometimes shown by figures on a form?" "If you look at the tax return or form 1040, it's pretty hard to tell until you get in an actual audit procedure, whether something is wrong. Usually looking at a tax return, unless it is completely blank." "Well, do the figures on the return *ever* lead you to further investigation?" Well, sometimes if I look at a tax return, I compare gross income to deductions, something along that line may lead me to come up with some kind of *suspicion* that there may be something wrong with the 1040." (The Court) "Let me ask you this. If you look at that and determine that the 1040 is proper and the figures were honest and correct, does that result in criminal investigation?" "No, it doesn't." (The Court) "Okay." (The court had cut off my front door attack. It was time to go around to the side.) "But it *might* result in an audit." (The Court) "Is an audit a criminal procedure or civil audit prior to any criminal references?" "Could you restate the question?" (The Court) "Is a simple audit prior to a criminal reference, is that a criminal proceeding or a civil proceeding?" "It is a civil proceeding." (Not one to give up, I persisted.) "Can a civil audit *lead* to a *criminal* proceeding?" "It can lead to a potential referral where I feel that there may be - there may be potential there, but that doesn't mean that there is." "A potential. What is the *potential* in a *criminal* investigation?" (The Prosecutor) "Your Honor, I'm going to object." "Objection is sustained." I felt that at least I got the jury thinking about how information on a return might later be used to prosecute somebody, and we would tie it up later with Charles' testimony.

Next Mark called Charles. Referring to a booklet printed by the government, *The Citizens' Guide to Individual Rights Under the Constitution of the United States of America*, Charles testified, "For instance, in the *Fifth Amendment* to *The Constitution of the United States* which says 'that no person' - then dropping says, 'that no person shall be compelled in any criminal case to be a witness against himself,' and this booklet pointed out that as applies to individual tax returns that no one is excused from filing a tax return because it is incriminatory, but that the privilege must be asserted on the return or it will be waived or lost." Charles covered other publications such as those which revealed political surveillance operations from the federal government as investigated by the Senate Constitutional Rights Subcommittee, Army Surveillance covering the years 1970 to 1974, and scandals including Watergate and the Special Service staff of the Internal Revenue Service. Under the staff, 29,520 tax returns were turned over to other government agencies pursuant to a request for information on the activity of the individuals. Charles covered his reading of *Reader's Digest* articles, exposing how IRS utilized elaborate spying equipment and how agents were sent to school to learn how to pick locks, and that the IRS maintained in Washington a staff of specialists in illegal snooping. "I violate state laws all the time," was a direct quote in one of the publications from Special Agent Thomas Minute. The impact it had on Charles was that it had made him "fearful that this awesome power might be used against me, especially since I am outspoken, lecturing against excesses and abuse in the government."

Charles testified from another congressional record exhibit, a letter from IRS in response to Senator Long's inquiry concerning the rights of taxpayers to which IRS counsel responded that, "Good faith challenges in the form of constitutional and other federally recognized privileges are of course recognized by the Service. For instance, the privilege against self- incrimination under the *Fifth Amendment* may be a proper basis by an individual taxpayer for refusing to answer specific questions or to furnish his records."

Another IRS special agent, Agent Boyd, had been interviewed in *Freedom,* a publication of the Church of Scientology. Charles explained the article. "If the IRS makes up its mind to go after someone, they do. If it comes down from higher up, he points out that in addition to questioning from the interviewer, there is *not a return in the world* that an agent can't either find something wrong with or even change to trip up the taxpayer."

The one I liked best, however, was the book, *Tax Fraud Investigation*, by attorney Ira Burman, formerly assistant to the regional counsel, midwest region of the IRS, who discussed a multi-agency organized crime drive, a method by which the Department of Justice organized and coordinated the investigative forces of a number of governmental agencies to pool all information in an effort to find some crime with which to charge an individual. Charles continued, "He points that 'in fact, one of the problems is that Justice names the defendant and then orders a crime be tailored to him. It sounds funny, but it's no laughing matter,' he says. He points out that 'between Internal Revenue Code provision 7206 and 7207 [false returns], the numerous crimes set forth in Title 18, the Federal Communication Regulations and the Labor Regulations leave almost *everyone* vulnerable - *there is a crime that fits every one of us.* The *only* uncertainty is whether the government will put you on the list to be investigated.' This increased the fear that already I had for my activities and for my vulnerability as a lecturer and author and printer and publisher. He goes on to say that 'We must all confront the fact that the Internal Revenue Service has lost its independence and is more and more becoming subservient to the Department of Justice, which in turn will carry out the wishes of the executive branch.' Now I tied this together. We'd already been through Watergate at that time and President Nixon had a blacklist of names and had requested information from the Internal Revenue Service of his political enemies. I didn't know to what extent that list might extend to other people in the government and I didn't know when my name might end up on one of those lists. So I determined that it was more than ever necessary for me to maintain the constitutional rights that I had to my private books and records in accordance with the Supreme Court opinions. Assert my constitutional rights on my tax returns because the tax returns are just a reflection of the books and the records. One is just the same as the other and the audit - it all comes out and so you can't expose one and not expose the other."

It was now Fields' turn. He thought he had Riely right where he wanted him. "Mr. Riely, you stated that during this time you were also involved as a publisher, lecturer and writer. Is that correct?" "During which time, Mr. Fields?" "The periods '71 through '74." "Yes, that's correct." "Okay, did you receive any compensation for this publishing, writing" - (McClellan) "Objection. Income is not the issue in this case." "The objection is overruled." (Riely) "Mr. Fields, would that be one of those questions that Special Agent Friedenberg said I do not have to answer?" (Do not get too smart, Charles; maintain that humility.) "I am asking you *now* , did you earn any income from your lecturing, publishing or writing from these things that you talked about?" "If that is one" - (McClellan) "Objection on his *Fifth Amendment* -" (The Court) "The *Fifth Amendment* is up to him to take. If you want to stand up there and advise him as to when to take it - [to Charles] if you wish to decline to answer on the basis that the answer might tend to incriminate you -" (Riely) "I will decline to answer on the grounds that the answer might tend to incriminate me." There it was. The irony of all ironies. Charles was on trial for failure to report his income on the 1040, claiming the *Fifth*. Now the prosecutor on cross-examination wanted to know that which Charles failed to report and Charles again claimed the *Fifth*, the Court stating that if he wished, he could. Not pushed further by the prosecutor, the issue was dropped.

But the prosecutor had another angle and brought out that some of the people Charles knew who had claimed the *Fifth* on the return had been *convicted*. It was Mark's turn again on redirect. "Mr. Fields asked you two questions about others who may have been convicted for tax offenses. Did this knowledge change your mind as to the law?" "Not when I inquired into the circumstances of the case." "The circumstances ... " (Fields) "Objection, your Honor." (The Court) "You've already answered the question." (McClellan) "Would you explain that, please?" (Fields) "Your Honor, I'm going to object to getting into other cases." (The Court) "He can explain it. Go ahead." (Riely) "There have been other people recently also concerned with things that have been going on in the country. Many of them I consider have made improper use of the Internal Revenue Service forms. Some of them - many that have been convicted that are used as cases in the government's motions, for instance, they were for cases in which people said that the whole revenue system was unconstitutional, and for that reason, they

146

didn't have to obey it. But I've never made that type of claim. That's not - the only reason I took the *Fifth Amendment* is because I was fearful of having my name on a list that is Nixon's black list."

Fields also attempted to discredit Charles' good faith reliance by bringing out that Charles had failed to take the prudent approach: seek the advice of an attorney. While Charles had not personally sought an attorney's advice, he had a simple answer: most of what he read and relied upon had been *written* by *lawyers, including Senators!*

Mark, concluding his closing argument, stated, "Mr. Riely has taken a stand on some issues, or has taken a stand politically, and has spoken and he has made it his lifestyle - he has testified that as for the years of 1971 on, and he is fearful and he was fearful that because of that, but it would go through some sort of retribution or some sort of unjust prosecution or some sort of punishment for that. That is why he asserted what he did on the stand. If that is wrong to do that, if that is evil and if that is bad purpose, then we certainly could attribute that to our forefathers and many of our great men that Mr. Riely relied upon, because all of them read something in what they believed to be right, and they believed it to be the law and acted upon whether or not they were told it was right or not. And nobody ever debated the law every time Mr. Riely asked them about the law. Mr. Friedenberg said, 'I'm not here to debate the law.'"

Indeed, it was for the court to instruct the jury on the law. The jury instructions, or charges to the jury, is an act which, but for the verdict itself, is the last act of the trial. It was with this act that Mark and I had planned our strategy and tactics. Reverse planning. That is what the military calls it. Mark and I learned well through our experience with combat assaults by helicopter and airborne jumps that you start with the landing zone or drop zone and work backwards. Same with a trial, be it civil or criminal. You better anticipate the law as instructed by the court and tailor your evidence to tie in with the instructions. To get the instruction you request, you must have not only legal authority, but some evidence in the trial that supports the instruction. Judge Copple instructed the Riely jury as follows.

"... You are instructed that the statutory requirement to file an income tax return does not violate a taxpayer's right against self-incrimination. The defendant's motivation in this case, the fact that he was engaged in a protest and a sincere belief that he was acting in a good cause is not an acceptable legal defense or justification. You are further instructed that, as a matter of law, the defendant, by submitting a Form 1040 containing the blanket declarations regarding his *Fifth Amendment* and other Constitutional rights, without stating specifically items of his gross income and any deductions and credits to which he was entitled, failed to file a return as required by law. It is not necessary for the prosecution to prove that the defendant knew that a particular act or failure to act is a violation of law. Unless outweighed by the evidence in the case to the contrary, the presumption is that every person knows what the law forbids and what the law requires to be done. However, evidence that the defendant acted or failed to act because of ignorance of the law is to be considered by the jury in determining whether or not the defendant acted or failed to act with a specific intent as charged.

"Now you are instructed that you are not to make any inference of guilt on the part of the defendant by the fact alone that he asserted his Constitutional rights under the *Fifth Amendment* as a United States citizen on his tax returns for the years 1972 through 1974. Information given on a tax return is testimonial and to infer guilt on the part of the defendant solely for asserting that right would make a hollow mockery of the exercise of this privilege itself. You are instructed that, even if the defendant erroneously or mistakenly asserted his Constitutional rights under the *Fifth Amendment* on the tax returns in questions, that if he did so reasonably and in good faith, then you must find the defendant did not act willfully. If you find that the evidence shows any of those elements to be present, then you must find Mr. Riely not guilty due to his absence of acting willfully.

"Now, good faith as used here means the defendant's reasonably based good faith belief that to provide the true dollar amounts of income and deductions as called for on Form 1040, the income tax return form, would tend to expose him to criminal prosecution due to furnishing such information. To find the defendant guilty, you must find beyond a reasonable doubt that such belief was not held in good faith.

"You are instructed that if a person wishes to assert his right against self-incrimination regarding specific items, you must do so on the tax return itself or forever waive the privilege. This is true whether there is a legal justification or basis for such claim or not. The assertion on the tax return form preserves that issue for later determination of the validity or invalidity of such claim as we are proceeding here yesterday and today .... "

The jury found defendant Charles Riely "not guilty" in all three counts of the indictment.

All brave men love, for he only is brave who has affections to fight for. Nathaniel Hawthorne

John Law Freeman. This wild looking man with the long, white beard, was traveling the country telling people not to file tax returns and not to pay taxes, for it was not only unconstitutional, but the second plank of the Communist Manifesto: a progressive income tax. After the Riely victory, he called to see if I would take a case in Alaska. In July, 1979, Mark and I flew to Fairbanks to defend Ralph Marshall, a bush pilot and alcoholic who had not filed in eighteen years. He had attended a Freeman seminar and Freeman was offering some kind of legal defense fund for those who got into trouble based on his advice. He doubted Marshall really fit the category, because Ralph had failed to file for so many years prior to John's speech. Ralph was, I was later to learn, one of the ten million IRS estimates who do not file when required. Part of the "underground economy." Ralph dealt in check as well as cash, of necessity; his clients were for the most part from the lower forty-eight.

As we waited to transfer planes in Seattle, Mark and I would look at Alaska posters, at each other, then say slowly, with wild eyes, "A-L-A-S-K-A." It was a dream come true for two Army Rangers who loved the outdoors. All the way up, Mark had put up with my Jimmy Stewart imitations from a movie, *The North Country*. Jimmy, a former gunfighter turned cattleman, drives cattle to the Yukon Territory with sidekick Walter Brennan. He sells the cattle and readies himself to stake out a gold claim. But there is trouble brewing; a town bully, Mr. Big, is knocking heads, controlling the town. Walter cannot believe Jimmy would walk away from putting a bully in his place. But Jimmy had put his gun fighting days behind him. He wants no trouble. Out of patience with Walter, he mounts his horse and says, with disgust, "Would you hand me my rifle?" So, all the way to Alaska, I am talking to Mark as Jimmy Stewart and he, in his good nature, is imitating Walter Brennan until it reaches a point where I am driving Mark crazy. (In the movie, Jimmy is later gunned down at the mining claim by Mr. Big, Walter killed. Jimmy, left for dead, gets back to town and handles things the old-fashioned way: with a gun.)

In Anchorage, Mark and I stayed with a law school classmate working for an oil company. He showed us a recent newspaper article about Alaska's leading tax protester Rock Smith. Rock was pictured in the paper, and I am impressed by his words and appearance. This guy cuts no slack for the *Monster*. Does not mince words. Steady as a *rock*. About as immoveable as a rock.

Looks like a rock, all 280 pounds. Rock's group, *Patriots in Action,* a "nonorganization" as he calls it, has found a home over a gas station and Mark and I drop in to see him, but he is not around. Little do I suspect at the time the major role Rock will play in my life during the next nine years.

On to Fairbanks. Our local counsel was John Rosey, a personal injury lawyer and hockey player from Michigan who drove his VW bus up the Alaska Highway in search of work. He found his niche winning six and seven-figure judgments for injured plaintiffs, mostly those crushed by large machinery. John became coach of the local semi-pro hockey team.

The good news for Ralph and us was the judge, James M. Fitzgerald from Anchorage. We found him hospitable and fair-minded. The bad news for Mark and me was Ralph. No doubt, he had spent all his tax money on booze. We could always find him at the Arctic Bar in downtown Fairbanks. We declined Ralph's many invitations to fly us in a small plane to the Brooks Range, not feeling secure with his flying ability, despite his claimed eighteen years as a bush pilot and hunting guide. He had trouble walking straight out of the bar. Besides, Mark and I had flown while in Anchorage in a small float plane and toured local glaciers. (Anchorage has the largest float plane airport in the world.) Ralph could not remember anything and had no records which might be introduced to show a low tax debt, thus providing us with an argument to negate willfulness: lack of greed.

Declining Ralph's weekend invitation for the Brooks Range, Mark and I struck out in one of Ralph's pickup trucks loaded with camping gear for Mount McKinley National Park. There, we camped and had our first confrontation with "Alaska's state bird," the mosquito. They were awesome. Their appetites were exceeded only by a swarm I slept with one night in a bamboo grove in Vietnam. There, for the first time, I had worn a mosquito net over my face while on ambush, which cut down on my vision, hearing, and sixth sense. I watched in utter amazement as I would coat the back of my hand with Army insect repellant that had always worked. The mosquitos accepted the repellent as appetizers, finishing with my blood.

The round trip to McKinley and the camping provided us time to more fully brainstorm the case. Without much help from Ralph, we hoped that Freeman might bail him out. Ralph could not very well explain the theory to the jury, but with his testimony of reliance on what Freeman preached and his belief in what Freeman said, offered not for the truth of the matter but for Ralph's state of mind, we had hoped that there was some chance at least that the jury would find the government had not met its burden of proving specific criminal intent beyond a reasonable doubt. But after hearing Freeman's testimony outside the presence of the jury, Judge Fitzgerald denied our request to have him testify, a major issue for appeal after hearing the verdict of guilty on all three counts.

What happened outside the courtroom proved more exciting. Some Alaska residents, the Olivers, had been having a running battle for years with the IRS and had driven to trial their VW bug worth maybe a few hundred dollars, at most. IRS had a lien and wanted to make a show of force for all tax protesters in attendance to witness. Two agents were attempting to seize the vehicle. The problem for them was the Olivers, wise to the agents' activity, took turns sitting in the car, figuring no one would tow it with a warm body inside. They were right. I complained to the judge, saying IRS is denying our client his *Sixth Amendment* right to public trial by their harassing operations. The judge refused to act. During a recess, I was in the U.S. Attorney's office and personally heard the agents complain to the Assistant U.S. Attorney that they could not tow the car. To this he replied, "They've got to leave sometime. Be patient. Avoid a physical confrontation." They disobeyed his orders.

We finished for the day at 5:00 p.m. and Mark and I, with John, headed for John's car. In the parking lot was the VW with the Olivers, surrounded by agents and onlookers, including Freeman. The tow truck waited. Freeman was giving verbal abuse to the agents and pointing at them. Photographers and reporters were there, a story in the making. With billy clubs, the agents broke the glass on driver and passenger side of the vehicle and dragged the Olivers out of the vehicle over the glass. Mrs. Oliver was screaming about her heart medication in the glove compartment. Through the struggle, pills were scattered with the glass. Freeman continued his barrage of screams, "Would you look at that? It's the modern-day Gestapo." Photographers took it all in. Mark, John and I watched, not knowing whether to be enraged or disgusted. Our heads appeared in the back of the nationally-circulated photos. In my first book, *April 15th,* I wrote on the back jacket, "IRS - the modern-day Gestapo," remembering our Anchorage experience and Freeman's words. Acts of terrorism such as I found only added to the fuels of fire of the tax rebellion. It proved the tax protesters all too correct and, as well, added to my commitment to defeat the *Beast.*

That was not the end of the Oliver incident. Several weeks later, IRS auctioned the vehicle in front of the federal courthouse. As crowds stood in protest, the VW was sold for $300 and the same agents photographed the crowd from the window. *Dossiers.* This was same tactic practiced by the Army, FBI and CIA during war demonstrations in the early '70s, an activity supposedly outlawed by the Privacy Act of 1974, which states in no uncertain terms that "No federal agency shall take notice of how any individual exercises *First Amendment* rights." As I was to learn in my own case against IRS for surveillance of me by two female undercover agents, the troops in Vietnam were correct when they said, "It don't mean nothin'."

I was back in Alaska in January, 1980, this time alone to try three cases back-to-back. Randy Knowles, Dan Emans, and Ed Telles, all had been charged with knowingly and willfully filing false W-4 exempt. Finally, I would meet Rock. The defendants had heard Freeman speak at one of the Patriots in Action regular meetings at Clark Jr. High in Anchorage. An Alaska tax attorney, Russ Nogg, to whom I had been introduced the summer before, would act as local counsel, preparing the defendants' testimony. It would be his first trial. Since Alaska, I had been to New Hampshire with Mark and alone to New Mexico and Detroit. I definitely preferred states west of the Mississippi.

"Mac, you'll love Randy Knowles," Russ told me on the phone. "How so?" I asked. "Medic in Vietnam, awarded the Silver Star. Twice. Plus two Purple Hearts, wounded twice. Was taking care of the wounded, ignoring the intense enemy fire, and then ignoring his own wounds. Infantry unit. Unassuming, humble. Was in my office yesterday. Nicest guy you could meet. The jury will love him." "Government know of his war hero background?" I asked. "I don't know, but mum's the word." "Right. See you soon."

Well, Major Mac, was this challenge enough? Three cases back to back. Randy sounded like a great one for jury appeal. Dan was, according to Russ, kind of a teddy bear. Telles, he said, might be a problem; the evidence in that case was strongest against the accused. I had mixed emotions about Randy: I was at the same time excited about representing a "brother boonie rat" and mad at the government for charging my "'Nam brother" under a tax law no one could understand.

Before my second trip to Anchorage, I had been put in touch through Charles and Peggy with William Cohan, an attorney in Denver. Bill had impressed Peggy. Peggy was assisting a tax protester defendant in a criminal case in Denver and was being hassled by good old Jake Schneider. Another tantrum. Bill, an impartial observer, had merely stood up and said, "Why don't you pick on somebody your own size?" (Bill, like me, hated bullies and loved being the bodyguard.) Schneider walked off in a huff. Bill continued to taunt him and Bill, no doubt, cut an intimidating figure. Although no more than 5'11", Bill's shoulders are big, for he used to bench-press 350 pounds. When we finally connected by telephone, he wanted to know how it was I was winning impossible cases. We immediately hit it off. Good chemistry. I said, "We've got to get together. I'm headed for Anchorage. Why don't you meet me there? Peggy will be there, too." "I'm headed for L.A.

and Anchorage is a little out of my way on the return trip," Bill said, "But I'll see what I can do." Russ and I went to the Anchorage airport to pick up Bill and spotted him as the guy with big shoulders riding the escalator with two young attractive females. The two girls who had been on the plane wanted to see Bill at some dance hall that night. But Bill had business and was scheduled for the red-eye flight home.

We headed for the Patriot meeting and heard the tail-end of a talk by Montana Red Beckman, favorite speaker in Alaska, who had run for Montana governor. Rock was M.C. and we met. I introduced him to Bill. Attorney appearances for tax protesters were rare, even in the courtroom. Attorneys avoided protesters like the plague. This I could not understand, considering our ethical obligation to take "unpopular cases." These guys sure were unpopular with the IRS, Justice Department and the judges. Rock asked each of us to speak.

Watching my ethics, I told the standing-room-only crowd that they would not hear about the cases about to be tried, but I performed best before a large crowd and wanted them in the courtroom. (They complied with my wish; the courtroom in all three trials had standing room only.) I peered out at the group, which ranged from housewives to Alaska sourdoughs. *Ordinary folk. Don't look like criminals to me.* Bill was next. He mesmerized the crowd, which surprised no one more than himself. Unaccustomed to public speaking but for the courtroom, he enjoyed the effect. The point of his brief remarks made at the most serious of times was that he could not understand how the government could treat as criminal obvious acts of petition for redress. "Civil disobedience is a proper form of political protest."

How well Bill knew. Not only had he been thrown out of law school and thrown into the Washington, D.C. street stockade when the United States invaded Cambodia, he was arrested at the White House when he attempted to gain entrance to see President Nixon. He was there to act as the President's "conscience." His services were offered for free. The son of a veterinarian, Bill had been dismissed from the University of Washington law school, but had regained entrance. He had played football at Stanford, graduated with a Master of Arts with honors in political science and economics. Like me, he was a lawyer in search of a practice. Fearless. The enemy of bullies. We later made a good team.

For Randy, I developed a technical defense. For added measure, I hoped to ambush the government with the war hero background. I expected they would be caught in total surprise and too inflexible to adjust.

Although Randy had attended the Freeman meeting, a fact not known to the government and not asked on cross-examination, he was without a tax protest motive. Randy was living in Kenai and working at the Union Oil plant there. In addition, he did construction work on the side and, like many Alaskans, some commercial fishing. Thus, unlike most W-2 wage earners, Randy had substantial "anticipated itemized deductions" as a result of capital expenditures, entitling him to a large number of W-4 allowances. Russ, good with a pencil, helped with the accounting.

A problem loomed for us with the Special Agent's report, a memorandum indicating, as was the case of Jim Friend, Randy's refusal to cooperate. Law abiding citizens do not hesitate to cooperate, the prosecutor would be expected to argue. But, like Jim, Randy was jumped at a bad time. It was Saturday and he was making ready to leave on a hunting trip and had packed his .45 in a shoulder holster, a fact the government would attempt to exploit. Although Randy was, like Charles Riely, the mild-mannered Clark Kent type, I had to totally destroy the Special Agent, present a technical defense, understandable and believable to a jury, and totally destroy the IRS' expert.

Trials, like football games, deal with momentum. And like a football game, with little action they become boring. This is especially true in tax trials. But a single event, a pass interception, or one question and answer on cross-examination can completely not only reverse the momentum, but grab the attention of the spectators.

A major challenge became the IRS' expert witness on W-4s, Alaska's own Doris Day, aka Arlene Patnoe. IRS had instituted a program of witness development including attractive females for jury appeal, believing attorneys would shy away from vicious attacks on females. Over the years, I cross-examined one lady from Ogden, Utah in about ten different trials. I had to be imaginative each time and come up with a different approach.

Patnoe was, I thought, her own worst enemy; she obviously played up to the jury with her sweet little smiles and pretty blue eyes, batting her eyelashes. *Yuck!* I trusted the jurors, men and women alike, would have enough sense to see through her Mary Kay Cosmetics. With her, I decided to be the West Point officer and gentleman: be patient with her self-serving editorializing, to a point, throw enough rope to allow her to hang herself, and eventually dismiss her with disgust. After all, this was but round one. I would face Patnoe at three trials dealing with much the same issue. She was the IRS district expert on W-4s, trained for the job. But my advantage: the government must prove beyond a reasonable doubt falsity; therefore, they must prove the amount claimed was not correct meaning, if logic applies at all, that the deductions were not available to the taxpayer. It was Peggy's idea: make them prove by common sense application the non-existence of deductions. Try and prove a negative!

Patnoe was but one of over fifty IRS Special Agents I would cross-examine from 1979 to 1988. I learned later that *dossiers* were maintained on me and my trial techniques and passed among Justice Department attorneys in Washington and U.S. Attorneys throughout the country. I had, like the guerilla warrior, to utilize different tactics. *Never set a pattern. Always keep the enemy guessing.*

After numerous tax protest victories, I watched with no surprise at the government's new tactic: do not call the Special Agents. Prosecutors had been learning the hard way what happened when they called their case agent to the stand. It would open the government to an attack it could sometimes ill afford. But by their new tactics, I could simply turn the scenario around to a no-win situation for the government. If a prosecutor did not call a Special Agent to the stand, his case agent who had investigated the case for one to three years, recommended prosecution and would sit at the prosecutor's table and assist the prosecutor, I not only called the agent myself, I made the government regret not calling him. Make them look foolish, or as if they are trying to hide something. Questions to a Revenue Agent or Officer called by the government might go something like this. "Sir, tell the jury please, of all the many IRS personnel in your district, who was assigned to investigate my client?" "Special Agent Jones." "And who, if anyone, in the whole world would know more about this case from the government's standpoint than Special Agent Jones?" "Well, no one I guess." "And that's Special Agent Jones sitting right there at the table [pointing]?" "Yes, sir." "Special Agent Jones investigated this case for how long?" "About two years." "And you're familiar with the duties and activities of Special Agents?" "Generally, yes." "And as you well know they interview witnesses, collect all the evidence to be used against the accused?" "Yes." "You've been on the case just a few months, is that correct?" "Yes." "Special Agent Jones been in good health during the last few weeks?" "Yes." "Any reason you know why, considering he has the greatest knowledge of anyone in the world, he sits at the table [pointing again] silent, rather than in the witness chair telling the jury the fruits of his investigation?" "I don't know. You'll have to ask him or the prosecutor." "Thanks for the suggestion. I'll do just that when I call the Special Agent to the stand." *Stick it in their face.*

Now this might have the jury curious. Common sense. *Yeah, why haven't they called the guy who knows the most? The guy testifying was brought in at the last minute.*

Of course, I may not in all cases get so far as the above, but at least set up the jury on the theme, and I caused for the prosecutor a no-win situation. If he objects and his objection is sustained for lack of relevance, then it appears he is hiding something. (Juries hate objections, but attorneys must be courageous enough to displease jurors in effort to maintain the evidence at an acceptable level.) If he does not object, I stick it in his face even more.

In some cases, I have called the Special Agent to the stand several times. Why not use him for the walking encyclopedia of the case, especially before I put my client on? If I know what is in his report or have a good idea, I can use him to impeach another government witness. Here is a guy who has sat through the entire trial. How can he *not* know? "Recall Agent Jones, your Honor." "Now Agent Jones, you have heard a few minutes ago the sworn testimony of Mrs. Doe [on the government's rebuttal case], correct?" "Yes." "And you know through your own personal knowledge that a portion of her testimony was given absolutely false, correct?" "What do you mean?" "I'll gladly clarify. She testified, did she not, that ...." "Yes, she did." "Was this to your knowledge correct?" "No." "How so?" "She told me a year ago that ...." "And you know that from your report you have maintained?" "Yes." "She gave no sworn statement?" "No." "But you took notes." "Yes." "And you had your secretary type from your notes a memo of interview." "Yes." "And according to your notes, as recorded for time immortal, Mrs. Doe said .... one year ago." "Yes." "I couldn't help observe as she said it that you didn't as much as flinch." (Prosecutor) "Objection. Counsel is testifying." "I'll be glad to withdraw and to rephrase, your Honor." (Court) "Go ahead, counsel." "Isn't it true, Special Agent, that if she testified falsely under oath, you didn't as much as flinch?" "I was reading something." "You did hear her testimony?" "Yes." "And did it not bother you?" "I don't know what you mean." "Tell the jury whether during the brief recess after Mrs. Doe concluded her testimony you approached the prosecutor or the judge, even to as much as inform them of your belief as to false testimony." "I didn't do anything." "No, nothing. Rather, such falsehood should remain in the minds of the jury so long as they serve an IRS purpose." (Prosecutor) "Objection, he's arguing again, your Honor." (Court) "Sustained." "Did you take an oath to support the *Constitution of the United States?*" "Yes." "As an IRS Special Agent, do you have hopes that the government will win this case, or do you merely have hopes that 'justice be done?'" "I don't know." That 'justice be done,' isn't that a mandate for purpose of protecting the dignity of this court?" (Prosecutor) "Objection. Arguing again, your Honor." (Court) "Sustained." "Are there other falsehoods to which Mrs. Doe testified that you wish to now bring to the attention of the jury before they retire for the evening?" "No, not that I can think of." "Do you promise to advise counsel and the court of any other falsehoods put before the jury that come to your attention?" (Prosecutor) "Objection. Argument." (Court) "Sustained." "Nothing further of this witness at this time, but I reserve right to recall."

The beauty of cross-examination is the leading question, one which leads the witness to the answer. "Is it true that; " "is it not true that [confusing];" "you did ..., correct?" "You did say ..., right?" The cardinal rule of cross-examination is: if you do not know the answer to the question, do not ask it. Recently, on the television news in Phoenix was a hearing concerning whether two dogs should be put to sleep as vicious. The dogs had mauled a little girl about age three who was playing in her yard, and proceeded to drag her across the street. A motorist who had witnessed the incident and chased the dogs away, testified. The dog owner, acting as his own attorney, cross-examined the eye witness. If the court were to find that the dogs were vicious, then they would, under the Arizona statute, be destroyed. The questioning went something like this: "Would you say my two dogs were acting vicious?" "Sir, if I hadn't come upon the scene, your dogs would have eaten that little girl." The witness never answered a "yes" or "no" type question properly, but so what? Damage was done. The dogs were ordered destroyed.

There is another rule that is Major Mac's corollary to the first rule: if you are daring enough and an IRS agent is the witness and you know how the IRS thinks and operates, take a chance. Sometimes the best defense is to be daring with hopes that something good will fall loose. Drop enough eggs in the basket and one is bound to break. At risk is the very real possibility that you will begin to dig yourself a hole which will become only deeper with each question. The corollary rule substantially tempered if you know the inner workings of the *Beast*. Intelligence. *The Special Agent's Handbook. The Revenue Agent's Manual. IRS' Regulations. The Code Book itself.*

In a criminal tax case, typically there are four types of IRS personnel who act as witnesses. They are the Special Agent of the Criminal Investigation Division, the Revenue Agent of the Audit or Examination Division, the Revenue Officer of the Collection Division, and the District Counsel, an IRS attorney. Most often, a special agent or revenue agent will act as a summary witness, summarizing for the jury the evidence and testifying, for example, that the total income was such and such amount, or the total tax due and owing was such and such amount. Most IRS personnel, whatever their title, appear arrogant and haughty on the stand. This is especially true with special agents who should be more confident, but hate finding the tables turned, and become paranoid. *You're mine, Special Agent, come a little closer. That's right, ease your way down the trail. A pungi pit? Oh no, that's just brush across the*

157

trail. But watch to your left over there. Do you see it? Is that a claymore mine hidden in the bushes? No, just looked like it. This foliage [this IRS regulation] is confusing, is it not? Over there, to your right, an M-16 muzzle? No, just a tree branch. Sure looked like one. Why are you sweating? Do you feel well today? And behind you. Yes. When was the last time you looked behind you? You didn't pass up a spider trap, did you? A trap door which might soon lift up suddenly from which emerges that vicious enemy, a written report prepared by you, which contradicts your lies. You're all mine, Special Agent.

Arlene Patnoe was a special challenge for me. This seemingly sweet Doris Day IRS expert wanted to put Randy Knowles, Vietnam Vet Brother, grunt medic, Silver Star winner, father of two little girls, and husband to his humble wife, Linda, behind bars for tax fraud. Over my dead body. Since I could not attack Patnoe by way of aggression or intimidation by shear force as would *Rambo,* I had to be patient and outfox her. I had to be smarter. Clever. Shrewd. But to the jury, it had to appear *Columbo*-like. "Now let me get this straight, Ma'am, I don't quite understand. Perhaps you can help me with ...."

IRS agents love to show off with their knowledge. Enough rope to hang. At issue was whether Randy knowingly and intentionally filed a false form W-4 claiming more allowances than that to which he was entitled. Confusion became a partial defense to the specific intent crime. What better way to show confusion than permit Patnoe, the expert, to give the jury a lecture on forms W-4, exempt status, exemption versus allowances, and anticipated itemized deductions? Anticipated! "You mean to say the taxpayer in deciding what he can claim on his W-4 has a right under the law passed by Congress and under the regulations written by IRS as their interpretation of what Congress intended, to anticipate in the summer of 1979, what final deduction he could actually claim come April 15, 1980?" "Yes."

I loved it. The logic of it all, even though the government had been so illogical. If you are going to claim the man filed a false W-4 in the summer of 1979, why not wait until *after* he has filed his return, *after* you look at what deductions he finally claimed, to determine whether or not he in good faith *anticipated* incorrectly or had intent to break the law? The *Monster* is as stupid as he is powerful.

My plan for the defense of Randy Knowles was this: a three-pronged attack. First, I picked away at Patnoe by asking the right questions to cause her to destroy the prosecution's position that Randy knowingly filed a false W-4. The rules were confusing. How could you intend to violate a law you did not and could not possibly understand? How can the government prove a negative that Randy

158

was not entitled to that which he claimed where the government pulled the plug too soon by bringing the case before Randy filed his return showing that to which he was actually entitled?   Second, I attacked relentlessly the smug Special Agent whom I suspected would and did lie on the stand. Third, the jury would learn of and the prosecution would be surprised by Randy's status as war hero. I confess I overlooked another angle which would have proven perhaps devastating to the prosecutor: Randy's wife, Linda.

Special Agent Chan did the best he could to show Randy an uncooperative criminal. He and a cohort, Robert Jewell, surprised Randy on a Saturday morning as Randy was preparing to leave on a hunting trip, armed with a .45 semi-automatic pistol in a shoulder holster. The Special Agent said Randy was uncooperative, but did answer a few questions such as where he worked and what he did on the side. Randy was in fact entitled to file thirty-six allowances for reason he had numerous anticipated itemized deductions warranting no further withholding for the remainder of the year. (He had also attended a John Law Freeman meeting, a fact never developed by IRS or the prosecutor at trial.) The Special Agent, feeling some desperation, lied and said Randy had said to him, "I know I'm entitled to file thirty-six. My accountant, Sam Bass, told me so." *Ouch.* This hurt our case; Bass would testify he never told Randy such a thing. The truth was: Bass never said it, and Randy never said that Bass said it. Chan was lying, I believed. With intensity I watched the Special Agent's expression. He was lying through his teeth. But how do I prove it? Technically, we did not have to prove anything, but the defendant remained silent at the risk of his own peril. I was mad. I felt we had made points with Patnoe, but now the case was slipping away. I had to totally destroy the agent's credibility or risk conviction for Randy. Otherwise, the jury might believe Chan and conclude that *Randy* was lying!

The courtroom, modern as it was, was designed like an amphitheater. The jury was seated semi-circled in tiered levels at an angle to the defense and prosecution tables. Under Alaska informal rules, unlike most federal courts, I was permitted to use the courtroom rather than be confined behind a lectern.   And, I was not required by Judge Fitzgerald to ask permission to approach the witnesses. Unlike the two prosecutors who had remained at their own will, or due to lack of confidence, behind their table as if trapped, I made full use of the space. An actor on the stage. With Patnoe I had moved from jury to witness, to my table to the jury, Perry Mason style. The closer I got to the jury, which was right up to the hand rail, the closer I could look them in the eye, and as well let them hear more distinctly the variations in the tone of my voice, the reverberations.

Picture now, as you face into the courtroom, the two tables,

159

defense on the left, prosecutor on the right. On the left at an angle facing in, the jury box in three-tiered levels. (Typically a prosecutor's table is closest to the jury; the prosecutor has the burden of proof throughout the trial). On the right, the judge's bench, high above everyone, and beside the bench, on the far right, the witness chair. The court reporter sits in front of the bench, where she can hear well the witness. This left, then, an amphitheater and a walkway from jury box to witness box. (I liked almost as much the antiquated "well" system I discovered in such courtrooms as Richmond, Virginia, in which the witness is in an enclosed box, a "well" in the center of the courtroom directly facing the jury on the right. To me, it should make the witness take the oath all the more seriously, feeling at center stage, as if *he* is the one on trial. And, if he is an agent, examined by me, he is on trial.)

With the stage set, I devised in a moment's notice my plan for the Special Agent. It is what I call the Johnny Carson/Ed McMahon technique. Remember, Johnny announces on *The Tonight Show* a book or directory or article concerning some off-the-wall subject matter and Ed, taunting Johnny, says in raised voice, *"Everything in the world concerning ... is right there in that little booklet. Everything!"* Johnny answers flatly, something like, *"Wrong, Camelbreath."*

Special Agents take great pride in the thoroughness of their investigation and the accuracy of their reports. *Pride cometh before the fall. A man's cause seems just until another man comes to examine him.* The cross-examination of the Special Agent went something like this. "Now, Special Agent, you have testified as I recall, that Randy Knowles told you on that Saturday when you paid him a visit that Sam Bass, Randy's accountant told Randy he could claim thirty-six alllowances?" "Yes, that's what I said." "That's what you said under oath, correct?" "Yes." "Is it still your testimony that Randy said those words?" "Yes." "You're absolutely certain?" "Yes." [The anchor in cement. Changing tone as if to go to another subject.] "By the way, Special Agents are required to prepare a written report in making a recommendation for prosecution." "Yes." "And you did so in this case." "Yes." "And that report contains the most important matters of the case." "Yes." "The most important evidence to be used against the accused." "Yes." "Everything important the government would need to refer to on this case is right there in that report." "Yes." "For example, Randy's W-2 wages are in the report, right?" "Yes." "And Randy's W-4 history is in the report, right?" "Yes." "Those were important matters, right?" "Yes." "Introduced as evidence against Randy, right?" "Yes." "And likewise, an important matter was Randy's statement that you testified to in this case?" "Yes." "In the report, correct?" "Yes." "And that was a very important matter, correct?" "Yes." "And that's why it's in the report?" "Yes." [How could he disagree with any one of these?] [Pause for effect. In combat, when calling in artillery, after bracketing the enemy, the command was fire for effect. Now that I had the witness bracketed, I teased the jury a little, paused and gave the witness, since I am such a nice guy, a chance to retract his statement, which I am confident he won't. If he does, I'll ridicule him relentlessly for making such a gross error] [Slowly, very distinctly with emphasis on each word.] "You're *absolutely certain* it is in the report?" [Remember, he already said one, all important matters go in the report, major premise; two, this was an important matter, minor premise; and ergo three, this must be in the report - conclusion.] "Yes." [Another pause for effect while I ponder. This is an act. I know exactly what I will do next. Peter Falk playing *Columbo*.] "Sir, do you have that report with you in the courtroom today?" [I know he must. If not, I'll have him get it for me.] "Yes, it's at my table." "Would you be so kind as to walk to your table and return to the witness stand with the report?" "Yes." He begins his walk and suspense builds. Now I am treating him like a five year-old. As he does what I ask, everyone, including me, wonders whether Randy's statement will be there. I am confident, yes. If no, I have a contingency plan: where are his hand-written notes; were they destroyed in violation of IRS procedure? "May I see the report?" He does not want to give it up, but if the statement is in there, I will take the wind out of his sail. My cursory review, made in a matter of seconds, reveals no such statement. I know just where to look, and just as I suspected, it is not there! "Well, can you locate the statement and direct me to it?" I hand the report back. "Yes." "You were certain it was there." "Yes, it's here, I'm sure of it." Now, not finding it on initial perusal, he begins to panic. Beads of sweat appear on his forehead. It is time to drive the razor-sharp knife into his back, the one I purchased at the West Point cadet store, one of only 3,000, serial numbered, the blade curved so that it misses the ribs and punctures the lung, air escaping; only air sufficient for a final gasp rather than enough for a cry out for his comrades. I turn my back on him, and slowly walk, looking dead ahead to the jury box, then looking at the wall, not the jury. My voice is the key, not my eyes. I stop and pause. "It's not there, is it?" "No, I can't find it." Seize the moment. Whirling around, rapid voice and pace back to him, I grab the report, hold it in the air, and in an outrage, again raising my voice, state, "It's not in there because it *never was!* It never was there because the words were *never* spoken by Randy!." [Here the prosecutor could object due to my compound question, but it would only cause more attention to the issue, attention he does not need.] "No, he said it. I remember he said it." "You're *positive?"* "Yes, I'm positive. I'm positive he said it." [Now

161

with total disgust] "Just like you were so *positive* it was in the report." He does not answer. He does not have to. He has no answer. He knows it. The jury knows it. Everybody knows it. The jury has discovered a liar. Now it is time not to say "I'm finished with this witness" or "no further questions, Your Honor." But instead I just slowly walk to my table with an air of disgust and sit down. The Special Agent snakes back to his table, totally destroyed.

Chan also testified that he was *sure* he told Randy that Randy could not consider any business losses in determining the number of allowances to which he was entitled. Again, no mention of the statement within Chan's notes and report.

It is noteworthy that the above was not merely drama, it was as much logic. Most folks do not know what a syllogism is, much less know how to apply one. I made use here of two syllogisms. The first demonstrated that the conclusion to be drawn was that Randy's alleged statement should have been in the report. The second was more subtle, but probably more effective due to the subject matter. The second was that since this agent could not be trusted on one matter about which he was so positive, how could he be trusted as to the other? The other, of course, had become the most important issue in the case: whether Randy *really* said that he relied on Bass when Bass testified he had not given Randy any advice.

When defendants testify, they usually give some background concerning their general education, training, and military service. Thus, the prosecutors were not surprised when Russ Nogg began to ask Randy generally about his background. They were lulled into a state of complacency, figuring they would hear a typical, boring litany about how someone joined the service and obtained an honorable discharge. During Randy's testimony, he stated in response to a question about his military service in a matter-of-fact, humble way that he had earned two Silver Stars and two Purple Hearts as a medic in Vietnam. We had rehearsed it enough. The trouble in rehearsing with Randy was that he was so unassuming and humble, it was unnatural for him to mention it without a prodding. Here he was, Randy Knowles, the family man, never before been in trouble, wife and two little girls, no intention of committing a crime, facing time in jail. Slight, glasses and mutton-chop sideburns. His presence was not what you would call imposing. No *Rambo* here. That made it all the more effective. The jury could then conjure up in their minds the image of this shy man risking his life under fire to save lives on the field of battle.

In my closing argument to the jury, I minced no words with respect to the credibility of both Patnoe and Chan (transcript):

Well, it got a little more exciting at the point we had Mrs.

162

Patnoe, the expert. She was qualified, well qualified. And I cross-examined her as to her qualifications, and conceded that she is an expert. Well, we found out she collects delinquent taxes, she secures delinquent returns. She wasn't collecting any or securing any on Randy because there was none to be collected or secured, becaues Randy was a habitual overpayer of his taxes as to withholdings. That's why. And she told about this special W-4 procedure. The large majority weren't entitled to W-4 exempt or a large amount of allowances. Well, there is a small minority. The large majority is not entitled. Where is the small minority? Well, I submit to you, there [pointing to Randy] is the small minority. His name is Randy Knowles. He was entitled, or if he wasn't he sure thought he was. And if he was acting with reckless disregard, gross negligence, that's not enough to convict him.

Well, it got real exciting when I asked her the definition of tax liability, and I led her into the little trap. She said she knew, I said, "You stake your reputation as an expert on it?" And she said, "I know for sure that is the definition." And then later she said, "No, I made a mistake, that's not the definition." Well, remember that point, and remember Mr. Chan, I am going to get to him [pointing] in a minute. Remember those little points when you think about Randy's testimony and when you think about how hard it is to be subject to cross-examination. Okay, I am not priding myself in how well I cross-examined her, and I am not going to compliment the government on how well they did with Randy, because most attorneys can do what we did. So take that into consideration. It's not hard to make a mistake when you are an honest person sworn under oath. It's not hard to be tongue-tied a little bit in your testimony.

Well, she was certain on tax liability, positive, and then she said, "No." And then she said there was a law that said -- now this got into a big issue here, it is an important issue -- and that is, she said there was a law that said you couldn't apply your business loss in determining your amount of allowances. And she never came forth with that law, and we still haven't heard from it from the government. It is not here anywhere. She said there was a law on that, and she quoted some section, and I showed her the regs, how she was wrong, and the code, how she was wrong in her definition.

Well, we heard from Mr. Chan. He didn't know for sure. Now he knew for sure one thing, he knew for sure when he was going to go get his notes that he told Randy he couldn't apply a business loss in determining more allowances. Remember how sure he was, and remember how long it took him looking through hits notes? And when we got to the bottom line, it wasn't in there.

Within a couple of hours, Randy's jury decided it was undecided. The vote was 7 to 5, which way we did not know. It did not matter. The attorneys were called to the judge's chambers where the foreman's note was read: "Hopelessly deadlocked." The prosecutors were taken back by the Silver Stars and Purple Hearts. "Jury nullification," they said cynically. Silver Stars. "No," I insisted. "The guy is innocent and the government and now some jurors still believe otherwise." The judge smiled and declared a mistrial. He said something like, "I think the jury was surprised to hear about the Silver Stars."

Rock flew Peggy and me to the Kenai Peninsula to a small town, Soldotna. At seven o'clock that night, Randy, Rock, Peggy and I were scheduled to speak. With only two hours notice in this small town of only one thousand, there had been assembled a crowd in the public school. Standing room only. There I met Linda and Randy's two little girls. I realized then what a great witness Linda would have made. Totally supportive of Randy, she could have testified about Randy's work habits and their tax returns. The jury, men and women alike, would have loved her. The little girls could have sat on the front row, watching with great interest.

I told the crowd I was disgusted with the *Monster* bringing charges against an American hero and that I was proud to represent Randy, a Vietnam Vet brother. I had high hopes that the prosecutors would see reason to dismiss the counts with prejudice so that we would not have to retry the case, subjecting Randy to a possible prison term. Rock and Peggy gave their typical Christian, patriotic speeches.

The prosecutors agreed to dismissal. One down, two to go.

Next up was Dan Emans and again, cross-examination of Patnoe. That weekend I studied the documents time and again and came up with my best defense: surprise. Dan had been more vocal and IRS would attempt to paint him a rabid tax protestor. Would the Monster expect a technical defense as in Randy, or a constitutional defense as Rock preached? I would deliver neither.

Mid-trial in Randy's case, Rock and I had a confrontation in the hallway during one of the recesses. It reached a climax as we were surrounded by spectators, "When are we going to hear about the *Constitution?* That's what all these Alaska Patriots in Action are here for. All this technical talk about allowances, deductions and anticipated itemized deductions is nothing but government lies. We want the truth." "Rock, I represent Randy and I call the shots. I'm responsible, no one else. If he's convicted, it's on my shoulders. No one tells me how to defend my client. The *Constitution* may be the best defense for others, but not for Randy. That's my opinion. If and when you're charged, you take the Constitutional defense. When it's your neck, you decide. When it's Randy's neck, I decide." Randy stood to the side, a little embarrassed. Rock and I were now encircled like an after-school fight. Peggy saved the day by doing the smart thing. She grabbed Rock's hand and my hand and said, "Let's form a prayer circle." We did. She prayed. Rock and I shut up. (When it came Rock's turn at criminal charges, he would keep his word.)

Although Dan was a teddy bear-type, I could also tell he had some pent-up feelings about IRS. Would he burst on cross by the prosecutor? I hoped not, but with my plan, we would never reach that point. Like Randy, Dan had filed a large number of allowances.

As I expected, Patnoe was really ready for me. Rather than be trapped in proving a negative, IRS copied my technique of using charts to show how many itemized deductions it would have taken for Dan to be entitled for exempt status, daring that we would come forward and claim so many. I did not take the dare. Instead, I made a flanking attack, developing a theme that IRS never put Dan on notice that his form was not correct. Unlike Randy, he received no letter, no second chance. The agents went to talk to him at work, but he was not around. That is not the American way. You first say, "Look buster, stop in the name of the law. What you are doing is wrong and could put you behind bars. Cut it out!"

Having decided on the theme - lack of notice - I repeatedly developed it as each witness took the stand. With the Special Agents who went out to see Dan, I hammered the point home. No contact. No notice. No government evidence of intent. Their intent was that of pure paper conviction based solely on the W-4's filed by Dan. No eye or ear witnesses who would testify that Dan was a tax cheat, tax protestor, or even that he did not like paying taxes. (Who *does* like paying taxes? If you dare complain to your neighbors about the tax system, IRS ears might pick it up and attempt to use it against you. Given that, you can either decide to keep your mouth shut, or if they do come after you, to stick it in their face and argue to the jury that sure, you do not like taxes, who does? And sure you complain about them, who does not?)

At the end of the government's case in chief in U.S. v. Emans, I moved for acquittal on grounds there was lack of sufficient evidence on the issue of knowledge and intent. There was insufficient evidence to as much as take the case to the jury, for under the test a reasonable minded jury could not have concluded based on the evidence presented thus far, that beyond a reasonable doubt Dan acted with intent to violate the law. The judge immediately agreed and dismissed, meaning Dan was again a free man. The standing room only crowd went wild, shouting and coming over the railing, congratulating Dan, Russ and me. Rock and Peggy were there, too. It was like something out of the movies where the underdog prevails in the end. *Jimmy Stewart* in *Mr. Smith Goes to Washington.* Two down, one to go.

In the third case, I had to take the attitude my imagination was not yet exhausted. I was able to do so. It was, evidence-wise, the toughest of the three cases. Patnoe again. Would they expect a technical defense or would they expect that since I knew they might expect a technical defense, I would not give them a technical defense? I let them guess and provided a technical defense, but with new approaches. I left some engineers on the jury purposefully. I would need their help with my application of logic. As it turned out, the jury was more logical than I, and was split, finding Ed not guilty on one count and guilty on the other. It made sense, finally, when I went back to examine the evidence. But in the end, Telles got probation and left for his job in Africa.

Soon after arriving back in Phoenix, Barbara received from Linda, Randy's wife, a beautiful note in which Linda expressed her love and sincere appreciation for Barbara's sacrifice in being without her husband for the salvation of Linda's husband. The home front sacrifice, known so well to both Barbara and Linda. For as Barbara awaited my return from combat duty with the *173rd Airborne Brigade (Separate)*, Linda was "patient and long suffering" awaiting the return of Randy from his tour of duty as combat medic with the *1st Infantry Division.* Reading Linda's prose, I could only think of Randy and what a "boonie rat" team he and I would have made. I was moved by Linda's letter to re-read Randy's Silver Star citations:

9 June 1968 - Republic of Vietnam. For gallantry in action while engaged in military operations involving conflict with an armed hostile force in the Republic of Vietnam: On this date, Private First Class Knowles was serving as a medical aidman with his company during a battalion-minus reconnaissance in force operation nine kilometers east of Lai Khe. At approximately 1300 hours, contact was made with an enemy force, and his unit sustained four casualties. Private First Class Knowles immediately began crawling forward to aid the wounded men who were pinned down by a hail of hostile rounds. With complete disregard for his personal safety, he manuevered from one individual to another, administering first aid as the insurgents' fire struck all around him. Although he was seriously wounded while helping his fellow soldiers, Private First Class Knowles continued to render aid until all were safely evacuated. His extraordinary courage, initiative and determination were instrumental in saving the lives of several of his wounded comrades. Private First Class

Knowles' unquestionable valor in close combat against numerically superior hostile forces is in keeping with the finest traditions of the military service and reflects great credit upon himself, the 1st Infantry Division, and the United States Army. By direction of the President....

1 December 1968 - Republic of Vietnam. For gallantry in action while engaged in military operations involving conflict with an armed hostile force in the Republic of Vietnam: On this date, Specialist Knowles was serving with his company as a medical aidman at Junction City, the battalion night defensive position. At approximately 0300 hours, the friendly encampment was subjected to intense hostile mortar and rocket-propelled grenade fire, followed by a massive ground assault. As soon as he learned that the battalion tactical operations center had received two direct hits by incoming rocket-propelled grenades, Specialist Knowles immediatley left his bunker and ran through the hail of hostile rounds to treat the wounded. After administering first aid to the three casualties at the bunker, he obtained additional medical supplies and ran to the perimeter. With complete disregard for his personal safety, Specialist Knowles braved the relentless enemy fire as he constantly moved about in the open, treating the wounded and organizing evacuation teams. After aiding many of his injured comrades, he returned to the battalion aid station and continued to render aid to the casualties there. Specialist Knowles also assisted in carrying five seriously wounded individuals to medical evacuation helicopters. His extraordinary courage and deep concern for the welfare of his fellow soldiers were major factors in saving the lives of many Americans during the encounter. Specialist Four Knowles' unquestionable valor in close combat against numerically superior hostile forces is in keeping with the finest traditions of the military service and reflects great credit upon himself, the 1st Infantry Division, and the United States Army. By direction of the President....

Randy also received two Purple Heart awards for his combat wounds. IRS had almost succeeded in putting behind bars Specialist Four Randall Knowles for a crime he did not commit. Almost.

Attack the heart by surprise on the headquarters of the enemy for thus he is easily defeated and his nerve center destroyed. Mao Tse-tung

WASHINGTON IRONWORKER   Chapter 9

The Alaska trilogy complete, I had now the confidence level to take on any IRS expert on any technical issue. Although I was helpful, no doubt, for Patnoe's training, she as well assisted me. I assumed I would never run into an agent quite like Patnoe, but each agent presented for me a different type of challenge. I had to size up each witness, and assess their strengths and weaknesses. A few years after the "Anchorage Three," Patnoe was promoted to Special Agent. Her husband also was with IRS and there was a time when she and her husband broke up, she had a boyfriend, and they all made the papers. Apparently, her jealous husband used IRS records and inside information to make things difficult for the boyfriend. But she continued to maintain a high position in the "Patriots Rogue's Gallery," maintained in the office above the gas station. There, Rock and others would post photographs, descriptions and tidbits of information on each of the agents. *Intelligence. Counterintelligence.*

One of the Anchorage district Special Agents was Bob Jewell, who had been involved in the investigation of Knowles, Emans and Telles. He became a laughing stock of the Patriots. Every time we saw him he was in a different disguise, and would yell over, "Hey Bob, how you doing?" He would ignore us and we would just yell louder, whether it was outside, across the street, or in the courthouse corridors, "Hey, IRS Special Agent Bob Jewell, is that you? You look a little different today. You didn't have a beard the last time I saw you." Jewell was indeed a real jewel of an IRS Special Agent. He was always snooping around, but struck me as having the competence of Peter Sellers' *Inspector Clouseau.* I caught him eavesdropping on my client and me in the Anchorage courthouse during the Pazsint trial (Chapter 16). Bob Jewell, *The Pink Panther.* Peter Sellers could have made a great movie about IRS agents, something on the order of *Dr. Strangelove.*

It was not long after "The Anchorage Three" that I received my opportunity to drill into the ground another IRS technical expert. I was thankful to Rock and to Peggy for the common sense attitude they had given me. Now I had a litmus test to be applied to my courtroom question: what would Rock or Peggy ask? How would they ask it?

Bill Hughes, ironworker, was another John Law Freeman seminar attendee and the IRS' next victim. Bill was charged in Yakima, Washington with separate counts of false W-4s. Bill faced several years in jail. Mark McClellan and I would defend. Judge McNichols presided.

Mark succeeded in moving the place of trial to Pasco, Washington, the tri-cities area of Richland, Kennewich and Pasco, where the Snake River meets the Columbia. Bill worked at a power plant and had also been involved in the construction of bridges. He was one of those gutsy guys who swings from girders, hundreds of feet above the ground.

The trouble for Mark and me was that the government suspected Bill had been active with the tax protesters, attending Freeman's meetings. We figured they had utilized undercover surveillance and perhaps had descriptions if not photos on many of the citizens who would dare exercise their *First Amendment* right of association or assembly by attending a meeting led by a controversial figure. We were concerned that the prosecutor would nail Bill on cross-examination, despite our good faith reliance efforts. We needed John Law, who was in prison.

I moved the court for a *subpoena ad testificandum*, a subpoena issued to a prison warden to bring a prisoner to the trial for testimony. I felt we had good grounds, in that we would present the reliance defense by having the jury hear it from the horse's mouth: John Law would testify and explain basically what was presented in the seminar. By this means, we would not have to rely on the defendant's memory and the jury would be able to see the impact a charismatic speaker like John might have. There was legal precedent for this argument, though I suspected judges were concerned that the speaker would so persuade the jury that tax protesters could never be convicted. My analogy was simply this: if an individual was on trial for being a Christian and had been converted through a Billy Graham crusade, would not it make sense to permit him, since he was a "newborn Christian," to bring Billy Graham? Graham would give testimony as to the sermon he preached and the invitation given at the end of the sermon. Impressed perhaps only with my imagination on the analogy, judges had never permitted Freeman to testify. Such was the case in the Hughes trial. Judge McNichols denied my motion, ruling as Judge Fitzgerald had in Marshall's case that John Law's testimony was not relevant. (Ironically, when I argued Marshall before the Ninth Circuit panel of three judges, Judge McNichols was a member of the panel as a visiting district court judge, a very common practice.)

John Law had been convicted in a criminal tax case in which he raised the *First Amendment* as the defense. He urged that his speech was protected where he suggested and even encouraged individuals to stop filing tax returns and file W-4 exempt, thus causing the end to withholding of taxes from paychecks. He was sentenced to a year in prison and had obtained a stay by a Supreme Court Justice pending his petition to the U.S. Supreme Court to hear the case. But the petition *(petition for certiorari)* was denied, meaning the court would not as much as hear the case. John was off to prison.

After serving his prison term, John was charged again for the same activity, where he was acquitted for exercise of his *First Amendment* right. What factual differences were there to the two cases? Virtually none. Oh, yes. Two different judges, two different opinions. *Luck of the draw.*

Mark worked extensively with Bill and came to me with his prognosis. "We've got problems, Mac. I fear Bill will do terribly on the stand. He can't keep his facts straight. He'll come across as elusive despite his honesty. He'll appear to be a dyed-in-the-wool tax protester. Without Freeman's testimony, we've got serious problems. Can we win without Bill taking the stand?" Now the greater burden was on me. It was like the general in WWII who was told by his intelligence officer at a staff meeting that they were surrounded. To his staff and subordinate commanders, the general, unflinching, readily announced his decision: "We attack!"

In that chess game called *trial strategy,* psychology plays a big role as it does in any form of combat. Is that defense attorney acting like he will not call his client just so I think he will not, and then he will surprise me and he will call the client, or is he acting like he will not call his client so I'll think he is *acting* like he will not, but I really believe it's only an act, and believe he will, but then he will not? *Circles have no ends.*

Leaning toward not calling Bill, but not absolutely certain until the time came, we were faced with a dilemma. How much should I attack the government's case? If I attack every inch of the way conceding nothing, then we look silly to the jury when Bill testifies and answers the obvious, what we should have conceded but did not. If an attorney loses the jury's credibility in one area, he does so at the risk of leaping into his closing argument with no credibility. *Can this guy be trusted,* the jury will think.

Mark and I liked Bill. Out of work by time of trial, financially destitute, he was in a real jam. His wife was petrified. Bill had a wife and small children to support, no income on the horizon, and faced a possible jail term. I had often been told by my wife that Mark and I had a two-man *Salvation Army* rather than a law practice. *Send me your downtrodden, your outcasts.*

We had seen no greater outcasts within the legal circles than the tax protesters. "Unpatriotic, communists, greedy, selfish, not willing to pay their fair share, thus shifting to us honest folk an even greater burden: lepers. "Attorneys shied from tax protester cases as hopeless. "Why don't you just plea it out, file your returns and ask

170

for the mercy of the court?" Mark and I liked to see it another way. The ethical responsibility to accept unpopular cases. Had not Clarence Darrow represented the Communists? A Christian had a duty to display the *Boys' Town* philosophy, exemplified by the words made into a song, *He ain't heavy, he's my brother.* Those were the words of a small boy arriving at *Boys' Town* late in the evening, carrying on his back another. Asked if he wanted any help with his load, that was his answer. *It's a long and winding road.*

Add to all of this the extra element: Mark and I simply loved representing the underdog against the bully. *David v. Goliath.* It took David cunning, surprise and one smooth stone to slay the giant. *The Monster.*

For Bill, then, Mark and I developed a combination technical defense. What is tax liability? (Bandwagon defense. Everyone was filing W-4 exempt at the job site.) And burden defense. (How can the government prove beyond a reasonable doubt he had criminal intent?) We were encouraged by the fact that a few construction workers were on the jury, the prosecutor was not vindictive, and the judge seemed fair-minded.

Mark called several bandwagon witnesses, co-workers who testified everyone was filling out W-4 exempt on the hood of pickup trucks at the job site. Word had spread that it was a proper means by which one could handle his tax affairs, especially if it was mid-year and you had, like Jim Friend, a lot of deductions from your dragging up from union hall to union hall in search of work. Construction workers often had to move across state lines in search of work, incurring high travel and away from home living expenses.

In my opinion, our best witness was the IRS W-4 coordinator from the state of Washington, flown in from Seattle. *The expert.* This man was the government's expert in the entire district on W-4s. Who can file exempt and under what circumstances. Although he was at the prosecutor's table throughout the trial, he was too confident to realize he was being set up with all the government witnesses. He would be soon faced with a no win situation, but too stupid to realize it. Blinded by his own ego. *We are surrounded. We attack.*

Under the old form for claiming exemption from withholding, the W-4E, the form stated at the top, "Exemption from withholding (of federal income tax) for use by employees who incurred no tax liability in 1974 and anticipate no tax liability for 1975." The employee would sign, "Under penalties of perjury I certify that I incurred no tax liability for federal income tax for 1974 and that I anticipate that I will incur no liability for federal income tax for 1975." The form was revised in May of 1977. No longer was form W-4E utilized. Instead, the new W-4 form encompassed allowances

171

to be claimed as well as exempt with line 3 stating: "I claim exemption from withholding (see instructions)." Enter "exempt." Again, the employee would have to sign "Under the penalties of perjury I certify that the number of withholding exemptions and allowances claimed on the certificate does not exceed the number to which I am entitled. If claiming exemption from withholding, I certify that I incurred no liability for federal income tax for last year and that I anticipate that I will incur no liability for federal income tax for this year." Within the instructions, employees were told:

Avoid over withholding or under withholding. By claiming the number of withholding allowances you are entitled to, you can fit the amount of tax withheld from your wages to your tax liability .... You may claim exemption from withholding of federal income tax if you had no liability for income tax for last year and you anticipate you will incur no liability for income tax for this year. You may not claim exemption if your joint or separate return shows tax liability before the allowance of any credit for income tax withheld. If you are exempt, your employer would not withhold federal income tax from your wages....

Many employees received only the top portion, without the instructions. Even those reading the instructions had difficulty in understanding what must have been written by a Philadelphia lawyer. To make matters more confusing, there is no reference on the 1040 concerning tax liability. What does it mean? If you owe someone, you have a liability. If you do not owe them, that is, they owe you money by way of a refund, then how could *you* have a liability?

In Bill's case, the government called an IRS service center representative to introduce Bill's prior returns. She did not know what tax liability was. "Not my department." I asked her to examine the returns and tell the jury where it appeared on the returns. "It's not here." Again, the government charged too early. With no 1979 return filed yet, there was no evidence of actual claimed itemized deductions. "What deductions can Bill claim for 1979?" "I don't know, but he claimed very little for 1978." "Would that prevent him from claiming more for 1979?" "No."

Likewise, the employer's bookkeeper did not know what tax liability was. "It's not within my job description." She handled thousands of form W-4s, but merely processed them. She did not care what the W-4 said. A paper shuffler.

Even Bill's prior accountant, who had tax return experience, testified, but did not know what tax liability meant. "I'd rather not say. It's really not part of my work."

We were now up to the last witness: the expert who came all the way from Seattle, the Revenue Agent. An eager beaver, the agent could not wait to show off his knowledge. *All these dummies. No wonder the government had to fly me from Seattle to this arid, hick town of Pasco, Washington.*

Before I delved into tax liability, I reinforced our bandwagon defense. The revenue agent had the knowledge I needed. "Sir, you are the W-4 coordinator for the entire state, correct?" "A big undertaking, yes." "Lot's of problem W-4s?" "Yes, over four thousand W-4 exempts currently." "That's right, four thousand. It must be a lot of work for you?" "Yes, but we handle it." "Bet you do, bet you do. You no doubt are the expert." "Yes, I think I am." "I mean, can you think of *anybody* that knows more about W-4s in the State of Washington than you?" "No." *You can lead a horse to water, but you can't make him drink. This guy is dying of thirst. He can't wait to show us how smart he really is.*

He had testified on direct examination by the prosecutor about how in his expert opinion, Bill was not entitled to exempt because he did not meet the first test: he had a tax liability for the prior year, meaning he paid some taxes even though he had received a refund. It was time for a homespun analogy. Again *Columbo.*

"Now let me make sure I get this straight. In you're opinion, Bill didn't qualify for exempt when he filed exempt because he had in fact a tax liability for 1978. Correct?" "Yes sir." "You know that from his 1978 return?" "Yes. Line 54 shows a tax." "Tell the jury whether it says on that line 'tax liability'." "No." "Now, tell the jury whether it says anywhere on that form 1040 tax liability." Pause while he looks. "No." "Anywhere on there does it say 'liability?'" "No." "So when Bill filled out his W-4, he was supposed to go to his 1978 return and find something that is not there, namely tax liability?" "No, it's on there, line 54." "Total tax." But where does it say a 'liability?'" "The moment he earned the money, it became a liability." "Well, first, let's get this straight. You admit that it doesn't say 'liability'." "Correct." "Thank you sir. Now, you mean to say if a man fills out a return in April 15, 1979 for 1978 and it shows a refund of $1,000, he has a 'liability' to the government?" "No, he *had* a liability." "How so?" "If he had a tax due of $1,000 but had $1,200 withheld, he had a liability of $1,000 and a refund of $200 because he overwithheld by $200." "I see, but when did he *incur* the $1,000 'liability'?" "The instant he received the money." "How would he know he had a 'liability' the instant he received the money." "He would know. Everyone pays some tax." "Everyone?" "Well, most people." "But not everyone, you might have sufficient deductions to offset your income, right?" "Yes." "A millionaire might pay no tax, right?" "It's possible." "And all this about instant tax liability, that *of course* is all explained on the form W-4 instruction form?" "No." "Looking here it says *'avoid over withholding and under withholding.'* That's what Congress wants us to do, right?" "Beg your pardon?" "The *law,* Congress passed the law, right?" "Yes." "And under the law, law-abiding citizens are to avoid over withholding and avoid under withholding." "Right." "And Bill Hughes over here, he didn't do it the way Congress wanted him to last year." "I don't understand." "Well, he was due a refund, meaning he over withheld. He's got a big refund. He messed up, I suppose." "No, we don't care if he over withheld." "Oh, I see. Only if he *under* withheld you get concerned. Your money, not his, right?" "That's correct."

"Now, getting back to this tax liability, can you tell us what it means?" "Yes." [He's now very excited.] "Great. At long last, what is the definition of tax liability?" "I'll have to read it from the regulations." "You mean it's not on the W-4 form?" "Right." "It's not on the W-4 instructions?" "Right." "It's not on the form 1040?" "Right." "It's not within the instructions for the form 1040?" "Right." "It's not within the Internal Revenue Service Code as passed by Congress?" "Right." "But it is in the regulations?" "Correct." "And in fact, that's the *only* place it's located, right?" "Yes." "And those regulations, those are those huge volumes that have thousands of sections?" "Yes." "And do you have one of those with you?" "It's over at my desk." "Would you please get that?" As he walked to the table to get this volume about three inches thick, I looked down, looking at my Defendant's Requested Instruction No. 34, that I hoped the court would approve and give to the jury as the law, "You're instructed that the word liability is not defined anywhere in the Internal Revenue Code and the following is the dictionary definition, a) the quality or state of being liable; b) something for which one is liable, such as an amount that is owed, whether payable in money, other property, or services." This was in Webster's Third New International Dictionary, unabridged, copyright 1971. In my Instruction No. 5, I had the Random House College Dictionary definition, "monies owed, debt or pecuniary obligation (opposed to assets)." Now we were going to hear IRS' *simple* definition.

"Do you have it there, sir?" "Yes." "Well, can you tell me the definition of tax liability for the purpose of the form W-4 where one states he incurred no tax liability for the prior year?" "Well, it's rather long and I'd rather just read it." "That would be just fine, sir." He proceeds to read, including the commas, semi-colons, periods, parenthesis, et al.

Section 31 point 3402 parenthesis small n parenthesis, dash one Employees incurring no tax liability period.

174

Notwithstanding any other provision of this sub part an employer shall not deduct and withhold any tax under chapter 24 upon a payment of wages made to an employee after April 30, 1970 if there is in effect with respect to the payment a withholding exemption certificate furnished to the employer by the employee which contains statements that parenthesis a parenthesis the employee incurred no liability for income tax imposed under sub dash title A of the Code for his preceding taxable year semi-colon and parenthesis b parenthesis the employee anticipates that he will incur no liability for income tax imposed by subtitle A for his current taxable year period. For purposes of section 3402 parenthesis small n parenthesis and this section comma an employee is not considered to incur liability for income tax imposed under subtitle A if the amount of such tax is equal to or less than the total amount of credits against such tax which are allowable to him under part roman numeral IV of subchapter A of chapter 1 of the Code comma other than those allowable under section 31 or 39 period." [By this time, some jurors are giggling; the judge suppressing a smile.] "For purposes of this section comma an employee who files a joint return under section 6013 is considered to incur liability for any tax shown on such return period. An employee who is entitled to file a joint return under such section shall not certify that he anticipates that he will incur no liability for income tax imposed by subtitle A for his current taxable year if such statement would not be true in the event that he files a joint return for such year comma unless he filed a separate return for his preceding taxable year and anticipates that he will file a separate return for his current taxable year period.

Now, some jurors are laughing out loud and the judge is smirking. I keep a serious face, biting the inside of my lip. "Sir, is that what an *ironworker* is to understand when he fills out a Form W-4 and claims W-4 exempt?" "I don't understand the question." Now more forcefully. "Sir, when an *ironworker* like *Bill Hughes* fills out at the job site on the hood of a pickup truck a form W-4 exempt, stating under *penalties of perjury* that he incurred no tax liability for the prior year and anticipates no tax liability for the current year, is what you just read as to the definition of tax liability what *he* is to *understand* at the time he signs that W-4 exempt form?" "Yes." The jury watches and listens in disbelief.

"I notice, sir, after the definition, some examples contained within the regulation, and the second example, a simple example showing a tax liability of $1,630 and income tax withhold of $1,700. It says, does it not, 'Although A received a refund of $70 due to income tax withholding of $1,700, he may not state on his exemption certificate that he incurred no liability for income tax imposed by subtitle A for 1970.' Is that what it says?" "Yes, that's correct." "A simple example, right?" "Yes." "Now go back to the W-4 instruction form. Do you see the example anywhere?" "No." "Is IRS in the business of helping people or confusing them?" "Helping them." "Any reason why a simple example such as that couldn't be contained on the W-4 instruction form?" "No, not that I know of."

I sat down, the jury still giggling to themselves. I did not crack a smile. I did not find it very funny. I was still mad. They want to put my client in jail.

Bill was found not guilty on all counts. In October of 1979 IRS had revised their form W-4, probably because of the several W-4 wins. Now the form stated "I claim exemption from withholding because (see instructions and check boxes below that apply)." The first box stated "Last year I did not owe any federal income tax and had a right to a full refund of ALL income tax AND [the second box] this year I do not expect to owe any federal income tax and expect to have a right to a full refund of ALL income tax withheld." If both boxes apply, then the signer is instructed to enter exempt. Our public servants, burning some midnight oil.

In response to my letters of complaint concerning IRS' proposed new W-4 form, which requires not only a Philadelphia lawyer but a CPA to figure it out, I received in May of 1981 the following response from Arizona Senator Barry Goldwater:

> Thank you for sharing with me your objection on legal grounds to the Internal Revenue Service's revised rule limiting withholding exemption claims. There are really two issues here.
>
> First, there is a legal one regarding lack of authority, which is being strongly pressed on the IRS. Second, we get to whatever merits the changed rule may have. Now, the IRS claims that any taxpayer can still claim any number of exemptions that is in reasonable bounds, but they say 99 or 100 exemptions is outside the ball park.
>
> Whatever the outcome, the recent taxpayers' revolt have demonstrated more clearly than anything else the enormous surge of public opinion for tax cuts. I am working actively to achieve sizeable tax reductions including tax indexing so that taxpayers will not rise into higher tax brackets simply because of inflation. In other words, the current ruckus would have done the country a lot of good by resulting in tax relief.

No such luck.

God is always with the strongest battalion. Frederick the Great

TEXAS PROFESSOR	Chapter 10

It was inevitable that the foreign triple trust would come to the center of attention in my practice, and in my life, personally. Little, however, did I ever expect the impact it would make on both, with the result an economically viable law firm and lasting friendships nation-wide. Not unlike an army leapfrogging from one military objective to another, absorbing, as does the amoeba the advantages of territory gained, *MacPherson & McCarville* developed from a firm of what IRS called "tax protest lawyers" in 1980 to a well-honed *Special Forces A-Team* of six lawyers in 1989, with two of the six certified tax specialists. (The popular television show, *The A-Team,* borrows its title from the Special Forces [Green Beret] concept of the twelve man A-Team. I was, in 1971-73 an A-Team commander.) The rapid growth of our firm in an age of fierce competition among lawyers was due in large part to the following factors: hard work (hours and effort), vision, seizing the initiative and exploiting the opportunity, rising to the occasion, luck, and the case of *U.S. v. Karl Dahlstrom,* which I would spend three months, off and on, trying in Seattle, Washington. My client and four of his "lieutenants" were charged in the first case in the United States in which the government attacked in a multi-defendant indictment and by conspiracy count the use of the "foreign triple trust" for tax avoidance. *Evasion,* the government called it. Messrs. Karl Dahlstrom, Bruce Ripley, Hy Conley, Dave Morris, and Gaze Durst were charged with conspiracy to defraud the United States by frustrating the purposes of the IRS and, in numerous counts, substantive counts as they are called, of aiding and abetting in the preparation and filing of false tax returns. It was the returns of members of the defendant organization, the American Law Association (ALA), and its spin-off, the American Law Education Society (ALES), members of which had filed returns and taken substantial deductions in conformity with the ALA program.

Having been through the gauntlet - West Point, Airborne, Ranger, Infantry, Special Forces, and Vietnam - I have not since been low on self-esteem nor confidence. I had not only made it through these confidence courses a survivor, I had always done well and even excelled. An *over achiever,* they call it. Rarely have I maintained self-doubts, subscribing to the principle of "power of positive thinking." I am, after all, to my clients priest, confident, and most often *bodyguard.* Bodyguard, no doubt, is my most important role for my chosen profession has been "the profession of arms." Not literally, of course, as in the armed services, but no doubt as trial lawyer, litigator, challenger to IRS abuse and excesses, I am engaged in conflict. Combat on a daily basis. As I hear facts from my clients and potential witnesses, I visualize trial exhibits - charts, just as in Vietnam as I viewed the terrain from a helicopter I would visualize topographical maps, routes of march and ambush sites.

I think, for the most part, linearly by time lines, either horizontal or vertical. Two dimensional matrixes. Sometimes three dimensional. I automatically transpose that which I hear into battle plans: strategy, tactics, avenues of approach or retreat, intermediate objective, final objective and counter-attack. I am without apology concerning my military background. Background? Who am I kidding? I walk, talk, eat and sleep military. I *am* military. It is in my blood. I have been a member of the profession of arms since first grade, and I left active duty with no regret due to boredom, a lack of combat, only to take up a new banner, not that of crossed rifles, *Infantry, The Queen of Battle,* but of the *Constitution* and the rights and interests of my clients, who are exposed and threatened on all flanks.

Command time. The essence of service for the infantry officer is command time. Platoon leader, company commander, battalion commander, brigade commander, division commander. By age 24, with only two years of active duty, I had commanded two out of five. In combat! Spoiled. Because I had served in Vietnam as a company commander for six months, that was, by Department of Army standards, equivalent to eighteen months command time stateside. Another ticket punched in my career pattern. (Aviators were found to be at a disadvantage, spending combat years commanding an aircraft of a few men as compared to 150 to 200 troops organized in a combat unit in Vietnam known as the company or squadron.)

With command time served, I was eligible upon my return from Vietnam in 1969 to teach ROTC at the University of Cincinnati, despite the fact that I had not as much as attended the Infantry Advanced Course. Spoiled, then, by all the responsibility and thrill of *combat company commander,* I was being asked, I visualized, by my Army superiors, to be patient. "Good job, Captain MacPherson, as company commander. Now we would like you to sit at this desk, go through more schooling, make major in five or ten years, serve as a battalion command staff officer, and, if you prove yourself, then we will put you on the list for battalion command. That, of course, will be after you reach the rank of lieutenant colonel. This will only take about 15 years." *Fifteen years! Meanwhile, I command a desk, go back to school, and be assistant to the assistant something. I've already been in school 16 - 1/2 years of my 25, or 66 percent. Someday, after battalion and brigade command, I might make general. That's only 25 years away. A quarter of a century!*

Never one big on patience, I decided to do something different. During my second tour in Vietnam, I had been tempted to extend again but I could feel, due to the climate and diet, that my body was becoming weakened. Nineteen months with one month break stateside. And dare I press my luck another six months with the boobie traps? Civilian employment in Southeast Asia as an engineer was a second temptation, but first I must complete my service obligation of at least two more years. My real dream was *to fly*. In combat. Gladly, I would have agreed to another Vietnam tour or two, had Uncle Sam been willing to train me as a pilot. Hueys, Cobras, Sky Raiders, even a Bird Dog Scout plane, though I fancied myself of the fighter-pilot mentality. *The right stuff. The eye of the tiger.* I did not want to just transport men and equipment or recon by air. *Shoot, move* and *communicate* is what I had been taught in the Infantry. Now I wanted to fly through the air, mostly shooting and moving. "Charlie Six, this is Sandy One. About one zero mikes [minutes] from your vacation haven and we got goodies for the gooks. Where you want them, ole buddy? We can give you time on target of three zero mikes, then we gotta tank up. Our little goodies for the gooks include hot stuff [napalm] and five zero mike [50 mm cannon)] See you soon, ole buddy. Prepare to pop smoke."

Without the 20/20 eye sight required of pilots for all branches of the service, I was destined to become a courtroom kamikaze. "Yes, sir, your Honor, I realize you can, if you choose, hold me in contempt and order me incarcerated, but I submit to you the following: if my conduct is as bad as you would have the record read, then my client is without effective assistance of counsel, an issue he may want to raise on appeal; and if, in fact, the jury does not see things his way, three judges may well agree with his position and you will be faced with retrial of this case." The judge whipsawed (ambushed) throttles down by the thought of a new trial granted by the court of appeals. My position, of course, is not without solid basis.

Seasoned bodyguard.

But, Karl Dahlstrom was not shopping in 1981, when we met, for a bodyguard, for he had done pretty well, or so he thought, as his own lawyer. Of course, his actions had cost him a federal indictment and a possible maximum sentence of over thirty years in jail plus over $100,000 in fines. *So wadda wanna do, make a federal case out of it?* It was Lincoln who said, "An attorney who represents himself has a fool for a client." ALA membership was estimated by the government to be from 600 to 800 members, most of whom had paid from $2,000 to $12,000 for ALA membership and the ALA program of the foreign triple trust. At least six million dollars had been traced.

For Karl, the state attorney generals had not as much as ruffled his feathers. A college professor, Karl was inspired, as was I, by a non-attorney, Norman Dacey, who had written a book *How to Avoid Probate.* I read it in 1973, well before law school, and had even used Dacey's forms to set up my own trust. Presented by Dacey is the simple theory of the *inner vivos* or living trust, by which individuals in most states can avoid probate. The theory is this: you can place all of your personal and real property into a living trust and name yourself as trustee with your spouse as successor trustee and children over 18 or a friend or family member as second successor trustee. The trust is a revocable living trust, meaning that you can change your mind at any time and revoke the trust. Beneficiaries of the trust are your wife, with successor beneficiaries children equally. You, as trustee, hold only legal title, but the beneficiaries hold beneficial interest. At the instant of your death, the property under the trust is not part of your probate estate for reason that you, as trustee, not personally, hold title for the benefit of the beneficiaries. Thus, it is not included in your probate estate and there is no delay or expense associated with any property that is covered by the trust. At the instant of your death, the trust evaporates with title to the beneficiary because now your spouse, who is named beneficiary, becomes trustee, and without a separation between legal ownership and beneficial ownership, the trust cannot exist. *Poof.* It evaporates.

As Dacey points out in his book, which has sold over 100,000 copies, lawyers typically will *not* advise such an arrangement because they want to rake in the probate fees. In many states, lawyers charge a percentage as high as 12% of the gross estate to probate it. Typically, to probate an estate means the filing of much paperwork by the lawyer's secretary and a couple of visits by the lawyer to the courthouse.

Based upon his research, Karl by 1977 had written *How to Avoid Probate, Gift, Inheritance and Estate Taxes, Etc.* and quoted in Chapter 2, "What Really Happens When a Person Dies," from articles appearing in the *Dallas Morning News, Business Week, Reader's Digest* and *Time.* In Chapter 4, "A Few in the Law Profession Speak Out," Karl quoted from *Los Angeles Times, Money,* and *Forbes* articles. One lawyer, Leo Cornfeld from Huntington, New York, wrote in *Money Magazine* in 1973, "Fees for handling estates often bear no relationship to the amount of time spent by the lawyer on behalf of the estate. This is a real racket in probate. It is a lot easier to exact an enormous fee from a dead man's estate than from a living client.... Courts and bar associations rebuke lawyers who try to change the deplorable system." (Is it any wonder that the vast majority of bar associations do not print a public service publication entitled 'How to Avoid Probate?' Lawyers are not about to pay fees to an organization which would promote a program robbing them of fees.)

Missouri was the first state to attack Karl, and an order was entered enjoining him from holding seminars there and giving advice concerning estate planning. Not chagrined, Karl cared little, for he had accepted a position as Professor of Mechanical Engineering at Texas A&M and had moved to Bryan, Texas. There he continued to promote the concept. Again he was sued, this time by the Texas Bar Association, a suit ending in a stalemate. They claimed he was practicing without a license.

"If attorneys would mislead us regarding probate and trusts, what other secrets lie within those dusty legal volumes," Karl queried. He learned of the Massachusetts Business Trust, or the Pure Trust Organization, and from that developed a system of tax avoidance by means of the Foreign Triple Trust. Between 1978 and 1981, Karl would conduct seminars for businessmen, CPA's and attorneys throughout the country, who would pay up to $12,000 for his packet of information and consultations. In addition, he preached the litany of tax protest ideas to which I had been exposed, but in a professional manner, quoting from the cases. The IRS hates nothing worse than the truth as long as it does violence to the taxation system based upon "voluntary compliance." Arm the people with knowledge and the government has problems. Remove the veil of intimidation and fear evaporates. Worse yet, people get downright cantankerous, making bold moves, confident in their new found knowledge. Karl to the IRS was becoming *dangerous*.

Karl would cite that often-cited case of *Gregory v. Helvering* , 55 S.Ct. Rpt. 266 (1935), that the legal right of the taxpayer "to decrease the amount of what otherwise would be his taxes or altogether avoid them by means which the law permits cannot be doubted." Within the "Taxpayer's Legal Defense" section of the ALA notebook provided to its members, Karl quoted from the Seventh Circuit in the case of *U.S. v. Dickerson*, 413 F2.d 1111 (7th Cir. 1969), "Only the rare taxpayer would be likely to know that he could refuse to produce his records to IRS agents." Karl included a copy of a UPI article from Memphis, Tennessee in which a tax lawyer was quoted as saying, "The worst mistake is to be cooperative [with the IRS] hoping the investigator will go easy on you. Never cooperate. What the taxpayer doesn't know is that the agent has taken an oath to overcome any love he might develop with the taxpayer during the course of any investigation. The worst thing a taxpayer can do is to be too cooperative. That can get him indicted." And, of course, Karl recited protection afforded by the *Fifth Amendment* as contained in *Maness v. Meyers*, 95 S.Ct. 585 (1969) and *Kastigar v. U.S.*, 406 U.S. 441 32 L.Ed.2d 212 92

S.Ct. 1653 (1972), in which the U.S. Supreme Court reaffirmed the principle that the privilege against self-incrimination can be asserted "at any proceeding, civil or criminal, administrative or judicial, investigatory or judicatory." *The truth.* How could IRS deal with truth? Based on his legal findings, Karl developed the thirty-question letter to be used by ALA members in response to a request for information by an IRS auditor. Shift roles. Taxpayer became *inquisitor.* Turn the tables, stick it in their face. The battle lines were drawn.

Meanwhile, I was struggling defending those alleged to be "rabid tax protesters" winning some, losing some. A client exposed to me the ALA program and I reviewed it in detail. The taxpayer forms, through a foreign creator in the Turks & Caicos Islands or Belize or some other "tax haven country," a foreign trust organization (FTO) number one. Property is placed in this trust for which the taxpayer receives units of beneficial interest. FTO No. 1 becomes trustee of FTO No. 2 and FTO No. 2 becomes trustee of FTO No. 3. The taxpayer does business with his FTO No. 2 and pays for services such as "consulting." This causes for the taxpayer a business deduction taken on the return. FTO No. 2 then has business dealings with FTO No. 3 to the end that the money eventually winds up in FTO No. 3. As a non-resident alien not doing business in the U.S., FTO No. 3 has *no* filing requirement and gifts or loans to the taxpayer money. Thus, the circuitous route. FTO No. 2, because it is receiving money from a U.S. source but is a non-resident alien, files with the Philadelphia Service Center a form 1040 NR, listing receipts, but also showing no tax liability due to expenses to FTO No. 3. Taxpayer *in substance* controls all transactions.

Phoenix attorney Steve Allen, I was told, was offering the program for $12,000. It was 1980 and time for me to consider a business entity or pay the tax man dearly. Trust or the traditional professional corporation? As much as the ALA program sounded technically correct, I was too cynical from my exposure to bureaucracy to believe that the IRS and the federal courts would ever accept it. If it could work for Dahlstrom and his ALA members, it could work for every businessman, thus cutting off substantial revenues to the public coffers. I had read enough appellate cases in which the courts interpreted Congress' intent, meaning the court *re-wrote* the law. Also, I saw immediately the attack the government would likely launch: *substance over form.* What was the FTO No. 2 *really* providing the taxpayer? And, what was FTO No. 3 *really* providing FTO No. 2? In theory, I felt it should work, *if* in fact there were real services to be provided. But under a typical scenario, be it a doctor, dentist or lawyer, what offshore activity really existed? Besides, as a guerilla warrior, I was not about to expose my flanks, allow the government to pick the battlefield. *Discretion is the better part of valor.* I chose the corporate form of business.

When I was a boy, we had a family doctor, Dr. Karman. He brought my mother and all of her children into the world. Plain Dr. Karman. Not Dr. Karman, M.D. P.C., meaning professional corporation. A perusal today of the yellow pages under doctor, lawyer, CPA, psychologist or psychiatrist reveals the business form for the professional: the corporation. Under the corporate concept, a single professional or several professionals together can form a corporation and reap tax advantages. The pension plan is but one method under which the professional deposits from the corporation to a pension plan a nice chunk of what would be taxable if there was no corporation. *Inc. yourself!* The doc now wears three hats: individual, corporate president, and trustee of the pension plan. So long as his transactions are arms-length at full market value, he can do business with himself and legitimately and legally reap the tax benefits. If there were not advantages, why all the PC's in the phone book?

I recall reading an article in the *National Law Journal* in the early '80s which described how a lawyer could purchase a new $18,000 Porsche automobile for in effect nothing after taking into consideration all the tax advantages. First, the investment tax credit. Second, the lawyer would borrow from his own pension plan and pay the plan interest, a personal write-off. One pocket to the other. And on and on and on. (Tax reform in more recent years has decreased but not eliminated the Inc. advantages.)

So, instead of calling Steve Allen for an appointment, I remained on the high ground, followed the ridge line, and paid a pension attorney $2,000 to Inc. me and set up my pension plan. (Now that Mac had a corporation, Mac as President had to find a lawyer to work for the corporation. After advertising and lengthy interviews, President Mac decided the best attorney in town for President Mac's corporation was Mac. At the interview, Mac accepted President Mac's offer and Mac was hired. President Mac and Mac had agreed upon a salary and each year around Christmas time, President Mac calls Mac into his office and counsels him concerning his performance in the past year and awards, if President Mac chooses, a bonus to Mac. Mac keeps President Mac happy and President Mac keeps Mac happy. President Mac decided to make Kirk McCarville Vice President and President Mac and Vice President Kirk decided Kirk would be good for the corporation and hired Kirk. Once in a while, Mac screws up and is called to the carpet by President Mac. But overall, the relationship has been a good one and the corporation has succeeded, adding additional attorneys hired by President Mac and Vice President Kirk.)

For years the IRS contested the one-man professional

corporation. A "sham," they called it. "Substance controls over form," they said. IRS kept losing the court battles and ultimately conceded. Business purposes aside from tax advantages are, as we all know, served by incorporating. For example, a corporation will be on everyone's mailing list for receipt of a corporate credit card. *Holiday Inn* offers corporate discounts to its corporate guests. "Good evening, President Mac, will that be cash or charge?" "American Express Gold Credit Card. See, it says President. Your corporate discount, please." *Ad infinitum.*

The pension plan must provide benefits to all employees, thus it was not long before innovative lawyers decided how to side-step the requirement. If dentists A, B and C had a corporation with five employees, the five would have to share in the profits by way of pension plans. Idea. A, B and C, instead of practicing as the ABC Corporation, formed a partnership between A, Inc., B, Inc., and C, Inc. The partnership, rather than the corporation, hired the employees. With no other employees of A Inc., B Inc., and C Inc., the profits (pension plan benefits) flowed 100% to President A, President B and President C. IRS challenged and lost in the famous case of *Kiddie v. Commissioner.* This caused Congress to change the law. Substance versus form? Not miffed, innovative lawyers decided again no employees by way of leasing the labor force from an employee leasing company. Again, Congress changed the law. *"The beat goes on...."*

What then does a P.C. have to do with *U.S. v. Dahlstrom?* A lot. Dahlstrom's program differed little on the substance v. form issue, except that professionals with a P.C. pay taxes on personal income (wages), whereas Dahlstrom's followers theoretically could go tax-free. Ironically, the counts listed in the Dahlstrom indictment were those of professionals who had paid taxes and filed returns, only taking, as the government would claim, overstated deductions by way of their payments for consulting services to the FTO No. 2. The Honorable Barbara Rothstein, former Washington State Assistant Attorney General and a Carter appointee, would preside. Her husband: Dr. Rothstein, DDS, PC.

I had another theory about the government's attack on Dahlstrom. Although he posed a threat to the collection of revenues by way of his providing to the professionals tax avoidance or even elimination through the use of FTO's, there were but so many professionals who could afford or were willing to pay the $12,000 membership fee. And, considering the forces of supply and demand, it was likely that the fee would go up just as it had from its original level of $2,000. No, the real threat Dahlstrom presented for IRS was an *informed public.*

Dahlstrom, unlike most attorneys and accountants, was telling taxpayers they had *rights,* rights they could legally utilize to thwart

184

IRS attempts to intrude into their personal and business lives. By exercise of these rights, the citizens would feel good about the exercise and IRS would be stymied. Because Dahlstrom was reaching the professional, this presented for the government a potential for the ripple effect. *The snowball.* Imagine, if you will, an individual who visits his dentist for a six-month checkup and is looking low. "Problem with your tooth?" the dentist inquires. "No, not at all," the patient answers. "It's just that when I finish here, I've got to be downtown to the federal building at 1 p.m. with all my books and records for the past three years. IRS audit. I got a letter in the mail a couple of weeks ago." Interested now, the dentist offers, "Didn't you know? Audits are voluntary, not mandatory. You have rights concerning that audit. You don't have to go if you don't want to. The *Constitution of the United States* says so, as well as Congress. Here, let me pull from my file what I used with great success: the thirty question letter."

Doctors, dentists, lawyers, Indian Chiefs, captains of industry are all in a position to influence patients, clients, business associates, and employees. The government cannot afford that the "cat be out of the bag." If citizens knew of their rights, they just might, with encouragement by the professionals, start exercising them.

Although for many years individuals have utilized tax havens, offshore trusts, and other romantic devices toward the end that they could reap the benefit of tax avoidance or even evasion, Dahlstrom was the first case in which the government litigated a conspiracy case with multiple defendants in an effort to shut down on the flow of funds offshore or alternatively, as in the case of Dahlstrom, the use of offshore entities with the claimed tax benefits onshore. Under ALA's program, money need not even leave the continental United States. Bank accounts were set up locally for the various FTO's.

Use of offshore banks to hide money from the government was highlighted by *60 Minutes* years ago, in the famous *Castle Bank Caper Case.* In that case, it was suspected that many U.S. citizens were squirreling away in the Castle Bank located in the Bahamas huge amounts of money and failing to pay tax on it. It was further suspected that the users of the Castle Bank included prominent attorneys and movie stars. The problem for IRS, considering Bahamas' bank secrecy law, was how to get the names of those who maintained an account at Castle Bank.

At the time, tax filers were required to check a box on their form 1040 as to whether or not they maintained any foreign bank account. IRS suspected that many had lied on the form by checking the box "no," when in fact they had an account at Castle Bank.

IRS' investigation led to information that one of the Castle Bank officers would periodically visit Miami where he would do banking business. With him he carried a briefcase. IRS felt the best way to find out the names of the individuals was to steal the contents of the briefcase. This, of course, would be a crime. So, instead of committing a crime, IRS hired agents provacateur. A private investigator was hired to assist in the crime and he in turn hired a prostitute who would befriend the bank officer and lure him to her apartment. While the bank officer and the woman were engaged in pleasantries (who says sex has nothing to do with taxes?), IRS hired a locksmith who entered the motel room of the banker and upon entrance also was paid to open the locked briefcase. IRS agents took the contents of the briefcase down to the IRS office, copied all the papers, and returned them, the bank officer none the wiser.

With this evidence illegally seized, IRS learned of U.S. citizens who maintained accounts with Castle Bank. They then checked the names against the tax returns to see if anyone had checked "no" in answer to the question regarding a foreign bank account. Mr. Payner, who had an account at Castle Bank but had checked the "no" box, became the government's victim.

Payner's attorney, of course, raised illegal search and seizure upon discovery of the method by which the IRS had gained the evidence. Violation of the *Fourth Amendment*, he urged. In addition, he moved to dismiss for governmental misconduct for the commission of a crime through agents selected by the government, urging that under the supervisory power of the court, the government must be deterred for its illegal acts. The district court agreed and dismissed and the government took an appeal to the Fifth Circuit. There, the court affirmed the illegal search and seizure holding of the district court without addressing the issue of due process violation and supervisory power of the court. The government again appealed and the U.S. Supreme Court agreed to hear the case.

Our highest court reversed the holding of the lower courts on the basis that Payner had no standing to raise the *Fourth Amendment* issue. The papers illegally seized were not his; they belonged to the bank. Thus, under strict *Fourth Amendment* analysis, he had no standing to complain about papers of another which were illegally seized, notwithstanding the fact that the papers were to be used as evidence against him. Because the Fifth Circuit had not dealt with the due process issue, it was not addressed by the Supreme Court.

Not only was I appalled by the decision, but I quickly developed in my mind a scenario which fits the holding. You are under investigation by IRS and they suspect that you have hidden assets. They have such lack of evidence, however, that they cannot even make a showing of probable cause to a magistrate by way of affidavit which would justify the execution by the magistrate of a search warrant. Stymied, IRS agents kidnap your young son, whom they believe might know the whereabouts of the assets. He refuses to talk. They torture him. He talks and leads the agents to the evidence which the government seizes and intends to use against you at time of trial. You raise illegal search and seizure and outrageous governmental misconduct, and you lose. You have no standing. Your son was kidnapped and tortured, not you. Only your son can raise the issue, and he is not charged.

Prior to Dahlstrom, an attorney by the name of Margolis, in Southern California, was charged individually for use of foreign trusts to save for his clients income taxes. Presenting his good faith beliefs and his good faith understanding of the tax law from his earnest study of the complicated code sections, he was acquitted. Reeling from the Margolis case, the government in Dahlstrom chose the "darling of the prosecutor," the conspiracy count, charging Dahlstrom and his lieutenants with conspiracy to defraud the United States and aiding and abetting in the preparation and presentation of fraudulent income tax returns. In a conspiracy count, the government will allege that any persons who had any dealings with the subject matter whatsoever are co-conspirators, whether or not you ever meet them, talked to them, or ever knew of their existence. And, as to any act of a co-conspirator, whether named or even known by the government, it can be used against all defendants, so long as the jury finds that there is a conspiracy and that the act of the conspirator was committed in furtherance of the conspiracy. The lesson there is: be careful not only with whom you have lunch, but with whom your luncheon date has dinner ... *ad infinitum.*

When I first read the Dahlstrom indictment, it, like many of its kind, sounded devastating, reciting within the overt acts section those acts committed in furtherance of the conspiracy, items such as Gaze Durtz's statements to the undercover agent, recorded on tape. In response to the agent's question as to why the ALA "taxpayer legal defense program" was necessary, he answered, "If they [the IRS] get a hold of your books or records, they could probably shoot holes in this thing .... Yeah, if they do, you're in trouble .... then you're talking about tax avoidance, *tax fraud,* and the whole thing."

Karl and I had many similarities, but the major two were these: we did not like bullies and we got excited about Constitutional issues. We believed that people deserved to know the truth. After meeting Karl in Bryan, Texas at his request and reviewing the ALA program including the seminar tapes and hearing what he expected from an attorney and from the case as a whole, I suggested he represent himself or hire F. Lee Bailey. Karl wanted not only to win, but to prove a point: the form of the transaction was just as important as substance. He wanted to send the government reeling and use the case as a springboard to educate a nation of citizens who had cowered in corners at the sound of IRS. He also was seriously considering joint representation, that is, having an attorney represent him and he himself participate in the trial, including questioning of witnesses. After all, how could anyone but Karl question the IRS' expert when Karl had researched the substantive tax issues for so many years, had written his book, given the seminars, and become the nation-wide expert? He had a point. Although I certainly was not shy about taking on the government's experts after having done my homework, I could see from the look in Karl's eyes that he was, like many of my clients, the "law library lawyer." A close cousin to the "drugstore cowboy." Rather than suffer the time, money and humiliation of law school, Karl wanted to play lawyer without the ticket. He did not want to pay Bailey's price which I estimated would be at least $100,000. Karl offered me the job. I accepted and was committed to a lengthy trial in Seattle, Washington during the months of November, December and January of 1981 and 1982. I would not see the sun shine but for my brief visits back to Phoenix.

Except for Bruce Ripley, who was represented by private counsel, the other co-defendants were represented by court-appointed counsel. Merwin Grant of Phoenix, with whom I had first practiced when I arrived in the Valley of the Sun in 1978, represented co-defendant Conley. In fact, it was Merwin who had referred Karl to me, having already been retained by Conley, who was then living in Tucson. Thus, Merwin and I commuted to Seattle, staying at first at the downtown athletic club where two of the defense counsel had a membership. One of the defense attorneys was a former IRS counsel. Irwin Schwartz, the head public defender in the Seattle district, was the attorney appointed for Durst. For the princely sum of $200, Durst had prepared the returns under the government's sting operation and paradoxically had become the government's strongest witness against us by virtue of tape recorders hidden on the body of the IRS undercover agent.

Frustrated by the growing number of professionals joining ALA and utilizing its program, IRS had commenced in 1979 a criminal investigation. At first, the agents, led by Donald Jenkins of the Seattle office, attempted to secure information by way of the IRS administrative summonses to banks, requesting financial information about the defendants and their various trusts. But ALA was too prepared, dug in by the teachings of Karl and the protections afforded citizens by Congress. At that time, the law provided when a summons was issued to a bank, the taxpayer could merely write to the bank within fourteen days and demand that the bank not comply with the summons. IRS had to give the taxpayer notice. Once the letter was received timely by the bank, the bank did not comply and IRS was forced to turn to the courts to petition for enforcement of the summons. This might take several months and if stays were granted pending appeal, several years. Karl and the others had stayed compliance. IRS needed bigger guns. The grand jury.

Jenkins' request to the Justice Department for a grand jury investigation was approved and IRS began the two-pronged attack: frontal attack by way of grand jury subpoenas to banks for financial information, including checks which would reveal the membership, plus infiltration of the enemy camp by Walter Perry, alias Vince Paoli, an IRS special agent who specialized in undercover work. Karl's attempt to prevent the grand jury from securing bank records on *First Amendment* grounds failed.

At a seminar in Seattle held by Karl, et al, a dentist, Dr. John Rickets, had attended and recorded the presentation, an introduction to the ALA program. An apparent loner and unmarried, Rickets decided to become *Captain Marvel* and contacted first an accountant, O'Leary, formerly with IRS, who in turn brought in Randy Draughn, IRS special agent. Convinced ALA was assisting others in violating the law, Jenkins devised a sting operation approved by his superiors. Rickets was the willing bait, who, playing himself, joined ALA. Paoli posed as a financial consultant in California, acting as Rickets' advisor. Paoli maintained a front company, renting an office with phone in Los Angeles.

Karl was so confident and up front, he offered that a member could bring to the training seminar his professional advisor, be it attorney, accountant, or financial advisor. Thus, Paoli was off to Karl's technical seminar, videotaped by Karl and held in Bryan, Texas, headquarters of ALA. Paoli even appeared in the video tapes! At the headquarters, Karl's "ALA college" facilities included a moot courtroom where he intended in the future to teach individuals how to go before the tax or district court and make arguments. *The threat.*

Rickets set up the trusts and needed a return prepared in the Seattle area and was referred by Conley to Durst, who became the weakest link in the defense. A confessed alcoholic, Durst became the center of Paoli's attention and in a motel room stated to Paoli, his concern about "tax fraud," if in fact, the government was able to pierce the veil of secrecy created by Karl's legal defense program. Taped to Paoli's body was a Nagra recorder.

Karl had never as much as met Rickets nor Durst. An attempt by Paoli to get Durst to back date documents to show a deduction for the prior year failed. but Paoli was making headway: if the jury found a conspiracy and Durst's statements were in furtherance of the conspiracy, then his statement concerning tax fraud could be used against *all* the defendants.

There was very little contact between Paoli and Karl. On one recorded call, Paoli asked Karl why he insisted that the members keep good records to which Karl responded, "That way, you can sleep at night," meaning you had done what the law requires with no loose ends and should have then no worries. But while Karl had been cautious, not so for his lieutenants. Morris provided one of his clients with false employer identification numbers to be used in connection with bank accounts. Durst suggested to Rickets that he set up additional trusts to make tracing by IRS of future transactions more difficult. Ripley and Durst told clients they should use "copy not" pens to sign checks so that IRS agents could not read them on microfilm records maintained by the banks. Morris told another dentist to use a false name on a non-resident alien tax return filed by one of the offshore trusts, and Durst counselled individuals to alter their social security numbers on trust bank accounts. *Badges of fraud.* Karl's name in connection with these activities was, as they say, "conspicuous by its absence." *Watch with whom you have lunch and with whom your luncheon date has dinner....* Thus, the government had its badges of fraud for jury appeal.

Perhaps worst was Conley's suggestion to a third party of outright fraud, a suggestion he and all defendants would sorely regret. At the Seattle seminar, Conley needed some assistance at the reception area and offered a young lady the position, stating that he would pay her $1,000 to sit at a table and register seminar attendees. He added that he would pay her in cash, "under the table, that way you don't have to pay taxes on it." (What questions should Karl's attorney have for her at trial, but for her lack of contact with Karl?)

Due to the rift between Karl and his lieutenants, and the ultimate spin-off organization of ALES, Karl was without knowledge of all of this behind-the-scenes nonsense. Just as in the doctrine of torts, or civil wrong, in which "the tortfeaser" (one who commits the tort) "takes his victim as he finds him," a defendant named in a conspiracy indictment "takes his co-defendants as he finds them." For example, if you strike an individual in the chest not very hard, but it turns out he has heart disease and dies from the blow, that is your problem, despite your lack of intent to kill. You have committed not only assault and battery, but you are now left with a homicide on your hands. Likewise with Karl. He was left with the traits, good and bad, of those lieutenants chosen by him directly or indirectly.

It got worse. Some of the lieutenants came up with a notion that since you paid $12,000 for the ALA program, you could put the program in one of your offshore trusts and then buy it back, take the deduction for the repurchase. What was it worth? How about the figure $50,000 even though you paid only $12,000 for it? Whatever the market would bear. If trust No. 2 required $50,000 as the price, then the taxpayer had no choice but to pay $50,000.

Even without the misdeeds of Dahlstrom's co-defendants, the government felt that they had enough on Karl to prove willfulness. First was the District Director letter, a letter written to Seattle area practitioners, critical of the ALA program. Karl responded with the fruits of his own legal research. The district director letter would prove to backfire on both the IRS and the Justice Department prosecutors for the reason that it demonstrated how complex international tax law was and that practitioners - CPA's, accountants and attorneys - were themselves confused. If the trained professionals, including those licensed by the State were so confused, how could it be that Karl could have acted with criminal intent?

Second was the legal defense program by which Karl taught members their common law, constitutional and statutory rights concerning IRS audits. "Obstructionists was how the program users were viewed by IRS. The program was viewed as a means to hide the truth, and who would want to hide the truth if he had done nothing illegal? A knowledgeable citizen would, Karl explained, if he simply wanted to exercise his rights. The government would also make much of the fact that the application for membership in ALA included a promise not to divulge ALA information in event of a civil or criminal investigation.

With input from the other attorneys in the case, Karl and I devised the ultimate strategy: only Karl would testify, with spill over effect to the other defendants, for after all, they had relied principally on Karl. He would present the good faith belief/reliance on law defense, together with reliance on counsel for the reason that attorneys and CPAs had become involved, some of whom had personally utilized the program. We would play for the jury the video taped seminars, both the introductory seminar held at hotels and the technical seminar conducted by Karl at Bryan, Texas. If necessary, we would call Special Agent Jenkins if the government did not.

The Justice Department sent from its tax division in Washington two prosecutors, Bietz who was seasoned but lacked luster, and Hayward with little experience, who had spent years in the catacombs of the Freedom of Information Act requests section of the Justice Department. It was Hayward who had commented to me about Jake Schnieder and his abilities to manipulate grand juries.

My pretrial motions were denied by Judge Rothstein, the two most important of which were to dismiss on *First* and *Fifth Amendment* grounds. Karl had advocated ideas, not action, I argued. He promoted an idea and provided the knowledge and the tools, including a form packet, but his advice was that members should seek the counsel of their own choice, attorney or CPA, or both, which is what many did, receiving endorsements from the professionals, with returns prepared by the CPA, who at the very least had knowledge of the source of the deductions. Karl had not as much as met nor spoken personally with the vast majority of member witnesses brought to testify against him.

There was very little activity with Karl personally beyond his research and seminar presentations. He gave little technical advice by phone, though ALA did assist members in setting up the trusts by traveling to Belize or the Turks & Caicos Islands in the event the taxpayer did not wish to take time out from his busy schedule. This, I felt, was the weakest part of my *First Amendment* argument: some activity, however minor, beyond advocacy. Relying on Freeman's case and that of the Black Panthers, I urged the district court to consider whether anyone would dare write a book advocating what he believed to be legal tax avoidance for fear he would be prosecuted for aiding and abetting in the preparation and filing of returns filed by those readers who had followed the advice and filled out the returns without personal advice from the author. In Freeman's second case he had been acquitted by the court because he had not prepared for his listeners a W-4 exempt, just as Karl had not prepared for his members the form 1040. The Black Panthers, who advocated that the President be shot, did not go so far as to insight imminent lawlessness. Listeners had a chance to think it over. Likewise for ALA members, admonished to seek further counsel. In filing the motion, I believed that the best shot on appeal, if necessary, was the *First Amendment* issue. Karl indeed had cloaked himself in the *First Amendment*, having been stung by the Missouri and Texas Bar suits. If the NAACP and United Mine Workers had a right to associate for their common good as declared by the U.S. Supreme Court in landmark decisions, then was not the same true for citizens seeking legal tax avoidance? That was Karl's theory. Through the association, the members could counsel one another without fear of prosecution from a bar association for practice of law without a license.

Under the *Fifth Amendment* due process clause, I raised the issue of "lack of notice of any illegality, an issue raised with success in an Indian case in North Carolina, *U.S. v. Critzer,* 498 F.2d 1160 (4th Cir. 1974). In *Critzer,* the Fourth Circuit held that in view of the uncertainty of taxability of certain income, the taxpayer must be exonerated for lack of willful intent to evade and defeat the income tax. Critzer had been found guilty of four charges of willful attempt to evade or defeat the federal income tax with respect to income earned from improvements located on land in which the defendant had a possessory holding, *land* which was within the Cherokee Indian Reservation in North Carolina. The court held at 1162, "... that the defendant must be exonerated from the charges lodged against her. *As a matter of law,* defendant could not be guilty of willfully evading and defeating income taxes on income, the taxability of which is so uncertain that even co-ordinate branches of the United States government plausibly reached directly opposing conclusions. *As a matter of law,* the requisite intent to evade and defeat income taxes is missing. The obligation to pay is so problematical that *the defendant's actual intent is irrelevant,* even if she had consulted with the law and sought to guide herself accordingly, she could have had no certainty as to what the law required." The *Critzer* court at 1163 concluded that "pioneering interpretations of the tax laws should not be sought or rendered in criminal prosecutions under Sec. 7201 [willful attempted evasion] but rather in civil suits."

Must a woman who sells her rare blood report the proceeds as income? That was the question presented in *U.S. v. Garber,* 607 F.2d 92 (5th Cir. 1979), in which Mrs. Garber was charged with income tax evasion arising from her failure to report funds received by her for the sale of her blood plasma. On rehearing *en banc,* the Fifth Circuit reversed the conviction, holding the failure of the district court to permit experts for the government and the defendant to testify as to the controversy which existed as to the taxability of receipt of such funds, and the district court's refusal to instruct the jury that reasonable misconception of tax law on the defendant's part would negate the necessary intent, resulted in denial of defendant's right to a fair trial. As to the first point, the court at 959 noted, "The parties in this case presented divergent opinions as to the ultimate taxability by an analogy to two legitimate theories in tax law. The trial court should not have withheld this fact and its powerful impact on the issue of Garber's willfulness."

On the second point, the court noted that the defendant had testified that she thought the proceeds from the sale were *not* taxable and that "by disallowing Nall's [expert's] testimony of the recognized theory of tax law that supports Garber's feelings, the court deprived defendant of evidence showing her state of mind to be *reasonable.*" But rather than reversing the conviction on the basis of "void for vagueness" or "lack of notice of any illegality as a matter of law," the Fifth Circuit reversed and remanded for retrial, leaving more confusion for tax practitioners and potential victims of tax prosecutions. Indeed, there was much disagreement within the Fifth Circuit, sitting *en banc,* three of the judges feeling that the question on appeal was whether the district court "should have dismissed the indictment on the ground that the taxability of the monies was too unclear to support criminal liability." If judges cannot agree, how can citizens as much as be brought into court, accused of violation of tax laws?

Even after the Dahlstrom case, the Fourth Circuit would again in

U.S. v. Mallas, 762 F.2d 361 (4th Cir. 1985) make it clear that they would not stand for a tax prosecution where there has been raised "novel questions of tax liability to which governing law offers no clear guidance." In *Mallas,* the defendants had promoted a tax shelter program based on deductions allowed to participants in coal mining enterprises. Reversing the convictions and acquitting the defendants, the court stated: "Because the defendants therefore could not have ascertained the legal standards applicable to their conduct, criminal proceedings may not be used to define and punish an alleged failure to conform to those standards.... The uncertainty of a tax law, like all questions of vagueness, is decided by the court as an issue of law. [citing *Critzer*]. To the extent that the Fifth Circuit has adopted a contrary approach in *U.S. v. Garber* [cite] we decline to follow that rule." The *Mallas* court found that the issue revolved around "notice" and "fair warning," finding that the government had failed to demonstrate any regulation, judicial decision, or even revenue ruling which would have put the defendants on notice as to their alleged illegal conduct.

Since there was not a case yet decided which would adjudicate the issues raised by the ALA program, then given *Critzer* and *Garber,* we urged Judge Rothstein, "how could it be said that Karl has been put on notice that his acts constitute illegal conduct?" "Denied. "Case set for trial." "Call your first witness." The battle lines were drawn.

Beitz at best was laborious. Slow to speak, slow movements. A turtle. Monotonous. No flair. One after another, ALA members were called to tell their story of how they joined ALA and relied upon the advice of CPA or counsel for the preparation of their returns. A "spring butt," I sprang out of my seat in an attempt to awaken the jury with raised voice. "Have you ever met Karl Dahlstrom?" "No." "Ever talk to him?" "No." "Ever see him?" "No." "Did he ever give advice to you?" "No." "To whom did you go for advice?" "To my attorney." "How about your CPA?" "Yes, my CPA also gave me advice." "And who prepared your return?" "My CPA." "To your knowledge, did Karl so much as *see* your return before it was filed with the IRS?" "No." "Did he ever mail them for you?" "No." "Before your return was prepared by your CPA, you told him about the ALA program?" "Yes." "And he said it was okay?" "Yes." "It was based upon his advice, not Karl's, that you filed the return." "Yes." "Did Karl Dahlstrom in any way aid and abet or assist in the preparation of your tax return?" "No." I would typically pick up the indictment and read the allegations right from the charges, asking whether Karl ever did any of those things, to which the answer was, as I well knew, "no."

Karl's trial, like many complex tax trials, would become a battle of the experts. First, on the government's side, Karl Krogue, an attorney, was called. His purpose: declare that in his opinion the "triple foreign trust" program of ALA was no doubt a total sham. It would not do for the taxpayer what Karl had claimed. What do I do with Krogue? Frontal attack in an attempt to totally destroy him, or sneak attack from the flanks or rear? I sized Krogue up, watching his demeanor on the stand, sensing he had a blockhead government employee mentality, despite the fact he was a private practitioner. I had a battle plan for this blockhead. Time and again it had been my experience that government tax prosecutors would call witnesses, usually IRS agents or attorneys, but sometimes private CPAs or lawyers, who were immovable. No flexibility. Never willing to concede an inch. The bottom line, I figured, with those types, was the hidden lack of self- confidence. Confident experts are willing to concede certain issues, hear the other side, and then, despite their concession, stick to their professional opinion. Those less confident will not give an inch for fear of providing an opening, an attitude which can cost them credibility with the jury.

Since we planned for our own experts plus Karl's testimony, including the findings of his exhaustive research, why take this blockhead head on? You beat your head against a brick wall and after a while your head is bound to start bleeding. Try to move a brick wall, you will appear a fool if it remains in its original position. But if you weaken the foundations at critical points, the wall collapses.

Such was the tactic employed by the Allies during the Normandy invasion in 1944. Bangalore torpedoes, long tubes of explosives, were placed under obstacles and beneath fortifications by combat engineers. Undermine the foundation and the fortification falls. The VC utilize the same technique with satchel charges. Their satchel teams became experts at first infiltrating the defenses made up of concertina wire, trip flares and claymore mines, and then placing satchel charges at key defensive positions, such as the tactical operation center.

Mindful of all this, I watched Krogue. Listening closely, I was patient to find an opening. He gave it to me. Not only was it his opinion that the program would not work tax wise, he swore that the trusts were *not trusts* in the legal sense. *Not valid legal entities.* I had him. Time for the Bangalore torpedo. I could, I felt, make him out a fool if he maintained that position. Karl had always taught "legal wise" versus "tax wise," meaning you might have say a trust or corporation legal wise, but it would not do what you desired tax wise. I had agreed with Karl.

On cross-examination of Krogue, I first asked, in my agreeable tone, the witness to state again that in his opinion the trusts were not valid. He did so. I asked him if he was positive, and he willingly placed his feet in cement. Digressing to other areas, I let the cement harden and later circled back to the trust validity question. After raising my voice, parading and pointing out some legal principles of trusts, he caved in and admitted sheepishly that yes, the entities were in fact "valid trusts." To rub it in a little, I pointed out that he was positive a few moments ago that they were not, and now he was sure they were, to which he again sheepishly agreed. Krogue's admission as to trust validity was significant because it was the government's position that *no* valid trusts were formed. The prosecutor had not been willing to concede to anything. Now their own expert had testified otherwise. Unknown to me, the issue would prove to be crucial in another way.

The government likewise attacked the "legal defense program" as a sinister plan to defraud the government of its revenues. They had apparently ignored an important fact: Karl taught members about rights under the *Constitution* and under statutes passed by Congress. How then can exercise of those rights be construed to be evil? With this issue I went on the frontal attack. Beitz, on direct examination, would ask witnesses about the defense program; on cross I would have the witness give in effect Karl's speech on rights. In addition, I had on hand the IRS Special Agent's Handbook, which recognized the very rights of Karl's program. After a few rounds of this, we heard no further complaint on the legal defense program. The government was forced to concede. Another chip out of their armour.

Our reliance defense was what I would call "side door." Karl had not paid an attorney for specific legal advice, but attorneys had become associated with the program. One was Steve Allen of Phoenix, who was so impressed he began to promote it on his own. Special Agent Jensen had interviewed Steve, but was probably somewhat intimidated by the knowledge Steve might have as an attorney, and had not asked him pointed questions. The government did not as much as know, for example, Steve's promotion of the program for his own economic gain, and that Karl had paid Steve some "finders fees" for Steve bringing some clients in for Karl before Steve went out on his own. Obviously, Steve believed in the legality as did Karl. Although Steve was relatively young and inexperienced, I thought he would make a great witness. A handsome young Mormon lad, he appeared honest and I got good vibes from him. I believed that he believed and what was most important, I felt the jury would believe that Steve believed. I could then draw an analogy: if Steve believed, then it logically follows Karl believed, and if Karl believed, it cannot be said that he acted willfully.

I had listed Steve as a witness and Hayward, who had read Jensen's memorandum of interview of Steve, laughed. I kept bringing up Steve in light conversations with Hayward, talking about how he "would blow the government out of the water with our reliance defense." With my bluster, Hayward must have thought it was a ruse, a feint, a demonstration, that I was bluffing. I would not call Allen at all, he assumed, believing Allen had nothing to offer.

The night before Steve was scheduled to testify, I announced to Hayward my witnesses for the following day, including Allen. "You better get ready for Allen," I told Hayward. "We'll blow you out of the saddle tomorrow." "Sure," he said, laughing and teasing back. "I'll stay up all night getting ready." After calling some preliminary witnesses, we had a recess and I left the courtroom to visit with Steve for a last minute coordination. I had him waiting in a room at the end of the hall. Usually, witnesses wait in the hallway or in the witness room just outside the courtroom. But Steve was my "secret weapon," concealed at the end of the hall. As I left for recess, I told Hayward Steve was next and he again laughed, "Sure, Mac." But when I had disappeared for a few minutes, Hayward got worried, walked down the hall looking for me, and came to the entrance and asked, "Who you got in there, MacPherson?" "Come on in. Steve, I would like you to meet Mr. Hayward, one of the prosecutors in this case. This is my next witness, Steve Allen." Hayward turned white. He looked at me in disbelief and then clutched, not knowing what to ask. We had about two minutes before court reconvened and Hayward scurried away, to show up later in the courtroom, out of breath. No doubt he had to run upstairs to get his notes on Allen, for whom he was totally unprepared. But that was only step one of the trap. I figured Hayward, in an attempt to belittle Karl's program, would take a chance and ask Allen if he had ever promoted the program himself, expecting an answer of "no." My mind game with Hayward had resulted in no personal interview of Allen by Hayward prior to the witness taking of the stand. On direct I only brought out Steve's attendance at seminars and receipt of finders fees, and his belief in the program. Hayward again turned white as he learned from the witness on cross-examination that Steve had been charging $12,000 to set clients up in a triple trust program, and that he himself had utilized the program.

In addition to Steve, I called a CPA from California and an accountant from Tucson, Neil Nordbrock. The CPA would later be brought under criminal investigation as would Neil. In addition, Neil would be hit with a $75,000 penalty for refusal to turn over accounting records to the IRS, a judgment I would succeed in reversing with the Ninth Circuit. Then Neil and his wife Evelyn would be charged in late 1988 with false returns for their use of Karl's program. (The saga continues; details in *War Stories, Part II.*)

Bruce Ripley had received some advice late in the game from attorneys who had thought Karl's program "imaginative." No red flags. And attorney Michael Pinatelli from San Francisco testified as our expert, giving his opinion that the program had merit. In addition, several CPAs and attorneys whose clients used the program with their advice, agreed, of course, it was not illegal, at least not in the black on a spectrum of white (legal) through gray to black (illegal).

A big issue in the case became what Karl actually said at the seminars. Undercover agents and clients summarized, but both the introductory and advanced seminars were on video tape. Since Karl believed in the legality, there was nothing to hide. We wanted the tapes played for the jury, but the government objected and the judge ruled against us. I was hot. "If a bank was robbed, the best evidence would be a video tape of the robbery; likewise if a crime was committed by Karl, it would appear on the tape," I had argued. Beitz no doubt did not want the jury to hear and see Karl evangelize. To get even, every time the seminars were mentioned by a witness, I offered the tapes in evidence, holding them up to the jury to see. The tapes had remained at the evidence table in front of the bench. "Your Honor, again we offer the video tapes of the two seminars as the best evidence of what happened." "Objection." "Objection sustained." I must have offered the tapes at least fifty times throughout the trial, daring Beitz to again object to the truth.

Not to be smitten by lack of tapes for the jury, Karl and I put on a "dog and pony show" for the jury. In essence, Karl gave his seminars, with me at the overhead projector showing the jury the same cases Karl had presented to his perspective clients, to CPAs and attorneys. Much of what Karl urged was on the issue of "substance versus form," Karl taking the position that form, according to the case he had researched, was at least as important as substance. The judge finally ruled by trial's end that the jury would be told that both substance and form should be considered as to any tax transaction. This was an important victory because Beitz had again refused to concede to anything, adopting the theory that the trusts were "total shams." With Krogue agreeing we had "valid trusts," and with the jury to receive the law on substance and form, Beitz had to switch horses midstream, which he did in closing.

For this I criticized him relentlessly and taunted him during my own closing. In addition, I asked the jury to consider if the government was indeed in search of the truth, then why had they time and again objected to the introduction of the tapes? I asked the jury to speculate as to why the government did not want the jury to see the taped seminars if Karl had in fact committed a crime. Here Judge Rothstein stopped me, admonishing me in front of the jury that my argument was not proper. This was, I reckoned, due to the general rule that jurors are not to be asked to speculate about evidence not introduced. But I had not done that. I had asked that they speculate about the government's *motive* in protesting introduction of the evidence, not to speculate about the evidence itself. Perhaps I was splitting hairs with the judge.

It was the Durst audio tapes which no doubt did us in. During the week of deliberation, the jury asked that the tapes be replayed. They found the defendants guilty on most charges. But the greater insult was the sentencing a month or so later. Some jurors showed up at time of sentencing curious. This was the first time I had ever seen such a thing. After the sentence was imposed, jurors were overheard commenting that, "Gee I didn't think it would come to this." *Too late to say you are sorry.* Dahlstrom received five years, Ripley four, Conley three, Morris two and Durst one.

It was appeal time. Karl, not satisfied with the results I had obtained for him, fired me and hired a Texas firm to handle the appeal. I had laid for them the foundation: the *First* and *Fifth Amendment* issues plus Krogue and the legal defense program. My prediction was reversal on *First Amendment* grounds because Karl had done little more than to speak and write.

Karl and his lieutenants were lucky. In a two to one decision, the Ninth Circuit not only reversed the conviction, but held the defendants not guilty. The government stupidly did not seek a rehearing *en banc* and sought direct appeal to the U.S. Supreme Court, which refused to hear the case. The opinion did not make clear whether the Ninth Circuit sided with the Fourth Circuit - issue of law, or with the Fifth Circuit - issue of fact. The Dahlstrom Court held that considering all of the evidence, there was not sufficient evidence for the jury to find the defendants guilty as charged, which sounds on first blush as if the court impliedly acquitted as an issue of fact, except that the court added: "We are convinced that the legality of the tax shelter program advocated by the appellants in this case was completely unsettled by any clearly relevant precedent on the dates alleged in the indictment. 'It is settled that when the law ... is highly debatable, a defendant - actually or imputedly - lacks the requisite intent to violate it.' [Citing *Critzer*] A criminal proceeding pursuant to Sec. 7206 [filing of false tax returns] 'is an inappropriate vehicle for pioneering interpretations of tax law.' [citing Garber]" So much for legal theories. Let us examine how evidence at trial came back to haunt the government.

As the Ninth Circuit noted, the government asserted "that the FTO's allocated by the ALA had no economic substance and were therefore blatant shams ... that the 'taxpayer defense program' could reasonably be found to be inconsistent with a belief in the legality of the tax shelter program ... [and] some statements made by appellant Durst [shows] that the appellants had guilty knowledge." As to the first government contention, the court noted "The government's own expert witness, Karl K. Krogue, testified that the trusts created through implementation of the ALA tax shelter program were *valid, legal entities.*" On the second issue, "even the government *concedes* however, that the actions recommended in the taxpayer defense program were *not unlawful.* We are unpersuaded that the appellant's advocacy of various lawful actions translates into proof that the appellants were aware of the illegality of their tax shelter program."

Finally, in dealing with the Durst statements, the court held that "they were clearly inadmissible as proof of the crimes charged against the other appellants" for reason the government had failed to establish "substantial, independent proof of the existence of the conspiracy." With circuitous logic, the court reasoned that there was lack of evidence on intent because the Durst evidence could not be used against the other defendants because there was lack of independent evidence of a conspiracy; and there was lack of independent evidence of a conspiracy because conspiracy requires intent; and there was lack of evidence of intent! Add to that this inconsistency: although Durst's statement, the court reasoned, could not be used against the other co-defendants, what about Durst himself - why then should he be acquitted if his statements were so inculpatory?

As will be seen, the *Dahlstrom* decision and its progeny has left a great deal of confusion on the "lack of notice" defense within the Ninth Circuit, the specifics of which will be discussed in *War Stories, Part II* . In my opinion, the court should have done one or both of the following. First, the court, like the Fourth Circuit, could have held that the intent of the taxpayer was of no moment, so long as he was not put on any notice of illegality and, therefore, could not be held to be criminally liable as a *matter of law.* Second, under *First Amendment* analysis, the defendants could not be guilty for, as the *Dahlstrom* panel noted in discussing intent:

> Even if the defendants knew that a taxpayer who actually performed the actions they advocated would be acting illegally, the *First Amendment* would require a further inquiry before a criminal penalty could be enforced.... Nothing could be more clear at this stage in the development of *First Amendment* jurisprudence than 'the principle that the Constitutional guarantees of free speech and free press do not permit a state to forbid or prescribe advocacy ... of law violation except where such advocacy is directed to inciting or producing imminent lawless action and is likely to incite or produce such action.' [citing Supreme Court case] Nothing in the record indicates that the advocacy practiced by these defendants contemplated

imminent lawless action. Not even national security can justify criminalizing speech unless it fits within this narrow category; certainly concern with protecting the public fisc, however laudable, can justify no more.

In the dissenting opinion by Judge Goodwin, who would lead the way in wetting down the "lack of notice defense" in the cases following *Dahlstrom* , mention was made of not only the Durst tape, but some of the other activities of co-defendants: use of blue "copy not pens," use of fictitious names as authorized signatures on bank accounts, use of a false name on a non-resident alien tax return, altering social security numbers on trust bank accounts to prevent IRS from tracing them. What now, I wondered, did the *Dahlstrom* jurors think, having spent three months in trial?

Rebellion to tyrants is obedience to God. Thomas Paine

ALASKA FISHER OF MEN   Chapter 11

"The black robes of the judicial system met the red, white and blue of the *Patriots in Action* Tuesday in an Anchorage court, and colorful is a polite word for what happened." Thus began the *Anchorage Daily News* article of July 8, 1981, entitled "Moody, Tax Opponent Tangle in Court." Judge Ralph Moody cutting off Rock's attempts to challenge the criminal tax proceedings brought against him, said in open court to Rock, "If you don't shut up I'm going to send you to jail." "Why are you prejudiced against me?" demanded Rock. "I find you in contempt, and sentence you to one day in jail," said Moody. "I appeal that ruling!" shouted Rock. "I find you in contempt and sentence you to two days in jail," countered Moody. Rock was brought before Judge Moody on a grand jury indictment alleging that Rock willfully attempted to evade taxes for 1976 and 1978 and that he willfully failed to file state income tax returns for 1975 through 1978. The grand jury alleged that Rock owed $483 for 1976 and $2,177 for 1978. Without evidence of a tax due and owing for the remaining years, the State was able to muster only misdemeanor failure to file charges. Of course, by the time Rock was charged in June of 1981, Alaska had repealed its income tax. But not retroactively. Rock's case was the first criminal tax case in Alaska history. The first and the last. *The alpha and the omega.*

According to the *Daily News* article, at the July 8th hearing Rock "said he hasn't decided his defense tactics yet except that he plans to call a thousand character witnesses." Then on July 17th, this *Daily News* headline: "Tax Protester Asks $1.3 Million in Suit Claiming Judge Violated U.S. Constitution." Rock had filed in the United States District Court in Anchorage a suit against Judge Moody, claiming the judge had denied him his constitutional rights during the arraignment. Rock was back before Judge Moody on August 27th. "Judge, I think you should disqualify yourself. I plan to collect $1.3 million from you and there is no way you can sit on this case without prejudice and bias." Moody responded, "Mr. Smith, just because you're prejudiced against me is no sign I'm prejudiced against you, denied." The trial was set for October 5th. And to complicate things, on July 22nd, the State's prosecutor, Assistant Attorney General Elizabeth Sheley, brought additional charges against Rock for "disorderly and contemptuous behavior toward Superior Court Judge Ralph Moody." According to the *Daily News* article of July 22, 1981, "Sheley refused to say why the State had decided to pursue the new contempt charges against Smith. 'It's on the books as a crime punishable by six months,' she said. 'It's within our discretion to prosecute without giving a reason.'"

Of course there was a reason. Rock Smith for years had been a nemesis to state and federal taxing authorities in Alaska. For years IRS special agents investigated him but the federalities declined prosecution, no doubt because the alleged tax due was so small. Without a substantial tax due and owing, how could they prove willfulness? But the vendetta banner was passed from the feds to the state for in fact the two IRS agents who had investigated Rock for years had left IRS employment for higher salary with the state. They were out to get Rock. In July, 1979 during my first trip to Alaska, I was shown the *Daily News* article of July 24, 1979 entitled "Fighter Tax Resister Takes on the IRS." Under the large photo of Rock, behind which was shown a form 1040, was this quote from Rock: "It's my conviction we're going to be able to get people to understand what their constitutional rights, privileges, guarantees and duties are, and return America to a constitutional government." When asked in the interview how he would classify himself politically, Rock had answered, "I don't exist politically." "You have no political philosophy at all?" "No." "Isn't that sort of impossible?" "It is to a slave, but it's not to a free man.... The Scriptures say, 'By their works ye shall know them.' So when we start talking about political, I say that anything political - by their works we know them - and they're all part of Satan. And I can't have anything to do with Satan."

Rock Smith is the son of an independent missionary who in 1937 took his wife, Rock, and Rock's brother to Ekwak, Alaska, which was a village of all natives except for a white couple who were teaching school. Rock was two years old. The first winter was spent in a native log cabin. The Smith family traveled to Ekwak, in western Alaska, by float plane, which at the time was the only way airplanes could land there. They were there for five years. Hear Rock's story in his own words.

"In 1945 my Dad got his first airplane, which was a J-3 on plywood floats. And, of course, then in the winter it was on skis, but he never did fly that airplane on wheels. By '47 when he got the Super Cruiser, why I was getting to be thirteen years old, and I had done a little flying in the back seat of the J-3. Dad then taught me to fly in the Supercruiser, and in the Spring of 1950, an instructor from Anchorage named Gene Effler, who was also pretty well known in Alaskan flying circles, came to Dillingham with his PA-11, which is a 90 horse Piper Cub, to teach flying. And there were a number of high school boys, my classmates, that he had come out there to teach to fly, and of course, I wanted to solo and get on with my flying education.

"I begged my Dad to let me be instructed by Gene Effler, because though my Dad taught me to fly, he was not rated, so I didn't have any time at all in a log book or any record or certification or anything that would lead to a certification in the way of experience. Of course, this flying at Dillingham took place at a little pond that was about 400 feet across, right in back of the town of Dillingham, and the aircraft was on skis. At the edge of this pond the ice area of the pond was smooth, but beyond the pond where the snow had drifted up, why it was quite rough. So when you landed with skis you didn't have any brakes, so you had to put it down on the first few feet of the pond so that as you slid across the pond, you would be slowed down enough when you hit the drifts, so it didn't take the landing gear off the airplane. So Dad told Gene Effler, 'Well, you take Rock out in the PA-12, our airplane, and give him a private pilot check ride. If he passes it, he can solo.' So Mr. Effler and I went out in the PA-12 and an hour later we were back, and Mr. Effler had nothing but praise for my Dad's teaching. Mr. Effler said, 'Well he passed it with flying colors. He's ready to go.' My Dad said, 'Let him solo *your* airplane.' So, Gene Effler said, 'No problem.' So we moved over into the PA-11 and went around the patch, as we call it, made three landings, and he got out of the airplane and I soloed. So when I soloed, I had an hour and thirty minutes of flying time in my log book.

"My first landing was on the lake. I didn't have any problem. I was really what any observer would think to be a seasoned pilot. My Dad had not only instructed me well, but I had been doing a lot of flying with him. And my Dad was a very exacting taskmaster, and he got to where he'd even let me sit in the front seat. My Dad was a 200 pound, six foot two man, and I learned to fly sitting in the back seat behind him so that I could only see out at about a 45 degree angle to the front. It served me very well. I could get in planes like open cockpit taildraggers, where you can't see over the nose, and I was right at home since I wasn't accustomed to seeing any more than I could see at an angle.

"From Dillingham my folks sent me to Eugene, Oregon to finish my high school, because my mom wanted me to have some access to music and of course, I wanted to play football, and they didn't have any of these things in Dillingham, or even in Alaska, at that point. How do you play football on the snow and ice? I went to Eugene and stayed with some friends of my folks there for one year and when I got there, of course, I went right over to Springfield, Oregon, to the airport, and rented an airplane from Milt's Flying Service.

"I did not yet have my full pilot license, but I could fly solo. I just rented the plane solo. Then I would fly over to the Eugene Airpark, where I would meet my school buddies and they would pay to go for airplane rides to help me pay for my flying. (I wasn't supposed to take any passengers up until I had my private license.)

I was a sophmore when that started. By the time I was a junior, I had my private license and by the time I was a senior I had my commercial license. In fact, I didn't graduate from Eugene High because I left school early.

"I finished my junior year and I can't remember if I started my senior year or not, but if I did, I didn't go very long, because I went to work in the woods out of Eugene, Oregon. I went to driving a logging truck. I played football in high school for two years. Even though I had never played any football or done anything with it before, didn't have any knowledge, I played varsity football both years. I was the heaviest football player in the state of Oregon and I played noseguard defense. It was a platoon system during those years. I was the terror of the center of the line in the Oregon high school football for those years. I weighed 265, was about 6'1". I didn't stay and graduate from high school because there was no challenge in school and I wanted to go to work and I was riding a motorcycle and some of the guys I was riding motorcycles with worked in the woods. I met one of their bosses, and said, 'Why don't you put me to work?' and for whatever reason, he thought that was a good idea and did!

"In high school, I wanted to be a motorcycle rider, airplane driver, stunt pilot, logging truck driver, cat skinner, commercial fisherman, and in fact, participated to some degree in all of the above. In 1954 I got maried in January to my first wife, Lucille, and went driving a logging truck. I was going to move to Oakridge out of Eugene, and I needed a housekeeper and one of the ways to accomplish that was to get married. I was nineteen. I was making $2.10 an hour, genuine silver dollars for every hour I worked and the logging truck drivers in central Oregon today are making about $10 an hour, which gives them about one-third the purchasing power that I had at $2.10 an hour.

"In about April of 1954, I purchased a Taylorcraft airplane from Milt's Flying Service. I topped the engine, and when I and my new bride went to Alaska, we went in style. The Taylorcraft was a 1946 model. 65 horse, and we loaded up the two of us and a good amount of baggage in Eugene, flew to Seattle where I landed at Boeing Field, which I was vaguely familiar with. After the tower cleared me to land, I landed on the taxiway. Cruising speed was about 100 miles an hour. As I taxied up to Bellaire Service, Art Bell was the guy that I knew there, why here came the airport cop, and he said that they would like to talk to me up in the tower, that I had just landed on the *taxiway*. (To this day, the general aviation runway is a small, insignificant path of concrete out in the center of a huge complex where they test Boeing 747 aircraft. The taxiways are much larger than the runways.) "My wife Lucille stayed with her sister in Seattle and I got in that Taylorcraft by myself and headed north, the plan being for her to come with my folks when they came later.

"I fished every summer in Alaska from that time until 1955 when we moved to Seattle and I went to work for Independent Delivery, and that was a motorcycle and sidecar operation, and resulted in a lot of traffic tickets. The Lord saw fit to give me lots of courtroom experience as I went to court to fight these tickets. In 1974, I was delivering oil one afternoon in Bellevue, Washington when I ran into a man named Doug, who handed me a pocket-sized copy of the *Constitution*. This was in July. I took that home with me that evening and read it after dinner, especially the *Declaration of Independence*. And I realized in 1974 we Americans were subjected to much greater tyranny than what the colonists had been in 1774. That got me started going to *Patriot* meetings and studying and learning about the founding of this nation, and I quickly realized that this nation was only great because it had recognized God the Father of Jesus Christ as the supreme authority over all things.

"In September I went to the job office and filed an exempt W-4. The next year, in 1975 in Alaska, I got involved in construction for the first time in my life, and filed an exempt W-4 there. The exempt W-4 was filed as a result of the information that I had researched and discovered that wages are not income, according to many definitions and various other things, plus the fact that I realized that I had been rendering unto Caesar when I didn't belong to Caesar. I belonged to God. And I didn't owe Caesar the first fruits of my labor.

"My first *Patriot* meeting was with the *Snahomish County Posse Comitatus,* and I found them by questioning Doug and getting the name of their chairman. That led to hearing Marvin Cooley speak, and Bill Drexler speak, and William Gale speak, and Jim Scott, the flim-flam man from Sacramento, California. Of course, when I went on this construction job, I wasn't the only one to file an exempt W-4, it seemed like a lot of the other guys on the job were interested in such things and after listening to what was said, they filed exempt W-4s too. From there I went to work on the Alyeska pipeline project in Alaska and drove a stringing truck for hauling 80 foot joints of pipe, driving a rig that was 105 feet long and stringing pipe along the pipeline right of way, which meant hauling it from the pipe yard to the ditches that had been dug. More than that, there was a lot of time to sit around and talk to various people and the drivers, construction hands of one kind or another, and there was a big movement afoot at that time, by 1976, to right these wrongs that had been perpetuated upon the American people. The misinformation that had been given was being set straight. Many people filed exempt W-4s as a result.

"I finished with the pipeline in 1977, associated with some

people who called themselves *IRS Checkmate* in Anchorage, Alaska, and in fact moved to Anchorage in 1976, where I married Carol in September of 1977. (I had divorced Lucille.) We started holding public meetings, entitled *'Patriots in Action'* in Anchorage in November of 1978. John Freeman was the big thing on the scene at that time. We brought him up in November of 1978. 1979 and 1980 saw the *Patriot* movement, not only in Anchorage, but nationwide, just grow to huge proportions with big meetings everywhere. In 1981 I was charged by the State of Alaska with four counts of willful failure to file and two counts of attempted tax evasion.

"In 1980 I had met Mac as he and a couple of other attorneys came to an Anchorage *Patriots in Action* meeting as they were preparing for a defense. We had three patriots charged in the Anchorage area with filing false W-4s and Mac came up to defend those cases. In 1981, when I was charged by the State of Alaska, the tale started being told in the *Northern Lights Glimmer*, which was the *Alaska Patriots in Action* newsletter. Just about two weeks before trial was due to start, Mac called me on the phone one day and said, 'Rock, what's going on? I just read in the newsletter that you've been charged with these tax crimes. What can I do to help?' I told Mac that that was a kind offer, but that there were no funds available for such participation, and that it was my understanding that the Lord was directing me to defend in the courtroom according to Matthew 10:19, where the Holy Spirit was going to speak through me. Mac informed me that the Holy Spirit had moved him to come up and help me if I wanted him to. Well, after tears being shed on both sides, we decided that that must be what was right, and so Mac came up and helped me *pro bono* defend the charges brought by the State of Alaska in 1981.

"I was charged with four counts of willful failure to file and two counts of tax evasion. I went to the grand jury prior to my indictment and talked to them about a minister being exempt from many requirements otherwise imposed, and just generally laid a big red herring for the prosecutor. As a result of that testimony to the grand jury, the prosecutor was all prepared to prosecute me for claiming status of a minister in connection with the tax charges. At the trial, that was never going to come out. But it's an interesting strategy that the Lord just led me into. I hadn't even thought about doing that, but when I was talking to the grand jury, that was what came out. That's what the Holy Spirit had me say, and in fact, while I was in front of the grand jury, I almost refused to let the prosecutor talk. I addressed all my remarks, questions and comments to the grand jury and pointed out how the prosecutor, by asking certain questions, was able to, if they could obtain the yes or no answer they wanted, would be able to distort the facts. It's obvious none of that meant any great deal to this grand jury, as they indicted me anyway.

"Following indictment, the prosecutor issued a summons and when I appeared before Judge Moody for my arraignment, he started right in with a loud harangue about how I was not to disrupt the court and talk and do these various things, and when he got done, I stood up and asked, 'Why are you prejudiced against me, Judge?' He said 'That's contempt!' And he imposed a one-day jail sentence as an attempt to prohibit me from saying anything further, and said, 'If you say anything else, I'll add to it!' At which point, I responded, 'I want to appeal that ruling.' He said, 'That's another day!' At this point, there was some conversation between the judge and the prosecutor and there was a public defender present who had been with me on another case earlier, and the judge got him to come up and sit alongside of me. However, I quickly instructed him that the judge is going to have to talk to me, that I didn't want him to be involved in this in any way, which he did. John Selemi was the name of that public defender. He is still a public defender and seen as one of the more successful public defenders in Anchorage.

"During this arraignment, the judge told me to go and see the financial responsibility office, pursuant to appointing me counsel. Since I had no intention of securing or even allowing public defender-type counsel, I didn't go to the office. He also said something about going and being processed at the jail. And I didn't do that, either. He certainly didn't make it clear that that was an *immediate* order of business, and as the arraignment ended, why he rescinded the contempt citation. I believed that that rescinded the other things he talked about, the going to the financial responsibility office, etc. However, within a day or two, Elizabeth Sheley, the Assistant Attorney General who was prosecuting my case, indicted me by information on three counts of contempt of court. One for being contemptuous in court, the second for failing to report to the jail, and the third, for failing to go the financial responsibility office.

"That led to an interesting four-day trial before another judge, Johnstone, where the jury was picked by myself and Ms. Sheley, and at the end of the defense, the judge dismissed the first and most serious charge, that of being contemptible in the courtroom. The other two counts were minor misdemeanors, traffic ticket type. At any rate, the judge held a reasonable man might disagree on the minor counts, so he let those go to the jury and the jury returned guilty verdicts on both of those counts. I asked the judge to defer sentencing, after of course moving to have the jury verdict set aside, based on the judge's observation during my four days in his courtroom. During his ruling time, Judge Johnstone said that indeed, my demeanor in his courtroom for four days had been exemplary and that I was more capable than 70% of the attorneys who practiced in front of him, and that he wished I would go to school so that I could help other people. He agreed to defer sentencing and ruled that the record would be clean if there were no reoccurrences within the next twelve months, which of course, there weren't.

"This trial took place, of course, prior to the 1981 tax charges trial. During the time between my arraignment on the tax charges in 1981 and the trial, I had several hearings trying to get Moody taken off the case. I was contending that he should be taken off for cause, saving my pre-empt for Judge Carlson. Following the contemptible behavior during the arraignment, I filed a Title 42, civil rights, lawsuit against him in federal court, alleging that he had interfered with and deprived me of my civil rights by his irascible behavior, and flagrant violation of the just use of the powers which a judge has. Of course, my Heavenly Father saw that I was unsuccessful in my attempt to get Moody dismissed for reasons you'll soon understand.

"As we went into that 1981 state tax trial, Mac was admitted as co-counsel without local counsel to endorse him, and basically we were deciding during the direct testimony of the state's witnesses who would conduct the cross-examination. After the little lady from the Voter's Registration Office testified as to where I lived, I got up to cross-examine her and I didn't realize at the time what a problem it would have been for them if the judge had thrown out that evidence, because they were busy trying to establish where I lived. And really, the only thing they had was on this voter's registration application, where I said I lived at 1708 Newnocka, which is where my wife lived, and lives today. So I asked this young lady if it was her testimony that the information she had just presented was information on this Rock Smith, and I pointed to Mac, sitting at the table beside me, and she confirmed yes, it was. Of course, there was pandemonium in the court and I moved to have her evidence stricken as being unfounded and I can't think of another word, but I guess you get the message. And of course the Judge just denied that out of hand and let the testimony stand, thereby establishing where Rock Smith lived when the records keeper didn't have any idea who Rock Smith was.

"Prior to my state tax trial, I was not without federal trial experience. At one point, I and seven others were arrested at the IRS building in their offices and charged with, "creating a disturbance." *The Anchorage Eight.* The IRS agents and the federal police officer who had arrested us testified at the trial before Judge Fitzgerald. We were unable to get a jury. By the time we went to trial, there were not eight of us, I believe there were six of us and after one day of trial, the judge dismissed the other five defendants and I stood trial alone, which took four days.

"After the prosecutor had put on his case and the federal police officer and IRS people had just lied through their teeth, it came time for the defense to put on its case, and I started putting on these witnesses who were up there with me, these five defendants who had been dismissed, and I would ask them particular questions about the day in question, which had occurred seven or eight months prior to the trial. When they answered, I would say, 'How can you be sure of that after this length of time?' And they would respond that they had listened to a tape the night before their testimony, a tape just like the one they had made, since all of us had tape recorders up at the IRS office on the day of the alleged crime. And that's how they could be so certain, since they only had to remember it since last night.

"It wasn't very long before the judge and the prosecutor had their tongues hanging out a foot, wanting to hear that tape. Well, we were happy to accommodate them and we put the tape on the tape machine and played it into the record, and after the testimony of these various government liars, that the work had all stopped in the IRS office, that we had created such a disturbance, that business could not go on as usual, when we started playing the tape, guess what we heard over the conversations being taped? The typewriters clicking! And the people going by talking about business. It was very obvious from the tape that there had been no disturbance at all. In fact, the most disturbing element of that 'wild fiasco' was the federal police officer who was very upset and out of control and actual hollering. Again, my Heavenly Father had a hand on me and my loud voice, and that was one time when I wasn't loud. I was cool and quiet. The federal police officer came across much more loudly on the tape than I did. And, also, his voice of course, was agitated, where the Lord kept me calm.

"After that trial was over, the judge spent forty minutes berating me for being a ringleader and being contemptuous of the government system, and so forth and so on, and what a bad guy I was, and I just knew he was going to say guilty. But, then again, my Heavenly Father intervened and suddenly the judge just switched directions and spent five minutes ruling that I was not guilty.

"Another time I was arrested for failing to display a driver's license to a police officer upon request. He had stopped me for running a red light, he claimed, which of course, I wouldn't do, and wanted my driver's license. I said, 'Well do you have a warrant? ' He said, 'No, why would I need a warrant?' I said, 'Well, the *Fourth Amendment* guarantees me the right to be secure in my person and if you want my driver's license, I'm not going to voluntarily give up any of my rights, so you're going to have to have a warrant, and then you can have my driver's license, no problem.' Well, he said, 'I don't have a warrant.' And I said, 'Am

I under arrest?' He said, 'Why would you be under arrest?' I said, 'Well if I'm not under arrest, then I'm leaving,' and I put the car in gear and started moving, and he said, 'Hold it, hold it, you're under arrest,' at which point I emptied out my pockets and got out of the car. Carol came around to the driver's side, got in, and drove off, left me standing there with this police officer. Well, we got into the police car, of course he frisked me first, and put me into the back seat of the police car. Then he got in and he said, 'Do you mind telling me your name?' I said, 'Not at all, I'd have been glad to tell you who I was anytime you asked.' I gave him my name, and then he called the dispatcher and told the dipatcher that he was headed for the bail magistrate with Rock Smith. After the dispatcher acknowledged, he punched the button again, and said 'Corporal did you hear that?' And the corporal came back on the radio and said, 'Yes. Unfortunately.' The bail magistrate turned me loose on my own recognizance and then the hearing started. What with one thing and another, it was seven months from the time I was arrested until this trial for failing to display an operator's license. In Alaska, the statutes say that I cannot be convicted of failing to display a license if in fact I had a license and would display it in court.

"So that's where we were headed, and the morning of calendaring, the morning of the trial, I was in the calendaring room, which is a very big courtroom there in the Anchorage Municipal Court system, and this judge was going to service the attorneys who were all milling up in front of the bar prior to servicing anybody else, and when she addressed the attorneys, I jumped up and I said, 'Judge, my case has been on the calendar longer than any of the rest of these, and I want to be assigned a judge now.' And she said, 'Well Mr. Smith, look at all the people in here,' and the courtroom was full, there were about sixty people in there. She said, 'Look at all these people that we have to deal with, Mr. Smith, you'll just have to wait your turn.' However, she did immediately assign me a judge and a courtroom, and as soon as that was completed, I turned to leave the room, and as I did, every single one of the people in that courtroom got up and left with me, because they were all there to witness what was going on in my case.

"We went down the hall to the courtroom and the judge there started a harangue, and I stood up to say something, and he said, 'Mr. Smith, I don't want to hear from you, I want to hear from the attorney that's sitting beside you,' and John Selemi had been appointed as public defender to help me in that case, and I had instructed him prior to going into court that he was not to speak in the courtroom, otherwise, I would not have him at counsel table. I did want him there for technical advice. So when the judge said that, I sat down and John Selemi stood up and he told the judge basically that he had promised that he would not speak, that I was going to speak for myself. So the judge then addressed me and I stood up to say something, he started talking and I sat down.

"Over the next twenty minutes, this happened several times and finally, the judge said he couldn't believe that I wouldn't show my driver's license because that's what he was trying to get me to do, was to show my driver's license so he could dismiss the thing. And of course, I wouldn't do that. He hadn't really given me a chance to refuse it and I hadn't really refused it at that point, but he was incredulous that such a thing could happen. He would ask me a question every once in a while and I'd stand up to answer him, he'd start talking, and I'd sit down, so finally, he said, 'Well Mr. Smith, you said you wanted to speak for yourself, and I've been asking you questions for twenty minutes and you haven't answered one of them.' So I stood up and I said, 'Well Judge, I've got some things to say when you say it's my turn.' And he started talking and I sat down. At that point, there was quite a long, pregnant silence, and he said, 'Ok Mr. Smith, it's your turn.' I stood up and started to talk, and he started to talk again, and I sat down. Realizing what he had done, he apologized and then he let me have my say. I told him among other things that I would not voluntarily waive my *Fourth Amendment* right to be secure with my license by showing it to them, and that I cared enough about America that I was going to give whatever it cost to exercise my God-given rights as guaranteed by the *Constitution*. He tried to argue me out of bringing my case to the jury, as he was just certain that I could not prevail in my position and on and on he went, but of course, I called his bluff. I didn't agree to do any of the things he wanted done, so he instructed the prosecutor to get a copy of my license from Juneau and called a recess.

"At that point, the prosecutor complained that he shouldn't have to do that, that the law clearly states it was *my* responsibility to display it in the courtroom, and the judge said, 'Well, he can wait until the jury finds him guilty, and then display and he's still overthrowing the conviction. We're just having a go-around for nothing.' So the prosecutor complained, but when we reconvened after the recess, the prosecutor said he hadn't been able to get it, so the judge invoked *Rule 43(c)*, which says that the judge on his own recommendation can dismiss the charges in the interest of justice. So, we'd had probably another two hours of the court's time, or more, over this thing, and Officer Gruhall, the arresting officer, of course, he started laughing at the government and their inability to deal with a *pro per* defendant, and that was the final laugh. Then the judge dismissed the charges and it was all over.

"Concerning principle objectives, a *Patriot in Action* by definition is an individual who loves his God and his country enough that he will pledge his life and his fortune and his sacred honor in order to return America to God-fearing constitutional government. In response to the question how do I join that organization, the answer is, you cannot join *Patriots in Action,* you just have to be one. *Patriots in Action* is a disorganization and it's an individual endeavor. Each one of us has to do our own patriot acting. *Patriots in Action* meetings took place for seven years in Anchorage, weekly meetings every Thursday at Clark Junior High, and at those meetings we held mock trials, we studied the *Constitution,* we talked about how to conduct ourselves when stopped by a policeman, which is the same procedure which was put into effect when I was stopped for allegedly running a red light, which charge was dismissed seven months later.

"The *Alaska Patriots* brought in guest speakers starting in 1978 with John Law Freeman. He was a real pied piper and really was the spark plug that ignited the *Alaska Patriots in Action* or at least led them to become such a large group. Probably, looking back from 1988, we were the most effective patriot group and effective, meaning that we were able to hold the bureaucratic onslaught at bay better than any other group in the United States. Also, due to the fact that one could not join the *Patriots in Action,* the organization couldn't be infiltrated, since there wasn't one. There was no member list, so that could not be obtained and a lot of things that happened to groups like the National Commodity and Barter Association, and many others, didn't happen to the *Patriots in Action,* since they did not have this central structure that the others did. John Law Freeman would stand up there and dance on the Constitution, on the stage, and say 'I'm above the Constitution, and the government's under the Constitution, and you just do what I say and if the government hauls you into court, you tell them that you heard me speak, and that's why you've done what you've done, just what I told you to do, and then they'll have to bring me in and let me testify to the jury and give them the same presentation that you're hearing.'

"Well, that was a wonderful idea, and of course, John was absolutely right. No jury in their right minds would convict anybody of a crime for doing what John Law Freeman said. He had one of the best presentations that I ever saw in the Patriot movement, and was certainly a pied piper and people rushed to follow him by the droves. The problem with all this was that he was only allowed on the stand one time, and sure enough, that defendant was acquitted. But, after the government heard him once, they never let him testify to the jury again. His testimony occurred in the case of a young man who had filed an exempt W-4 and was charged under section 7205. This young man was acquitted. Whereas there were five of them charged, four of them pled and only the fifth went to trial. I believe that case was defended by the old gentleman from Missoula,

Montana.

"John was then charged himself as a conspirator with these four people who had filed W-4s. He was convicted, even though one of the first people had been acquitted. Why John Law Freeman was convicted and in fact was sentenced to a year and I think did his nine months in jail as a result of that, I'll never understand. He raised the *First Amendment* on appeal and lost. Then he was charged in another state, filed a motion to dismiss based on the *First Amendment,* and it was granted. Then, I think he was charged again in Washington or Oregon and lost in that case, went up to the Ninth Circuit and he lost that one on *First Amendment* grounds. I think it was a close case.

"John Freeman one day decided that he needed to find where the income tax had come from. So he started looking in the law books and he couldn't find it there. Then he looked under the bed, and he looked in the refrigerator, and he looked everyplace he could think of, and he couldn't find the source of the income tax amendment, so he looked in the Communist Manifesto, and there it was, Plank II. 'A highly progressive or graduated income tax. You shouldn't file an income tax return because it's illegal, immoral and does everything but make you fat.' The reason that he got so irate about this was because he looked around at his little red-headed grandson one day, and he said, 'NOOOOO, this is not going to be imposed on my grandson!' And he undertook to fight the income tax.

"He held himself out as a lawyer, which he was. He said a lawyer is one who knows the law; a bar member is one who practices court decisions. Well, he knew the law and he had a client come to him in Medford, Oregon, right after he first got started. This client had been charged with drunk driving, and John said, 'Well did you do it?' And the client said, 'Yes.' And he said, 'Well I don't defend people that are guilty. If you want to get acquitted of that, you're going to have to go find an attorney that's got a favor coming. You just start interviewing attorneys, and when you find one that will guarantee you an acquittal, then you know he's got a favor coming at the court, and he'll get you acquitted.'

"After John's big success, why there were a number of Mr. Freemans around: there was David Freeman, and Mac says some of them even looked like John, with white beard and all. I don't know about that, but it turned out that you could have John Law Freeman speaking in three different parts of the United States on the same night! There was a Bob Freeman.

"In 1978, the building inspector came to the property where Carol and I were living, and seemed to believe that our carport was newly constructed, even though he hadn't been there. In fact, I think the workers were still working on the back porch. So he wanted to come on the property and inspect this building project, and I informed him that if he didn't have any warrant, he better not cross the curb line and come onto the property, that I was ordering him to keep off, and my position was as a manager of the property. He informed me that he would come on the property, that he'd go get the cops, and I said, 'Well just be sure that you got a warrant with you when you come back, and then you won't have any problem. We believe that the law must be obeyed.'

"Well, he did come back with a policeman. I wasn't there, and he came up, walked up on the property and tacked a 'cease and desist' notice on one of the legs of the carport. Just then Carol recognized what was happening and went running out and told him to get away from there unless he had a warrant. Where was his warrant? He said, 'I don't need a warrant, I've got the police officer.' And Carol said to the police officer, 'Where's your warrant?' He said, 'I got a badge, I don't need a warrant. I can go anyplace I want to and do anything I want to in the municipality of Anchorage.' Then he refused to identify himself. He gave her the badge number and that's all he would give her. And of course all they were there to do really was to post that notice which Carol tore down before their very eyes. They made all kinds of threats against her for such a thing.

"As a result of this, some of us went out to the Municipal Building permit office, or whatever it's called, and confronted the head man of the building permit department. And we asked him what was going on that his boys, his underlings, were out running around harassing the people without warrants, and all these things. He proceeded to get upset, since we had tape recorders running and witnesses to this, and we put him on notice that he was bound by *Article 6, Para. 3* of the *Constitution* to uphold the *Constitution*.

"Skipping ahead, we found this building inspector head. It was at Christmas time. The original incident occurred in October. A week before Christmas he was down in the lobby of the Captain Cooke Hotel, and we confronted him as he came out of the liquor store, and he was on company time. It was during work hours. And we said, 'Why Mr. Strandberg, what are you doing in here? Aren't you working today?' 'No,' he said. 'I took the afternoon off.' So we called his office and found out that he hadn't taken the afternoon off at all. We wrote that up and confronted him some more with it.

"What this eventually came down to was that the building department could not get on this property to make an inspection of what they perceived to be new construction. So they went to court and they finally got a court order prohibiting Rock Smith from interfering with their inspection of the property and the court, in their wisdom, provided that they needed to give notice in advance before they were going to make this inspection so that all parties would be forewarned. Well, when they arrived at the house to make their inspection, the building inspectors were joined by two cars of policemen and all the flack jackets and the works. They found forty openly armed Christian patriots lined up along the perimeter of the property and the patriots informed the police and building inspectors that they did not have any right on this property and that this was *church* property and that they were going to stand right here. This is where the showdown was going to be, this was going to be it because they weren't going to give in. After a few minutes of arguing back and forth, finally the police and the building inspectors and all the 'officials' decided to withdraw and that was the last confrontation over that particular issue. About a year and a half after that, the court sent out a notice that they were dismissing the action for lack of prosecution. So that is where that ended."

Obviously, Rock was a well-honed litigator by the time I reached Anchorage in October of 1981 to assist with his state criminal tax case before Judge Moody. After I had offered my assistance to Rock *pro bono* by telephone from Phoenix, Rock told me that he had been led by the Holy Spirit to defend on his own and that the Holy Spirit through Rock would be in charge of the case. Thus, I was somewhat surprised when Rock called back and asked that I come up and lend technical assistance. I agreed, but Rock made clear to me that I was not in charge of the case; I was there only to assist. This for me was difficult at best, but I felt I would just do the best that I could.

Thus, on the first day of trial I appeared in court with Rock, and Rock moved for my admission as "co-counsel." This was unheard of; judges do not permit defendants and an attorney to be "co-counsel." Furthermore, under the local rules, out of state counsel must associate with a local attorney. But Rock took the position that since he was his own attorney, he could sponsor me. The judge agreed so long as I would agreed not to ask for a continuance. I was in agreement, and right after the judge ordered my admission, I made a motion for an evidentiary hearing and the judge was outraged, thinking that I had broken my promise and was attempting a continuance. The hearing was denied and Rock and I were threatened on numerous occasions with fines for contempt of court.

We took three days to select the jury and I gave opening statement in which I brought out before the jury that, "This is the first case of its type. No one in the State of Alaska had ever been charged with an income tax offense. Alaska no longer has an income tax." Prosecutor Sheley objected and the judge cut me off. With the help of Rocky Streble, we had a technical defense: Rock did not owe the taxes they claimed he owed.

Rock and I took turns in cross-examining the government's witnesses, most of whom were record keepers. Rock has described how the voter registrar identified me as Rock Smith. My recollection is that it was not the voter registrar but a payroll clerk for one of Rock's former employers. It makes no difference which witness it was; what is important is this: the jury, judge, prosecutor and even Rock and I were being set up. What was happening was that Rock and I were adamant on the issue of the government's failure to tie the documents offered to Rock Smith. Then followed the bank witnesses. Rock had banked at several banks, and I asked the bank witnesses whether or not they knew for a fact that the records they had brought to the courtroom concerned the Rock Smith sitting at the table. They said they did not know. I then asked if they had ever met Rock Smith? Did they even know what he looked like? And they answered, "No." We objected for lack of foundation - that the records were not tied to the defendant - but the objection was overruled and Judge Moody ordered the records admitted.

During a brief recess I was examining records in preparation for the next bank witness, Rock and I sitting at the defense table. Rock handed me a bank signature card bearing what appeared to be the signature of Rock Smith and whispered, "This isn't my signature. I never had an account at this bank." The bank was in the Seattle area, where Rock had lived for a period of time, and I closely examined the signature card and answered, "Come on, Rock, you must be mistaken. It looks exactly like your signature," comparing it to other signature cards. Rock said, "No, there's a mistake, I'm sure of it. I never had an account at this bank." My adrenaline skyrocketed. In a flash I could see in my mind's eye what was about to happen: the prosecutor again would bring a bank witness who had never met Rock and over our strenuous objection the documents would likely be admitted against Rock Smith despite the fact that the records had nothing to do with this Rock Smith. They were the records concerning whom we later called "Seattle Smith."

As the bank officer was being examined by Sheley, Rock and I were over at the defense table, again whispering. "Rock, what do you think, maybe I shouldn't persist too much with my objections as before because perhaps the judge will not admit the records without a more precise foundation laid by the prosecutor and witness." "No, let's object to the hilt," was his response. I did so. The records were admitted and the stage was set for a "gotcha" about which defense attorneys dream. The plan was this: we will locate Seattle Smith, subpoena him, and when the government finishes its case in chief, I will rise and announce, looking at the jury, "Your Honor, the defense calls as its first witness - Rock Smith." Everyone will wait for Rock to get out of his chair, but he will not move, and I will pause. As patience grows thin, I will move to the door and ask Seattle Smith to take the witness stand. By this method, we would bring out the government's lie and hopefully totally destroy their credibility with the jury.

The plan was much like the closing argument I had heard about by a defense lawyer whose client was charged with murder. The lawyer argued that his client did not commit the murder and then stated confidently, "The person who did commit the murder will walk through that door in thirty seconds," pointing to the large double doors of the courtroom. All the jurors, of course, as in a tennis match, simultaneously turned their heads to the door and waited the thirty seconds. No one appeared and the defense lawyer then stated, "If you believe that someone would walk through that door, then you held a reasonable doubt as to whether my client committed the murder. Thus, you must acquit him."

During the evening recess, it took me five minutes through the telephone information operator to locate Seattle Smith. He agreed to fly to Anchorage on a ticket we would provide. He would fly to Anchorage the next day and would take the stand the second day. As Sun Tzu proclaimed:

Nothing is more difficult than the art of maneuver. What is difficult about maneuver is to make the devious route the most direct and to turn misfortune to advantage. Thus, march by an indirect route and divert the enemy by enticing him with a bait. In so doing, you may set out after he does and arrive before him. One able to do this understands the strategy of the direct and the indirect.

The next morning before calling her next witness, Sheley said she had some preliminary matters to bring to the court's attention. After discussing perfunctory matters such as exhibits and witnesses, Sheley said, "Oh, by the way, Judge, we have a *slight* problem. We need to withdraw the records from the Seattle bank because we discovered that they don't pertain to Rock Smith." Judge Moody sat up straight, unbelieving, and said very dryly, "You *sure do* have a problem." As it turned out, Seattle Smith had cold feet, called the bank to see what was going on, and the bank officer in turn called Sheley. We had lost the element of surprise. It was now time to make the frontal attack. I was ready to spring up and move for a mistrial, but remembered that Rock was in charge of the case and first consulted with him. Sheley and the judge were engaged in a dialogue concerning how the situation could be remedied. "What do you propose I tell the jury," Judge Moody was saying, while Rock and I were again whispering at the defense table. "Don't move for a mistrial," Rock commanded. "Why not?" "Just do what I say," Rock responded, confident. "Well then how about a motion to dismiss for prosecutorial misconduct?" This he okayed and I stood, lashing out at Sheley for incompetence, explaining to the court that I

218

was able to locate Seattle Smith in five minutes and that the prosecutor has a duty to protect the accused. She obviously was vindictive and had no desire as the record reflected throughout this case to protect the rights of Rock Smith. At this point, Sheley began to cry, but she wasn't much of an actress. Strange how tears flowed as I lashed out at her, but as soon as it was her time to speak, she again regained composure, complaining that I had personally attacked her. I later retorted there was nothing personal about it at all. It was simply a vicious, vindictive prosecution and should be dismissed.

After much bantering back and forth between Sheley and me, Judge Moody, appearing perplexed, finally said, "I don't see any choice but to declare a mistrial," and he did so. He brought the jury back in and dismissed them. I suggested each side file a brief concerning their legal position and the judge agreed. Thus, I went back to Arizona to do considerable research on double jeopardy. The U.S. Supreme Court has interpreted the double jeopardy clause of the *Fifth Amendment* to the *U.S. Constitution* to mean that where a defendant moves for a mistrial during trial, the prosecutor can commence a second trial. Likewise, where the jury is unable to reach a verdict. From my research, I found, however, that where the court on its own declares a mistrial or the prosecutor causes a mistrial without motion of the defendant, that the defendant cannot be retried. Had I moved for mistrial, I would have waived the issue! There was Alaksa Supreme Court case law in our favor. Thus, I prepared and submitted a brief on the double jeopardy issue and went back to Alaska to argue. Rather than reach the legal issues, Judge Moody, in King Solomon-like fashion, ruled that the state could proceed with the second trial *if* they paid Rock's lost wages and my attorney fees. "Mr. MacPherson agreed to try a case *pro bono,* but he didn't agree to try a *second* case *pro bono*." The Judge asked Rock and I for an estimate of the total to be paid by the state and we said, "Thirty-five thousand dollars." Sheley refused to pay the fare and the case was dismissed.

Undaunted, the *Beast* would later indict Rock in federal court for conspiracy and income tax evasion. Named as his co-defendant would be his wife, Carol, for her refusal to cooperate before the federal grand jury investigating Rock. Rock would represent himself; I would represent Carol. (But that is another *War Story* reserved for *Part II.*) *The Northern Lights Glimmer,* a newsletter of the *Alaska Patriots,* had reported in September of 1981 Rock's proceedings before Judge Moody of July 7. On page 3 of *The Glimmer* it was stated: "Rock seems to hang right in there, giving God ALL the praise and glory for strength and strategy." Divine providence? Let the reader decide.

I hold it that a little rebellion now and then is a good thing and is as neccessary in the political world as storms in the physical. Thomas Jefferson

NEW YORK CARPET LAYER Chapter 12

Larry Ranucci, an Italian carpet layer from Long Island, New York became in 1981 Bishop of the Life Science Church of New York. Millions of dollars were funnelled through the church in a multi-level marketing plan designed by Larry to bring not just religion to the masses, but the glory of tax exemption. *Church of the Immaculate Deduction.* City of New York policemen, garbage collectors, police detectives, bus drivers. It was, as a television news special called it, "God v. the IRS." I would spend three months trying a conspiracy case in Manhattan: Larry Ranucci; his daughter Lorraine Schneider; Frank Ebner, "legal liaison"; Joe Rodi, former city policeman; and Harvard Tapen. (For personal reasons, Donna was severed from the case.)

"Hey, Larry. So what's happening?" "Mac, how are you? So what are you going to do already?" "Listen to me Larry. We're going to put tax exemption for churches, the lawyers and the whole system on trial."

I had to love Larry Ranucci. He was Italian. And, as ethnic groups go, I love Italians, especially those from the Northeast. Their looks, their devout Catholic roots, their food, their expressions, talking with their hands. (Didn't *all* Italians live in the Northeast?)

My first contact with Italians was in 1955, when our family moved to Greenwich, Connecticut. Born and raised in Cincinnati, I had never been out of Ohio except for military school at Millersburg, Kentucky and on a fishing trip to Burnside, Kentucky. My stepfather, Kurt, an architect, wanted to get to know my brother and me before he wed my mother. Burnside, on Lake Cumberland was the selected spot. We stayed in a motel, rented a boat and fished without much success. I was ten, Doug was fourteen.

I distinctly remember at age 7, my mother asking what I wanted for my birthday. "A father." She laughed. She was a beautiful woman and had been a model. Why hadn't she re-married or even dated much? My sister Margo, brother Doug, and I reckoned no one could meet up to my father. This, I could believe. He was strikingly handsome and apparently successful in business: public relations and writing. At age 29 he collapsed and died of a heart attack in an elevator in Philadelphia. We had been living in Orland, outside of Philadelphia, and he commuted by train. I was two years old. My mother returned with her three children to Cincinnati and began work, including house-to-house Avon sales. I remember at age five going with her door-to-door.

Initially, Doug, Margo and I attended public school at North Avondale Elementary School, at the top of our street, Warwick Avenue. Doug had a run-in with the teacher and we were all transferred to St. Thomas Aquinas, a private Catholic school a few blocks away. I had attended kindergarten at North Avondale and was now in first grade. I did well, but felt an outcast. A loner. We were the only non-Catholics in the school. And, I had to contend with some bullies. I was a new kid in school and was an easy target. The bullies were bigger. After school I was harassed walking home the same route as three bullies, who were a couple of grades ahead of me and much bigger. I decided that discretion was the better part of valor and began to take the path of least resistance, a different route. As school ended I stalled getting my books and then slipped out of the building and headed in the opposite direction. It took me twenty minutes instead of ten to walk home, but it was worth it.

Mid-year in my first grade my mother decided to put us all in Catholic boarding school. I had mixed feelings. I was now well-adjusted and doing well at St. Thomas Aquinas, but the thought was exciting: away from home, on my own, wearing a uniform! *Time* magazine had pictured on its cover Douglas MacArthur and my grandfather, a self-made man and devout Republican, had often criticized Truman for firing MacArthur, the West Point graduate, WWI hero, WWII hero, and Korean War hero. "I shall return." "It was 1951 when MacArthur was fired and then gave his farewell speech to Congress, ending with "Old soldiers never die, they just fade away." *Life* and *Saturday Evening Post* were part of our household. MacArthur, Eisenhower, and Billie Mitchell. These were my heroes. Without a father, I needed some heroes.

Doug and I entered St. Aloysius Military Academy, a Catholic school run by nuns. Father Schroeder was in charge, the only male on the staff. Daily lessons included catechism, but the doctrine was similar to the Episcopal Church my family attended. In fact, we were "high Episcopal" so the major differences were our non-recognition of the Pope and no Latin. Again, I was a loner and perhaps because of it, decided to excel. I was first in my class, but was not to participate in First Holy Communion. Not Catholic, no communion. No ticky, no laundry. Yet, I knew the catechism better than anyone.

Bedtime was worst. It was then that I thought of my family and home and was quite homesick. During weekend visits, my mother would either first pick up Margo at nearby Brown County School for Girls, also Catholic, and Margo would spend the day at our school, or Doug and I were picked up and taken to visit with Margo. Sunday evenings at 4 or 5 p.m. were the saddest. On furloughs,

Doug and I rode the bus to Cincinnati where my mother would pick us up at the bus station. I was proud of the uniform. I became accustomed to the discipline.

During the summer, after my second-grade year at Fayetteville, Doug, Margo and I were at Fort Scott Camp, also Catholic. I learned that St. Aloysius would not reopen for the fall. My mother had found another school for Doug and me, Millersburg Military Institute (MMI) in Millersburg, Kentucky. Margo would attend a Catholic girls' school in Cincinnati and sleep at home.

At MMI, non-sectarian, I lived a more normal life and was not near as homesick. Of course, I was older. Two cadets shared a room and I had a buddy, Charles Brawley. He and his sister attended Fort Scott in the summer as well. Chuck was not studious like I was, but was a fearless daredevil. Small and wirey, he loved trouble. He and I did crazy things like slip out the window at night, climb down a porch and go AWOL. We had nowhere to go, we just wanted to prove to ourselves we could slip out and slip back in undetected. In fact, we planned our escape back to Cincinnati, a plan never executed. A railroad track ran through town about one hundred yards away. We took note of the freight train times and figured how we could slip out, hop the train, and be in Cincinnati before we were as much as missed.

We did other crazy things just to relieve boredom. One weekend, Chuck's mother left him a birthday cake which we took to our room and hid it. One of the teachers, Captain Steel, had a boxer dog named Tonker that wandered the halls. We heard the scratch, scratch noise of Tonker walking down the hall on the hardwood floor and opened our door, inviting Tonker in. We then fed him the entire cake, let him out the door where he wandered down the hallway, near the rooms of other cadets, and started throwing up.

Our rambunctiousness did get me in trouble in fourth grade. We were, during our afternoon play, always exploring off-limit areas. This one included the field house where the bleachers were folded against the wall and we decided to play tag, running along the tops of the bleachers, leaping from one to the next. In chasing Chuck, giggling, I lost my balance and fell headfirst for the gymnasium floor. In a natural reaction, I stuck out my right forearm to block the fall and it struck the hard floor first. Knowing the trouble we were in, we decided to keep it secret. But the pain became unbearable and I reported it. I had a green stick fracture of the bone and had to wear a cast for several months.

In the third grade, my teacher for all classes was a Mrs. Rawls, but in fourth grade I had several teachers, all men in uniform. They were given Captain rank. The head of the junior school was Major Betts. He and his wife lived in an apartment in the complex. We wore Eisenhower jackets to class and changed to play clothes immediately after class. Again, I excelled academically.

My Millersburg experience exposed me to the cultures and mannerisms of the South. We bussed or trained to nearby Paris, Kentucky, not far from Lexington. This was tobacco and horse country. On Saturday we were given town passes and went to the drugstore with an old time soda fountain, where we bought comic books and drank cherry cokes. We also fought a lot with the "town kids," the "townies." Church attendance was mandatory and with no Episcopal church in town, Doug and I settled on the Methodist. The preachers were fiery fundamentalists. Margo and my mother would visit once in a while, sometimes bringing aunts and uncles and my cousins Mary Ann or Jimmy and Nancy. I was now, at age nine, an experienced soldier.

My brother's best friend was a scrawny redhead kid named Billy Promberger. One day I watched with astonishment as Billy stood up to a hot shot bully, twice his size. He was shoving Billy around, but lightening fast Billy shot for his legs and scored a takedown, knocking the bully to the ground and jumping on his chest before Captain Steel broke it up. I was impressed.

On Thanksgiving leave I was back to North Avondale playground in Cincinnati. We had a street bully and some other kids on the street were saying how "Sandy's going to whip him now that he has been off to military school." For ten-year olds, military school was like somebody joining the Marines. I was not saying anything, hoping their dares would die down and the bully would ignore it all. He did not. The kids on the block had seen me in uniform and the bully was going to call my bluff. Dare I back down now? He shoved me a few times, "So I hear you're home from military school. Where's your uniform? You going to whip me now, soldier boy?" He was much bigger, I was not a tough guy, and I did not look for fights. What to do? Simple, I copied Billy Promburger, shooting for the legs, catching the bully by surprise. His head hit the ground with a loud thump and he began to cry. It was over in a flash. He bullied no one after that. After all, if he were to do so, he risked retribution from the old soldier from Kentucky. (I was to learn a lot more about Billy's takedown years later in plebe wrestling class and as an intramural wrestler at West Point. West Point's intramural program is high calibre, akin to junior college intercollegiate programs.)

At the end of my fourth grade, my mother and Kurt were engaged and I left MMI with sadness. It had become a second home and I was now well-schooled in religion as well as academic subjects.

The night before we left Cincinnati by car for Greenwich, I could not sleep. I was ready for the adventure of a small town on the Connecticut coast. After visiting D.C. and Annapolis on the way, we moved into an apartment across from Greenwich High School, where my brother attended. My sister and I rode our bikes to Julian Curtis Elementary School, a couple of miles away, where I began fifth grade.

Again I was a new kid, my slow Southern (by comparison) drawl gave me away to initial ridicule, but soon I made friends and loved the small town atmosphere. I could go anywhere in town on my bike. ("Up the avenue," not "downtown.") I would see Bert Parks ("Miss America" host) on his motor scooter on the avenue, Bud Colliere ("Beat the Clock") taught Sunday School at the Episcopal Church we attended. Margo's boyfriend was Danny Guerrieri, very Italian. The Guerrieris became for Margo a second family and were sorely disappointed when Margo married Kerry Nevin, an orthopedic surgeon from Long Island, who had attended Dartmouth. (Danny, who expected to go to Annapolis, attended the University of Rhode Island. His good friend and Margo's classmate, Pete Kraus, was, under one thousand to one odds, my first roommate plebe year at West Point. Danny's younger sister married another West Pointer.)

After two years in Greenwich, my mother's second marriage did not go well. She divorced and we returned to Cincinnati. But Margo, heartbroken to leave, lived at the Guerrieri home for a couple of years, then returned to Cincinnati where she graduated from high school. She attended the University of Connecticut Nursing School and worked at Greenwich Hospital. I returned to Greenwich one summer, staying with my friends, the Derkasch family. (Dr. Derkasch was our family doctor and a physician at Greenwich Hospital. His son Bob, my best friend in Greenwich, became an orthopedic surgeon and he and Kerry crossed paths during a residency in Cleveland.)

The Guerrieris, then, were my first real exposure to the Italian-American family. Mr Guerrieri owned and ran the Putman Barbershop at the top of Greenwich Avenue, across from the Pickwick Hotel. Of course, living in Connecticut two years, I came in contact with many Italians and came to love their ethnic heritage and culture. At West Point there were many cadets from New York and the New England states.

But it was Larry Ranucci who taught me about "the short-arms disease." He and Ebner and I would go to lunch in Manhattan after visiting the prosecutor, reviewing file cabinets of documents. "Larry, why is it Ebner never offers to pick up the tab at lunch?" "You see, Mac, Ebner's got the short-arms disease." "The short-arms disease, what's the short-arms disease?" "You see, Mac," demonstrating. "He's got money in his pocket, but his arms are so short, he can't get his hands down to the money ... Mac, it seems like there was a time when," was the introductory clause to everything Larry had to say in response to my many queries concerning the facts of his case. He had a long story to tell.

Larry's true ambition in life, in addition to becoming independently wealthy, was to help other people. Multi-level marketing was, he felt, the key to success for the common man. As a carpet layer, he had done well. His wife, a real estate agent, and he had acquired a nice home in Long Island on a canal near a golf course. They had a son and three daughters and the American dream was theirs. But an avid reader of *The Power of Positive Thinking* and other such books, Larry had a driving ambition to do better and to share with others the methods of his success.

A student of Earl Nightingale and Norman Vincent Peale, he listened to tapes, becoming an enthusiastic marketer and a motivating public speaker. His Italian emotion, charisma and natural good looks, coupled with his driving ambition, were his major assets. He had a big funny bone and loved to tell jokes to me and to my three sons, and I am sure to many others. But to the U.S. Attorney's Office in New York, he became public enemy number one, a serious threat to our taxation system based upon *voluntary compliance*. Larry had tried multi-level marketing through organizations destroyed by the government. Glen Turner's *Dare to Be Great*. Koskot and others. Was the writing on the wall for Larry?

Under multi-level marketing, individual salesmen (account representatives?) create a "down line," thus building their wealth by means of a pyramid. They receive a certain percent of the profits from those monies brought in through all members of the down line. Hypothetically, tremendous profits can be reached, due to the geometric progression of multi-level marketing. For example, if an individual brings under him but five individuals who each, in turn, bring in five individuals and you go "six levels deep," you have a total of 15,625 in your "down line." Many multi-level marketing programs have been attacked on the basis of no product or service actually rendered but merely a "Ponzi scheme" by which money keeps changing hands with no real economic purpose served, such as the sale of a product.

In 1981, Larry was invited to attend a meeting in New Jersey at which another Italian spoke, Frank Conti, "Archbishop Francis John I," "Dr. John" and "Father John," later charged with evading $790,900 in taxes on income of $1,710,000 between 1978 and 1981. Indicted with Conti were Joseph Borriello and Guy Santeramo, a former police officer. Larry knew Conti through Koskot. This time the issue was tax reduction or even elimination by means of a loophole in the law: the church. Since Congress cannot make a law prohibiting a religion or discriminating in favor of one religion over another, then, again hypothetically, every man can be a minister and every man can have his own church. While charitable organizations such as foundations must apply for tax exemption status under *Sec. 501(c)(3)* of the Internal Revenue Code, churches are exempt from such application under the Code. This is a little-known fact. While IRS, in testing the deductibility of charitable deductions found on a tax return will refer to their cumulative listing of organizations which have received IRS blessings through the *501(c)(3)* application, the truth of the matter is that churches need not be on such listing. They are automatically exempt if, in fact, they are a church. Which then raises the question of: what is a church?

Because of the proliferation of mail-order ministries, IRS began to develop a questionnaire mailed to questionable churches for their completion and return to IRS. The questionnaire, in and of itself, violates the *First Amendment* for reason that it asks questions about beliefs.

Kirby Hensley and the ULC had been practicing this concept for a number of years. Form your own church! As a minister, you could either take a vow of poverty and be totally exempt from taxes, or give to the church up to 50% of your earnings and take a charitable deduction for that amount. You could hold services in your own home, dictate your own creed and programs of ministry, and perform marriages and baptisms. Under the *First Amendment*, the state could not encroach upon your beliefs, however different. The problem for IRS was that Hensley's concept had strong foundation in the law. Who is to say what is a religion without doing violence to the *First Amendment*?

In 1981, ten Brannif Airline pilots were indicted with tax evasion in Fort Worth, Texas. IRS claimed the pilots signed a "vow of poverty" and agreed to turn over all their earnings to the church. A church building, complete with steeple, was purchased in Grapevine, Texas. I was called to represent Gerald Ross, a Viet vet brother who had flown bombing missions over North Vietnam as a Navy pilot. (Details in *War Stories, Part II.*)

At the New Jersey meeting, and at other similar meetings which launched Larry and others into the ministry, the attendees watched a short film clip presentation by William Drexler, an attorney from Minnesota. Drexler described his winning criminal tax case in which he was charged with willful failure to file federal income tax return where he had filed claiming the *Fifth*. Then he went on to describe the religious exemption under the law and the Life Science Church. The Life Science Church, Drexler explained, had, in fact, a letter from the IRS agreeing to its exempt status. *The proof was in the pudding.* (It was later discovered Drexler had actually purchased or otherwise obtained the original Life Science Church from another minister.)

Intrigued by the message, Larry did what any reasonable person would do: he checked it out. First he read the Code himself to see if what Drexler was saying was, in fact, the law. He asked an attorney about the Code sections and it appeared Drexler was correct. After studying and talking it over with others, Larry was more excited and wanted to meet Drexler, which he did in New York. At that meeting, Drexler was impressive, but did not bother to mention to Larry that he had been disbarred in Minnesota. His promotions, in fact, emphasized not only his status as an attorney, but as a former Justice of the Peace. Hence, the early beginnings of the Life Science Church of New York. (The Life Science Church, no different than the Catholic Church or any other religion, could be broken down into territories. With Italian names like Ranucci, Petroza, Rodi and Jania, it could appear to the public as a church mafia.)

Beginnings for the Life Science Church of New York were modest, Larry, conducting meetings and seminars. But not to Larry's surprise, people began to sign up, paying $2,000 "donations" to obtain the instructional materials, the forms. As the church grew, it acquired property near Long Beach, Long Island, where services and meetings were held, marriages and baptisms performed.

As the Life Science Church became more popular nation-wide, articles began appearing in newspapers such as the one entitled "Church Challenges IRS to Court Battle Over Pledge of Tax Salvation for its Converts."

...The IRS insists the beat-taxation plan doesn't work. "We will not allow income signed over to a church to be considered as charitable contributions when the church simply acts as a conduit and pays out the money on your behalf," a spokesman said. But Larry Ranucci, a former businessman who is bishop of the Long Island, New York branch of the Life Science Church, said, "We have hundreds of members who can show how it has worked for them." He challenged the IRS to bring court action against the Life Science Church or any of its affiliates. "I've already invited them to send a representative to one of our meetings to try to prove where we are wrong, but they've refused," he said ....

Dr. Ranucci added that he thought a church that worshipped the Constitution was much more worthwhile than the Church of Lesbians, one of those granted tax exemption by the IRS.

To bolster his case that his church members beat taxes anyway, he produced pay slips that showed that no federal, state or city taxes have been deducted and copies of tax rebates ....

Dr. Ranucci said the Life Science Church was not against taxation, only unfair taxation.

"Rich people like Richard Nixon, David Rockefeller, the late Lyndon Johnson, and John Wayne have avoided paying taxes in this way for years," he said. "We are just offering the ordinary guy in the street the same chance."

The battle lines were drawn.

But Bishop Ranucci and Life Science Church of New York were not without legal authority through case law, or practical authority by way of major nation-wide ministries. Even before the Jim and Tammy Bakker of *Praise the Lord* and *Heritage Town, U.S.A.*, including the millions of dollars allegedly spent by the Bakkers for their personal use, including the air-conditioned dog house, there were numerous articles concerning the amount of wealth held by TV and radio preachers and their extravagant spending. For example, one article addressed the Reverend Ike of the United Christian Evangelistic Association, Reverend Billy Graham, Reverend Rex Humbard, Reverend Oral Roberts and Reverend Robert Schuller. The title of the article was "TV Preachers Now Using Show Biz Razzle-Dazzle to Rake in the $Millions." Under Reverend Ike's picture is the caption, "Reverend Ike was the most flamboyant of the TV evangelists. He preaches love of money, wears $700 suits and has 16 Rolls Royces." The article reported on the holdings and salaries of each of the ministers. Humbard, for example, was living in a $200,000 home.

As the Life Science Church of New York grew, its organizers and leaders became bold in their challenge to the government. But it was not IRS who launched the first attack. No doubt the Attorney General of New York, Robert Abrams, felt pressure as a result of the substantial City of New York publicity. AG investigators were lurking about, attending seminars, signing up as ministers, using body recorders.

But before Abrams fired the first volley, almost $8.4 million had flowed to and through the Life Science Church of New York! Of that, $2.7 million went to Ranucci and his family, $1.2 million to the Life Science Church of California, which was Drexler, and $5.7 million to the Life Science Church of North America, a spin-off organization of the Life Science Church of New York, which consisted of four trustees: Ranucci, Petroza, Ebner and Rodi.

If the truth be known, it is the state government that can launch more quickly a vicious attack than the *federalities*. Although the feds raise images of Elliot Ness and J. Edgar Hoover, the *Monster* becomes tangled in its own tentacles. *Bureaucracy*. IRS will investigate for two or more years and then it takes two or more years for the Justice Department to make up its mind to prosecute. The case is then sent from the Justice Department back to the U.S. Attorney's Office for either further investigation or the indictment itself. Hence, tax indictments are returned three to six years after the years under investigation, with six years the maximum under the statute of limitations. If a Grand Jury is involved, the investigation may itself drag on for years. In the case of the multi-count indictment brought against Drexler, the San Diego Grand Jury investigated at least four years. This was likely several Grand Juries. Dahlstrom had two. Where one Grand Jury runs out of time on its term, there is a choice between extension of the term or review by a second Grand Jury. Evidence collected by the first is merely summarized by a Special Agent appearing before the second.

The state, on the other hand, a much smaller bureaucracy, can mobilize at will without so many layers of approval. The New York AG's office took the dare laid out by LSC: "We are a church; therefore, our ministers reap tax benefits as any other ministers; it's the law; treat us differently and the *First Amendment* is violated." These positions were, of course, not without merit from ULC's victory to IRS Revenue Rulings upholding the vow of poverty. Common sense analogies applied as well. Does a Catholic cardinal live in modesty? Does Billy Graham drive a Chevrolet Malibu or something more expensive, and if something more expensive, how is that justified, considering that he needs but basic transportation? Are Catholic nuns granted vow of poverty status where they are required by their order to work at a public hospital? (Yes, in one case.) If the sister's salary is assigned to the order, is she required to pay taxes? Where is the line drawn?

Even IRS' internal memos in Washington pointed out the confusion of the law and lack of IRS applying and enforcing the law with consistency. They knew they wanted to stop the growth of "mail-order ministries," but they had to find easy targets. They could not afford to lose for the risk would be opening of the flood gates.

The cynical, of course, would immediately claim "sham." How can a City of New York policeman be a minister assigning his wages to his "sacerdotal order?" *The proof is in the pudding.* What, pray tell, is the difference between the police officer and the nun, so long as their intent is pure and they carry out their religious duties with the same spirit and attention? No difference. But therein was the key. The policeman typically did not in substance "look, talk, act, walk or smell" like a minister of any religion. As in so many of the IRS conflicts, the issue boiled down to substance versus form, economic reality and business (here religious) purpose.

Enter the attorneys. No, first enter one Frank Ebner, would-be attorney, whose wife was a probation officer for the state. Frank's job - "legal liaison." Frank would handle the lawyers. As LSC grew and became wealthy, it needed legal counsel. Ministers had trouble with W-4 exempt. Legal counsel was needed to write threatening letters to the employer. LSC advertised and hired Jay Cohen, who had been a county prosecutor. Cohen, anxious to make the split to private practice, was in need of a steady retainer. Not a tax attorney, he would quickly learn.

Cohen, finding the religious loopholes as claimed by LSC did, in fact, exist, gave to LSC, as I would later argue before the jury, no red lights. Not even flashing red lights. No yellow lights. I would ask the Ranucci jury, "If it was so dead-in-the-water wrong, so dyed-in-the-wool black, so sinister, then why did these many lawyers never cry 'Stop in the name of the law'?"

As Cohen got flooded, and as state and federal investigators began to put on the pressure, LSC needed someone to back up Cohen. Someone less intimidated, with more experience. Enter one George Delmarmo from New Jersey, a wheeler-dealer, heavy-set type. George, whether from greater courage or smaller brains, was not intimidated by IRS. Or anyone, for that matter. Including, as it turned out, the federal judge. With a voracious appetite, he was always ready for Larry to take him to an Italian restaurant and talk. And talk they did.

While the multi-level plan was the brainchild of Ranucci, Delmarmo would, after the state court order against the church, come up with a new idea: IANDRO. International Association of Non-Denominational Religious Organizations. As employers and IRS auditors were showing their muscle, George concluded the obvious: strength in numbers. IANDRO members were entitled to legal counsel paid for by IANDRO. It was a form of prepaid legal insurance, but more than that, IANDRO would litigate as necessary test cases and be watchful for the benefit of its members the trends in the law. Research. Articles by minister lawyers of the Catholic and other faiths. Of course, Delmarmo's idea was not without financial benefit to Delmarmo. *Necessity is the mother of invention.* And if invention turns a profit, so much the better.

When Abrams filed suit in New York City Supreme Court to enjoin LSC under consumer fraud statutes and to appoint a receiver, even Delmarmo felt out gunned. It was time to call in the big guns from Madison Avenue. First Seth Siegel and then Marty Garbus. Garbus, it was said by George and Seth, was a well-known successful litigator concerning *First Amendment* issues. But he was not cheap. (Was there such a thing as a cheap Madison Avenue firm?) No sweat. Ebner, the legal liaison, knew well how to deal with lawyers. Keep them in line. "Bishop Ranucci, you keep bringing in the flock. I'll handle the lawyers." A million and a half dollars and several years later, Ebner was still talking and Ranucci listening, but the game had become not just about financial survival; they each faced a lot of years behind bars. Ebner still called the shots. Larry was the mouthpiece, Ebner the brains. (During the trial, I repeatedly and jokingly told Larry that if he loses and if the judge wants to really punish him harshly, the judge will require Larry to share a cell block with Ebner. Larry did not find it very funny.)

Ebner would bring out at trial that of $1.4 million, the Garbus firm received $900,000, Siegel $150,000, Delmarmo $150,000, Cohen $100,000, Stromer $34,000, Larry Greenapple $12,000, and two other lawyers $54,000. That is a lot of money paid to attorneys without so much as a *yellow light*.

On April 27, 1982, Judge Seymour Schwartz of the New York Supreme Court in Manhattan entered his opinion at the conclusion of a trial on the Attorney General's request for permanent injunction, enjoining Ranucci and others from continuing with alleged fraud and pyramid scheme of the LSC. According to the judge's order, investigator Edward Martinez, acting under cover, attended a seminar of LSC's Freedom Foundation in January of 1980 and subsequently became an ordained minister of the LSC. The "donation" at that time had risen to $3500 and perspective members were told that it would rise $100 in each succeeding month. Petroza and James Rotollo "informed investigator Martinez that he would receive a 10% commission on payments made by any new minister he recruited into the church." At one of the three training sessions attended by Martinez, Joseph Dalconzo and Carmine D'Onofrio taught Martinez and others how to draft church bylaws, constitution and trust agreements. In another meeting, he was informed that "Ebner, as legal counsel, would deal with ministers' problems with banks and real property tax. Mr. Ranucci then described how a Life Science Church minister could become a *millionaire* in one year by recruiting new ministers who, in turn, would recruit new ministers, thereby receiving commissions on all recruitments at an ever increasing level which would make him a millionaire."

Delconzo testified that he and Ranucci agreed that Delconzo, upon payment of $10,000, would become a director of LSC and would have his own organization. Under the church's marketing program, Delconzo testified, a minister recruiting other ministers was a "missionary representative" entitled to receive 10% commission on each payment by a new minister and after recruiting two ministers in a single month he became a "missionary supervisor." The commission rose to $500 for each recruit after the first two recruits and, as director, Delconzo received 40% of the money paid by those he recruited. Delconzo had received approximately $95,000 for the 20 people he had recruited.

At trial, the AG presented what the court regarded as "some of the nation's leading tax experts: Jerome Kurtz, former commissioner of the Internal Revenue Service; Father Charles Whelan, professor of law, Fordham University Law School, an expert on church exemptions; Stanley Weithorn, author of a definitive treatise on tax-exempt organizations; and Howard Schoenfeld, special assistant to the assistant commissioner for exempt organizations of the Internal Revenue Service." The AG had challenged every facet of LSC's claim of complete legal tax exemption, including the "vow of poverty" by which "a minister would claim authority to expend church funds for his family's food, clothing, shelter, personal expenses and even for spiritual retreats to Las Vegas."

Because of the *Fifth Amendment* dilemma - anything produced and any testimony given during the trial of this, a civil case, could be used against any of the church leaders in a criminal case - the respondents rested without producing any witnesses. In fact, the church, under Garbus' leadership as attorney, refused, and rightfully so, to produce any documents subpoenaed by the Attorney General on *Fifth Amendment* grounds. By striking the first blow civilly, rather than criminally, the government, whether state or federal, gains a tremendous advantage, especially if it succeeds in obtaining a freeze on all assets of the respondent, fixing them in place. By this blocking maneuver, the *Monster* then proceeds to "divide and conquer" by leverage of the criminal investigation and prosecution. Any defendants should feel free, of course, to come forward and "turn state's evidence." Which is what happened. Reverend Charles Respoli signed a sworn affidavit on July 5, 1980 that he joined the church because he believed "in the doctrines, principles and beliefs of the church which are the *Constitution of the United States* and the *Declaration of Independence* " and that he was not "a defrauded consumer of the Life Science Church Freedom Foundation or any of the named respondents." When charged with a felony, Respoli cut a deal with the government. Respoli had ironically appeared in one of the newsletters.

I first heard about the Life Science Church and Freedom Foundation from a fellow sanitation man. I am now off the tax roles and have a great feeling of relief from it. I admit when I heard about the organization, I was very skeptical about it, but by attending meetings and talking to various organizations, all my fears were relieved. I now feel that this is the most important thing I have ever done in my life. I am now spreading the word to my friends so they can also reap the same rewards.

But even before Respoli's agreement to turn on his fellow

ministers, the die had been cast. Judge Schwartz's order of April 27, 1982 enjoined Respondents:

from directly or indirectly engaging in the following illegal fraudulent and deceptive acts: (1) soliciting funds from the public for ministers' credentials; (2) selling or offering to sell ministers credentials; (3) engaging or attempting to engage in a chain distribution scheme as defined in Sec. 359-FFF of the General Business Law; (4) engaging or aiding anyone in engaging in the unauthorized practice of law; (5) continuing to use the name "college" unless and until proper authorization is obtained from the appropriate state agency." In addition, the court appointed a receiver to establish a fund for restitution to "victimized consumers."

Garbus' appeals would fail and the receiver would drag his feet, paying out around $75,000 to attorney and accountant cronies each year. A federal indictment was returned in 1984. But Garbus, after first entering an appearance to represent all defendants, would bow out, claiming a conflict of interest. After several years and almost a million dollars in fees.

So it was in the fall of 1984 that I received a call from Larry, with a brief story of the indictment and the question of would I be interested in the case. If it would cost another million dollars, he could not handle it. I flew to New York where I met with Ranucci, Ebner and Petroza. It was an amazing story. Garbus had lost the case, but his firm was now taking up the entire ninth floor of a Madison Avenue office building, having moved from a portion of the eighth. With a million dollars over a few-year period, I told Larry I could well expand my firm and take up one floor of a high rise. "Sure you don't have another million to spend, Larry?" He laughed, chopping on his stogie. Unshaven, now overweight, Bishop Ranucci was obviously distraught by the entire situation. It was bad enough he was indicted. The grand jury had indicted as well his daughter Lorraine and had brought his son before the grand jury, granting him immunity and forcing him to testify against his own father and sister This was the Southern District of New York. Rudolph Guillano, the United States Attorney. These guys were not shy. *So wadda ya wanna do, make a federal case out of it?*

Marty Perschetz, prosecutor, was aggressive, but not personally vindictive, an advocate with whom I could joke. Ironically, he was a schoolmate of Lorraine's. They had attended the same high school in Long Island, but never known each other. No conflict there.

When I heard the facts of the case, I believed there was hope. Besides, the plea offer was: "plea to the indictment." Larry had relied on the laundry list of attorneys, beginning with Drexler. At no time did any of these lawyers say, "Stop in the name of the law," though I was in for a surprise when I insisted on calling Cohen to the stand. In addition to Cohen, I would call Delmarmo and Stromer, who Larry had heard give lectures on exempt status for ministers and other tax technical matters. Peter Stromer of California was ULC's advisor and had also given some advice over the years to the LSC of New York. Garbus would wonder who would call him, if anyone, and he and Perschetz as well would worry about Ebner's habit: telephone tape recordings and hidden body mikes. It was significant, I felt, that if the program was so illegal, why had not any attorney advised them to simply quit? Instead, Garbus on tape had said after Schwartz' order, "You need to get more 'churchy-churchy,'" meaning beef up your marriage ceremonies, baptisms and special missions.

LSC already had its "fish for the poor program." Church leaders, including Ranucci, Petroza, and Jania each had parsonages on the water and expensive boats. The houses and boats, of course, were owned by the church, and on Sundays the ministers went fishing, donating the catch to the poor. By this means, the church leaders continued to bolster their substance argument in which they, but for the multi-level problem, stood in a better position than the garbage men and police officers, for the church leaders, in fact, did work for the church full time. *They could afford to.*

Another paradox was that through the church membership there truly developed fellowship outside of the common goal of tax reduction. A church with an initial premise of tax exemption became through its meetings an individual contact, a true church. *Too little too late.* And was the entire tax litany of the church too much for a jury to swallow? Remember, those jurors had paid through the nose their "fair share." An additional paradox: Larry's genius in applying multi-level marketing was no doubt the worst thing that he had done.

But with all these problems, by far the largest was the question of whether Larry could testify. Schwartz had frozen assets and Larry was under court order then not to spend those assets. After the Schwartz order, Garbus had cut off the receiver's attempt to obtain from Larry information concerning the location and form of assets. *Fifth Amendment* objection. In addition, LSC was able on *Sixth Amendment* grounds raised by Garbus, to expend LSC funds for attorneys. But for no other purpose. But how would Larry live since the order in 1982? (The appeal attempts had failed.)

If Larry took the stand and presented the defense of good faith belief and reliance on the law and attorneys, what could be asked of him concerning his good faith compliance with the court's order to freeze assets? Indeed, how had he lived during the past several years; on his wife's real estate income alone? Or, had he expended church assets in direct violation of court order? Given that Larry was a charismatic speaker, dare we risk Larry *not* testifying?

Garbus' motion for release for the case was pending when I entered the picture. Garbus offered a $60,000 refund which was far more, he said, than what was really owed from the last retainer. All defendants were agreeable that that money could be paid to retain me, but then Garbus wanted a full release and satisfaction, a promise that no one would sue, signed by all defendants. They would promise as to any and all causes of action "from the beginning of the world ...." New York lawyers. They want to cover all bases, starting from the beginning of the world less ten days to the end of the world, plus ten days. Ebner refused, wanting to reserve his options, figuring that if he went to jail, he would have plenty of time to become a jail house lawyer and keep Garbus' firm busy defending. Poetic justice. My recommendation was "take the money and run," but Ebner, the spoiler, was adamant.

I represented Larry, while the other defendants were all represented by court-appointed counsel called CJA's, under the Criminal Justice Act. I was the general, the spearhead, lead counsel with a greater experience with this type of case. For the most part, counsel got along. We were a team. *Cooperate and graduate.*

Perschetz' opening was devastating. He walked backward, along the rows of tables, shouting and pointing at each of the six defendants as he walked past, repeating the most serious allegations of the grand jury. An aggressive style. I liked it. *This enough of a challenge for you, Major Mac? The fast lane. Manhattan. Five defendants. Conspiracy and numerous counts of aiding and abetting in the preparation of false returns. It's time again to rise to the occasion. Fight fire with fire.* As in Dahlstrom, the government had not charged any of the defendants on their own returns.

I was first to give opening and countered with a surprise to Perschetz and probably the jury. *Take the starch out of Perschetz' shorts.* I began with the story of Kerby Hensley and California Universal Church, and its winning case against IRS. That was, after all, where the story of Ranucci and LSC had started. I then developed the Drexler story and how Larry had done what a reasonable person would have done: acquire the services of not one attorney, but several over the years. Drexler, Cohen, Siegal, Delmarmo, Garbus, Greenapple, Stromer. No red lights. No flashing yellow lights. No danger signals. No "stop in the name of the law." How could it be all that sinister, yet these lawyers, including a Madison Avenue type, never told LSC to cease, "Go out of business, forget it, you are not a Catholic Church or Billy Graham? The public and the courts will never buy it." The cynical will answer. "To protect their fees." Maybe, but would a lawyer risk malpractice and even criminal prosecution to protect fees? After all, how were the attorneys any less the co-conspirators if in fact the LSC program was so coal-black? The truth of the matter, I submit, is that LSC, ULC and other such ministries were navigating, no less than Dahlstrom, in unchartered waters. Were they, like Dahlstrom, merely pioneering new tax law? Unlike Dahlstrom, however, there was civil case law precedent through the U.S. Tax Courts in which numerous decisions had been reached where the taxpayer minister lost on his claimed exemption. Perschetz had, in fact, argued these cases in response to my pretrial motion to dismiss under the *Dahlstrom* due process/lack of notice defense.

I, therefore, developed for Larry the only viable defense: the truth. Larry believed and relied. It was his belief and reliance in good faith, thus negating the requisite willfullness. This was a question of fact for the jury, one that could be difficult for us without Larry's testimony. How do you present Larry's good faith belief and reliance unless Larry takes the stand? And, do you risk that he will be hammered by the prosecutor on cross? These were classical decisions of strategy and tactics of the courtroom battlefield. If Larry was to stay off the stand, I had to present his belief and reliance through other witnesses.

Perschetz was upset after my opening. He wanted a ruling from the judge that the attorney/client privilege was waived by the defense I had raised and that he was entitled to subpoena the attorneys, obtain documents, and interview them now, in advance of their being called by me as witnesses, assuming I was going to call them. Would I call them? He could not be sure. I argued that the door was not yet opened. No waiver occurs until the client takes the stand and waives the privilege by his testimony concerning conversations with the attorney. Alternatively, we could call the attorney and the client waives the privilege. Compounding the issue was the fact that all defendants were clients of one or more of the attorneys. Hence, attorneys for the co-defendants argued that even assuming for sake of argument that Ranucci had waived the privilege, their client had not. Given this morass, the judge, Judge Broderick, former police commissioner of Philadelphia, decided to maintain a wait and see attitude, ruling no waiver yet. Perschetz could in the meantime proceed with subpoenas for records to the attorneys in the event we call them, or in event the judge permits Perschetz to call them.

A stickler for detail, Perschetz was always well-organized with a platoon of assistants. He had another assistant U.S. Attorney, an experienced paralegal who had helped in the trial of the Reverend Moon, plus several IRS special agents full-time. He had boxed himself in somewhat, at least as to Delmarmo, who originally represented Tappan. Perschetz was moving for Delmarmo's withdrawal as counsel for reason he was a potential witness, having given advice to some of the defendants. The story was that once

Schwartz had ruled Delmarmo told Ranucci and others on the steps of the courthouse that they were not enjoined technically from continuing their activities. Thus, they formed the Life Science Church of North America, continuing with church activities. This became a big issue at trial, Perschetz arguing how could the defendant claim good faith and reasonableness if they had violated a court order? To this, our response: Delmarmo's advice.

The case became more cat and mouse for reason that no one, *including me,* knew for sure what tapes Ebner had on anybody. Was he taping me? Ebner initially represented by CJA, fired him after hearing his opening. Ebner then proceeded as his own attorney with the CJA attorney remaining by his side for advice. This, I thought, was Ebner's dream come true. Not only was he now a criminal defense trial attorney in a major federal conspiracy case in Manhattan, five other attorneys became dependent on him for information! He and Larry kept me busy on weekends, listening to scores of tapes of Cohen, Delmarmo, Stromer, and Garbus. Garbus would not as much as talk to Ebner anymore and was leery about me. "Are you taping me, Ebner?" Garbus would ask. At a post-indictment meeting before my involvement, Ebner had been caught surreptitiously taping a strategy session between Garbus and the other defendants at the conference room of Garbus' firm. Garbus was enraged and stomped out.

The tapes, which could be used to impeach any witness who failed to testify consistent with what was recorded, provided not only leverage over the witness to whom we refused to divulge the tape transcripts, but caused Perschetz at least a little bit of consternation. The element of *surprise.* Which attorneys will he call? Will he in fact put *them* on trial? I decided to be flexible. Try first to manipulate the attorneys to testify in our favor, holding the tapes at bay. If they became too protective of their own skin, I was prepared to lower the boom. It was my hope that at least one would take the *Fifth,* thus providing a scapegoat for Larry and the rest. A way for the jury to rationalize Larry's innocence without Larry's testimony. I subpoenaed Cohen, Delmarmo and Garbus.

Stromer was a separate category. He was on our side and agreed to help all he could. The Stromer tapes to which I listened were those of his speeches to ULC and LSC members, tapes about which he knew. I needed to study his method of dealing with the church tax issues. He was our expert. Judge Broderick, Catholic, grew weary mid-trial of my analogies of the Catholic church: the vow of poverty, expenditures for Catholic real estate, and personal expenditures for the benefit of Cardinals. He reached a point where he adamantly stated there would be no more analogies to the Catholic church.

The trial then, lasting two and a half months, was one in which I needed to be prepared for anything. Strategy could change at a moment's notice. After a few weeks, I had become accustomed to the routine. Drive to Long Beach, Long Island railroad station. Take the train to the City, then the subway, walk several blocks. It was a two-hour commute one way. On the return trip, Larry, Ebner, Petroza and I often drove back discussing strategy. Because of the trial length, I had taken my whole family. For the boys, New York was like living in a foreign country. The New York accents, the food. Greek diners, armed guards in the grocery stores. No children permitted in the department stores. No sunshine for days. Soda pop machines that dropped a cup which is then filled, rather than delivering a can. Old buildings. Miles of traffic jams. Sephardic Jews.

I had loaded Ryan and Nathan, then ages 10 and 5, into the Cesna 205 aircraft, a 1963 6-seater with the two middle seats removed. The plane, akin to an old Chevy station wagon, converts to a camper with the middle seats removed, leaving the boys leg room to sleep on top of the luggage. Cruise speed is 160 miles per hour. On our first day, after skirting storms we reached after dark Woodward, Oklahoma. On the second day, again skirting storms until we stopped in West Memphis, Arkansas, we traveled across Tennessee, landing at Lynchburg, Virginia. It was then dark and we continued on north through Washington D.C., Baltimore and Philadelphia, landing at Republic Airport, 30 minutes from Long Beach. It was 9:00 p.m. when we landed, after skirting the JFK Airport traffic, flying out over the Atlantic.

Lorraine had moved out of her house in Long Beach due to the receiver's court action for seizure of assets, including the house. It was a Life Science asset, he argued, despite Lorraine's and her husband's partial funding of the house by separate funds. Larry and I had hoped we could appease the receiver, hold him at bay, and use the house during trial. Barbara and Scott had flown to Newark, New Jersey, where Larry had picked them up and drove them to the house, which had belonged to Rocky Marciano. Then he picked us up at the airport.

The receiver, an attorney appointed by the court, had retained another attorney and an accountant and had done very little to the end that "defrauded consumers" were to receive restitution. Several years had passed and there was little to show for their efforts, due in part, at least, to Larry's *Fifth Amendment* stonewalling. To collect assets, the receiver needed to find them, and to find them they needed testimony from Larry. For one year alone, the attorney for the receiver, no doubt a cronie, had been paid $75,000 in fees. Larry's boat, a twenty-six foot speed boat, its whereabouts known for years by investigators, had not been seized. Nor Larry's Excalibur automobile, worth over $20,000, and that of Rodi.

After the receiver had told me we could stay in the house, we received one day a seizure notice demanding we immediately vacate. Barbara hired a realtor and learned of life in the big city. If you were Catholic, you could not rent or buy from the Jews, and vice versa. A clear violation of federal fair housing law, of course, but I had more important battles at hand. Once Barbara revealed that MacPherson was Scottish, not Irish, and that we were Protestant, not Catholic, we were shown a rental property a block from the beach. The owners were Jewish and we were in the middle of a Sephardic neighborhood catty corner from the Jewish Temple and down the street from a Sephardic school. As I drove to the train station each morning, I passed young Sephardic Jews dressed in black, with black hats, pigtails and unshaven.

A second logistical problem was schooling for the boys. Scott, at the top of his class in Glendale, was finishing eighth grade. Ryan, 4th, and Nathan kindergarten. Barbara's visits to the local public school resulted in a demand by them for $2000 per child. Extortion. We were "migrants," not full-fledged citizens. Again, I had more important skirmishes, and we turned to the Catholic school which, after interviewing Barbara and the boys, welcomed us with open arms and at only $90 total per month. Sister Kathleen was a gem of a Christian woman, and Scott and Ryan, though complaining that they missed Arizona and their friends, adjusted well. I could only grin, having little sympathy in remembering my training in the Catholic schools, for which I had always held deep respect due to the discipline. Catholicism was, after all, a very disciplined religion. Nathan stayed at home. Kindergarten was not required and Nathan was well advanced due to home schooling by his mother's efforts.

The schedule became fixed. At 6:00 a.m. I rose, caught the 7:02 train, and arrived at the courthouse by 9:00 with court starting at 9:30. I did not reach home until after 7:00 p.m.. Then it was walks or jogs on the beach and more trial preparation. I saw little of the family except weekends, some of which were spent exploring the northeast in the 205 for material for my other books: Martha's Vineyard, Nantucket, the Coast Guard Academy, West Point, Naval Shipyard at Norfolk, Virginia, where I visited my sister Margo and her family, and a trip to Chattanooga, Tennessee where I gave a speech during the "Justice Symposium." Speakers there included former Congressman George Hansen of Idaho and Baptist preacher McCurry of Georgia.

"If forced to, you can stand on your head for three months," I told the boys. "Consider this a visit to a foreign country and experience the cultural differences. Don't forget it. Grin and bear it. Remember, you are ducks in the rain." My boys did well, but were glad when it was time to head back to Arizona: sunshine, arid climate, new buildings, everyone spoke English (except in the Hispanic communities), swimming pool in the backyard, no guards in the grocery stores, canned pop and pizza that was without grease.

Perschetz first called a long line of witnesses who had joined the program and paid $2,000 or more. They had not been very "churchy-churchy" but I was able to develop a theme of good faith belief by these common folk. I had to take chances and calculated risks. "And you joined the LSC, accepting the tax advantages of being a minister and believing that to be legal?" Without a recess between these witnesses, I was able to score points with the last witness, a black man, Robert E. Young, who was very friendly to Larry and to the church. Young had submitted an affidavit in the State case, contradicting an Attorney General affidavit, claiming it to be out of context. Young stated in his affidavit:

> I was asked by a member of the audience what he would get for $3,500. My reply was that for $3,500 one would receive a minister certificate, a church charter, all necessary training to set up your church legally and properly if you qualified. I never stated they should establish their own churches in order to avoid paying income tax. Furthermore, I told them that if avoidance of income tax payment was their sole motivation for becoming a minister, then they would not qualify.

Young also denied placing "plants in the audience" for the purpose of asking specific questions that would encourage new recruits to join. Perschetz was unhappy with the way things were going. These LSC ministers, all of whom were "defrauded victims" of the LSC, believed that the program was legal. And for good reason. The attorneys, the IRS revenue rulings, the Code itself.

Next, Perschetz called another minister, a police detective. This witness had the demeanor of a detective and I suspected an ambush. I was getting bad vibes. Perschetz did not attempt to "take the wind out of my sail" by asking before I could my litany regarding belief and then, somehow, to his benefit, removing the sting from the testimony. *It was too easy. I was being set up. My hairs were on end. The antennae. My sixth sense. Walking down the trail, sensing the presence of something unnatural. Do the smart thing. Leave the trail, strike out in a different direction.* I asked of the detective no questions.

Despite the points I had made with some of the witnesses, Respoli was a zinger. He had been high on the church hierarchy and had the inside tract. He pled to one felony, the remaining counts were dismissed, but as is the general practice, sentencing would await until *after* the Life Science Church trial so that the prosecutor and judge could decide how much assistance Respoli had given.

240

His testimony was complete with an explanation of the multi-level program, including charts which must have cost the government thousands of dollars. Respoli laid it all out. How do you impeach a turncoat? He had no prior record. The best I could do was point to the article in the Life Science Church newsletter and Respoli's guest editorial:

I know some of you have been discouraged because you have received nothing but correspondence from the IRS regarding your 1040 refund and request for more information, etc., but still no refund. I had much the same response from the IRS - UNTIL NOW!! Through the guidance and help of the Life Science Church on the morning of February 9, 1981, at approximately 11:00 a.m., I received in my mail a REFUND CHECK from the IRS in the amount of $2,292.82. I had requested a refund of $2,093.87. The rest, $198.95 was INTEREST. I almost ran out of faith and then the Lord smiled down on my church. My prayers are that your church too would be blessed this way. Keep your faith. Reverend Charles Respoli.

In addition, Respoli, along with Rodi, had been one of the ministers featured in a series of major network newscasts in New York City, "God v. The IRS." The ministers and their wives had been interviewed in the living room of their homes.

The next best thing to direct impeachment was to use an analogy. If Respoli had admitted to knowingly and willfully violating federal law by lying under penalties of perjury that his return was true, correct and complete, then why should the jury now trust his oath under penalty of perjury? It was the same technique I had used on those ministers who claimed at trial they had *not* believed the program to be legal, yet had claimed their charitable deductions on the tax return. It was yes-win situation for us. Either the witness believed it was legal at the time the return was filed, thus supporting Larry's belief, or the witnesses did not believe it was legal, therefore violating the perjury oath on a return. What makes the witness any more believable now? The approach likely did little good as to turncoat Respoli because we had nothing to refute his testimony but that of the Defendant's, and who would dare take the stand? In addition, a multi-level program was described by Respoli fairly accurately. What was missing was the distribution of the millions of dollars. Despite the $1.4 million to attorneys and other costs, Larry and family had still received approximately $2,660,000. Too much for the jury to swallow?

But for the turncoat, the multi-level marketing in the millions, I was thinking we would have a heck of a good shot at this case.

That might sound silly, but the gist of the government's action was supposed to be the church issue, an issue for which standing alone I felt we had a fighting chance. After all, had not I succeeded time and time again with the reliance and due process/notice defenses? The government, realizing their burden, is always in search of what I call "the icing on the cake." For example, in Drexler, in which he and his son were charged in San Diego before Larry's trial, before even the New York State action, the charge was conspiracy, mail fraud, and wire fraud. The icing? Defendants had back dated documents. It is one thing to argue tax law nuances, but outright badges of fraud? Back dating. False names, false social security numbers. Cash under the table. Use of cash rather than checking accounts. Obvious under reporting. Flight. Obvious inconsistency. Bribes. Extortion. Threats to witnesses. These elements make for a viable prosecution. (Another problem in Larry's case was the flight of funds to a Cayman Island bank account.) A prosecutor loves a case in which he can comfortably argue that he has proven offense elements not beyond a reasonable doubt, but beyond *all* doubt. This was not Perschetz's argument.

Larry and I decided Larry would not testify. Delmarmo did the best he could to help with his testimony, but lacked the jury appeal. Cohen threatened to bury us if I called him, but I had to take the risk, believing I had the leverage with the tapes. I thought I could control his testimony. I was right to a point, finding myself ambushed by Ebner's incompetence. Cohen, in the latter days of his representation of the church, had written a letter critical of LSC and warning them as to law violations. Ebner had never showed me the letter. "Slipped my mind." I saw it for the first time when Perschetz used it on cross-examination. It was not what I would call devastating for reason it was written late in the game long after Cohen had assisted LSC with their major thrust for which he had been handsomely paid. It was Cohen's self doubts, especially about the vow of poverty, that caused LSC to bring in a bigger gun, Delmarmo.

Judge Broderick's ruling concerning my analogy with the Catholic church had spoiled an additional defense maneuver. We had intended to tail a Catholic lawyer who is a self proclaimed *First Amendment* expert and lives under a vow of poverty, Father Waylon, who had testified in the state case. Where did he eat? Sleep? What were his work and recreational habits? As a witness he may have been useful as well to explain why the Cardinal had to live in a mansion and be transported in chauffeur driven limousines. That was a vow of *poverty?* No "net benefit shall inure to any individual," so states IRS' church exemption rule. "Net benefit" meaning *after* reasonable expenses of the church. Wasn't it reasonable for Bishop Ranucci, the head of the church of 3,000 strong, to drive an Excalibur and fish in a luxury boat at the expense of the church? Personal benefit likely would have become the major issue had it not been for the multi-level plan, money shipped to the Cayman Island account, the state court order and violations of the court order.

Peter Stromer did an admiral job as expert, but again the judge limited us in his testimony. Elmer testified and was hammered, causing the other defendants to stay off the stand but for Petroza. Petroza did his best by his attempt to show "churchy-churchy" by a video of the seminary graduation. A candlelight procession. Did the jury think it a bad joke? Probably; some of them were smirking.

The last card for me to play was Garbus. It became dare and double dare with Perschetz and me. If I did not call Garbus, should Pershetz at the risk that I had the tapes? If I did not call him, was it an attempt at ambush, a set up to allow Garbus to either hand himself to the jury as the scapegoat, or act defensively to protect himself by his reliance on the ambiguities of the tax law? Either way, Larry benefitted. Was I bluffing with the tapes to which I eluded? Yes, for the most part, I was. "You should get more churchy-churchy" was the best I had. But what more, if any, did Ebner have?

Again, my nemesis was Ebner. He had some tapes but nothing akin to a smoking gun. The best was Garbus' advice after the order to get more "churchy-churchy," thus the seminary and other improvements. It was too little too late. After the Cohen spider trap, I felt Garbus for me was too risky. After all, his name was all over the documents, especially the lawsuit, and I had developed a Garbus reliance defense without his testimony. He would be unhappy with me calling him and would likely state that he had warned the LSC not in writing. In closing, I could blame the government; they could have called him. (After Cohen, the court ruled the attorney/client door was now opened.) We had no burden, it was on the government and never shifted. No red lights, no flashing yellow lights, no "stop in the name of the law." And the Madison Avenue law firm was paid almost one million dollars for advice to the Life Science Church of New York.

After a couple of days of deliberation, the jury found for the government. Larry got seven years, Ebner five, the remaining defendants two. (Under parole standards, they were eligible for parole after service of one-third of the sentence.) No one ever said it would be easy. Later, Perschetz, who had considered private practice in Arizona, wrote from Florida. His coming out card. Another good prosecutor through the revolving door. During his tenure in New York he had succeeded in fulfilling through a criminal prosecution the political agenda of the federal government. Destroy the tax protest movement, especially the mail order ministry.

Let the people think they govern and they will be governed. William
Penn

| TEXAS HOUSEWIFE | Chapter 13 |

The war story of Karen Verlander of Victoria, Texas, illustrates
several ironies. Charged with willful failure to file federal income
tax returns in Laredo, Texas, she had been a dutiful wife, signing
Fifth Amendment returns prepared by her husband, Rick, who was
a Marvin Cooley follower. Marvin, of Mesa, Arizona, gave
seminars across the nation. The *Fifth* was all Rick's idea. Karen
took no notice of tax matters. "Here, Honey, sign this." "What's
this? No figures, only objections?" "Right. Perfectly legal. A man
from Arizona said so. Also, attorneys say it's okay."

The irony was, Karen, who was not working, had more income
than Rick because of oil and gas royalties from trust property
received from her grandmother. A construction worker, Rick was
in and out of work throughout the years in question. Thus, Karen
was charged while Rick was not.

Mark was in Southwest Seminary at Fort Worth and needed
some financial assistance, so I brought him in on the case. I
attacked relentlessly the IRS agents on lack of evidence concerning
knowledge and intent. Karen and Rick testified and we obtained in a
few hours not guilty verdicts. Rick accepted full responsibility.
(He would have made a good Army officer! *You can delegate
authority but not responsibility.*)

Which raises the question, why are spouses forced to sign a
return they do not understand? Who *does* understand? Often, only
one spouse takes responsibility for the preparation and filing, yet
both are legally responsible under the law. At least one case holds
that even crossing off the jurat, the statement made under penalties
of perjury, does not prevent the government from charging for a
false return. Also, so long as the return is false in any material
matter, there need be no tax due and owing. Since material is
defined by the courts to mean, though very technically speaking,
failure to leave off a deduction, this then causes the return to be false
in a material way. What sense does this make: charging an
individual for filing a false return where they failed to report a
deduction which would have resulted in a lower tax due and owing?

And what of the individual who misses the filing deadline of
April 15? Does he not face a dilemma beginning April 16, since it is
a crime to file late? By filing a return late, he provides the
government with two-thirds of its case in chief, considering the
government must prove that he was required to file, failed to file,
and willfulness. The late return provides clear evidence of the first
two elements.

Add to all of this the community property confusion. The states of Arizona, California, Texas, Nevada, Idaho, Louisiana, New Mexico, Washington and Wisconsin are community property states, and the federal government gives deference for tax purposes to community property law. Thus, in say Arizona, a wife who is not working, and believes she earns no income and does not file and her husband likewise does not file, could technically be charged with willful failure to file because one-half of his income is hers for purpose of meeting the filing requirement.

My theory to all of this nonsense is that the system is not designed to readily collect revenue, which could be done through an excise tax on goods, and made progressive in nature if desired by a sliding scale on the type of goods, but that indeed the government, through its paranoia of the *Master - We the People* - feels an urgent need for the upper hand by way of a *dossier* on every person, living and dead. The thumb theory. Place the people under your thumb. Right where you want them. *Gotcha.*

As further illustration is the recent plea for social security numbers for children ages four and over. The rationale by IRS is that too many divorced parents are each claiming the child as a deduction. *The end always justifies the means.* On television ads, the Social Security Administration asks for parental and teacher assistance in registering children at school for social security numbers. Into the system. *The mark of the beast. Into the mouth of the beast.*

There are two obvious fundamental reasons behind registering children with the fed. First, the government intends to cut down on the underground economy by registering children at an early age to facilitate keeping track of them as they become bread winners. Second, once the child is registered for one purpose, he is registered for all purposes; e.g. conscription. "Four years old in 1988. Let's see, now, four plus fourteen equal eighteen. 1988 plus 14 equal 2002. Our computer matching program in 2002 will evidence those 18 years of age who have failed to register for the draft. Hello, this is Big Brother calling ...."

By bluff and intimidation. A standard operating procedure of IRS. Bluff in many instances through lies or half-truths. "Your children over four must have a social security number." Wrong. If you intend to claim them on your return as an exemption, then if you fail to list the social security number you can be penalized five dollars per child. In other words, if you have five children, it's $25.00 per return, the price of privacy for your children. The price of liberty. Of course, the government maintains that continuing threat: willful failure to supply information, *26 U.S.C. Sec. 7203*, a misdemeanor. A doubtful prosecution, but possible. *The wheel that squeaks the loudest gets the grease.*

245

Again, technically speaking, in addition to the civil penalties of five dollars per child, IRS could charge an individual with willful failure to supply information by failure to supply the social security number. Of course, if there is no social security number to supply, then could the charge stick? This is akin to the statute which from the appellate decision has never been utilized: willful failure to keep records. I know of no such charge brought, but technically IRS will say if you fail to keep your church receipts intentionally, you have committed a crime. One year in jail.

In 1962, the government brought a case against a gentleman in Hawaii who protested against the Census. *U.S. v. Steele*, 461 F.2d 1148 (9th Cir. 1962). The man stood on street corners, handing out information to those passing by, encouraging them not to comply with the Census request, taking the position that the Constitution required only an enumeration, a head count. He was singled out for prosecution, despite the fact the government knew that others had failed to comply, but were not as vocal as Steele. In reversing the conviction, the North Circuit set forth a standard: where others are similarly situated and have not been prosecuted and the defendant has been prosecuted for his exercise of his constitutional right, or on other impermissible ground, then the case warrants dismissal for selective and discriminatory prosecution. No doubt, the appellate courts realized the floodgates that would open by the lack of ability of the government to prosecute the most vocal tax offenders. Despite the well-reasoned holding in *Steele*, since the *Steele* decision, the courts have refused to follow it in tax protester cases, stating that the Justice Department was justified in bringing a case against the most vocal offender.

One method by which to end at least temporarily this madness, almost overnight, is this: all those receiving an audit notice refuse the audit. Thus, the need by IRS for lies. The audit notice is a fraud. It leads the recipient to conclude that he must comply. The truth is, audits are voluntary, not mandatory.

Of course, refusal may lead to disallowance of deductions and notice of proposed deficiency of additional tax, interest, and penalties, which in turn means a right to petition the Tax Court. Query: If the tax court is now backlogged by some 50,000 cases, which take an average of two years, what will be the backlog in revenue at least temporarily lost if all brought under audit refuse to comply with the audit? The flank attack. Not anarchy. Congress intends that you should, as *Master*, have the right to refuse an audit and a right to petition for redress of grievances by means of the Tax Court. No doubt, if all refused audit, Congress would scurry in a hurry to pass new laws. But what would they pass?

Fear is the foundation of most governments. John Adams

ARIZONA SENATOR	Chapter 14

As a result of a newspaper article appearing in the *Arizona Republic* on June 18, 1986, the Ethics Committee of the Arizona State Senate convened the morning of June 23, 1986. (Arizona is probably the only state whose legislative body will call committee meetings merely as the result of a newspaper article. Also, its capitol city, Phoenix, is probably the only capitol city with two major newspapers owned by the same family. The *Arizona Republic* and the *Phoenix Gazette,* euphemistically known as *the RAG.*) "Legislator owes $500,000 couple claim" read the front page headline, with a subtitle, "State Senator cheated them out of business, home, elderly pair say." According to the opening statement by the committee chairman, Senator Hal Runyan, "Information contained within [the *Republic* article] cast dispersions upon the integrity of a member of this body, Senator Bill Davis, and brought into question possible misuse by Senator Davis of his title and office as a legislative officer to effect personal financial transactions." Simply put, the article alleged that Davis, resting his credibility upon his position as state senator and his former position as Baptist minister, ripped off an elderly couple, the Shipleys. Davis' mistake was in ignoring the article, rather than hitting it head on.

Runyan went on to say, "It should be well understood that the inquiry of the Ethics Committee is concerned solely with the issue of whether Senator Davis has misused his office or has conducted himself in any manner that renders him unable to perform the duties of that office." After hearing objections by Davis' attorney, Phil Goldstein, concerning lack of due process because the Senate rules did not provide for such a procedure as was being undertaken, the five committee members proceeded to question Davis about the allegations. Runyan then proposed that an independent investigator be appointed for "ascertaining whether there has been a misuse of office by Senator Davis" and report back to the Committee within thirty days. It was so moved and passed.

Thus began the Senate investigation of Senator Bill Davis, an investigation which became an inquisition, demonstrating how false allegations contained in a newspaper article can hold hostage an elected official. But no ordinary elected official. Did Davis have enemies on a national scale, or was that a mere "crackpot conspiracy theory?" Was it mere coincidence that the article appeared a few months before the Republican primary and that almost immediately after the article, without Davis' side of the story yet made public, Jan Brewer, a Republican house member, announced to the public

247

that she would run against Davis in the primary? And before all was said and done, Davis would be accused of promoting offshore trusts for the purpose of tax avoidance. What that had to do with his ability to sit as an Arizona Senator only the investigator, "Judge Ridge," could answer. Others would answer: "smear tactics."

Davis had committed at least two political mortal sins, neither having anything to do with the allegations contained within the article. First, he was not a *good old boy team* player. As former Baptist minister and a man of principles - God, country, family - he, like fellow Republican State Senator Wayne Stump, was not a political hack. Neither could be bought off by the political power brokers. *Jimmy Stewart. Mr. Smith Goes to Washington.* Neither senator, as the RAG repeatedly complained, was effective nor deserving of their constituents. Davis and Stump, the RAG charged, refused to demonstrate a concilliatory spirit and were an Arizona embarassment. Davis' second mortal sin was that he dared take on the abortion power brokers.

Stump, who always stood by his principles, apparently had not presented for the power brokers a serious threat. At least he had not filibustered. Stump had introduced such "cockamamie" legislation as proposing that Arizona should, in compliance with *Article 1, Section 10* of the *Constitution,* require that only gold or silver be legal tender for debt, and proposed that jurors in all criminal cases be instructed that they had a right to decide the law as well as the facts. *Jury nullification.* "Anarchy," the power brokers called it. Stump, the papers said, could not as much as be taken seriously. Davis was more aggressive, daring to filibuster against funding for Planned Parenthood, a scene from *Mr. Smith Goes to Washington.* Although the Senate agreed to fund the pro-abortion group, it decided against funds for abortion which, to Davis, begged the question. Obviously the funding of non-abortion activities for Planned Parenthood would free funds from non-abortion activities to be used for abortion activities. Substance over form. Had this conduct placed Davis on the national hit list of the far left? Bill concluded "it had."

A second conspiracy theory of Bill's dealt with disgruntled employees at a restaurant owned in part by him. He had replaced the manager. Behind it all, as I would discover, were allegations of major drug dealings. Before my representation of Davis would end, one witness would be murdered on the front porch of her home in Peoria, a bedroom community of the greater Phoenix metropolitan area.

I had followed Davis' political career through the RAG. He served for two terms in District 17, adjacent to Stump's District 16 in Glendale, where I resided. Both districts are extremely conservative. *At least someone is trying to be a spoiler for the*
248

power brokers, I thought.

I first met Wayne when I flew Barbara and Scott one evening to Prescott, Arizona, in the mountains, where I was to speak at a meeting of the Arizona Patriots, a loosely-knit group headed by a former TV and movie star Ty Hardin. I flew the small Cherokee 180 aircraft which our firm had at the time, landing at the Prescott airport. I had talked to Ty a few times on the phone and we had really hit it off, believing in the same religious and Constitutional principles. Ty had starred in the movies *PT-109* and *Palm Springs Weekend,* plus a regular TV show of which I was a big fan back in the '50s during the era of popular adult westerns. Along with *Maverick, Sugarfoot* and *Cheyenne,* I made a habit of tuning in to *Bronco Lane,* alias Ty Hardin.

For some years, Ty was a TV preacher on a cable station in Phoenix and had left the ministry to preach on his own, carrying the message of constitutional, as well as religious, issues. With our common interests, we became friends, but I saw little of him. He printed a newspaper, *The Arizona Patriot.* In the 1988 election, enemies of Wayne would attempt to blackball him by his association with Ty, the Patriots, and "Free Men" who, it was claimed, were engaged in both violent and non-violent forms of anarchy.

In 1982, a Patriot rally was held at Estrella Park outside of Phoenix with speakers including Ty, Martin Larsen, a regular columnist especially on tax issues with the national weekly newspaper *Spotlight,* and my clients Charles Riely and Jack McLamb, City of Phoenix police officer. I spoke briefly as well. Later, articles appeared in the RAG concerning the Free Men and an alleged plot to assassinate Governor Bruce Babbitt, a member of the Trilateral Commission. Reminiscent of the Gordon Kahl technique, I thought. Where you cannot pin anything on dissidents, create a threat, call up the FBI, and no doubt you will develop something. And indeed they did.

Apparently there were some factions within the Arizona Patriot group that were quite militant and prone to violence. In the mountains outside of Kingman they plotted, according to the FBI undercover agent who lived with them for several months, to rob an armored car and to blow up the IRS Service Center in Ogden, Utah. In 1987, several were charged, but not Ty who, at the time, had left Arizona.

As the Kingman case was being readied for trial, I received a call from a RAG reporter who wanted to know more about McLamb's involvement. I saw it coming. Governor Evan Mecham was already under serious attack by the media on the far left and McLamb had been a supporter and voluntary bodyguard for him during the vicious race for governor. The press would attempt to play the game of guilt by association just as they had with my

249

"illegal tax protester" clients. For tax protesters the chain was this: a *Fifth Amendment* filer is an illegal tax protester; an illegal tax protester is a member of the Posse Comitatus; a member of the Posse Comitatus is associated with Gordon Kahl who murdered two U.S. Marshals; therefore, an individual who files a *Fifth Amendment* return advocates the violent overthrow of the United States government. For Mecham, I suspected the story to run backwards: anarchists to Hardin to McLamb to Mecham. In fact, in one article about Mecham before the Kingman incident, in which it was brought out that Mecham's wife was a former John Birch Society member, there was more talk and photos regarding McLamb than Mecham! Taint Mecham with McLamb's background. I immediately recognized a repeat performance. I could just hear the *Republic's* publisher, Pat Murphy, telling this reporter, "We need more dirt on Mecham. Check out this Kingman incident. See if we can tie Mecham in with these extremists bent on doing violence to duly-appointed officials."

In the Kingman case, a transcript of a conversation taped surreptitiously by the FBI agent had been discovered by the defendant and became public record. (It should not have become public record; probably some inside help through court personnel.) "What can you tell me about McLamb's involvement in the conspiracy?" I was asked by the reporter. "We have information that he was at a motel meeting in Phoenix with Hardin and some of the defendants and at that meeting there was a discussion concerning the destruction of the IRS Service Center in Ogden, Utah."

I could not believe McLamb would be knowingly involved, so I called the reporter's bluff. "No way. Read to me some statements by McLamb or by those in his presence." "Well, the transcript is not clear as to *when* he arrived." Jack later told me that he arrived as the meeting was about to break up. I warned the reporter that if he would not be fair to Jack, Ty and the governor, I promised to call a press conference with Jack and Ty and stick it in the RAG's face if the article implied knowledge by Jack. Without hard evidence, the RAG backed off, mentioning McLamb arriving late and no mention of Mecham. Since Ty apparently had been present during this discussion, I assumed they had little other evidence against him or they would have indicted him. I concluded that even if Ty had agreed to the principle of the plan, thus technically making him a conspirator, he was smart enough to not carry out any act (overt act) in furtherance of the plan. He in no way participated. Also, apparently Ty never appeared at the armed encampment outside of Kingman during the one-year period when the FBI undercover agent had become part of the group.

Thus, the Davis case had been no different: by lies and innuendo draw the RAG to the story, coordinate stories with the editorial page columnists and editorial cartoon authors, create public sentiment against the accused, try him in the press (who has the power and money to rebut in print the bogus allegations?) and remove the man from office by one means or another. Besides, stories of political corruption create headlines, and headlines sell newspapers. This was not unlike a tactic utilized by the VC: mortar a neutral village at night, enter the village the next day with medical care, and blame "the American capitalist pigs." To those scenarios, there is only one defense: we attack; fight fire with fire. Because Davis could not compete with the printed media, we later decided on an indirect attack: use the TV media to keep the printed media in line and, within the printed media, use smaller town papers - Glendale, Scottsdale, Mesa - to keep the RAG in line. After the Duke Tully fiasco of 1985, the RAG was still gun-shy when it came to its credibility. It had become a laughing stock of Phoenix. Tully had resigned as publisher after it was discovered he had for years been impersonating an Air Force fighter pilot with a heroic war record. Tully had not as much as served in the military and was banished to North Dakota. He had not only worn a Lt. Colonel's uniform at the governor's military ball and other formal functions, but the decorations as well. For the uniform and each ribbon, he could have been charged at least with misdemeanors under federal law. No such luck. The prosecutor, U.S. Attorney McNamee, declined to prosecute. Of course, McNamee was appointed by President Reagan, and considering that Tully and Republican Senator John McCain of Arizona were best of friends, and that Tully had contributed to McCain's campaign, it does not take a quantum leap in logic to conclude that Tully likely contributed as well to Reagan, or at the very least was a staunch supporter. No special prosecutor appointed in that case, as in the case of Ollie North.

As if Tully was not enough cause for lack of credibility for the RAG, the RAG supported "good ole boy" Burton Barr, who had been Republican leader in the House for over 20 years, in the Republican primary race for governor. Mecham beat him. Then the RAG supported Democrat Carolyn Warner over Mecham. In a three-way race between Warner, Democrat Bill Schultz, and Mecham, Mecham had prevailed. Mecham had become the nemesis for the RAG. But Davis would prove for the RAG the test run at political assassination, Davis' political life destroyed by the RAG two years before Mecham faced off with Barr.

First it was Warren C. Ridge who was elected by the Senate to investigate the Davis allegations. Ridge had been a Superior Court judge in Phoenix in 1970 through 1972, so should by all counts have been well qualified. Was it mere coincidence that his partner, Donald G. Isaacson, had been the Senate Rule's Counsel in 1975, majority counsel in 1975 through 1982, a former member of the

251

House, and a member of the Barr's legislative committee 1982 through 1985? A rich plum to pick. Isn't it nice to know people in high places? The firm's practice includes "legislative and administrative." And was it mere coincidence that Isaacson was a lobbyist for the Arizona Licensed Beverage Association at a time when Davis declined to vote on a bill in favor of the association? Conducting less than a thorough investigation, Ridge submitted his rambling, disorganized report of over sixty pages. Ridge was not an investigator; he was a one-man grand jury who, rather than acting as an "independent investigator," unbiased, became Davis' principle accuser.

On August 12, 1986, the Committee met to review Ridge's report and hear Davis' response. Ridge had forty days to submit his report; Davis had three to respond. Davis had hired, at the suggestion of the Senate president, attorney Phil Goldstein, known for the defense of politicians. While Goldstein initially appeared to have "the eye of the tiger," his performance in Davis' mind began to seriously wane. Had Goldstein, a member of *the club,* been called off by the political dogs? Was Davis too hot an item to risk the future of a law firm with a political orientation? Of course money, perhaps, had something to do with it, considering Davis already owed Goldstein $5,000. Goldstein had accepted the responsibility. RHIP. *Rank hath its privledges as well as its responsibilities.*

Goldstein did not as much as show up at the August 12 hearing, nor ask in advance for a continuance or more time to respond to the Ridge report. He filed an incomplete response, and sent a substitute, "Mr. Chairman, my name is Jim Myres. I'm a last minute pinch hitter after court appointments and illness took first and second string away ... the Senator and I can't perceive any good that can come from any further questioning of this Board ... I first saw this file last night at 9:30 p.m." Because Goldstein had complained about lack of due process, Runyan berated Myres, "The *Constitution of the State of Arizona* says that the Legislature, the Houses of the Legislature are the ones that determine the fitness of the people who sit in the body. Do you feel that that alone does give the Senate of the State of Arizona and this Ethics Committee the right to probe matters such as we are now probing?" Feeling trapped, Myres answered, "It is a philosophical, legal matter, absolutely you have the right, and obviously you have the right and none would be heard not saying you do have the right. When you exercise that right, there should be either substantive or procedural, probably both, [due process] guaranteed so that you all can rest assured in your minds that you know the rules you have to play by and if somebody accuses you of not playing by the rules, you have the opportunity to fully defend yourself. That should be of concern to you."

There were no rules of procedure, no road map. The Senate was making up the rules as it went along. Also, the Senate "Rules of Ethics" covered only bribes and improper disclosures. Did the Senate, under the *Constitution* and its own rules, have authority to take any action? Fearing public adverse opinion, the Senate gave Davis and his attorneys more to answer the Ridge allegations.

On Wednesday, August 13, I was vacationing with my family in San Diego when I first heard from Davis. I had met Bill at a dinner meeting of the Arizona Bipartisan Political Action Committee where we both spoke, he about Planned Parenthood, the inner workings of "the club," and how to get (independent) Republican conservatives like himself and Wayne Stump elected. I addressed with some anger an issue hot and heavy on my heart: secular humanism in the public schools. Scott in seventh grade had come home with an English assignment: "write your own obituary." Ryan in grade five had writing assignments such as "who do you like better, your mother or your father, and why." "Of your brothers and sisters, who do you like better? Why?"

After discussing Bill's case with Barbara and the boys, we agreed that we should return to Phoenix no later than Saturday the 16th, which we did. Then on Sunday the 17th, I met with Bill, Charles Riely, and other strategists at my office. First, I had to get a handle on the case and then quickly develop a strategy for the week of the 17th. We had but *three days* to prepare for the hearing on Thursday the 21st. It was doubtful, we predicted, that the Senate would give Bill additional time to prepare, despite the fact that he had new counsel on board. By telephone from San Diego I discussed briefly the case with Phil Goldstein, who was glad to be out; he had other pressing matters. He did not have much to offer but to say that due process rights were clearly at issue, an issue he had already adamantly raised with the Senate, to no avail.

The Committee was made up of five Senators, Runyan, Kay, Lund, Guitierez and Osborn, all non-lawyers, though Kay had graduated from law school and become a stockbroker. I had asked Bill to size up the Committee for me, and it was his prediction that, of the five, Runyan and Kay were definitely against him; Guitierez and Lund were more fair-minded; and Osborn was a question mark. Kay was, Bill told me, a pompous ass know-it-all who took himself too seriously and liked to make long, legalistic speeches, showing off his law degree. There was an additional problem with Kay: one of his staff attorneys, Michael Braun, was married to Kevan Ann Willey, who had broken the initial June 12 story in the *Republic*. Bill had already charged Willey with "pro-abortion bias." Also, Kay had already stated publicly that he found Davis' testimony before the Committee thus far "incredible."

In addition to these problems, we faced the heavily-biased

253

Republic and Gazette. "Bill Davis: The Senator Should Resign" had been the editorial appearing in the *Republic* on August 13, bringing out one of "Judge Ridge's" latest allegations: Davis had threatened an auto dealer with introduction of legislation which would curb the use of auto dealer plates, a threat made in retaliation for the failure of the dealer to reveal the identity of one of his employees who had been observed by Davis and another senator in a clear act of stealing campaign signs from the roadway. The allegations about Bill were false, which we would show by way of the Arizona Automobile Dealers lobbyist, with whom Bill had spoken, and Senator Wessel, who had heard Bill speak with the lobbyist on the phone. The Senate, with help of the media, further ambushed Bill by Senate President Stan Turley's release to reporters of another false story: that Davis had secretly sought through Turley secrecy of Ridge's report in exchange for Davis' resignation. Davis had never made such a request, but had spoken on the phone with Turley, merely seeking advice concerning his options. Davis' statements to Turley had been purposely twisted.

We were thus up against insurmountable odds and had but three days to prepare, in essence, for trial, facing four hundred pages of the Ridge Report allegations *and* with scores of witnesses to interview. Add to that this simple fact: Davis had no money. When the first story broke, his creditors called in the loans and the dominoes began to fall. Davis was bankrupt. After meeting with Bill and hearing his plausible responses to the Ridge allegations, I believed in his innocence and agreed to take the case *pro bono*. It was a political hot potato, but then I was not a politician. Never have been, never will be. I felt that a man who had the courage to filibuster against abortion was a man worth defending. And on the fee issue I had another idea. Tom Collins, Maricopa County Attorney, had recently been charged by a grand jury for his abuse of power for his investigation of Duke Tully, publisher of the *Republic*, which had time and again taken Collins to task in print. Collins was charged by the grand jury, but Melvin McDonald, his private attorney, had succeeded in obtaining a dismissal on grounds of grand jury abuse. (McDonald, who had prosecuted the Cayman Island *Bryan* case as the United States Attorney for the District of Arizona, had left office for private practice. *Bryan* is discussed in *Chapter 18.*) Collins succeeded in having the county award him attorney fees for his defense. Why should the same not apply as to Davis, I figured. Since Davis was now indigent, it stood to reason the Senate should agree that he receive adequate counsel, paid for by public monies. The Senate refused.

With the snowball effect against Bill, we had to seize the initiative. The plan was this: seek removal of Kay for reason that he had already decided the case without all the evidence in, and because there was an appearance, at least, of impropriety due to the relationship between Braun and Willey; schedule a press conference for Monday afternoon the 18th and at the conference build some credibility with the media by presenting evidence of at least one false allegation in the Ridge Report; and hold another news conference before the hearing, offering at the conference witnesses with personal knowledge, witnesses who could refute allegations. We had to reverse the momentum. By use of the news conference, we could hold the *RAG* at bay, keeping them at least on middle ground on the stories because the stories would also appear in smaller newspapers, such as the *Glendale Star* and on television.

"State Senator Accused of Wrongdoing Vows to Fight 'Like Trapped Animal'" was the headline in the *Gazette* on Tuesday, August 19th, with "Senator Davis Accuses Ethics Panel of Bias" appearing in the *Republic*. As the articles pointed out, we also asked that Ridge be removed as the investigator for reason that he had submitted a report "replete with ... false, misleading and fraudulent statements." I would show Ridge that "it takes two to tango." I hoped that, by showing some of the glaring errors within a few days time, we could convince the Committee to give us more time to respond to the allegations. I produced at the news conference clear evidence of one false allegation: Ridge had stated that the man who had stolen Davis' signs had never been prosecuted, but I had in hand the certified copy of the court judgment in which he pled guilty to several offenses. How complete a job had this former judge done, considering that the conviction was a matter of public record? "MacPherson also blasted Ridge for inaccurately including in his report that a case had been dropped against an employee of Bell Ford, a Phoenix automobile dealership. The employee, Vincent Joseph Henn, was suspected of tampering with campaign signs belonging to Davis and others. He pleaded guilty and was fined $32 for tampering with signs owned by Sheriff Dick Godbehere, according to court records produced by MacPherson," the *Republic* reported. "MacPherson called Ridge's account of the Henn affair 'the tip of the iceberg ... as to lies .... MacPherson also complained that Davis had been the victim of a 'witch hunt.' He said that the media have treated Davis unfairly and that Davis thus far has been denied his Constitutional right to cross-examine witnesses."

The next day, August 19, 1986, no doubt reeling somewhat from our attack on the 18th, the *Republic* fired back with its editorial with this headline: "Bill Davis: Senator Should be Impeached." As to our request for the removal of Kay due to the appearance of impropriety, the editor wrote, "MacPherson said he had no knowledge that anything improper occurred, but said he had subpoenaed Willey and Braun because there is 'an appearance of impropriety and conflict of interest.' This is pure nonsense, *chutzpah*, on a grand scale. Willey has never made any secret of her marriage to Braun, so why did Davis and his lawyer wait until now to bring it up?" Of course, the editorial ignored the fact that I had not come on board until Sunday the 18th, *one day before* we requested Kay's removal.

The *Glendale Star* on the 20th had been much more fair to Davis with headlines: "Senator Maintains Innocence - Violation of Rights Claimed, Additional Thirty Days Sought." In addition, they made clear one of our *Fifth Amendment* due process issues: the right to examine *in public* Davis' accusers. The Senate had issued at our request subpoenas for witnesses permitting us to take depositions, but there was no provision for a hearing at which we could examine the accusers *in public* . We had drawn an analogy to the recent nomination hearings for Supreme Court Justice William Rehnquist, at which witnesses were questioned by a panel representing both sides of the issue. It was simple, common sense.

With the *Republic and Gazette* owned by the same family - the Pulliams - the *RAG* had a double-barrelled shotgun pointed at Davis. First was the headlines on the 20th from *Gazette* columnist, John Kolbe, "Davis Report Reveals Portrait of a Sleazy Flim-Flam Man." In summary, Kolbe wrote "In line with this record, Davis now has the breath-taking audacity to ask us to pay his lawyer's bills (it's bad enough that we have to pay them for Tom Collins, but at least his actions, however dubious, had a semblance of official authority to it) and to give him another month (which surprise! will be after the September 9 primary) to respond to the charges. According to Senate President Stan Turley, Davis was so desperate to keep this slimy portrait from the public that he offered to resign from the Senate in return for keeping the Ridge Report secret. Turley wisely refused. But for once *Senator* Davis, as he would like you to call him, has a good idea. Or at least *half* an idea. He ought to quit before he stinks up the Senate anymore." This, the best of journalism from Phoenix, the capital city of Arizona. Second was the *Republic* editorial on the 20th, "Bill Davis - Senator Should be Impeached."

It was time for round two, the second news conference, which we held on Wednesday the 20th, the day before the hearing. In addition to the news conferences, Bill and I had been working about eighteen hours a day interviewing witnesses, some by formal deposition, others in secret. I felt I needed the element of surprise against Ridge and his report and utilized the feint and demonstration. Under the rules, we had subpoenas issued to various witnesses, which we served on only those who would not agree to meet with us privately. As to those subpoenaed, we had to give Ridge notice so that he could send an underling attorney from his office to sit in and hear the best we had to offer. I suspect we lulled Ridge into a state of complacency because, as I handled the few depositions, behind the scenes I was interviewing our key witnesses, on tape, with their consent. I then had our word processors transcribe the tapes, thus producing in effect an informal deposition. I also secured affidavits from some other witnesses. We were prepared at the second news conference to produce some of the witnesses in an attempt to begin to show "the other side of the pancake."

On the 21st, the *Gazette* headlines read "Bias: Senator Blasts Phoenix Newspapers, Seeks Boycott," while the *Republic* read "Embattled Senator Urges Boycott of 'Slanted' Papers." Of course these slanted papers were, by the very headlines, slanting the news for reason that Davis' request for boycott was but a small part of the conference. The major thrusts were the witnesses. The *Republic* did report "Davis was flanked Wednesday by four people who spoke on his behalf. . . One of the four people who accompanied Davis was Dan Miller, former lobbyist for the Arizona Automobile Dealer's Association. He blasted both the *Republic* and the Ridge Report for accounts of an incident involving Bell Ford. 'It was completely written up wrong,' said Miller.... Miller said Wednesday that Davis *never threatened* the Arizona Automobile Dealer's Association but merely suggested that legislation was needed to curb abuses of dealer plates. The second witness, Bob Bullis, had worked for the elderly couple, the Shipleys, who alleged that Davis had cheated them. But Bullis told the media that he knew the Shipleys' business, which was sold to Davis, 'was not financially sound.'" In other words, Davis, not the Shipleys, had been defrauded. We had evidence that the Shipleys had misrepresented on their financial statement the accounts receivable of the business, which accounts were uncollectible in the amount of over $75,000.

But again it was time for the *RAG* to give a "tit for tat" with Benson, the editorial cartoonist, showing Davis wrapped in an American flag, holding a Bible, standing in front of a "re-elect Bill Davis sign," looking up to the heavens and stating "Ethics, financial responsibility, full and open disclosure, honest business dealings, impeccable standards of personal conduct and integrity - I ask you Lord - since when have these been requirements for public office?" On the 20th, Davis had predicted, as reported in the *RAG* , "If they [Senators] are afraid of the *Republic and Gazette* , they'll have to slap my hand or maybe do something worse. If they do it on what's fair, ... they'll have to clear me."

On the 21st, we spent from 2:00 p.m. to 10:00 p.m. before the Senate and the hot, media camera lights. I submitted to the Senate our response to the Ridge Report, outlining first the false allegations and supporting them with transcripts or affidavits of our witnesses.

It was my plan to conduct in public a hearing at which I would have testify before the Senate witnesses in our favor, and demand that we be given opportunity to cross-examine the accusers in public. We began with a rocky start.

First, after I gave an introductory speech as to what we had accomplished in a short period of time and that we intended to call witnesses, I was told by Runyan that we would be permitted to call witnesses and be heard fully, but that first he wanted an update from "Judge Ridge." (Ridge had not been a judge for years.) After Ridge gave his update, standing behind his report, I stood up and said the first witness I wanted to call was Ridge, himself. I intended to bury him with his incompetence in public, for God and all the world to see. The cameras rolling, Runyan indicated he would not permit me to call any witnesses; this was not a courtroom. To which I responded, "Five minutes ago, you indicated that I could call witnesses." "But I've changed my mind. I won't permit it." "That's the problem with this Committee," I fired back. "You change the rules as you go along." In retrospect, I should have had the witnesses for our side sign up and ask to address the Committee on their own. I do not think it would have made any difference in the outcome, but it would have made more clear what a kangaroo proceeding it indeed was.

So after eight hours of arguments and some testimony by Davis, a lot of behind-the-scenes political machinations and final political speeches by all five members as to why they were voting the way they were voting, the result was exactly what Bill had predicted, with this the *Phoenix Gazette* headline the following day: "Senate Panel Rebukes Davis - 'Slap on Wrist' Given Over Financial Deals." To add insult to injury, Runyan announced as they read the rebuke that he was advised the Attorney General's office was conducting a *criminal investigation* into Davis' conduct. This was but days before the September 9 primary. The loan dissenter, Peter Kay, wanted the Committee to recommend censure for Davis, which we urged later would have been better because it would have afforded at least the rudiments of due process. To take the action of censure or any stronger action such as impeachment, both houses of the legislature would have to convene in a special session. "He should either be exonerated or reprimanded or censured or whatever," Kay said. "This begs the question. I think that's shirking our duty." There is indeed a paradox here, considering that Kay, whom we attempted to remove and who was most against Davis, was in favor of an outcome which would in the end provide Davis the greatest Constitutional protections. Maybe Kay had, indeed, learned something in law school. But no doubt the majority of senators, not just on the Committee, but acting behind the scenes wanted to put Davis to rest. They figured with the criminal investigation and the rebuke, however mild, the voters would boot Davis out on the 9th, which they did two to one.

The Committee had five choices: it could have cleared Davis or recommend that the legislature take one of four actions - reprimand, censure, expulsion or impeachment. Instead, it had issued an eight-point statement which accused Davis of exercising "poor judgment" and of conduct "beneath the standard of behavior the public has a right to expect of an elected official." Lund, recognizing that there were no ethics rules written as statutes require, and no rules of procedure, said that Davis had been "a victim of a maiden voyage." The *Glendale Star* had the last to say in the way of editorials with its "Clear the Clouds" on the 27th, criticizing the lack of due process, believing that:

> The Senator should be given a fair trial, that the Ethics Committee should practice what its name implies and give Davis a chance either to clear his name or be punished according to fair and impartial findings. It has been easy for the Ethics Committee to come up with their vague rebuke of Davis. They had the staffs of the *Arizona Republic/ Phoenix Gazette* working for them - this includes the reporting staffs, editorial staffs, and columnists.... The incident leaves everyone in the dark except those newspaper columnists who believe Davis is a 'sleazy flim flam man.' This is the time for the Ethics Committee to get its ethics together.

And what of the income tax allegations? After the offshore trust promotion allegations were flatly denied by Davis, in effect putting Ridge's feet to the fire, we never heard another peep about taxes or offshore trusts. This, then, brought to a close the Davis case. Well that is, except for the murder of Katherine Buyse, former employee of Davis whom we had intended to call as a witness. Buyse had been shot on her porch in Peoria at 1:00 a.m., apparently by her ex-boyfriend, Ralph Lawrence, who had previously fired at Buyse and Buyse's new boyfriend. But in addition to Lawrence, several police officers were charged, entering guilty pleas to illegal use of the state law enforcement's computer system. Lawrence, a former police officer, had asked his fellow officers to help him track down Buyse, which they did by means of computers. The officers were prosecuted under state law, pled guilty, and were granted probation. Kathy Buyse, age 21, was dead. Thanks, *Big Brother.*

Attack the enemy from all sides, firing and drawing the enemy out, requiring each flank of the enemy to participate in the dance, with the result that the enemy column is rendered immobile. Che Guevara

NORTH DAKOTA BRAKEMEN   Chapter 15

One of the few criminal tax cases tried in state rather than federal court was the "Fargo Five," five railroad brakemen from Fargo, North Dakota, charged with willful failure to file their tax returns under North Dakota law The trial was to take place in Bismarck, the state capital. "Oh no, how can we get a fair trial with so many state employees in Bismarck?" I protested with our motion for trial in Fargo. Motion denied.

So, in January of 1986, with Barbara assisting me again, I checked into a hotel in snowy, downtown Bismarck. Our defense was good faith belief: wages were not income and filing of a tax return was voluntary, not mandatory. *Ok, Major Mac. Not enough challenge lately? Suffering from delayed stress syndrome? Need a charge of adrenaline, that natural high provided in Vietnam by way of sniper bullets overhead?*

My clients had believed enough in their premise that they had filed suit against the state for adjudication of the issues, a suit still pending at time of trial. In response to the suit, the State Tax Commissioner, Kent Conrad, had made a statement that he believed the defendants had acted "in good faith," a statement made on television:

> I think they believe, they sincerely believe, that it's unconstitutional to have criminal penalties for people who fail to file their tax returns. Unfortunately, they will find out that it is legal; then they will have followed the advice to fail to file and put themselves in legal jeopardy; they will find that the legal jeopardy, in fact, does have merit, and they will be in trouble.

I had a video tape which I intended to offer at trial. This was an interesting twist in that I could call the principle accuser of my clients as a prime character witness. I, therefore, subpoenaed Commissioner Conrad, who, it was said, intended to run for U.S. Senate the following fall. (He did and lost.)

The investigator's report had but one intent witness, a railroad supervisor, and I was able to take the sting out of his testimony. With the investigator's report in hand, I used my *Tonight Show* tactic: if it happened and it was important, it was in the report; everything important in this case is right there in that report. No other direct evidence of intent. I had set the government up on inability to prove beyond a reasonable doubt intent. Evidence was lacking, but dare I risk it all without taking the fight to them? I thought not. My clients would each testify on their reasonableness. The basis for their beliefs was at stake.

On the voluntary issue, I succeeded in having two state revenuers contradict one another. The first, a male, agreed that the State of North Dakota follows the federal pattern of taxation and that the state's system of taxation is "based upon voluntary compliance." The following witness, his supervisor, having been sequestered during the earlier testimony, disagreed. Nice move. Another chink out of the *Monster's* armor. If the agents could not even agree as to what state policy and law was, how could it be said that these defendants acted intending to violate the law? Now for the spider trap.

State Tax Commissioner Conrad did not show, and as I was requesting an order to show cause why he should not be held in contempt for his failure to comply with my subpoena, the judge questioned the relevance in any event of his opinion about the defendant's good faith belief. I was not sure I needed Conrad's testimony, except to drive the nail in the coffin, considering that I had him locked in by the video tape. Certainly, he would not impeach his own testimony from the video tape. What was he going to do, say he did not mean to say what he said, and look like a complete idiot, our would-be Senator? The court denied my efforts to introduce the tape. Not able to get in this evidence, I felt it was crucial to make my clients' actions look reasonable. They had received a letter from an attorney who had agreed that their position had merit, but the letter was received *after* the due date of the subject return. But the government had made a fatal error. They had set themselves up by having admitted, over my strenuous objection (a ruse), evidence of the brakemens' failure to file in the subsequent year, which involved the time frame of the letter. The trap was set. Now to spring it timely. It is these small, tactical moves concerning evidence that can spell the difference between victory and defeat on the courtroom battlefield.

Prosecutors oftentimes ask of a defendant if he sought the advice of an attorney or an accountant before choosing his course of action or inaction, expecting an answer in the negative. This is especially so in what the government believes to be "frivolous" cases such as "wages are not income" or that "the tax system is voluntary, not mandatory." (Wages are not income, so the argument goes, because income is defined by the courts as gain from labor, property or capital. Wages are monies paid in equal exchange for services, thus not gained. What is your body worth? Interest on a bank deposit, for example, is gain. IRS says the system is based upon "voluntary compliance." What they mean is "you are required to volunteer," which of course does not square with Webster's notions about "voluntary.")

A prosecutor of Chinese heritage in another case had taught me what I had forgotten from my days in Vietnam. The spider trap. In that case, I should have known better, but did not demonstrate enough caution. I wanted the Special Agent testifying to stay away from the fact that my client had spent money on a new pickup, evidence which I felt would be prejudicial in the minds of the jurors, especially when the prosecutor got around to arguing at time of closing the "greed" of my client. I asked precise questions on cross-examination of the agent, confining the witness. But when he saw an opening, he reached in his coat and pulled out a document concerning the precise question, a document also revealing the truck purchase. I took the document, had the judge order the witness to be more responsive to my question, then moved to strike the answer. But the cat was out of the bag. It was an underhanded trick in that the question had nothing to do with the purchase of the truck.

Not so with my spider. A letter from an attorney. I took a chance. The prosecutor might not ask the question. But since our prosecutor was the head criminal trial attorney for the North Dakota Attorney General's Office, I figured him to be predictable. He was, and asked the question, "Did you ever seek advice from an attorney." (Note, he failed to confine the question to a *time frame*.) My client answered, "Yes, I have the letter right here," pulling it from the pocket in his jacket. "Attorney Guy Curtis from Nebraska. Should I read it to the jury?" "Objection." Too late to say you are sorry. The court would not admit the letter, but did permit my client to read its contents! Trapped, the prosecutor only compounded his wound by questioning the true existence of the attorney. I knew the attorney existed, having met him in Denver at a National Commodity & Barter Exchange conference. In closing arguments, I made mention of the fact how the prosecutor had attempted to raise some doubts as to the attorney's existence, but had not come forth with evidence. "Why didn't the investigator return to the stand and report no such attorney listed in the telephone book in Imperial, Nebraska?" Stick it in their face.

Interviews with jurors after the verdict revealed that they did not much like the defendants and their testimony, but for one who was quite humble. They did not like what the defendants had done or had failed to do by not filing. But the government, they concluded, had not met its burden. With several state employees on the jury, the government had failed in its production of evidence of intent. Five not guilty verdicts.

There was a true paradox to all of this. We had moved that the case be tried in Fargo rather than Bismarck, fearing that our jury panel in Bismarck would be predominantly made up by state workers. State workers sitting on a failure to file state income tax case! They would see the defendants as a threat to their job security. And, after losing the motion for a change of venue, and seeing the panel, I became more concerned. There it was. A good number of state employees on the panel. It could not be avoided. Our motion to exclude all state employees from the panel had also failed. Next, I considered that Bismarck, North Dakota must be about the most conservative state capital in the country, and what would these conservative people think about five railroad workers making trouble for the government by their failure to file tax returns? After all, everybody knew that you had to file a tax return, right? If you did not, you went to jail. Taxes and death, the only two things that could not be avoided. It was, however, their conservative attitude as law-abiding citizens that worked to our advantage. The law, they concluded, favored the defendants. However they might disagree with the law they, through their own conscience as law-abiding citizens, they could not violate their oath, nor violate the law as instructed by the court.

In addition to instructing the jury on the burden of proof and beyond a reasonable doubt, the court instructed that if from the evidence the jury could draw either of two conclusions, guilt or innocence, they must of course adopt the conclusion of innocence. "The fence post instruction," as I like to call it. Sitting on the fence post, one must fall to the side of innocence. In fact, in Scotland, there are three verdicts that can be rendered: not guilty, guilty, and not proven. To the Scots, not proven really means, "Don't do it again."

Without a strong case of intent, the government had failed to push the jury off the fence onto the side of guilty. Straddling the fence, not liking the defendants, not liking the position that they had taken, but sworn by oath to follow the law as instructed by the court, a law with which they disagreed, the jurors found that the government had not proven its case.

Nothing is easy in war. Mistakes are always paid for in casualties and troops are quick to sense any blunder made by their commanders. Dwight D. Eisenhower

VIETNAM HELICOPTER PILOT   Chapter 16

At Rock Smith's state trial, I met a humble man who ran to McDonalds, and returned with hamburgers for our lunch. At the end of the day, he was there again, ready to lend a hand. Jim Pazsint was a husky, outdoors-looking guy, made for Alaska. He appeared strong as a bear, stubborn as a mule in his slow, deliberate ways. I remember his maroon Ford pickup truck with "Boniface Texaco," a station on the corner of Boniface Parkway and DeBarr in Anchorage. What I did not know at the time I met Jim was that he was a Vietnam vet, a helicopter pilot who, after a year and a half in Vietnam and a tour of duty at Ft. Richardson outside of Anchorage, had left the Army as a captain. He and his wife, Holly, owned the station and I would later represent him twice in federal court, not on tax charges, but for "assault" upon a federal officer for Jim's citizen's arrest of a revenuer, an IRS collections officer.

Holly was pregnant with her second child, due any day, when she made that frantic call to Jim. "Jim, there's a black man here at the door alone and he's wearing a plaid jacket, says he's from the IRS. He's in a little blue car and he won't go away." "I'll be right there," was Jim's answer, as he jumped into the pickup and sped down Boniface to his house, but a couple of miles away. He grabbed his .44 magnum revolver and also had a back-up .22. *God, I hope she's not harmed,* Jim thought. He could be there faster than the police if Holly was under any threat. Jim had seen combat action flying the Huey Slick.

It couldn't be the IRS. They had contacted Jim and Holly before, looking for a delinquent return, and were told by letter not to call or visit, but to communicate in writing. *And what are those stories in Anchorage and elsewhere that Holly talked about?* She had recently seen on a television series how assailants pose as meter readers, telephone repairmen, etc., in effort to gain entrance to a home while a housewife is alone. Rapists had made a game of it, and it had worked.

A black man? There were not many blacks in all of Anchorage, and one with the IRS? *Chances are a million to one,* Jim thought. *Besides, this was the lunch hour. What would an IRS man be doing knocking on the doorstep at the lunch hour alone? They always travel in pairs.* Coming up to Chena Avenue, where he would make a left turn and go to the third house on the right, Jim was saying to himself, *God, let her and the baby be okay.* As Jim approached the corner, he saw a car speeding out of the intersection, not stopping at the stop sign. Obviously in a hurry. It was a blue car, and a black man was the driver. Jim honked and waived, attempting to get the driver's attention, but he turned right, heading up Boniface. No markings on the car showing that it was a government car. *Don't IRS agents drive marked cars? Aren't they white?* Jim had to make a split-second decision - go to Holly, or give chase to this man. He made a u-turn and gave chase, figuring the man had not had sufficient time in which to do harm to Holly. He pulled behind the speeding blue car, honking and waiving the driver to the right of the road. Rather than pull over or at least slow down, the driver sped up, causing Jim to give chase. Jim, still wondering whether he should go back to Holly or continue with the chase, again made a split decision. Arrest this man, who has assaulted my wife by half scaring her to death. Jim was no stranger to split decisions. And to danger. He had seen his share of combat in Nam, rescuing many a grunt in trouble.

Jim sped up, pulled to the left alongside the small car, honking and motioning the driver to pull over. The driver continued. Jim pulled up further and forced him off the road onto the icy shoulder. The man stopped and Jim pulled the truck alongside, getting out of his car, and noticed the man was getting out of his car, heading for Jim. Jim had his .44 Magnum pointing skyward and with him a backup .22. As he came around the truck, the man was headed toward him until he saw the gun. "Get to the back of the car," Jim shouted. The man obeyed and Jim made him spread eagle against the back of the blue car, where he began to frisk him. Then Jim paced up and down the street which was outside an apartment building, saying he was excited and he had to think. He waived cars down to come assist him and get the police. "I'm placing you under citizen's arrest for assaulting my wife," he told the man.

Jim had arrested Joseph A. Skeete, an IRS collection officer. The police arrived and told both men to come down to the station, which they did. Soon after, Jim was charged by a federal grand jury with forcibly impeding, intimidating and interfering with a federal officer. He faced a maximum of ten years in prison and a $50,000 fine. The caption of the case, that is the title, prior to the section which begins with "The Grand Jury charges ... " stated "Assault upon a federal officer."

Jim had a defensible position akin to that of Jean Hylton: state statutes provided for a citizen's arrest. The problem for Jim was that a citizen had to witness a misdemeanor or have a good faith belief that a felony had been committed. A citizen then proceeds at his own risk in arresting another. If the person arrested is a private citizen, the risk is civil suit for false arrest; if he is a federal officer, the risk is jail for obstruction or assault.

The prosecutor, as expected, would raise issues such as "Why didn't Jim go to Holly if she was the major concern? Why not take down a license plate and report it to the police?" But men trained in combat are trained not so much to think, but to *react*. "Now wait a minute here, let me think this one over. Do I really want to charge this hill with an enemy machine gun nest to my front? Stop, guys, I gotta think this over. Do I call in artillery to repel the VC at the wire? What happens if some shells accidentally land within my perimeter?" "Black Hawk Six, this is Wolf Three, approaching your position. I'm at 1,000 feet and ten clicks and got a load of twenty mike-mike for your guests. Well, what's that I see? You guys aren't taking incoming, are you? Let me think this one over a minute. I don't want the slick and my crew put in jeopardy." Indeed the Armed Forces of the United States have spent millions of dollars to figure out the best method to de-program thinkers, causing them to become actors. *Haul ass up the hill.* "Up the hill, down the hill, through the hill, can't stop, no stop, can do, here we go, all the way...."

Other than the charges themselves, what frustrated me the moment I met Jim again were two things. First, I saw something I had not observed at Rock's trial. This man was very intense. A walking time bomb. When I learned of his Vietnam experiences, it made sense: delayed stress syndrome. Why not have a psychological defense? It was the honest-to-God truth; Jim was not driving down Boniface, he was commanding that slick back in 'Nam, coming not to the rescue of Holly, but grunts in a fire fight. I am thinking, *Jim again dove into combat.* It had been over ten years since Jim left, but were not all the studies showing a latent period of ten years or more? While this defense struck me as the most honest and viable initially, the problem was President Reagan had just been shot by Hinkley, who had been acquitted on insanity grounds. "Not guilty by reason of insanity," was the verdict. Delayed stress syndrome from Nam vets was less drastic a defense and led to freedom, rather than confinement to a psych ward. It was a form of "temporary insanity." But dare I risk jury backlash from the Hinkley incident?

Secondly, Jim had a tendency to editorialize and never shut up. He was friendly and liked to talk, and he was mad as hell deep down inside. These factors, coupled with delayed stress syndrome, could prove a volatile mix, come time for cross-examination. My gut reaction was I could not put Jim on the stand. Compounding this problem was the fact that Jim had been to some Patriot meetings and had a book rack at his gas station of Irwin Schiff's book, *How Anyone Can Stop Paying Income Taxes*. Schiff had been prosecuted twice, jailed the second time on a tax evasion charge. As in Jean Hylton's case, the government would likely raise tax protest motive. Decisions, decisions. Not split second, but decisions upon which a man's future rested. It was my responsibility to prevent Jim from doing ten years in the pokey.

Before my involvement, Jim had been representing himself and already there was adverse publicity, due to underhanded tactics by prosecutor Jerry Miller, Assistant U.S. Attorney from Anchorage. An article appeared in the Anchorage newspaper with the headline that Jim Pazsint owed the IRS a half a million dollars. This was the government's way of retaliating against Jim for the article that previously appeared, an article which made Jim look like a folk hero. In that article, there appeared a picture of Holly with the family dog and a picture of Jim. Now the government had its own illegal means of making Jim look not like a folk hero, but the bad guy.

Under the rules of discovery, a prosecutor must make available to the defendant any and all documents he intends to use in his case in chief. Anything saved for cross-examination by way of surprise need not be disclosed. Also any information exculpatory to the defendant, which means which would help the defense, must be disclosed. Some prosecutors have an "open file policy" by which they disclose everything, which is as it should be. If, indeed, the government has the confidence level to proceed with the charges, they should have nothing to hide, and every opportunity should be afforded the defendant.

Many times files contain reports by IRS unfavorable to the defendant which will not be relevant at time of trial. For example, there might be an FBI report in which an FBI agent concludes, however erroneously, that the defendant is associated with the *Posse Comitatus*, the group allegedly responsible for the murder of two U.S. Marshals in North Dakota. This is obviously a hot item for the media, but it certainly does not do much to guarantee the defendant a fair trial. Even if the evidence is not used, and even if jurors claim they will not be biased by hearing such allegations, it is difficult to "unring the bell."

In Jim's case, IRS had begun to proceed civilly and, since Jim had not, in their mind, been cooperative by disgorging, indicating that he was willing to discuss the matter but it must be done *in writing,* IRS revenue agents had prepared a report in which they were disallowing all deductions, just adding Jim's gross receipt from the operation of the gas station. Jim *owed a half million dollars* to IRS, they claimed. Imagine, if you will, any business not allowed as a deduction all the costs of its operation. Obviously the tax was well overstated.

Reeling somewhat from the folk hero article, Miller and his boss, Michael Spaan, U.S. Attorney, political appointee and key hatchet man, no doubt devised together or separately a simple plan: deposit the entire file with the clerk, thus making it public record, and tip off a reporter. Even if the reporter is not tipped off, knowing the interest in the story, Spaan and Miller must have known full well that reporters will periodically review the public file. Their only excuse for such action: Jim, at the time, was representing himself and they wanted to cover themselves as to the discovery rules since Jim was not an attorney. Hogwash. Jim had been in contact by phone and in writing to make arrangements to review the file. Jim, as his own counsel, had just as much right as any attorney to sit down with the prosecutor or the agent or both, or to just be handed the file in a government office and review it. Instead, Miller dumped the file on the clerk making it *all* public record, and the article immediately appeared. The article headlines made mention of the alleged one-half million dollars owed! My motion to dismiss for prosecutorial misconduct would be denied at all levels. Miller's action was a clue to me that Miller, like Powers, would stop at nothing. But Miller was a lot more clever than Powers, and thus more dangerous. Not clever enough, however, for round one.

While I had concentrated pretrial on case law dealing with assault on a federal officer and citizen's arrest as a defense, I initially and for a long time "missed the forest for the trees." I discovered a federal case in which a shoot-out occurred at a black funeral, white men first firing. No identification. No "Halt. FBI." One black man fired back and it turned out his victim was an FBI agent. Lack of knowledge of identity was no defense, except that it is to be considered on state of mind and the government's attempt to prove beyond a reasonable doubt willfulness. In other words, if you get into a fight in a parking lot of a grocery store and punch some guy out, and he is a fed, you risk prosecution and five years in the pokey. (It is ten years if a dangerous weapon is involved.) What this body of law all meant to Jim's case, then, was that lack of Jim's knowledge that Skeete was, in fact, an IRS revenue officer was not a complete defense. It would be for the jury - a question of fact - whether Jim really believed or had reason to believe he was not a federal officer.

Embroiled in these legal nuances, I had failed to make a determination with what, exactly, Jim was charged. *Forest for the trees*. Under the case number, it read "Assault on a federal officer." But under "indictment" in what is referred to as the body of the indictment, the language of the Grand Jury read after the preamble, "The Grand Jury charges ..." that Jim had "impeded, intimidated and interfered" with a federal officer.

Miller and I both tried the case as an assault, and I had even submitted an assault jury instruction. But somewhere in the middle of the case and before closing argument, a light turned on: *Jim is not charged with assault. He is charged with impeding, intimidating or interfering*. When I made my final conclusion through research at the Anchorage law library, Rock Smith and Rocky Streble assisting me, I submitted new instructions and complained that Jim was *not* charged with assault. Miller was less clever than he believed. And the judge? Why do judges persist with obviously erroneous conduct? Is it the purpose of harassment of citizens, realizing that, even if the litigant wins on appeal, he will suffer great humiliation, trauma, stress, not to mention expense? Why not be fair to both sides as "referee?" Should not a tie or close case go to the defendant, considering that he is presumed innocent and every burden is upon the prosecution? Such circumstances I have faced many times in both criminal and civil matters, tax and non-tax cases.

The trial had proceeded as expected, with little factual dispute. Witnesses had watched the arrest from an apartment building, their reaction recorded by the police when the witnesses called by phone the emergency number 911. Officers arriving on the scene had testified that Jim's arrest method was proper and safe, just as they would have done. They even took Skeete into custody initially. Jim went voluntarily to the station. It did not help that his driver's license was a "constitutional driver's license," a matter brought up at trial over our objection. Although Miller agreed to my pretrial motion in limine - to keep out evidence - that the issue of tax returns or civil liability would not be brought before the jury, Miller brought in the garbage truck and dumped whatever bits and pieces he could find to demonstrate that Jim was involved in the tax protest movement. This, he hoped, would demonstrate motive.

We called a black man, Jim's mailman, whom Jim had taken on a fishing trip to the outback, Jim flying a Cesna 185 bush plane. We wanted to make sure the jury did not believe Jim somehow was prejudiced against blacks.

Miller called a neighbor who testified that Jim had cursed out the windows on a Sunday morning, threatening the man. Holly would testify that she and Jim had been awakened by the sound of a lawn mower and Jim was half asleep when he yelled out the window. (Watch your conduct in public, readers. Your neighbors may become your prime accusers. Whenever the FBI conducts any security investigation, the first folks they talk to are neighbors. IRS investigators do the same.)

There was a lot of other *quid pro quo* - this for that - punches and counterpunches between Miller and me, but the key witnesses had been Holly and Skeete. As usual, I felt I had to destroy the IRS agent, but here it became even more important because the accused would not be testifying. Too risky, we determined. Miller, with a Baptist preacher type approach, pious, smug attitude, would, I felt, turn hot-headed Jim inside and out. Especially on the tax protest issues. Jim had attended numerous *Patriots in Action* meetings. The burden now on my shoulders, as I liked it, I focused on Skeete.

269

"You were on your way to see Jim, whom you knew worked at the Texaco station?" "Yes." "You knew the Texaco station would be about a mile down the road?" "Yes." "And you had no reason to believe that Jim was at home rather than at the station?" "No." "And instead of going directly to the station for Jim, you decided instead to go to the home with the hopes that you might surprise a lone housewife?" "No." "Well then why did you first go to the home?" "Because it was on the way." "Yet you did want to see Jim?" "Well, I wanted to see Jim *and* his wife." "You did get letters saying to deal only in writing?" "Yes." "And as you saw this truck attempting to pull you over, you saw that it was a Boniface Texaco truck?" "Yes." "You concluded that the man driving was Jim?" "Yes." "So of course you just pulled over to the side?" "No." "Why not?" "I wasn't about to have a meeting by the side of the road." "Oh, I understand. So you instead just waved back and pointed ahead, showing that you would pull over at the apartments?" "No." "Why not?" "I didn't want to have a meeting on the side of the road." "Oh, so you just pointed in the direction of the station, meaning you would meet him at the station?" "No." "Why not?" "I didn't think of it."

It was the government's claim that Jim knew Skeete was, in fact, an IRS agent. Part of my cross of Skeete went like this. (Transcript.) "You testified, sir, that Jim said 'I know who you are.' Is that what he said?" "He said 'I know who the hell you are.'" "But he didn't say 'I know who the hell you are. You are from the IRS,' did he?" "He said 'I know who the hell you are.'" "Did he ever say 'I know you are an IRS agent'?" "He never said those words, sir, no."

With Skeete I wanted to bring out that Holly had cause for fear due to the fact that Skeete was wearing a strange checkered jacket that an IRS agent would not normally wear, that he was at the door and would not go away, and appeared very nervous, as one who was about to commit a crime. Skeete denied that he wore the checkered jacket, claiming he wore a brown corduroy jacket. Ironically, Skeete attended the same church as the Pazsints and Holly observed him at a church service after the incident but before trial wearing the checkered jacket. But it was a swearing match. On the issue of Skeete being nervous, I forced him to change his testimony as follows. (Transcript.) "Is it fair to say, considering you had been with the IRS for four months and this was your first day out on solo visits, that you were a little bit nervous that day?" "Yes." "And you demonstrated that nervousness to Mrs. Pazsint in her doorway?" *"No."* "Well, when did your nervousness stop, when you got out of the car?" "I was nervous." "My question is, you felt nervous, did you not, when you were standing in front of Mrs. Pazsint at the front door?" "There was a reason for that."

270

"Just answer my question - yes or no?" "Yes." "Were you nervous?" "Slightly, yes."

I did everything I could with Skeete to demonstrate his lack of consistency in his testimony, his propensity to lie in order to bring about a favorable result for the government. Since Jim was not going to testify, I had to make my points with Skeete. He repeatedly changed his story. (Transcript.) "Do you recall that you said that Jim said 'Who the hell do you think you are to threaten his wife,' and then told you that you were under arrest?" "No. I remember the part about threatening of his wife and the arrest part, I don't remember that precisely." "When do you remember that happening?" "I remember it happening off to my left, a slight distance off to my left, spoken back to me." "And this is *before* he frisked you, right?" "No. *After* he frisked me, as I recall." "Sir, do you recall writing a report on this matter?" "Yes sir." "I would show that to you. Page four indicates, does it not, it says 'Who the hell did I think I was to threaten his wife, and he told me I was under arrest. He frisked me, standard police style, and I assumed I asked if I could show him my credentials and he said he knew who I was.' Is that your statement?" "That's my statement." The timing was important because it was the government's position that Jim's reference to the threat was an *afterthought* for purpose of justifying the arrest.

Miller also called the police officer, and on cross-examination I brought out the state law concerning the right of citizen's arrest. Anchorage police officers, in fact, carry with them a form to be filled out by a private citizen who wants to make an arrest. This is to protect the police department from suit for false arrest. The complaint is filled out, given to the police, and the police take the person into custody. The officer explained that if a misdemeanor takes place in the presence of the officer or the citizen, that is sufficient for an arrest and, as to a felony, since it is a more serious crime, it need not take place in view, so long as the citizen or the officer has probable cause to believe that the offense was committed. (Transcript.) "When the police officer makes an arrest without a warrant, he must reasonably believe that a crime has been committed, based on all the facts and circumstances known to the officer at the time." "That is correct." I developed analogies between how the officers would react to a situation and how Jim, in fact, had reacted to Skeete, including pursuit of a fleeing car. (Transcript.) "What is the manner that the police might use to stop the vehicle?" "Road block, forcing the car off the road, whatever force becomes necessary depending on the crime." "Is it not true that an individual fleeing from a scene might give an officer a further indication of probable cause?" "That happens, yes."

On redirect examination, Miller, obviously feeling that he had lost

271

some ground with this police officer, attempted to regain the momentum. (Transcript.) "Isn't it a fact that the standard for a police officer making an arrest is a far different standard than for the private person making an arrest?" "There are a couple different standards." "And as far as a citizen's arrest for a felony having been committed, isn't there a distinction between a police officer being able to arrest on the basis of probable cause where a felony has been committed, whereas in fact a citizen must know that a felony has, in fact, been committed before he can make an arrest for an incident outside his presence? Do you know that distinction?" "I don't know the distinction, no." "Assume that you are home with your wife and while you are at home, an Internal Revenue officer came to your door and your wife answered the door and there, in your presence as a police officer, assume that the Internal Revenue officer asked your wife whether or not he could discuss tax matters with her and she declined. And thereafter the officer asked whether or not she had income for a couple of years and she indicated that she was pregnant. And assume further that officer said that this related to prior tax years when she couldn't have been pregnant and your wife told this officer that she would have to discuss taxes with you, with her husband, and the officer then handed her a business card and left. Now you, as a police officer, who has tried to make arrests, would you have any authority or ground whatsoever to go out and interfere with a man's traveling on his business to the next stop or any place else that he was going?" "Objection, Your Honor. Unless he has qualified this man as an expert, he cannot ask him a hypothetical question such as this. The question is improper." "But I can ask him what he would be lawfully authorized to do as a police officer," Miller responded. The court's decision, "Overruled. You may answer on the basis of the way the question is asked and what you would be authorized to do as a police officer." The officer responded, "Under the scenario that you presented, as a police officer, I would *not* arrest that subject for anything." "Why would you not arrest him?" "Because I would have no reason to arrest him." "You would have no authority to arrest him?" "Correct." Now it was my turn again. "I have a few, Your Honor." *What do I do now? This has become a see saw. We stuck it in their face. They stuck it back in our face. If I let it drop here, we look bad in front of the jury. It's time to take the calculated risk and stick it back in their face.* "Sir, the prosecutor asked you a hypothetical. I would likewise like to ask you a hypothetical a little bit differently. I would like to assume the following facts, and that is that your wife is nine months pregnant and has had some difficulties with the pregnancy. The baby is due any day. She is known to be high-strung at times like this; very emotional. She has had some medical problems in association with the pregnancy. And she has also told you that she

272

is afraid of black men, just generally, and has read a lot in the papers recently about how individuals entered homes saying that they were security officers and it turned out they were not security officers, and then in turn raped women, etc. And you get a phone call from her mid-day and she rather frantically tells you that 'There is a black man here at the door who says he is from the IRS trying to get in the house. He won't go away. He is out in front in a small blue car.' You thereupon rush home from work a few miles away and just before you get to the house, you see a small blue car pulling away with a black man in it and you ask him to pull over to the side and wave him over. And at that time, he speeds up the car and begins fleeing from you. Now I ask you, based on those facts and circumstances, would you, as an officer believe that you might have reasonable cause at least to stop that man?" *Please say yes, sir, please say yes. ""*"Yes." *Take it and run.*

Since we were not putting Jim on the stand, I decided to put his character in evidence as best I could: military background, combat service in Vietnam for a year and a half, involvement in community activities including church, Little League baseball coach, and nominated president of the state Little League organization. This, as it turned out was a mistake. The government in turn brought in evidence concerning Jim's failure to check with customs when he brought a plane to Alaska through Canada. *Tit for tat.* I was still wondering had I done the right thing not calling Jim. In a final effort to get the jury to understand who Jim really was and what he was really about, his true character, I had Holly testify about a newspaper article with photos showing Jim's plane which crashed into a tree of a playground. In the photo beside the plane stood some children who had been playing. Jim, on short final to his emergency strip, the school playground, saw in the last seconds of the landing the children playing. Rather than risk the children, he pulled the stick back, aborting the landing on the playground and crashed into the trees. He was fortunate he was not killed. As the caption of the article pointed out, as soon as he got out of the plane, his first words were "How are the children?"

It was time again for Miller to retaliate. (Transcript.) "Mrs. Pazsint, have you ever attended any of the Little League functions when your husband was coaching these boys?" "Yes." "Baseball and picnics?" "Yes." "Have you ever seen him take out a paper dollar bill, five dollar bill or ten dollar bill and display it to those youngsters and tell them that it was no good?" "No. I understand that they got one if they hit a home run." "It is your testimony that you have never seen him tell any of those boys, or your son for that matter, that paper money of the United States is no good, that normally having money backed by gold or coin money is good?" "I've never seen him say that, or heard him say that, no." "Has he ever said that to you?" "Just, has he ever said that to me? We both agree on that." *Be cautious, readers, as to your political beliefs. Watch what you read. What you read and what you believe may someday be used against you in a criminal tax case.*

Did the jury feel that Jim was "hiding behind petticoats?" After hearing the guilty verdict, and after the jury was released from the courtroom, we all sat stunned. Sick. Rock and the other supporters sat in the courtroom. Holly held her baby girl, Heather. Jim's son, age 12, sitting in the front row, was crying, his hands over his face. Jim went over, pulled his hands away and said, "No. You're going to watch this. Every minute. This is the system I fought for and was willing to die for. Learn how fair it is not." The tears streaked down his son's cheeks. The shock over in a moment, we all became mad and disgusted, no longer sickened. If looks could kill, the judge, Miller and the U.S. Marshals standing like vultures would all be dead. My wife, Barbara, who had assisted me with the trial preparations, sat beside Holly and Heather. Heather, no doubt sensing the mood, began to whimper. A big Marshal moved down the aisle into Holly's row and began to lift Holly out of her seat. Barbara leaped out of her seat, shouting, "You get away from her. You don't touch her." The Marshal jerked back, astonished his authority would be challenged. Other Marshals began to move in. I stared in disbelief, watching the judge from the corner of my eye. "Holly, you sit down," Barbara commanded. Holly, who was halfway out of her seat, sat down, frozen. Jim, Rock and everyone else in the courtroom, caught by surprise, watched in disbelief. My thoughts were of Section 111. "Whoever forcibly impedes or interferes with the official performance of a federal officer shall be convicted of a five-year felony." "You're not going anywhere. That baby is what this is all about, the reason we are all here," Barbara declared without hesitancy. It happened so fast. I was caught by surprise. The mood of us all was courtroom riot. The Marshals had now turned their faces to the judge as if to plead what to do next. I turned a hard look to the judge. It was his call. *Okay, judge*, I thought, *your move. Now what? Charge my wife for felony obstruction? Hasn't she done no less than Jim or Jean Hylton? Go ahead. Charge us all. I'll see you rot in hell. God will not be mocked.* Prudently, the judge waived off the Marshals. Jim was released pending sentencing and we all left the courtroom.

Back in Phoenix, I did further research on my gut reaction: the case could not go to the jury on assault when Jim had been charged with impeding and intimidating. Assault in the title was mere surplusage, not part of the indictment. A U.S. Supreme Court case from 1887 supplied the support: *Ex parte Bain* , 7 S.Ct. 781 (1887).

Why, then, since I had such ample Supreme Court authority, did the judge not grant my written motion for new trial? It was crystal clear and, indeed, a judge of the Ninth Circuit panel would later comment as I approached to argue following a more complicated case, in response to my comment "This case, I trust, is far more simple, your Honor." "Yeah. It's like shooting fish in a barrel." The district court judge had given Jim three years, stayed sentence pending appeal, and the Ninth Circuit reversed. We were back to square one, with another decision: do we do it differently this time? The element of surprise? Put Jim on the stand?

The sentencing had been bizarre. Jim fully cooperated with the probation officer, who insisted however, despite Jim's denial, in reporting to the court that Jim had been a leader of a tax protest group. According to an April 15, 1982 *San Francisco Examiner,* a daily newspaper, "Pazsint is a township leader in a group known as the Allodial Freeholders. This group is a spin-off of an older tax protest group, Posse Comitatus, which openly advocates armed resistance to government attempts at taxation." (Transcript.) Jim, representing himself at sentencing, stated to the court, "This, of course, puts me in the light of being an armed enemy of the government, and this is certainly not true. This was pointed out to the probation officer, Mr. Richardson, and in fact I will draw the court's attention to information that is already in the prosecutor's file which was made part of the record. And I would like to call Mr. Davis to the stand to show that I have no relationship whatsoever to this group." W. Clinton Davis then testified about "Scion Township" and "Liberty Township," of which, according to Davis and Jim, Jim was not a member. According to Davis, there was a public notice published in the *Anchorage Times* three times that the township was formed in March of 1981, a notice signed by Davis himself. The Liberty Township was similar to Scion Township referred to in the article. By formation of the township, Davis and others were declaring that the state had failed in its duty under *Alaska State Constitution, Article 10* to protect the rights of Alaska citizens. Despite Jim's denial and evidence to the contrary, Richardson had persisted in writing in his report that, considering Pazsint's activities such as with the township group, if those activities go unchecked it "could become serious and progressively impair his ability to function as an independent citizen." The court refused to strike it from the report.

Spaan argued for three years incarceration or, alternatively, two and a half years suspended with a five-year probationary period. In support of Spaan's argument, he told the court "if you look at Mr. Pazsint's brief that he has submitted, when talking about his conduct in the 1978 audit and his contemptuous attitude, Mr. Pazsint writes 'If this is the case, then a vast majority of attorneys that deal with the IRS have a contemptuous attitude of the law.' [*Agreed.*]

275

And it goes on on page 3 and adds, 'More often than not, actions by IRS agents are outside of the law and merely bluff.' [*Agreed.*] He goes on at page 5 and describes what happens to him, not realizing that he did pull a dangerous weapon on a federal official, but he writes in the main that, 'Defendant is a victim of circumstances not all of his own choosing....' The presentence report indicates that there is a paranoia almost, some sort of distrust of the federal government [*Vietnam, Watergate, Iran-Contra?*] and Mr. Pazsint needs this belief checked in order to deal in this society, and that he is rabidly anti-government. And this isn't just one incident in question. There is a prior history of his dealings with the IRS and his inability to deal with the people in customs.... I think your Honor also, in sentencing, has to take a look at the general deterrence. I think from the fact that there have been newspaper articles, there has been a certain segment of society that might think Mr. Pazsint is a folk hero, that it is important that federal officials, the government officials who are doing their duties in a law-abiding way can feel that society will not accept the fact that people could assault them with a dangerous weapon, and that is wrong. It is not the way to deal with problems with the federal government. Mr. Pazsint, if he was wrong, could have left his guns at the service station. He could have talked to Mr. Skeete. He could have talked to Mr. Skeete's boss. He could have sued the IRS *[lots of luck],* or he had other less violent remedies available to him. I think it is important to look at that, your Honor, and when fashioning a sentence, attempt to deter this sort of dangerous conduct so that in the future we don't have to worry about being lucky and that the Defendant and federal officials aren't killed, and that they don't have weapons brandished at them." The judge gave Jim three years!

The retrial went much the same as round one. In the final analysis, we again made the decision: Jim would not testify. Again, a disappointing verdict, but again the appealable issues. On the second appeal, we raised issues including dismissal for prosecutorial misconduct: the attempt by Miller to try the case in the newspaper. The Ninth Circuit turned a deaf ear. Jim served eight months in a minimum security prison. It was like being back in the Army: loneliness, hurry up and wait, boredom. Would it have made a difference had Jim testified? A question I will not learn to forget.

To sin by silence when they should protest makes cowards of men.
Abraham Lincoln

ARKANSAS PUBLISHERS	Chapter 17

There might be something said for an alleged tax protester who has not filed a federal income tax return for eighteen years or more: the government may have trouble in proving *knowledge*. Such was the case of Anita Lowery, about whom it was alleged that she well knew she was a person required to file an income tax return. The government could produce no evidence of returns ever filed by Anita, thus no evidence that she knew the requirements of filing or how to file a tax return. Typically, the government will offer into evidence a taxpayer's history, including his prior and subsequent returns, if any. But the government is limited in its storage capacity. It normally cannot produce the actual returns beyond five years. Evidence of the assessment and payments is usually available by way of the "certificate of assessments and payments" (C of A) which is produced from the microfilm on storage in Martinsburg, West Virginia. Only minimal information is put into the IRS computer system: the year involved, amount of tax assessed by way of self-assessment (filing of the return) or other means, such as Tax Court litigation, date of assessment and history of payments. Where no return is filed, the entry made is "no record of return filed." Often, IRS will, in addition to the C of A, produce a "certificate of no record of return filed."

Anita was charged in 1988, with her husband Ajay Lowery, the government alleging the couple were publishers and owners of a nation-wide tax protest tabloid, the *Justice Times,* of Clinton, Arkansas, formerly the *Tax Strike News,* of California. Even assuming, for sake of argument, that the Lowerys were the publishers, did this mean ownership of the publication and that the receipts to the publication were receipts to be attributable to the Lowerys personally? Is it not true that newspapers and magazines typically have publishers separate from owners? And even if the receipts to the *Justice Times* are attributable to the Lowerys, by what percent are they attributable to Ajay and Anita individually? Arkansas, the state in which the Lowerys were charged, unlike California, their prior alleged residence, is *not* a community property state, where one-half the earnings of each spouse is attributable for tax purposes to the other spouse. Without the testimony of the Lowerys, or an inside stooge, how could the government prove income, even assuming ownership? In other words, without a partnership agreement, how could the government prove beyond a reasonable doubt the amount of gross income attributable to each defendant so as to prove an essential element: "required to file."

Add to this the irony of the fact that the checks received by the *Justice Times* were made out to the *Justice Times* and deposited to the *Justice Times* accounts with the endorsements by stamp "A. Lowery." Ajay or Anita? The jury could, at most, draw an inference that, since Ajay and Anita were on the signature cards, they each had a right to the income, but by what percentage? Without the ability to prove a percentage, the government merely assumed fifty percent.

One would think IRS could and would mount a more sophisticated attack against a couple who, for fifteen years or more, had been "leaders in the illegal tax protest movement." Not so. IRS special agents investigated for five years and developed mere misdemeanor charges, lame at best.

After discussing strategy on the case, the Lowerys and I decided I might be useful as a witness and, since their two court-appointed counsel were both aggressive and bright, we made the joint decision: I would act in the role of consultant. I flew to Little Rock, and the five of us spent two days brain storming, playing out the various scenarios. The two attorneys made an excellent team, one with more trial experience, the other with more knowledge in tax matters, having been formerly IRS counsel. Also, the former IRS lawyer knew personally the special agent in charge of the investigation, having worked with him on numerous cases. Thus we knew the personality traits, work habits, abilities and frailties of the enemy. This was poetic justice since many times IRS utilizes under-cover agents or informants. One would think IRS would have infiltrated the *Justice Times*, a prime tax protest target, and mounted a much stronger offensive. Perhaps the Justice Department decided against aggressive tactics, fearing a *First Amendment* counter-attack.

The big questions were whether to put Ajay on the stand, and would I be needed to testify as to the defendants' character: their reputation for truthfulness and veracity in the business community. I had been a subscriber and advertiser in the *Justice Times* and had written articles and spoken at meetings sponsored by the Lowerys. In short, I knew their reputation in the business community for being truthful and honest individuals. In addition, we assumed that, with my background and present occupation, I would lend credibility to their character.

During the investigation, the IRS special agent had sent me a request for information. From bank records he had obtained the name and location of many subscribers and advertisers. I claimed the *First Amendment* and referred the agent to my counsel Bill Cohan in Denver who had defeated IRS in their attempt to obtain bank records by way of grand jury summons in another case. IRS was investigating another tax protest organization, the National

Commodity and Barter Exchange (NCBA), headed by John Granbouche in Denver. The Tenth Circuit ruled the subpoena violated the *First Amendment* rights of NCBA members and contributers, and that the government must therefore demonstrate a "compelling need" for the information, which it never attempted. After receiving my letter about Bill, NCBA, and the *First Amendment,* the agent never again contacted me, nor did he call Bill as I had suggested.

To show intent, the government might, we thought, attempt to introduce various *Justice Times* issues. Even if the Lowerys did not testify, I was prepared to counter the introduction by explaining that, as a law-abiding citizen, I was involved with the *Justice Times*, which was, after all, a *First Amendment* exercise by us all. The West Point combat vet, constitutional lawyer would not hurt, the attorneys thought, for appeal to the jurors in the federal District Court, Little Rock, Arkansas.

The government, for whatever their reasons of strategy, perhaps fearing opening of the *First Amendment* door, introduced in evidence only one of Ajay's songs, the transcript only: "Cut the Thievin' Hands off the IRS." So he and Anita did not testify and the lawyers therefore did not need my testimony. I watched as the prosecutor had no response to the judge's request for evidence of Anita's knowledge of filing. At the close of the government's case in chief, Anita's attorney had moved for dismissal for lack of sufficient evidence. Finding no evidence of knowledge for reason there was no evidence that Anita ever had filed a tax return, the case against her was dismissed.

Through our intelligence sources, we learned of the IRS's investigative technique of the Lowerys, especially Ajay. We did not discover why, during the location of *Justice Times* in California for many years, neither Ajay nor Anita had not been prosecuted for failure to file their federal income tax returns. But not long after the newspaper moved to Clinton, Arkansas, it came under IRS surveillance. IRS, as we discovered, "rode herd" on the activities of the Lowerys and the *Justice Times*. First they collected the article entitled "Rally Marks the Move of Anti-IRS Paper, To Hills of Arkansas" appearing in the *Arkansas Gazette* on Saturday, May 2, 1981. Reporter Sonny Rhodes began, "The *Justice Times*, the journal of the national tax revolt, is moving from California to the Arkansas Hills, which have a tradition of disdain for federal revenue agents, and an anti-internal revenue service rally at Leslie (Searcy County) marked the occasion Friday." Under the sub-heading "revenue fighters," Rhodes wrote that the Lowerys "did not oppose income taxes, because the federal constitution allows them, but they do oppose the IRS and what they consider excessive taxes." Anita was further quoted as saying, "The IRS are thieves. They can steal from people without due process of law, and the federal courts have said that the IRS codes supersede the constitution." The Lowerys reference to the fact that the progressive graduated income tax is the second plank of the Communist Manifesto was also mentioned by Rhodes.

To the relocation of the *Justice Times* and the revenue hating Ozarks, the Northwest *Arkansas Times* responded with its "Editorial-Opinion" on Sunday, May 3, 1981: "Coming on top of Arkansas' other problems, word that the *Justice Times,* a national organ of the anti-tax movement, has moved from California to Leslie, Ark., can hardly be looked upon as the best possible news." Then on July 11, 1983, an individual unknown to Lowery, and perhaps unknown to IRS, wrote to IRS, complaining about the Lowerys' anti-tax sentiments. (The letter we obtained through our sources did not bear the author's identity.) Attached to the letter was an article entitled, "Publisher calls Kahl, champion of freedom!" Included was Ajay's statement that "the personal income tax is unconstitutional." At the end of the article, circled and underlined by either the IRS or the author of the letter, was another statement attributed to Ajay, that "there are slightly less than 40,000 subscribers to his newsletter, published monthly at a subscription rate of $20.00 a year. His wife, Anita, is managing editor." No doubt IRS agents quickly calculated $800,000 a year in gross receipts to the newspaper and no tax returns filed by either the paper or the Lowerys.

The author of the letter thought, no doubt, that he was doing his "patriotic duty" by forwarding the information to the IRS. He asked IRS, "Does Lowery pay his taxes? Refer please to recent July 4th statement to news (Associated Press) enclosed. This man and wife, Anita, daily go about telling everyone that listens, 'to pay income tax is unconstitutional.' They use their home phone, at home rate, and operate their business, *Justice Times*, from the same number at the lower home rate among other things." Little did this self-indulging informant know that he was rendering little service to IRS for reason IRS utilizes "clipping services," or personnel within IRS, to clip from newspapers articles in which individuals criticize taxes, IRS, and the government in general. Contained on the letter was the following IRS handwritten notation: "Is this person in the T [tax] Protester program? Should they be?" If they were not already, they soon would be.

Under its' "Intelligence-News Clipping" program IRS obtained from Memphis, Tennessee, an article appearing in the *Commercial Appeal* newspaper. By IRS "routing slip" dated May 5, 1984, Memphis CID forwarded the article to Little Rock CID, "Lowery Hopes 'Tax Sanity' Will Reign.'" The article described Ajay's decision to run for president in 1984 and showed Ajay beside his van which has on the side a picture of an "Eledonkephant," which is portrayed as a "political animal eating money and depositing deficits." The article points out that "Lowery hasn't filed a tax return in more than a decade."

Likewise, IRS collected an article in the *Arkansas Democrat* on July 15, 1984, "Opponent of IRS Forms New Party" which described Ajay's criticism of IRS for compelling taxpayers to provide information, then using that personal information against them in prosecuting fraudulent tax cases. "What kind of government uses force to control its people?" asked Ajay.

Ajay Lowery, born in Indiana in 1925, one of nine children, describes his father as a "hard working industrial worker." Ajay grew up during the depression, and when he turned seventeen, he joined the Navy, serving almost four years during World War II. Ajay, like many constitutionalists, got involved in constitutional issues and taking on the IRS as a result of a show of force by IRS. Back in 1970, a time when he and his family were struggling to make ends meet, and Ajay was filing returns and paying the taxes he believed he owed, an IRS agent claimed erroneously that Ajay was not paying all he owed and seized from his bank account $40.00. As Ajay puts it, "Since that time, I have determined that I am one of those people who has no obligation to the IRS."

In 1983, Ajay decided to start a new political party - United Sovereigns - in an effort to bring attention to the need "to restore our nation to justice and sanity." On promotional brochures he wrote:

> Government has become a MONSTER! Our 'Government' has become a ravenous monster!... constantly feeding itself, at our expense. Many of the same conditions that led to the Declaration of Independence in 1776 HAVE REAPPEARED TODAY and we are now losing our freedom at a TERRIFYING RATE. We will only have a future if we *draw the line* and take positive *action* to put government BACK IN ITS PLACE! That place is as the SERVANT of US THE PEOPLE. GOD ALONE is the Supreme SOVEREIGN, the RULER, the FINAL AUTHORITY. 'WE THE PEOPLE' are SOVEREIGN *under* GOD. WE are the FINAL AUTHORITY, the RULERS. You have no king. YOU ARE the *king*. YOU are the *ruler*. WE ARE A FREE PEOPLE.... WE ARE GOING TO ELECT TRUE AMERICANS, men and women who will regard their oath of office as SACRED. Men and women who will make themselves available to their constituency *on a regular basis* instead of spending most of their time *scratching one another's backs* and SPENDING AMERICA INTO OBLIVION!

281

In describing "Ajay who?" and why he is running for president, Ajay stated in his brochure that he:

is the publisher of the JUSTICE TIMES, the national voice of the second American Freedom Movement for the past ten years. *He is a common man,* mostly self-educated, a graduate of the school of hard knocks. Mr. Lowery has *never had any political grooming* - but *maybe that's good.* He has never been a Congressman or Senator. He has never been a Governor of any State ... he has never been the Vice President. On the other hand he has never had a part in *fomenting war* ... he has never voted for *deficit spending* ... he has never helped to create *double digit inflation.* ... or a *$200,000,000,000.00 deficit.* He was not born with a golden spoon in his mouth ... he is not a lawyer..he is not in any position to buy votes or repay political favors ... he is not a peanut farmer...and he is not an actor. In short, HE IS NOT A POLITICIAN. *A.J. Lowery is just a common man who loves his God and his country and the principles which made America great! AND HE HAS DETERMINED THAT SHE MAY BE GREAT AGAIN.*

On March 24, 1988, IRS Special Agent Tom Bryan interviewed Mr. Jay Jackson, Editor and Publisher of the Van Buren County Democrat. Jackson had attended a meeting of the Choctaw Shrine Club at seven o'clock on a Tuesday evening at the Blue Bonnet Restaurant at Clinton, Arkansas. There he heard Ajay speak and wrote a brief article in his paper entitled, "Income Tax Unconstitutional, Choctaw Shrine Club Told." Jackson wrote that Ajay told the shriners "that he has not filed an income tax return in ten years" and "I am not breaking the law."

Thus having collected all the financial information from the bank, the news articles, and Ajay's record album with his anti-tax songs, the government was ready for the prosecution of Ajay and Anita Lowery. Or so it thought, for, according to our intelligence sources, the criminal investigation file as to Anita was quite thin. I suspect IRS charged Anita only because of its uncertainty as to what happened to the gross receipts received by the *Justice Times*. IRS had no evidence as to the expenditure of the funds but for business expenses of the paper. Therefore, since the agents could not prove that the Lowerys owned the paper or that the funds to the paper were in fact distributed for the personal benefit of the Lowerys, the agents no doubt hoped the jury would infer from the evidence that each defendant received one half of the proceeds to the newspaper, thus requiring each of the defendants to file a tax return. This was only the beginning of the several technical problems for IRS.

As a "God send," the Lowerys received competent, aggressive, court appointed counsel. One of the attorneys, former IRS counsel, not only knew the inside tricks of the IRS, but as well was quite knowledgeable of the technical aspects of the case. He could not believe it: how could IRS prove income as to either of the defendants? In his opinion, they could not. Thus the additional irony in the case of the Lowerys and the *Justice Times* became this: here Ajay, at least, had openly admitted certain beliefs, assuming the newspaper reports were correct; yet, with all of this "fan fare," including Ajay's candidacy for presidency in 1984 and his song "Cut The Thievin' Hands Off The IRS," the case would boil down to a *technical defense*: How could the government prove beyond a reasonable doubt that the Lowerys were required to file a federal income tax return?

First was the calculation of "gross income" which in the case of a business which has inventory, as did *Justice Times* (newspapers, books and pamphlets), means "gross receipts" less "cost of goods sold." If the cost of goods sold, a technical computation which takes into account inventory, is high enough, an individual or a business, whether it be sole proprietorship, partnership or corporation, may not even be required to file. This is true even if the gross receipts are a million dollars! That is right: a business can receive a million dollars in gross receipts and, under the IRS code and regulation, may not be required to file a tax return because its gross receipts less cost of goods sold, which is in effect gross profit, is to be considered as gross income for the purpose of the filing requirement. Did IRS take into account inventories? Did IRS utilize the appropriate accounting method which could make a big difference? As the Lowerys' counsel pointed out in their pretrial memorandum:

To illustrate the effect of different methods of accounting, assume that *The Justice Times* received only one payment in either 1982 or 1983 of $60.00 which was a check received in December, 1982 , for a three year subscription beginning January 1, 1983. A cash basis business would reflect income of $60.00 in 1982 while an accrual basis business would recognize no income in 1982 and would recognize $20.00 of income in each of the years 1983 through 1985. Assuming the business could even use the cash basis, it would grossly distort the business income - 1982 would appear to be a very profitable year since it had income of $60.00 with no expenses while each of the three subsequent years would (assuming no other items of income or expense) reflect losses from deducting the cost of producing the newspaper without recognizing any corresponding income. The correct 'gross income' of the business could only be computed using the accrual method because the receipts would be allocated in the same years to which they applied and reduced by the cost incurred in each of those years.

Understand all of that? If not, do not be embarrassed, because it is likely that special agent Tom Bryan and those revenuers assisting him likewise did not.

Once IRS gets beyond the hurdle of accounting method, they must take into consideration inventories to properly calculate the cost of goods sold to the end that gross income can be properly calculated. For you CPAs, the Lowerys' defense counsel, after rendering to the court three examples on the impact of beginning and ending inventory upon cost of goods sold, wrote:

From the foregoing examples, one can readily see that the calculation of inventory has a significant effect upon the calculation of "cost of goods sold" and, hence, the calculation of "gross income." Any increase in beginning inventory serves to increase "cost of goods" sold and decrease "gross income." Conversely a decrease in beginning inventory serves to decrease "cost of goods" sold and increase "gross income." An increase in ending inventory will decrease "cost of goods" sold and increase "gross income" while any decrease in ending inventory will increase "cost of goods" sold and decrease "gross income." The failure to include inventory and "cost of goods sold" calculations produces an incorrect and highly speculative "gross income" figure which, in this case, would serve to remove a necessary element of the government proof required, to wit whether any Defendant had sufficient "gross income" to require the filing of a return. (Did you pay close attention to all of that, Special Agent Bryan?)

Assuming IRS can overcome the above technical hurdles, they are then faced with the division of income. It is well settled that the government cannot arbitrarily assign ownership of assets or business income between the alleged partners. Since the IRS had no evidence of a partnership agreement - either oral or written - they had no evidence that a partnership even *existed.* Thus the argument: only when a partnership has been proven beyond a reasonable doubt by the government to exist is one to consider the distributive shares to the partners." For purposes of determining a partnership, federal tax law gives deference to state law, Arkansas in this case. Under Arkansas law are the rules for determining the existence of a partnership, including examination of the question of whether or not the individual received a share of the profits or holds ownership to any capital of the business. Again, the IRS had no evidence. What they had was, at most, a "mom and pop operation," like the grocery store that mom and pop might operate without evidence of ownership. When money is received in the cash register, to whom is it attributable, mom or pop?

In fact, in many civil tax cases, taxpayers claim a partnership between husband and wife because it might be advantageous. As defense counsel wrote, "The taxation of so-called family partnerships has been a thorny issue for the Internal Revenue Service for many years. Whether a partnership even exists is generally contested by the Internal Revenue Service because it has been historically used as either an income shifting device (i.e. diverting income from a high tax bracket taxpayer to a family member in a lower tax bracket, e.g. a child) or as a means to get a previously unemployed spouse credit for social security as he or she approaches the age of retirement (e.g. changing what was a previously sole proprietorship to a partnership so a husband or wife who had not paid FICA taxes may pay for a minimum period to receive social security upon retirement).

For example, in one tax court case, *Kjorvestad v. United States*, the taxpayers were trying to prove that a family farm was a partnership between the husband and wife and was an effort to avoid including in the deceased husbands taxable estate, one half of the farms value. It did not work, the Tax Court stating that it "acknowledges the value and importance of Selma Kjorvestad's [the widow] contributions to the farming operation, but tax law has not progressed to the point where such services can be recognized for tax purposes without first finding the necessary intent to form a business partnership." Since intent then is the test and without the testimony of the Lowerys, how could IRS prove beyond a reasonable doubt a partnership? Despite this paradox - the tax law favoring the alleged tax protesters - the judge refused to dismiss the case as to Ajay and submitted it to the jury. (The government had evidence that Ajay filed returns prior to 1970.)

For two days the jury deliberated on Ajay, telling the judge they were hopelessly deadlocked. He sent them back. Finally they reached what I predicted and feared: a compromise verdict. Not guilty on one count and guilty on the other count. The not guilty count was the one for which Ajay allegedly had received about twice as much income as the guilty count. As a prosecutor who lost a criminal tax case once said, "I don't understand electricity, the Holy Ghost, or juries." At sentencing, Ajay put the government and judge on notice that it would be useless to grant him probation *if* the probation was conditioned upon his agreement to file tax returns and pay taxes. He received no jail time and no probation, but was fined $10,000. The case is now on appeal. (Update in *War Stories, Part*

II.)

For the overall defense in the Lowerys' case, credit is due John Lilburne, known as "free born John." For, as I wrote in *April 15th* concerning the establishment of the right against self-incrimination:

If to James Madison goes the credit for authorship of the Fifth Amendment in the *U.S. Constitution,* equal credit is due John Lilburne for the first "Freeborn Englishman" to put to practice the right within our English court system as early as 1649, more than one hundred years before the American Bill of Rights. Lilburne was tried before eight common law judges, the Lord Mayor of London, the recorder of London, four sergeants at Law and twenty-six other special judges, including city alderman and members of Parliament. As with modern day tax resisters, Lilburne's strategy was "to challenge every step of procedure, pick to pieces each bit of evidence against him, depict the court as his oppressors, and appeal to the jury over the heads of the judges." The charge against him was for high treason: publication of "seditious" pamphlets. While in the tower on another charge, he wrote that "the government was tyranical, usurped unlawful." His defense was technical: they might prove the publication, and show his name thereon, but without his testimony, they had no proof of authorship. Time and again, when asked by the court to confess to authorship, "Freeborn John" refused to accuse himself.

As with John Lilburne, in the case of the Lowerys the government could prove the *Justice Times* had been published, and perhaps even prove that the Lowerys were the publishers or editors, but they could *not* prove ownership and allocation of monies received by the publication. For all this, what difference, if any, has the reader found between Lilburne's 1649 "seditious pamphlets" and Ajay Lowery's 1981 song "Cut The Thievin' Hands Off The IRS?"

For years and years our government has used
As a method collecting - the rack and the screws
They say you'll go to jail, if you don't confess
We say "Cut the thievin' hands off the IRS."

Chorus:
We're gonna get rid of the IRS
We got no use for the rack and the screws
Or their inquisitorial abuse
Cut the thievin' hands off the IRS....

The surest way to prevent seditions if the times do bec̲ ̲ ̲
away the matter of them.   Frances Bacon

CAYMAN ISLAND BANKERS   Chap.

In *April 15th* , I gave readers a "behind-the-scenes look" at the impact of the *Fifth Amendment* upon attempts by special prosecutors and the U.S. Senate to unravel the flow of funds through Swiss, Caymanian and Panamanian bank accounts, and offered readers the "missing link" to the pipeline of Iran-Contra funds through my latest client, an alleged CIA operative, *The Colonel.* I revealed the latest use of offshore tax havens - the Cayman Islands, Virgin Islands, Bahamas, Turks and Caicos, and the Netherlands Antilles, and introduced readers to offshore banking. (An update of the latest developments in *The Colonel's* situation will be rendered in *War Stories , Part II* .) I also told readers of the story of Jack Bryan of U.S. Tax Planning, Cayman Islands. Jack had been charged in a four-count indictment with money laundering by sending $50,000 and later $65,000 to the Cayman Islands. He had been caught in a government sting operation. Having received $50,000 in cash for a deposit in the Caymans Islands, Jack had gone to several different banks with amounts less than $10,000 and used fictitious names in wiring the money. His purpose in using less than $10,000 at different banks was to avoid the bank's report to the IRS on the currency transaction report (CTR) form, Form 4789. The target of a joint IRS and FBI sting operation, Jack, co-worker Larry Schmidt, and two Phoenix attorneys were indicted by a Phoenix grand jury with conspiracy to conceal material facts in a matter within the jurisdiction of the IRS, and concealment of the matter, plus two counts of wire fraud.

In the original indictment, a grand jury alleged that the defendants had conspired to willfully attempt to evade federal income tax and to knowingly and intentionally defraud IRS by impairing IRS in its collection of data and reports of currency transactions in excess of $10,000, knowingly and intentionally concealing from IRS a matter within its jurisdiction, and knowingly and intentionally causing banks to fail to file the CTR. In causing the failure to file the CTR, the defendants had, the grand jury alleged, attempted tax evasion. Part of the object of the conspiracy and part of the scheme to defraud then, the indictment alleged, was federal income tax evasion. But in pretrial motions Bill Cohan and I urged there could have been no income tax crime committed for reason that the last overt act of the conspiracy was January 20, 1984, well before the filing date of April 16, 1984. ("Wild Bill" Cohan, attorney from Denver, "Cohan the Barbarian" joined forces with MacPherson and McCarville, PA on the case.) Not only had a return not yet been filed, but none was

..quired to be filed. The government, I urged, had "pulled the plug too early." Rather than waiting until April 15 and having Jack assist in the preparation of a false tax return which would be filed with IRS, the government felt it had enough with the transmission of the $115,000 to the Caymans, with Jack recorded on video camera stating, (Transcript) "See, if somebody else gets in trouble, then they see that [ownership by the U.S. taxpayer of the foreign corporation] and it's, it's an *obvious sham* if they've got all the paperwork and all the stock and everything. Now some of them are gonna want to have the stock certificates, but it's important that you tell them they gotta keep that away from themselves someplace hidden." Jack's company, U.S.Tax Planning Services, had indeed assisted the undercover agent with formation of foreign corporations in preparation of loans back to the agent for purpose of laundering proceeds from cocaine sales. U.S.T.P. had, in effect, become an offshore bank.

But after the government prosecutors received our pretrial motions to dismiss or, alternatively, to strike the tax evasion language, they went back to the drawing board and had the grand jury render a "superseding indictment" in which the objects of the conspiracy were reduced from four objects to two objects, in which there was *no* mention of tax evasion. Even with removal of the tax allegations, the government's theory was not clear, and we persisted in our request for clarification, considering the superseding indictment alleged a scheme in which "The loan transaction was a sham designed to lead authorities, should they ever inquire, to believe that the monies that were wired were a loan and, therefore, non-taxable rather than taxable drug profits." We asked whether the scheme involved the loan transactions or the currency transactions. The court refused to require the government to answer more specifically, and the case proceeded to trial without clarification on the record as to the *object* of the conspiracy and the *scheme* to defraud by wire. The end result was, we later argued to the Ninth Circuit, that "at the choice of the government and with endorsement from the court, the case was tried and the defendants were convicted on but one scheme: one founded upon the currency transaction violations."

This was no insignificant technicality. After the jury had found Jack guilty on all counts, the Ninth Circuit reversed, holding that no crime had been committed. The law at the time required bank officials to file CTRs with IRS where the bank had received cash in excess of $10,000. There was no law that precluded a citizen from breaking up a $50,000 transaction into amounts less than $10,000 and taking those amounts to separate banks. The Ninth Circuit panel wrote:

It is patently clear from the language of 31 U.S.C. Section 5113(a), that a currency transaction report is not required to be filed with the Secretary when the amount of the currency transaction is less than $10,000.... We conclude that the reporting act and its regulations did not impose a duty on [defendants] to inform the banks involved of the nature of their currency transaction. We believe that the application of criminal sanctions against [defendants] here would violate due process.... Even though money laundering furthers the goals of those who may be engaged in criminal activity, it is not our function to rewrite the law or the implementing of currency reporting regulations promulgated by the Secretary. If Congress or the Secretary wish to impose a reporting duty on financial institution customers, they must do so in clear, unambiguous language. We cannot impose the duty by implication.

But that did not end the case. The Ninth Circuit found that there was no reporting requirement, thus no crime under Counts One and Two, the conspiracy and "concealing a material matter within the jurisdiction of the IRS charges." In addressing the wire fraud counts, the court stated that those also must be dismissed "since the appellants have not illegally concealed a matter within the jurisdiction of the IRS. The wire transfer of funds from the Cayman Islands to Phoenix could not have furthered a scheme to defraud the IRS." In its petition for rehearing, the government urged that the scheme alleged in Counts Three and Four were *different* from and *independent of* any concealment of material facts from IRS as alleged in Counts One and Two, the government claiming that the wire fraud scheme involved "converting income into a loan through the use of a sham Caymanian corporation." But here is where the government had shot itself in the foot. In effort to avoid the tax issues which we had raised pretrial, the government had totally *abandoned* any scheme but for the CTR scheme. In fact, I had succeeded in obtaining an answer from the government to our Bill of Particulars, an answer in which the government stated that the wire fraud counts "are the substantive violations" of the conspiracy count and since the conspiracy count had nothing to do with tax fraud and evasion and only with CTRs, it logically followed that the wire fraud count *must fall* with the conspiracy count. "Again," I wrote before the Ninth Circuit, "the *only* objects of the conspiracy count to which the wire fraud counts are inextricably tied, were: objects regarding currency transaction reports!" The government did not succeed in its "switching horses mid-stream," the Ninth Circuit apparently seeing right through its attempt to do so, denying the petition for rehearing. The government did not attempt to seek a rehearing from the entire Ninth Circuit panel, nor did it petition the U.S. Supreme Court for certiorari.

But that did not end matters for Jack Bryan. He, along with twenty-one others, was later indicted in Dallas, Texas with an indictment similar to the *Dahlstrom* indictment, conspiracy to defraud the IRS by aiding in the preparation and filing of false tax returns and numerous substantive counts concerning tax returns of various individuals. Three of the defendants were attorneys. I would be called to represent several of the defendants. Use of offshore trusts and corporations was the issue. Details and results in *War Stories, Part II.*

During the trial in Phoenix, Bill and I determined that it was necessary to take the *offensive.* First, the government was alleging that the loan transaction that Jack had arranged for Rex Reynolds, whereby Rex was to receive a loan from his offshore corporation, was a total sham. Yet Rex had signed a promissory note and was at the time of trial in default of the note. There were principals in the Cayman Islands who were the corporate responsible individuals, and when I contacted them, they agreed that Reynolds was in default and informed me that they wanted to sue Reynolds if I felt the matter was collectable. The individuals, of course, were involved with the management of Jack's company, U.S. Tax Planning Services. Therefore, we prepared and filed a suit against Reynolds in effort to demonstrate to Reynolds, the court, the prosecutor, and the jury that the loan was not, as alleged by the government, a sham transaction. It was a bona fide arm's length transaction by which the taxpayer - Rex Reyonlds - was indeed liable on a note that he had signed, having received the proceeds of the loan.

The main prosecutor, U.S. Attorney A. Melvin MacDonald, was outraged, suggesting that I should be sanctioned under *Rule 11* of the *Federal Rules of Civil Procedure,* whereby Congress authorized federal judges to sanction attorneys by award of attorney fees and costs against an attorney who would bring a vexatious or frivolous lawsuit. MacDonald also moved *in limine* in effort to bar us from bringing before the jury the matter of the lawsuit. My plan was to bring out on cross-examination of Rex the fact that he had signed the note, had received the money, and had not paid back the loan and was long ago in default on the loan. Of course, we had to serve Reynolds with the suit prior to his testimony, which we did, which took away somewhat from the element of surprise. The court agreed with MacDonald and ordered that we could not bring the matter out during trial.

There, of course, was never a *Rule 11* proceeding brought against me, and perhaps for good reason. First, we had good legal basis for the suit. Secondly, Reynolds as a paid informant for the government had actually stolen some money from Jack. This man

Reyonlds had a felony record as long as your arm and was a real gem of an informant, having done considerable time in the pokey.

On another front, Bill thought it wise to sue the four federal agents and the informant Reynolds for violation of *Constitutional* rights of our clients because the agents had obviously entrapped Jack and induced him to break the law. The law regarding entrapment is simply that the government cannot suggest to an individual a crime, but must find an individual who already has propensity to commit the crime. Jack, at the time he was brought $50,000 in a paper bag by one of the undercover FBI agents, had never been involved in either money laundering nor cocaine operations. (Details of the sting operation are contained in *April 15th*.) Bill prepared and had filed in the United States District Court for the Central District of California in Los Angeles a suit seeking $150 million in damages. The *Phoenix Gazette* on April 12, 1984, reported by the article headline, "$150 Million Suit Filed Against Four Agents." The article reported that MacDonald brought the suit to the attention of U.S. District Judge Earl H. Carroll and hurled "unethical conduct" accusations at me. "'He [MacPherson] filed a lawsuit as representative of the Board of Directors of the sham corporation (U.S. Tax Planning Service),' MacDonald alleged. 'He's now stalking the courtroom dropping subpoenaes on government agents.' MacDonald sought court sanctions against process servers he said were attempting to locate the federal agents through his office."

Of course, either MacDonald or the *Gazette* had their apples mixed with oranges for reason that as pointed out above, there were two separate suits. The article went on to point out that, "The lawsuit alleges Bryan and Schmidt were drawn into the conspiracy through subterfuge, rewards and intimidations by government agents Julian Miller, Raymond Campos, John Lughney and John T. Thrasher, and by confidential informant Rexford Reynolds. ... Bryan and Schmidt claim they were defrauded into participating in 'a charade created and orchestrated for the personal benefit' of the federal agents and 'paid for by the taxpayers.'"

Later, when U.S. Tax Planning was unable to continue with funding on the suit, we dismissed it. But Jack, Larry and the two Phoenix attorneys, Duane Varbel and Roy Osborn, were of course ultimately vindicated by the Ninth Circuit, which ordered their acquittal, and indeed the government had launched an expensive fiasco "paid for by the taxpayers."

State a moral case to a ploughman and a professor. The former will decide it as well and often better than the latter because he has not been led astray by artificial rules. Thomas Jefferson

| IOWA PIG FARMER | Chapter 19 |

The case of *U.S. v. Harold Haspels,* United States District Court for the District of Iowa, was a criminal case that never should have been recommended for prosecution, much less gone to trial. It is an excellent example of the left hand not knowing what the right is doing. The blind leading the blind. "And if the blind lead the blind, both shall fall in the ditch." Matthew 15:14. "Missing the forest for the trees." I love the paradox of the over-zealous IRS Special Agent: so thorough he misses the obvious. Again, I would try a case in which the case agent who investigated was not available for trial. Here, it was transfer, not resignation. A transfer I suspected caused by malfeasance in office.

I faced the lack of an investigative agent with mixed feelings. On the one hand, it provided for the prosecution and the new agent a lack-luster attitude if they were in need of an excuse to find one. "That SOB former Special Agent. He botched the case. Now we've got to try it. If we lose, it's all his fault." *No pancake is so thin that it doesn't have two sides.* Without the investigative agent present, I could not, in desperation if need be, attack a live, warm body. My attack would be against the IRS as an institution, a *Monster* the jury could not see nor hear. If they could not see nor hear the *Monster,* would it appear real? Quite a challenge. Charged with five counts of false tax returns, Harold Haspels, an Iowa pig farmer and family man with two children, faced twenty-five years in the pokey.

So the lack of a case agent in *Haspels* was received by me with a mixed review. Rumor was the investigative agent was not well liked within the IRS and the U.S. Attorney's office. Judge O'Brien who presided over the *Haspels* case, it was said, was not fond of the investigative agent, Special Agent Anderson. The judge had heard another tax protester case in which the defendant proceeded *pro se.* As is typical, the rule had been invoked, meaning sequestering of witnesses. Witnesses were not permitted in the courtroom except to testify. They were not to hear the testimony of others. Nor were they to discuss their testimony with anyone except their counsel. These admonitions were given by Judge O'Brien at the time the witnesses as a group were sworn in, and again after each witness testified, including Anderson. After testifying, Anderson violated the court's order, going back to the IRS office and discussing his testimony with other agents who were called as witnesses. Lucky for him, he was not jailed or at least fined for contempt when Judge O'Brien, outraged, called him back to court for a confrontation. As a result, I believe Judge O'Brien would not have much faith in the credibility of Anderson. This, I hoped would work in our favor as to at least pretrial motions, since Anderson would not come from his new IRS location in California for trial unless my client spent the money for a subpoena. Air fare plus $35 a day witness fee.

The prosecutor, Lester Paff, was not the vindictive type and had no axe to grind with Harold or with tax protesters, for that matter. I could tell that the more he reviewed the volumes prepared by Anderson, the more he realized that Anderson had missed the forest for the trees.

Cut and dried, was how Anderson saw the case. Anderson had concluded that Harold was a rabid tax protester, had been a pig farmer for years, and had reported, with help of a local CPA, his income from farming. He and his dad had some joint effort on grain production, his dad providing the land and Harold the labor. Harold had reported gross receipts from farming of over $100,000 for the years prior to the five indictment years. Little tax was paid each year due to substantial deductions for each of those three years. Unknown to Anderson was Harold's legal trick with the aid of his accountant - a pre-purchase of feed in December to offset income. Harold was, by this traditional tax deferment method, thrust into that vicious circle of year-end write offs. First, come December he needed $40,000 in deductions to pay little tax. Therefore, he needed $40,000 in cash for feed purchases, which meant another trip to the bank for a loan and slim equity-to-debt ratio. Second, a December grain purchase is but a roll-over, postponing the inevitable. To continue the postponement, a farmer must make the December purchase the following year, and the next year and the next, assuming the revenue and the resultant tax liability warrant it. Do it the first year and you are trapped. One of those games people play to beat the tax man. But, like the ice man, no matter what, the tax man cometh.

Why Harold was first called to civil audit, we never learned, but it was mighty suspicious, the revenuer must have thought, to see Harold's gross receipts from farming suddenly go from over $100,000 to less than $20,000. Had Harold retired? Sold the farm? Perhaps Harold could have nipped a criminal prosecution in the bud by disgorging at audit his use of the foreign triple trust. *Dahlstrom* again. On the other hand, unfortunate is the man who tells all at audit to discover he has provided the government with their best witness: the taxpayer. Silence *can* be golden.

Suspicions aroused, lack of cooperation by the taxpayer, and Harold's file found its way to the Criminal Investigation Division with a tax fraud referral from the civil auditor. *We have ways of*

293

making you talk. The Fuhrer will see you. In the morning you will be shot. Anderson, through his use of the IRS administrative summons to banks, farm suppliers and hog buyers, began to build a strong case against Harold: unreported income. Bank records revealed deposits. Banks maintain for five to seven years all records of deposits and withdrawals on microfilm. Bank secrecy law requires it. (Another oxymoron; the only secrecy that is afforded is that to government investigators, not the depositor.) And here, Anderson struck a roadblock. Harold had stopped depositing the receipts through his bank. Another badge of fraud. Only crooks use cash. Underground economy. Anderson was only slowed down. Bank records for prior years showed hog buyers, hog buyers which perhaps, just perhaps, made purchases from Harold for the years under investigation. Good guess, Sherlock. As evidence was building on the revenue side, likewise through old checks written by Harold to suppliers, the deduction side was building. Anderson was hot on preparing for Harold his return, which Harold could, of course, mail to IRS from a jail cell. But where had all the money gone?

Through the paper trail, Anderson learned of Harold's use of warehouse banking whereby Harold had payments made out to the National Commodity and Barter Association (NCBA) in Denver. NCBA paid directly to creditors Harold's bills and promised to Harold and other depositors confidentiality from government snoopers. All deposits were 100% secured by precious metal, as in the happy days of all U.S. federal reserve note holders prior to departure from the silver certificate.

A check with Denver CID told Anderson NCBA meant hard-core illegal tax protesters. According to a national IRS memo, these guys had plotted to kill a federal judge in Texas (a lie), who indeed was murdered. Harold was already guilty by association. After NCBA, Harold used NCE, a spin-off organization run by Lowell Anderson, an individual Special Agent Anderson discovered was a known illegal tax protester from Wyoming. One of the CPAs Lowell had used had been convicted of willful failure to file a federal income tax return and spent time in jail. The greater the association, the greater the guilt. At Agent Anderson's request, the post office was busy checking Harold's mail on a daily basis, recording the sender listed on the envelope, place of postmark, and postmark date. Mail cover, they call it. It requires no court order, just a simple request from IRS to their buddies at the post office. And then there was Harold's brother-in-law, another known illegal tax protester, who would appear on radio and TV calling the system "unconstitutional." They were everywhere, those illegal tax protesters, and Harold in the middle.

Let's see, Harold, who owns all that farm property and all those vehicles, Anderson must have thought. *Anderson's check revealed a trust. That's it. Harold is conveying assets to trusts with the specific intent to keep those assets outside of the reach of the IRS, a potential felony under 26 U.S.C. Sec. 7206. Fraudulent conveyance. Trust to defraud creditors. Newly discovered badges of fraud. Besides that, the trusts which made reference to Wyoming were never registered in Wyoming, nor in Iowa, for that matter, and there were at least six of them. Trying to confuse us IRS agents, that's what Harold's trying to do.*

Being such a thorough investigator, Agent Anderson checked with IRS to see what returns, if any, were filed by the trust. None, of course. "So much for that potential defense," he thought. "Harold can't claim that the income was reported by another entity such as the trust, nor can I find any corporations that Harold used. He's entered the underground economy. These trusts are just a sham to attempt to cover up his tracks or, alternatively, to offer an excuse for non-filing and non-reporting."

"What say ye neighbors and friends about the habits and beliefs of this pig farmer, Harold Haspels?" First Anderson visited with Harold's neighbor, who was also his minister. Sure enough, Harold did not like our tax system. "The government doesn't deserve our taxes," Harold had told his minister. "We discussed tax issues in the parlor of our house in the presence of our wives and it got rather heated. I could not subscribe to any of his tax views. We always argued about it."

"Wonder what the dentist might know, now that I've got his name from bank microfilm from a check Harold had written." There, the receptionist told Anderson that Harold often paid in cash. When asked why, "Harold said that way the feds can't get you," the receptionist told Anderson. "Beautiful. It all adds up. I got him boxed in now. I got him by the short hairs. No. No sense taking a chance. After all the work on this case, I'm gonna nail his coffin shut. I'll pay a visit to his hunting buddies." "Yes sir, " said the hunting buddy. "I remember around the campfire Harold complaining about taxes. How he seriously considered going out of business. Just wasn't worth it anymore."

Overly confident now, Agent Anderson completed his report recommending prosecution of Harold Haspels for five counts of willfully and knowingly filing with IRS false returns, a report well received by his superiors, IRS District Director, IRS District Counsel, and ultimately the Tax Division of the Justice Department, which made the final decision. Grand Jury indictment in Iowa. With Anderson the sole witness testifying before the Grand Jury, Les Paff had a Grand Jury indictment and Harold was summoned to court to answer to the five felony counts. "This is a bullet-proof case," all the government personnel must have thought.

"This is a great case, Harold. You ought to be able to win, but I sure can't promise that," Harold heard from me, some one thousand miles from Sioux City, Iowa. He had come to visit me in Phoenix to talk about the case. "Just like Paul Harvey, we're going to tell the judge and jury the rest of the story." And tell them we did. First the judge.

Harold had utilized the foreign triple trust program, one promoted by Lowell Anderson of Cody, Wyoming. I had met Lowell in 1980 during the *Hughes* trial in Pasco, Washington. At the motel along the Columbia River, the tax protesters were holding a seminar and Lowell was one of the speakers, preaching about the *Fifth Amendment* return.

In 1983, Lowell, his wife Carolyn, attorney Art Tranakos, accountant Don Perry, attorney Don Pilgrim, and others were charged with conspiracy to defraud the Internal Revenue Service and several substantive counts. The conspiracy claimed that the defendants had not only defrauded the IRS but as well those whom the defendants advised. Lowell had basically copied the Dahlstrom program with his own version of how the foreign triple trust program could work and, as well, NCBA's program with his own NCE. A huge man, he would never go to trial. In the winter of 1986, trying to pull a calf from the womb of its mother on his Wyoming ranch, Lowell keeled over and died.

Art had been an IRS District Counsel and was one of the handful of lawyers willing to try tax protester cases. I had met Art in 1979 at a log cabin in Montana during a meeting with Charles Riely, Rocky Strebble, Peggy Christensen and others, and I liked him from the start. There were other lawyers present. We had gathered to discuss defense strategies in tax cases, not unlike attorneys, I am sure, who represent those who engage in other forms of civil disobedience; e.g., abortion, Vietnam protests, and nuclear war protests. Art had an amicable, never-give-up attitude. He was not connected with Lowell's program but would give advice from time to time to Lowell's clients, advice not about the tax reduction efficacy of the program, but rather collateral matters such as how to convey real estate property into a trust. Called before the Anderson Grand Jury in Laramie as a "non-target," Art testified, only to subsequently find himself on the defendant end of an indictment. He faced ten years and, worse still, risk to his bar license. According to Grand Jury testimony, he did work with Lowell's clients in the promotion of traditional tax shelter programs for which Art would also come under attack. Like Scott McClarty of Atlanta, Georgia, perhaps it was only a matter of time before Art would have been prosecuted, not for any wrongdoing but because he had thumbed his nose at the *Beast*. At the Houston meeting in 1982 when I was surveilled by two female undercover agents, providing the basis for my suit against IRS, Art suggested to the crowd of three hundred "get out of banking. Don't leave agents a paper trail."

Scott, another fearless Vietnam vet who had won a number of acquittals for tax protesters, was charged in Florida with obstruction of justice. No love lost between Scott and the Justice Department, nor between Scott and judges. Judge Hauk from California, visiting in Hawaii on a criminal tax protester case, had jailed Scott for contempt. When I was later before Hauk, back in California, he referred to Scott as "that monkey."

Scott and I had mutual respect, but different styles. He launched frontal attacks, whereas I sought the ambush. Despite his Vietnam vet status, I felt I was always the smarter guerilla warrior, Scott allowing the *Beast* to pick the battlegrounds where the *Beast* was assured a victory.

But the Florida case proved a government snafu, in which the judge saw through the government's vindictiveness. Scott was acquitted by the judge at the end of the government's case in chief. Not without risk. He had faced ten years and loss of his trade license.

Harold, his wife, sister and brother-in-law had attended a seminar in Sioux Falls, South Dakota, at which Lowell had preached the advantages of the offshore triple trust program: avoidance of probate, viable estate planning, limited liability, and tax reduction or avoidance, not necessarily in that order. After Harold signed up, Lowell recommended a CPA from Denver to prepare returns, Don Perry. Harold discovered that Perry himself apparently had utilized the program.

Despite the fact that Colorado and Wyoming IRS had investigated the Anderson indictment defendants for many years, the inter-working of the program seemed a mystery to Agent Anderson. He even interviewed at length Don Perry. No doubt he had tired after seeing and assembling the bank and other third-party records. The trees were in Iowa but the forest was further west, in Colorado and Wyoming.

Harold had transferred his farm into an offshore trust, number one. Number two, he thought had filed 1040NR's with the Philadelphia Service Center, but IRS claimed none were to be found. CPA Perry had applied on behalf of the trust for an employer identification number, EIN. IRS in fact had assigned numbers to the trust and had written one of the trusts requesting information as to why a return had not been filed. For one year the trust answered that there was insufficient income for that year and as to the second year's request, answered that 1040NR's had been filed with the Philadelphia Service Center. This evidence showed use of the program, evidence ignored or not discovered by Anderson within his own bureaucracy.

Throughout the pretrial process, I was attempting to negotiate with Les a no-contest plea to a misdemeanor. I felt it a shame Harold should spend money for a trial, go through the risk and trauma. If he were to win, I told him, he would still not recover his financial and emotional loss. The price of doing business. The price of citizenship. A chance to walk into the mouth of the *Beast*.

For Harold, even if the government were to agree to a no-contest plea, it was a struggle. Principle versus practicality. "Mac, tell me this, am I guilty of anything? I believe this thing to be legal. CPA's, attorneys involved, I don't understand." No, Harold could not understand. It was the nature of the Beast. Body count. The mentality of McNamara and his whiz kids.

My experience had been that rarely would the Justice Department downgrade a criminal tax case from felony to misdemeanor. But Les would try his best. When justice declined the no contect request, Harold expressed interest in a misdemeanor plea, a straight plea versus no contest, despite the fact that he would have to admit guilt to something. "Harold, if you plead guilty to anything, you're going to have to admit guilt in front of that judge, under oath." "I just don't understand, Mac, I just don't understand." I did. The Justice Department said no and we were set for trial.

One day before trial, Les, perhaps seeing now more than ever as he prepared for his opening statement and his witnesses the next day, what a nightmare he had on his hands, asked me in the hallway of the courthouse that afternoon if Harold would consider a misdemeanor plea. Harold and I sat on a bench in a marble-covered entrance way. "Yes" was his answer. The Justice Department's reply: "no." The next day we proceeded to pick the jury.

An ambush was in store for every witness called by the prosecutor. I had interviewed most witnesses prior to trial. Those I was unable to locate I collared in the hallway. A lot can be accomplished in thirty to sixty seconds. "You find Harold to be an honest man in your business dealings?" "You bet." "Ever hear anything bad about him?" "Nope. I got no complaint. Harold's a good man."

First came the taxpayer's history: the old returns, subject returns, and comparisons. No doubt, Harold had failed to report substantial farm income, and for good reason, as he could attest. The preacher had strong views against Harold's attitude. The government, he thought, deserved our tax dollars. How about for murder of the unborn through subsidization of abortion? What did his church think of that? A political matter for Congress. No business of the church. No Patrick Henry, this man of the cloth. It was of no surprise to the jury that Harold left the church to join another, despite the fact that the church did take a strong position on *Second Amendment* rights, rights to bear arms.

298

The hunting comrade. He agreed it was but small talk around the fireplace. (Watch what you say after a few beers around the campfire; it may be evidence used against you. *Big Brother* is watching. The deer and fish are bugged.)

My greatest concern was for the dentist's receptionist. How would the jury react? Harold could not remember saying such a thing. I had no basis upon which to attack the grandmotherly witness. Her memory of Harold's words were etched in stone; she, like the other witnesses, had signed a sworn statement. (Special Agents often handwrite the statement for the witness to sign. By this means, any slant is in favor of IRS. The Agent first interviews the witness and takes notes. Then the statement is prepared. Sometimes a tape recorder is used, which only means the verbal questions will have the proper slant. Defense attorneys are endlessly challenged.)

I struggled with how to handle the witness. With all this talk of offshore trusts, 1040NR, NCBA and NCE, the verdict could turn on one alleged statement. "That way the feds can't get you." Was I missing the forest for the trees myself? Then it came to me in the motel room on the eve of the woman's testimony. Associate attorney Pat Sampair was assigned the not-so-easy task of preparing Harold for direct and cross-examination. (Harold's most popular question to me, "I don't understand, Mac, I just don't understand. Why do they want to put me in jail? I'm just an Iowa pig farmer who believed what these lawyers and CPA's told me.") My room adjoined that of Harold and his wife, Beverly. I was studiously reviewing documents, witness statements, and Harold's returns, preparing to outguess the government and prevent them from outguessing me. Laughter from the other room.

I was forgetting, despite my stay at the farmhouse with Harold and his family, that Harold was a kidder. A dry sense of humor. He would matter-of-factly understate the obvious and overstate the not so obvious. Typical of farmers. "But I would rather punch cows than dudes," as an old Idaho rancher once told me when I was preparing for him a study on whether or not he should supplement his income with a dude operation. During a telephone call to Harold once, I reminded him that I was doing my best to support his farming operation. I had bought bacon and sausage at the grocery store. There was a serious drought and Harold had nothing but despair. I then went on to talk about government subsidy of farmers and how the farmers had been trapped by government involvement, that funds used to flow freely, but in times of deficit spending, the Feds were not apt to support the farmers as they used to. "Yeah, I wish a trickle, at least, would fall my way," Harold said matter-of-fact like, using the natural drought as a metaphor for a budgetary drought.

It was the laughter from the other room that woke me up. That is it! Harold was kidding! When in doubt, present the absolute truth. Besides, just as often as the dentist was paid in cash, he was paid by check. On cross, I could bring out something along those lines. "Ma'am, you have, do you not, the records of account showing payments by the Haspels?" "Yes." "And how often did they pay by check?" "Can't tell by my ledgers." "Ma'am, let me show you these exhibits then. They appear to be checks endorsed by you in favor of the dentist, checks drawn apparently on the Haspels' account...." Beverly to the rescue: she had pulled the checks and suggested to me the tactic. Would a man hiding from the Feds be stupid enough to use checks half the time?" "And Ma'am," [*Columbo* now] "just one last question. About that statement of Harold's, 'that way the Feds can't get you,' you've known Harold for a good many years, right?" "Yes, sir." "He comes to the office now and then?" "Yes, sir. It's all here on the ledger." "And you know him to be somewhat of a *kidder* ?" "Yes, sir." (I knew the answer from my hallway conversation. What's the prosecutor going to ask? How can you tell when he's *not* kidding?)

The best was yet to come. *Divine providence.* You hope and pray for the breaks, but when they come, it is up to *you* to seize the initiative, drive home the point. Always alert, always responsible. The commander must be watchful of an opening.

Throughout pretrial discovery, we had asked the court to order the government to produce any evidence from the Philadelphia Service Center of forms 1040NR filed by Harold's various trusts located in the Turks & Caicos Islands. We feared the worst. I learned through my pretrial investigation that located in the Turks & Caicos Islands was Max Ellsworth, working for Lowell and responsible for the filing of the returns as trustee of the various trusts. Apparently there had been a falling out between Max and Lowell due to funding, and I was hearing horror stories such as stockpiles of 1040NRs sitting in the Turks & Caicos. The best, I concluded, would not be worth the effort to travel to the island and attempt to discover more. Don Perry would testify that the returns were prepared, but even he had no copies! The prosecutor's position was no such returns were ever prepared, much less filed. The preparation and filing of the 1040NR's was crucial to our defense: it showed the farm income was in fact *reported.* Another irony of the case was that Agent Anderson actually met with Don and interviewed him but had not asked the right questions. I obtained the transcript in discovery.

Now the revenue agent who had calculated Harold's tax liability based upon information collected by Agent Anderson was testifying. Since the year-end feed purchase was not needed due to use of the trust, Harold had not made the purchases, thus causing, by disregarding the trust as the government did, a large alleged tax liability. In fact, Harold and his dad both owed a lot. Then my cross-examination: "To this day, IRS has not located any 1040NRs, isn't that correct?" (Why did I ask such a question? I wanted to anchor the government in its position, or did my subconscious know different?) The agent answered, rather surlily, "No, that's not correct." Somewhat astonished, I responded, "What? What do you mean? Please explain." The hairs on the back of my neck having risen, sensing that I had the enemy at bay. "Yesterday we received a document indicating a 1040NR had been filed for one of the trusts," he replied. Now, no holds barred. I am going straight through the line, bayonet fixed. *Fix bayonets, men.* This was the ultimate cry of the Infantry. *You will close with and kill the enemy.* Facing the witness, standing next to the jury on my right, I could see with peripheral vision the prosecutor begin to squirm in his seat. He was shuffling through papers and then it appeared. He was pulling out the return. *Maintain the suspense of the moment.* "And where might this 1040NR discovered yesterday be?" (An answer I already knew. To the right, my peripheral vision told me the jury was eyeing the prosecutor, who was still fumbling nervously with his papers. The jury, too, was tense, sensing the urgency of the situation. Suspense. The prosecutor likely did not know whether to stand and speak or slip under the table. He did neither, continuing with his visible squirming. As the *Herd* would say, "That officer doesn't know whether to shoot or go blind." The agent's answer, "The prosecutor has it." *Now, do the natural.* I turn to my left, as if there is a choice of prosecutors, which there is not. "You mean this prosecutor sitting over here has had the 1040NR since yesterday?" "Yes." "Your Honor, I ask that the document be handed to the witness ...."

Outside of the presence of the jury I move to dismiss for prosecutorial misconduct, which is denied. But I could tell that for the Judge his Christian patience had been worn rather thin. "I had planned to give it to them today," came the lame excuse from the prosecutor. The court ordered the Special Agent to immediately call Philadelphia and have Fed X'd further information. I was not finished with this issue. The wound opened, I had the salt shaker in hand.

In an effort to redeem himself, the prosecutor called the next day the Special Agent who described his many diligent efforts with the Philadelphia IRS and gave a progress report. "No known 1040NR's located - except for the one we found yesterday." This was the same agent with whom I had engaged in small talk during a recess concerning an incident in Philadelphia I had read about a year or so previous. 1040NRs were reportedly blowing down the street. Bundles of returns were scattered, having fallen off the back of a truck, transporting them between IRS offices. "Never worry about your tax return; it is strictly confidential."

"Special Agent, the Philadelphia Service Center is the only recipient of forms 1040NR." "Yes." "Any forms filled out from overseas are filed in Philadelphia, correct?" "Yes." "So, if a 1040NR is mistakenly sent to another service center, IRS would forward it to Philadelphia?" "Yes." "Thank you." About to head back to my seat, "Oh," Peter Falk's *Columbo* style, "Just one last thing, wasn't it in Philadelphia that returns were blowing down the street, bundles of returns having fallen off the back of a truck?" Groping, his response, "Yes, but ah, that wouldn't have been Harold's returns." More serious now, with authority, "Sir, how do you know of your own personal knowledge that of thousands of returns scattered through the Philadelphia streets, Harold's 1040NRs were not included?" "I don't." "I thought so. Nothing further, Your Honor."

Don Perry, Art Tranakos, Bev and Harold all testified for the defense. They all did well, but Bev was my favorite. Not feeling well, she did not testify as long as I would have liked, but the Midwestern small town farmer image portrayed by Harold and Bev was classic. Bev had set up the books for the various trusts with Don's help. Don had actually flown in from Denver, sat down at the kitchen table of the Haspels' home in Rock Rapids, Iowa. Bev had dutifully kept immaculate records.

I also called a reputable businessman and friend of Harold's to talk about NCBA and NCE. This gentleman had attended the Anderson seminar and believed the trust program to be legal, but did not need them for any tax avoidance. Instead, he had purchased shelters through Art. And, in addition and what was more important, he had purchased an interest in the Turks & Caicos Island Bank set up by Lowell. A real bank with real money. What a reputable, law-abiding believer in the program. I wanted to show to the jury that law-abiding citizens utilized warehouse banking for security. In event of disaster, the Federal Reserve notes (FERNS) were backed by precious metal, unlike your neighborhood bank. In other words, you deposit $1,000 with NCBA or NCE and they guarantee that at any time you want your money, you can if you wish have it in precious metal, just like the good old days when $10 Federal Reserve Notes were called silver certificates. Also, NCBA and NCE would if you wished make payments directly to third-party creditors, thus providing the same checking account-type service of ordinary banks. Of course, they also made a claim of privacy, which paradoxically made them an IRS target, resulting in potential disclosure.

On cross, the prosecutor, not understanding my point, asked, "Couldn't you just hide the gold under your pillow?" "Yes, I guess so," the gentleman answered. *Hm, I* thought, *do I let that sit? No,*

I don't like it. "Sir, if the gold you wish to retain is under your pillow, could you write checks against it?" "No." "It would be pretty hard, wouldn't it?" "Impossible, I'd say." "Thank you, sir." (There was no re-cross by the prosecutor.)

The evidence closed, both sides resting, it was now time for the jury instruction conference with the court. Since Harold had relied in the preparation of the returns upon the advice of a Certified Public Accountant, Don Perry, we felt that we were entitled to the standard instruction contained within the "Bible" of federal civil and criminal practice: *Devitt & Blackmar's Federal Jury Practice & Instructions,* (Devitt is a federal judge in St. Paul.) That instruction reads with slight modification as follows:

> The defendant has introduced evidence that he did not prepare the tax return in question and that it was prepared for him by accountants who held themselves out as persons qualified to prepare federal income returns for others. If the defendant provided these accountants with full information in relation to his gross receipts from farming during the year and the defendant then adopted, signed and filed the tax return on form 1040 as prepared by the accountants without having reason to believe that it was not correct, then you will find the defendant not guilty. If, on the other hand, you find beyond a reasonable doubt that the defendant did not provide full and complete information to the accountants or that he knew that the return as prepared by the accountants was not correct and substantially understated his gross receipts from farming, then you are not required to find the defendant not guilty simply because he did not prepare the return himself, but rather had it prepared for him by another. *Devitt & Blackmar, Sec. 35.18.*

In a nutshell, what all this really means is that under the law, if the jury believes that you have given everything to your accountant and have no reason to believe that he has caused an error, then the jury should acquit you. What is confusing is that a paragraph beginning with "If on the other hand,..." addresses the burden of the government once you have raised a reliance defense. Although this instruction addresses a "defense of the accused," the accused has no burden of presenting a defense. Although Harold testified, the reliance defense could be raised by way of the testimony of the accountant only at the risk the jury would find the defendant did not give all information to the accountant. It depends on your case facts.

The judge would not give the accountant-reliance instruction, despite its prominent place within *Devitt & Blackmar.* "That's a directed verdict for the defendant," he said. (A directed verdict is one given in a civil or criminal case at the end of the plaintiff's case in chief, or at the end of all the evidence. In criminal cases, it is called a judgment of acquittal. It can also be given in both civil and criminal cases at the close of all the evidence. It is a finding that, based on all of the evidence submitted, there is not sufficient evidence from which a reasonable jury could conclude [in a criminal case] beyond a reasonable doubt that the defendant committed the crime. In a civil case, the standard is by preponderance of the evidence, or in the case of civil fraud, by clear and convincing evidence. "No sir, I beg to differ," I responded. "The jury could still find the defendant guilty if they find beyond a reasonable doubt that Harold did not provide full and complete information to the accountants or that he knew that the returns prepared by the accountants were not correct and substantially understated his gross receipts from farming. Still a question of fact to be resolved by the jury, they could find Harold and his accountant both less than credible. They could find that in effect, the two knew that they were violating the law and agreed or conspired to violate the law. I don't think the evidence supports such a conclusion, but the jury is certainly free to draw its own conclusions from the evidence presented. That's why they're here." Not persuaded, the court refused the instruction but did give a more general "good faith belief of accused" instruction found in *Devitt & Blackmar* at Sec. 35.12:

If a person in good faith believes that he has paid all the taxes he owes, he cannot be guilty of criminal intent to file a false tax return. But if a person acts without reasonable ground for belief, that his conduct is lawful, it is for the jury to decide whether he acted in good faith or whether he willfully intended to file a false income tax return. This issue of intent as to whether a defendant willfully filed a false income tax return is one which the jury must determine from a consideration of all the evidence in the case bearing on the defendant's state of mind.

After closing arguments, it was late and the jury deliberated only a couple of hours. Then, for the first time ever I heard this request: each juror wanted a copy of the instructions to take home and study. I found this encouraging, feeling that if the jurors truly understood the instructions, we would win. Believing the jury to be attentive and somewhat astute, I found that *I* had missed the forest for the trees.

I have a habit of using a chart in both opening statement and closing argument in an effort to help the jury clarify the issues by teaching them in school room fashion. Usually I put up the elements, one, two, three. Here, I felt it was not necessary. The government must prove each and every element beyond a reasonable doubt and the three elements here were that Harold had signed the returns under penalty of perjury, that the returns were false or incorrect in some material way, and that he had acted knowingly and willfully. I learned later that the jury spent more time deliberating for failure to understand the law, believing despite my admonitions to the contrary, that Harold had a burden along with the government. They found immediately that the government had not proven willfullness and were ready to acquit Harold, but they were stumped because they were not sure whether the returns were correct after hearing conflicting testimony between the IRS agent's CPA, Don Perry, and attorney Art Tranakos. In discussing the case, one of the jurors then came across again the burden instruction and pointed out that Harold had *no* burden of proving anything and that since the government had not met its burden, they must acquit Harold. This they did after deliberating one-half of the next day. Harold was a free man on a case that should never have been investigated and prosecuted, much less gone to trial.

Despite the willingness of the local prosecutor, a reasonable fellow, not vindictive toward Harold nor the issues, the Justice Department maintained the *tar baby* syndrome. The same government that brought us the Vietnam quagmire. The inflexible, bureaucratic blockheads. "Yours is not to question why, yours is but to do or die." Sun Tzu wrote:

During the early morning spirits are keen; during the day they flag; and in the evening thoughts turn to home. And therefore, those skilled in war avoid the enemy when his spirit is keen and attack him when it is sluggish and the soldier is homesick. This is control of the morale factor. In good order they await a disorderly enemy; in serenity a clamorous one. This is control of the mental factor. Close to the field of battle they await an enemy coming from afar; at rest an exhausted enemy; with well-fed troops hungry ones. This is control of the physical factor.

The enemy must not know where I intend to give battle. For if he does not know where I intend to give battle, he must prepare in a great many places. And when he prepares in a great many places, those I have defied in any one place will be few. For if he prepares to the front, his rear will be weak and if to the rear, his front will be fragile. If he prepares to the left, his right will be vulnerable, and if to the right, there will be few on his left. And when he prepares everywhere, he will be weak everywhere. Sun Tzu

WINTER OFFENSIVE	Chapter 20

Outnumbered almost two to one, Hannibal, in the Battle of Cannae in 216 B.C., defeated the Roman Army. How? The double envelopment. Through planning and superb execution, Hannibal completely annihilated the Romans. To secure his flanks from envelopment by the numerically superior Roman force, Hannibal placed along the riverbanks his front detachments of light infantry whose mission was to screen his own disposition, as well as to disorganize the Roman attack. The enemy sought to crush Hannibal by shear weight of numbers in a frontal attack. But massing his cavalry on the flanks and instructing his infantry in the center to feign weakness and fall back in the center, Hannibal succeeded in sucking the Romans into double envelopment or encirclement. A true leader, setting the example where most required, Hannibal was in the center, slowly giving way and withdrawing so as to perfectly entice the Romans into the trap. Hannibal was the bait. Imagination and ability had triumphed over numbers.

Forty-six years after the Japanese attack on Pearl Harbor, December 7, 1987, "Obscure Law Allows Discharge of Taxes Through Bankruptcy" was the title of an article appearing in the economic section of the *Arizona Republic*. Its author, Earl Zarbin had, like many, previously written "Examples of debt that cannot be discharged under Chapter 7 (bankruptcy) are ... federal and state income taxes." In response, I had written to Zarbin, pointing out his error, an error for which he "should feel no embarrassment. The truth of the matter is this: most attorneys, when asked, will state that federal and state income taxes cannot be discharged. This would include bankruptcy attorneys. I was under the same impression until a client straightened me out."

Intrigued, and somewhat disbelieving, Earl called me. He had, indeed, felt no embarrassment, for reason he had relied upon an attorney in drawing such an erroneous conclusion, an attorney he preferred not to disclose. "Check it out, sir," I advised. "I am curious myself as to the response you will get. Come visit with us and we will be glad to show you the law, the actual court cases, the words from the mouths of the judges, and then you can call the lawyers and IRS. See what they have to say." Earl took my advice and met with me and two other attorneys in our office, Pat Sampair and Kevin Rattay. Seeing the cases, some of which were copied for him, Earl believed I was right, but would follow-up as I had advised.

First, he called attorney Richard Lee who heads the Bankruptcy Section of the State Bar of Arizona and wrote that Lee "agreed with MacPherson's assessment that most attorneys are unaware that income taxes can be discharged through bankruptcy. Lee said he knows it can be done. 'I've done it,' he said, 'and the IRS was quite astonished to have me do it to them.'" Next, IRS. "Oliver Robinson, Public Affairs Officer for the Phoenix District IRS Office, agreed that federal taxes can be discharged through bankruptcy. 'Yes, under bankruptcy, taxes can be discharged,' he said. But he cautioned, 'There are rules that must be observed.'" Rules, indeed. But we, like no attorneys before us, had not only mastered the rules, we were ready to make them available to the general public, something the IRS had, for obvious reasons, failed to do.

In continuing with his article, Zarbin wrote, "MacPherson was delighted to learn taxes were dischargeable. He sees the Internal Revenue Service as a bully and has published a book, *April 15th: The Most Pernicious Attack Upon English Liberty* , in which he 'traces the history of the government's extraction of private information under the guise of tax collection from citizens under oath.' 'What I like about this (the discharge of taxes in bankruptcy) is you ambush the IRS,' MacPherson said. 'You have to develop a strategy. It's like a chess game. You have to figure out what moves you can make.'" (As it turned out, Earl and I had a lot in common concerning the government; he was a Libertarian, believing the less government, the better.)

Although Earl's article covered only the rules under Chapter 7 and did not state that, even where a tax return is not filed or fraud is involved, tax debts can be discharged under Chapter 13, the flood gates were at least cracked. Time was, I felt, they be opened wide. Time, indeed, considering the law had been in existence over twenty-two years. Like most attorneys, I had been a victim of a bad rumor and was never forced to deal head-on with the issue, not until about four years ago when a client, an airline pilot from San Francisco whom I had represented on a criminal investigation, had told me it could be done.

The pilot had become involved in the church issue and I had succeeded in getting the case dropped after winning on a summons enforcement case. The District judge had ruled IRS cannot obtain by IRS summons the W-2 (Statement of Earnings) of United Airlines because IRS already had the W-2s in its possession.

Constructively, at least. The judge was astonished to learn, through my cross-examination of the agent, that IRS does not have a W-2 matching program. Pure bluff, it is, when IRS misleads the public to believe they have on file your W-2s. Ask yourself this: if IRS has your W-2 readily available, then why do they ask for a copy to be attached to your return? "Yes, Your Honor, we have them all right; they are in a warehouse in boxes," was the agent's response to inquiry from the court. "You mean they can't be retrieved by name or social security number?" "Well, they could be, but it would take a long time. There are millions and they are not organized alphabetically, nor by social security number." (The law now requires that employers mail the W-2s to the Social Security Administration which, in turn, places the information on microfilm, available for retrieval by IRS agents on a request basis. *Big Brother* has not yet developed a nation-wide matching program, but is working in that direction.)

So this pilot, no longer facing possible jail and fine, but saddled with a tax debt he could never pay, had learned - how, I do not know - that taxes could be discharged through bankruptcy. "What are the sections of the *Bankruptcy Code,* and I'll look them up," I asked. "Sections 507 and 523," he responded. I checked it out. Sure enough, he was right. Not long after I had occasion to do further research and give three clients written opinions regarding dischargeability. But they were not serious about it.

It was not until December of 1986 that I became "dead in the water" serious about the issue. I was then retained by a construction worker, Dennis, who worked at the Bechtel nuclear power plant in Palo Verde, Arizona, just outside of Phoenix. Dennis had a serious tax problem: wages of about $40,000, tax debt of $50,000, and no assets. Under a payment plan with IRS, considering the interest running, he could never pay it off. $50,000. It was time to get real serious about bankruptcy as an *offensive weapon.* The client owed $50,000 because of his use of what IRS had declared an "abusive tax shelter:" investment in greyhound racing dogs. He was litigating the issue in Tax Court. His current attorney, one of the best known tax attorneys in Phoenix and a certified specialist, had given this simple advice: "pay up." By my nature - the pit bull - I was not about to have my client fork over $50,000 without a fight. But why hit your head against a brick wall? *Outsmart them.* Since many claim that Tax Court is but a "kangaroo court," IRS had succeeded in choosing for the client the battleground, a battleground favorable to the enemy. (To get into District Court and a jury trial with a refund suit, the law as written by Congress declares that one must first pay the tax, an impossibility for Dennis and for most when the stakes are so high.)

The guerilla warrior will never allow the enemy to pick the

battleground. Time, then for the chess game. The ambush. First, however, the bait: by a payment plan, IRS is led into a state of complacency during the 240-day requirement waiting period. The taxpayer must wait 240 days after the assessment. (My experience has been that most bankruptcy lawyers do not know what an assessment is, much less when it occurs.) The IRS is then drawn down the 240-day path into the horseshoe ambush. Smoking and joking along the trail, paying no attention whatsoever to the M-60 hidden up on the knoll just up the trail, the trail, itself, a *field of fire*.

While I waited the 240 days for Dennis, our firm received many calls and new clients as a result of the *Republic* article. Consumer response to the bankruptcy article encouraged me to mount an all-out winter offensive: a radio campaign in which we would offer free brochures. If the IRS, bankruptcy bar and tax bar would not educate the public, we would. With radio, we would employ a two-prong attack: paid advertising plus appearances. But the premier radio talk shows in Phoenix, KTAR and KFYI, first expressing an interest, never invited me. What is going on here? IRS says they are owed $50 billion dollars to which taxpayers have confessed. In addition, there is at least $150 billion owed by the non-filers. Certainly, there are many in Phoenix who got stung by the abusive tax shelters. Why no interest in such an issue, especially a few months prior to that *day of infamy* - April 15?

When I get stonewalled, it merely causes me to be more tenacious. First, the radio ad:

> Income taxes *can* be discharged in bankruptcy! That's right! If you can't afford to pay IRS taxes and have been given little hope by IRS, accountants and attorneys, there *is* a potential solution. You may have read the recent article that appeared in the *Arizona Republic* : "Obscure Law Allows Discharge of Income Taxes Through Bankruptcy." MacPherson & McCarville, Phoenix attorneys and certified tax specialists, have prepared a brochure on discharge of income taxes in bankruptcy. For *your* free copy, call MacPherson & McCarville today at 866-9566. 866-Ninety-five Sixty-six. You won't get this information from IRS publications. For your free brochure on how taxes can be discharged in bankruptcy, and for other tax advice, call MacPherson & McCarville, attorneys at law, at 866-9566. That's 866-Ninety-five Sixty six. Do you want to continue paying taxes you don't have to pay? The decision *is* yours.

In response to the ad, we received around three hundred requests for the free "'Bankrupt' the IRS" brochure, including many requests from attorneys and accountants.

The next step, intelligence gathering. What did IRS say about discharging taxes in bankruptcy? I secured IRS' own publication on bankruptcy, 908, a fraud upon the public! Publication 908, despite its introduction concerning its comprehensive treatment of bankruptcy, dedicates at page 7 only two paragraphs to "Discharge of Unpaid Tax." The publication does recognize that "claims against an individual or for other taxes predating the bankruptcy petition by more than three years may be discharged." But no encouragement is given "tax debtors" by IRS pamphlets and, I found through my intelligence gathering, IRS personnel handling the free IRS information hotline mislead callers into believing that taxes cannot be discharged.

Through my "undercover intelligence agent in the field" I obtained a copy of IRS' internal manual, IRM 57(13) 4.42: (1), "Dischargeability of Taxes in Bankruptcy," which outlines for members of the IRS Special Procedures staff the procedure to be followed in bankruptcy cases. IRS' own manual had confirmed our research. *The proof is in the pudding.* I had recalled the movie *Patton* in which George C. Scott played the general, and after his first defeat of Rommel in North Africa in 1942, shouted on the battlefield, "Rommel, you beautiful bastard, I read your book!" With our good intelligence, we intended to maintain the initiative.

By June 6, 1988, an article by Martin A. Larson entitled "Secret Exposed" appeared in *Spotlight.* The article began "I had always been under the impression that debts to the Internal Revenue Service (IRS) could not be discharged through bankruptcy. However, I have now learned through Don MacPherson, a Phoenix lawyer, that such is not the fact." On that same day, an article I authored appeared in the *Arizona Business Gazette,* "Tax Debts Can Be Discharged in Bankruptcy Proceedings." There, in addition to outlining the rules under both Chapter 7 and Chapter 13, I wrote, "For twenty-two years, IRS, many lawyers and CPAs have led people to believe in a fiction - that in no way can tax, interest and penalties be discharged by filing a petition in Bankruptcy. As Luke said in *Luke* 11:52, 'Woe unto you lawyers, for ye have taken away the key of knowledge ....'" In addition, a series of articles appeared in *Justice Times* and in *Full Disclosure.* The cat was out of the bag.

By now, we were handling thirty tax cases in bankruptcy and by July 1988, we succeeded in discharging $52,000 for our client, a mechanic in Kingman, Arizona. We knew it could be done; now we had done it. Time now for continuing the momentum. In a new radio ad campaign in Phoenix, I would tell of the success of our Kingman mechanic.

But what is this? Another message from the front lines. Our intelligence source - *"acting surreptitiously"* - had broken the IRS code, deciphering for us IRS Message 150, dated June 15, 1988.

The enemy had written that Publication 908 was "out-of-date and could mislead taxpayers" and that "any existing stock of Pub. 908 (11/82) should be disposed of." Was it pure coincidence that the message was written not long after the numerous articles beginning in December of 1987? Millions of copies of an IRS publication ordered destroyed!

On another front, I had become discouraged. I had received very little response to my news release mailed during the winter offensive. A few small-town newspapers had printed an article but publications such as *Money* , *Barons* , and *Time* had shown absolutely no interest. I was being stonewalled by "the establishment media." Meanwhile, attorneys and accountants nation-wide were writing to us asking for assistance; their clients had brought them one or more of the articles. Some of the attorneys, embarrassed to admit it, had stated in their letters that they had filed bankruptcy for their client but had *not* attempted to discharge the tax debts. In addition, bankruptcy specialists locally were calling for advice (what is an assessment?), and our cumulative total of discharged tax debts had risen to $300,000. Our ad in the *Justice Times* , in which we had placed an ad prior to obtaining any discharges, began "Oh, ye of little faith." *Matthew* 6:30.

Time again for action. First, a new ad with a description of the $300,000 victory. That would make believers out of them. Second, a letter to newly-appointed IRS Commissioner Gibbs, complaining about Publication 908 and offering my *pro bono* assistance in re-writing it, and further asking about the accuracy of Message 150. Had my *"undercover agent"* been set up by a double agent? Had IRS really ordered destruction of Publication 908? Third, coordination of efforts with *lion tamer* Dan Pilla: expose IRS "Message 150" through Dan's monthly newsletter, *Pilla Talks Taxes* (1-800-553-6458), thus making effective use of one of those West Point "principles of war:" *maneuver*.

Fourth, a turning movement. Seattle, Washington, I knew, had been a hot-bed for tax shelters in the early '80s, due in part to high salaries paid aeronautical engineers and others employed in the aerospace industry. Victims caught in the fifty percent tax bracket vice. Why not a radio ad in Seattle, after associating with a local attorney who could handle the bankruptcy cases? Plus, I had a man working "undercover" in the Seattle area. Through his informal survey, he had discovered, among other things, that bankruptcy attorneys were advising clients or potential clients that taxes could *not* be discharged. We would mount, then, a new offensive in Seattle.

The station chosen, KING, initially refused to run our ad. That is right. The station, touted as a leading talk station, flatly refused. Undaunted, I mailed to the station manager the articles and brochures to convince them that this attorney was not some kind of kook with some off-the-wall idea. Convinced, they ran the ad. What followed was sniper fire. That *crack, crack, crack* of the Communist AK-47, bent on snuffing out this soldier's exercise of his *First Amendment* rights. Pulling the trigger? Paula Selis, Assistant Attorney General of the Washington Attorney General's Office. She threatened suit against KING and they abdicated; the "king" of talk radio surrendered unconditionally. Ran in the face of enemy fire. This so-called champion of *First Amendment* rights.

Admittedly, my first reaction was to file suit in federal court, raising the *First Amendment* issue, and seek an injunction against the Attorney General's Office. But should principle fall in the face of practicality? Why mount the frontal attack, expose your flank, and over-extend your supply lines? If I were to maintain the momentum of the winter offensive, I could ill-afford to become bogged down in Seattle, a swamp land of bureaucratic mentality. I had remembered well that mentality in the AG's attack against Karl Dahlstrom. And I had not forgotten Napoleon. Bogged down in Russia, his winter offensive of 1812 had cost him the campaign. Hitler repeated the error in 1944. "The only thing we learn from history is we don't learn from history." That is, unless you are Sun Tzu (China, 500 B.C.), Mao Tse-tung (China, 1927), or Che Guevara (Cuba, 1959). *Guerrilla warriors.* No, my answer would not be by frontal attack. *There is more than one way to skin a cat.* Aerial envelopment. (Airborne or air mobile operation.) The side door, the back door, feints, demonstrations, surprise attack .... (Update and details in *War Stories, Part II*.)

Who is Che Guevara? Who was Castro's Guerrilla warfare mastermind, copied from China's Mao Tse-tung, who in turn copied from China's Sun Tzu who wrote in his *The Art of Guerrilla Warfare* the following:

They do not engage an enemy advancing with well-ordered banners, nor one whose formations are in impressive array. This is control of the factor of changing circumstanses. Therefore, the art of employing troops is that when the enemy occupies high ground, do not confront him; with his back resting on hills, do not oppose him. When he pretends to flee, do not pursue. Do not attack his elite troops. Do not gobble proffered baits.

Liberty lies in the hearts of men and women somehow. When it dies there, no Constitution, no law, no court can save it; no Constitution, no law, no court can even do much to help it. While it lies there, it needs no Constitution, no law, no court to save it.
Learned Hand

SUMMATION

So there you have it. Between all of the tax and courtroom mystification, you have the "flesh and blood" of battle-tested, stalwart individualists, the strategy and tactics of their "champion of a just cause." Within the courtroom drama you have all the frailties of human nature, the prides and prejudices of the jurors, the vindictiveness of prosecutors, the smugness of judges, the tenaciousness of defense attorneys. It is proven fact: the men and women of the Internal Revenue Service *can* be beaten. If you remain, in spite of this revelation, fearful, it is *your* choice. This is not to say you should feel now the expert in tax matters. We have barely scratched the surface. But at the very least, you should have learned that the *Bully* has a soft belly, an Achilles heel, and is mentally and physically *lazy*. Not only a coward, he is a *paper tiger*. Oh, yes, the *Monster* will continue, of course, to win eighty-three percent of his cases, but *your* chances of being one of his victims are slim to none. First the odds: 35,000 to one. Second because you have read this book and you know what to expect and you *know* how to stay out of trouble, you will *not* be so stupid as to become one of the *Beast's* few victims.

In 1983, the American Bar Association formed a Commission on Taxpayer Compliance which has, since then, completed an annual "Report and Recommendations." The Commission is made up of lawyers, CPAs, social scientists and business executives, and its purpose, according to the 1987 report, "is to recommend ways of improving compliance with federal income tax laws with the goal of reducing the tax gap that now appears to exceed $100 billion per year." Recommendations include decreasing opportunities for non-compliance of tax laws "by increasing the scope of withholding of taxes at the source, by increasing the reporting of third party payments, and by increased sharing of information among government agencies." The "moral climate for compliance," the committee concludes, should be improved. "Influential individuals in all fields have a responsibility, in the Commission's view, to speak out publicly against tax cheating. Business and professional groups, unions and civil organizations, and public officials should actively encourage compliance. With this broad public leadership, the Commission believes that the moral climate condoning tax cheating can be reversed." You then can expect, readers, that at your next Lions or Kiwanis club meeting, or at your next church service, you will be admonished to no longer tolerate tax cheating, in effort to dispel the attitude that "a little cheating on taxes is okay." In my view, the Commission with its annual reports begs the question, "misses the forest for the trees:" The American public can no longer *afford* to tolerate a tax system which it views as inherently unfair. The solution, then, is a system which is *fair*, or no system at all. But the only "fair" system is one which collects *absolutely essential* revenues by means other than the progressive income tax, such as a flat tax, tariffs, the sales tax, or even the lottery. Of course, this is all improbable, due to the fact, as Charles Riely long ago observed, "We have the best Congress money can buy." The result, then, I predict, is this: a growing tax rebellion, more covert than overt. And with the greater tax rebellion will come no change in the tax law except that which gives the *Beast* the stronger hand. Do not be deceived, dear reader: the 1988 *Taxpayer Bill of Rights* is but lip service from a Congress still intimidated by the *Beast*.

In *War Stories, Part II* , learn more of the training and testing of a "constitutional warrior," from West Point to Airborne and Ranger schools. Make a night jump with Special Forces, onto a 10,000 foot elevation drop zone! Read of Dennis Ryan, the Sante Fe Railroad conductor acquitted on felony charges of retaliating against a witness who testified against him in a tax case. The witness had felt threatened by a poem written by Dennis! A Nevada casino worker is acquitted on charges of failure to file. An IRS informant in Illinois trespasses and steals from the garbage of a dentist in effort to launch a tax prosecution. A state judge rules that the *Fifth Amendment* returns filed by a chiropractor and his wife satisfy, under state law, the definition of a tax return and dismisses the charges. A Montana plumber is acquitted of tax charges. Four Montana construction workers held in contempt of court for their refusal to give to IRS any information are ordered to jail, but the Ninth Circuit reverses, holding the order violates their *Fifth Amendment* right. In Alaska, a businessman is held in contempt for his failure to disclose to the court and to IRS the names of banks at which he has an account. The Justice Department drops the case on appeal. Two brothers in Minnesota are tried and acquitted on tax charges. "Major Mac" sues IRS for illegal surveillance, and takes the issue on appeal before the Ninth Circuit. An Indiana couple is acquitted of state tax charges. A tax case in California becomes a major drug case in which the government alleges that the client is part of an international drug cartel, responsible for the murder of a DEA agent in Mexico. One of my clients, a witness for another client in a criminal case, is murdered. Several criminal investigations are dropped against American Law Association

314

members. *The Colonel's* creditors seek to have him brought before a federal bankruptcy judge on involuntary bankruptcy in an attempt to force *the Colonel* , an alleged CIA operative involved in Iran-Contra, to talk. The message of "jury nullification" is spread by an attorney, and other "brothers of the bar" seek to have his license pulled. A Montana man is charged, along with his wife, for their failure to report the sale of a $6 million mine. An Arizona woman uses her knowledge of tax laws and her record keeping to defend against county charges that she should be placed in the Arizona State Mental Hospital, "the ash can." An Idaho rancher, convicted of a tax crime, turns the tables on a private plaintiff in a suit for fraud, where the tax evidence is brought out before the jury. An Arizona accountant reverses a $75,000 tax judgment, but faces, with his wife, charges of false tax returns. A pet store manager is charged with child molestation and claims he has been framed by young kids wanting to take over the store. "Arizona's fighting governor" is impeached and fights back. The "courtroom commando" engineers a new bankruptcy counter-attack. And after the draft board receives "Cohan the Barbarian's" letter, he does not hear from them again. Read, "from A to Z," the procedures IRS agents follow in a real criminal investigation.

Was Les Kaegler murdered by the CIA, or by "Mister Big," the drug dealer? Read the research update and advice concerning use of offshore banks for "profit, privacy, and tax protection." Rock Smith, "Fisher of Men," is joined by his wife on federal tax charges. An Hawaiian investor causes jurors to admit that they failed to follow the court's instructions in a criminal tax trial. *Fifth Amendment* advocate Marvin Cooley again faces tax charges. IRS threatens to bring tax charges against the pastor and elders of a Presbyterian church in Tennessee. Just how far can you push IRS and not be prosecuted? The saga continues in *War Stories, Part II* .

Thomas Jefferson asked:

What country can preserve its liberties if its rulers are not warned from time to time that its people preserve the spirit of resistance?

My research in preparation of this book led me to the writings of some of my military and political heroes - Billy Mitchell, Eddie Rickenbacher, Douglas MacArthur, Clarence Darrow and Thomas Paine, author of *The Rights of Man*. Paine, it is said, made a living as a troublemaker. *A muckraker*. As well, my research led to a book I received upon my departure in December of 1969 from Vietnam, a book entitled *The History of the 173rd Airborne Brigade: the Fourth Year*. Within the inside cover were written, no less, the words of Thomas Paine:

These are the times that try men's souls. The summer soldier and the sunshine patriot will in this crisis shrink from the service of their country, but he that stands it now deserves the love and thanks of man and woman. Tyranny, like hell, is not easily conquered; yet we have the consolation with us that the harder the conflict, the more glorious the triumph. What we obtain too cheaply, we esteem too lightly; it is dearness only that gives anything its value. Heaven knows how to put a proper price upon its good; and it would be strange indeed if so celestial an article as freedom should not be highly rated.

(General George Washington insisted that Paine's words be read aloud to the combat troops during the Revolutionary War.)

I have never fancied myself to be any more, nor less, than *a Soldier.* Having been battle tested, combat honed, I left the Regular Army and the potential of an illustrious military career for this simple reason: I did not want to be a "desk commander." (My West Point classmates are now full colonels, regimental commanders; commanders, one is a general.) Besides, a career soldier must, by necessity, be a politician, and to be a Regular Army politician one must, to at least some extent, be what the "Brown Shoe Army" officers called "a dog robber," meaning robbing a dog of its job, a lap dog, a "brown noser." Thanks, but no thanks. (After World War II, the U.S. Army, I sadly report, abandoned the "Eisenhower jacket," the "Sam Brown belt," officer "pinks" (trousers), the belted jacket, khaki colored tie, rank insignia affixed to the shirt collar, and the brown shoes. I was, no doubt, born twenty years too late!) It was from Western Australia that Sir Eric F. Smart stated:

> I did not choose to be a common man. It is my right to be uncommon if I can. I seek opportunity, not security. I do not wish to be a kept citizen, humbled and dulled by having the State look after me. I want to take the calculated risk: to dream and to build. To fail and to succeed. I refuse to barter incentive for a dole. I prefer the challenges of life to the guaranteed existence; the thrill of fulfillment to the staid calm of utopia. I will not trade freedom for beneficence nor my dignity for a handout. It is my heritage to think and act for myself; enjoy the benefits of my creations and to face the world boldly and say, "This I have done."

Until *War Stories, Part II,* "Keep your powder dry," and remember what Frances Bacon noted, "The best armor is to keep out of gun shot."

About the Author

Donald W. (Mac) MacPherson

Occupation   Trial attorney.

Firm   MacPherson & McCarville, P.A., Phoenix. General civil & criminal practice, especially tax, personal injury, business law, litigation & bankruptcy.

Qualifications   Board certified specialist - tax law. Board certified specialist - criminal law.

Experience   Tried over 50 criminal tax cases in 24 states. Criminal, tax & constitutional law.

Latest Credit   Developed expertise in discharge of income tax debts in bankruptcy. Firm discharged $500,000 in 1988.

Public Speaking   Appeared on television & radio talk shows; featured in major newspaper articles. Seminar speaker. Involved in conservative political issues, from abortion to gun control.

Military Background   West Point, Airborne, Ranger, Infantry, Special Forces, SCUBA, Jumpmaster. Platoon Leader & Company Commander, 173rd Airborne Brigade, Vietnam. Awarded Bronze Stars, Air Medals & Vietnamese Cross of Gallantry with Silver Star.

Family   Married to Barbara 19 years. Three sons: Scott Ryan, Nathan.

Interests   Flying, sailing, Christian education, military history, politics.

Tax Fraud & Evasion: The War Stories, Part II. Softbound, 320 pages.
The criminal & civil tax drama continues...

• Montana	Miner	• California	CPA
• Arizona	Conductor	• Arizona	Farmer
• Minnesota	Engineer	• California	Crop Duster
• Idaho	Rancher	• New Mexico	Chiropractor
• Montana	Plumber	• Indiana	Defense Worker
• Alaska	Businessman	• Alaska	Housewife
• Minnesota	Plumber	• Arizona	Accountant
• Illinois	Dentist	• Kansas	Professor
• Hawaii	Investor	• California	Grandmother
• Tennessee	Preacher	• Nevada	Casino Worker

April 15th: The Most Pernicious Attack Upon English Liberty (2nd
Ed., 1988). MAJOR MAC's first book traces the history of the government's
extraction of private information, under the guise of tax collection, from
citizens under oath. Read actual trial transcripts, plus a detailed look behind
the scenes of **Iran-Contra** & MAJOR MAC's client "The Colonel," an alleged
CIA operative working with **Lt. Col. North** and **Gen. Secord**. Softbound,
over 250 pages.

ORDER NOW AND SAVE !	Quantity	Price per book	$2.00 P&H per book	Sub-Total
War Stories, Part II *		$17.95 *		
April 15th (2nd Ed.)		$12.95		
War Stories		$17.95		

* $14.95 for orders received prior to
1/1/90, publication date.

TOTAL:

Send **check** or **money order** to:

MacPherson & Sons Publishers, Ltd.
3404 West Cheryl Drive, A-250
Phoenix, Arizona 85051

(602) 866-9566